T0304666

MANAGING GROWTH IN MINIATURE

Managing Growth in Miniature explores the history of the way economists think about growth. It focuses on the period between the 1930s and 1960s, tracing the development of the famed "Solow growth model," one of the central mathematical models in postwar economics. It argues that models are not simply efficient tools providing answers to the problems of economic theory and governance. The Solow model's various uses and interpretations related to the ways it made things (in)visible, excluded questions, and suggested actions. Its success and effects ultimately also owed to its fundamental ambiguities. Attending to the concrete sides of economic abstractions, this book provides a richly layered and accessible account of the forms of knowledge that shaped the predominant notion of "economic growth" and ideas of how to govern it.

Verena Halsmayer is a senior research and teaching fellow (*Oberassistentin*) at the University of Lucerne's Chair for Science Studies. Her dissertation, on which this book is loosely based, received the Best Dissertation Award of the Faculty of Historical Cultural Studies at the University of Vienna.

HISTORICAL PERSPECTIVES ON MODERN ECONOMICS

Series Editor: Professor Harro Maas, Walras-Pareto Centre for the History of Economic and Political Thought, University of Lausanne

This series contains original works that challenge and enlighten historians of economics. For the profession as a whole, it promotes better understanding of the origin and content of modern economics

Other books in the series:

H. Spencer Banzhaf, *Pricing the Priceless: A History of Environmental Economics* (2024)

Till Düppe, *The Closed World of East German Economists: Hopes and Defeats of a Generation* (2023)

Erwin Dekker, *Jan Tinbergen (1903–1994) and the Rise of Economic Expertise* (2021)

Jeff E. Biddle, *Progression through Regression: The Life Story of the Empirical Cobb-Douglas Production Function* (2020)

Erwin Dekker, *The Viennese Students of Civilization: The Meaning and Context of Austrian Economics Reconsidered* (2016)

Steven G. Medema, Anthony M. C. Waterman (eds.), *Paul Samuelson on the History of Economic Analysis: Selected Essays* (2014)

Floris Heukelom, *Behavioral Economics: A History* (2014)

Roger E. Backhouse, Mauro Boianovsky, *Transforming Modern Macroeconomics: Exploring Disequilibrium Microfoundations, 1956–2003* (2013)

Susan Howson, *Lionel Robbins* (2012)

Robert Van Horn, Philip Mirowski, Thomas A. Stapleford (eds.), *Building Chicago Economics: New Perspectives on the History of America's Most Powerful Economics Program* (2012)

Arie Arnon, *Monetary Theory and Policy from Hume and Smith to Wicksell: Money, Credit, and the Economy* (2011)

Malcolm Rutherford, *The Institutionalist Movement in American Economics, 1918–1947: Science and Social Control* (2011)

Samuel Hollander, *Friedrich Engels and Marxian Political Economy* (2011)

Continued after the Index

Managing Growth in Miniature

Solow's Model as an Artifact

VERENA HALSMAYER

University of Lucerne

CAMBRIDGE
UNIVERSITY PRESS

Shaftesbury Road, Cambridge CB2 8EA, United Kingdom

One Liberty Plaza, 20th Floor, New York, NY 10006, USA

477 Williamstown Road, Port Melbourne, VIC 3207, Australia

314–321, 3rd Floor, Plot 3, Splendor Forum, Jasola District Centre, New Delhi – 110025, India

103 Penang Road, #05-06/07, Visioncrest Commercial, Singapore 238467

Cambridge University Press is part of Cambridge University Press & Assessment, a department of the University of Cambridge.

We share the University's mission to contribute to society through the pursuit of education, learning and research at the highest international levels of excellence.

www.cambridge.org
Information on this title: www.cambridge.org/9781316515181

DOI: 10.1017/9781009092340

First published 2024

A catalogue record for this publication is available from the British Library.

A Cataloging-in-Publication data record for this book is available from the Library of Congress

ISBN 978-1-316-51518-1 Hardback

Cambridge University Press & Assessment has no responsibility for the persistence or accuracy of URLs for external or third-party internet websites referred to in this publication and does not guarantee that any content on such websites is, or will remain, accurate or appropriate.

Contents

Figures

Introduction

At the beginning of 1970, Amartya Sen prepared an anthology of selected readings in *Growth Economics*. What qualified the collection for publication with Penguin Books, known for inexpensive paperbacks, was its promise of a larger audience. While the field of growth economics did not even exist ten years earlier, it was now so central to the study of economics that Sen could note that "an undergraduate can no longer go through his economic theory course without meeting 'the rate of growth' face to face and without noticing its well-cultivated, if somewhat wayward, charm."[1] Straining to finish his survey-like introduction, he wrote a letter to Robert Solow, a former colleague at the Massachusetts Institute of Technology (MIT). Solow was well known for a model he had published in 1956. This model had been essential in stabilizing the specific, "technical" notion of a "rate of growth" that Sen talked about. In his message, Sen thanked Solow for clarifying in previous correspondence that the motivation of the model "was to trace full employment paths."[2] This clarification concerned the very status of the mathematical model as a "model." It could be read both as representing the actual workings of capitalist economies and as sketching some imaginary world that was purely hypothetical or could possibly be established in the future. In his reply, Solow conceded that "my general discussion in the 1956 article was ambiguous, for the simple reason that it wasn't clear to me at the time exactly what I was doing."[3] While Solow viewed his fifteen years younger self as somewhat confused, I read this anecdote differently. It attests, in a refreshingly honest manner, to the essential ambiguity of models. It is widely held that mathematical models made economists formulate their theories in a determinate and precise way. But their mathematical forms needed to be given "economic" meaning. At the same time, these forms essentially framed what "economic" meant. As for Solow, it took him some time to settle on what his model was all about.

The exchange points our attention to the tricky connection between models and a world outside their narrow confines – not only in economics but in many other fields in the arts, sciences, and engineering that involve languages and practices of "modeling." In principle, as the philosopher and historian of science Marx W. Wartofsky has noted, "anything may be taken as a model of anything else." The essential feature of what he has called a "modeling relationship" is that "it is *being taken as a model* which makes an actual out of a potential model."[4] In this book, I want to find out what made Solow's model a "model" and what that meant. I do so from a historian's perspective: Attending to other forms of economic knowledge-making and their settings between the 1930s and 1960s helps me think of modeling as a concrete practice and investigate the model's specific material and medial characteristics. At the same time, this approach allows me to tell episodes from the history of "growth" as an economists' problem. Overall, this book seeks to contribute to scholarship puzzling over the character, relevance, and effects of economic abstractions. My central argument is that models were more than figures of thought, expressions of social imaginaries, or rhetorical strategies. Due to their specific mathematical forms and to economists' way of treating them as tools, they exhibited certain practical qualities that made them rather efficient carriers of a specific way of reasoning. The central ambiguity and openness that characterized their status as models decisively contributed to their dissemination. As did Solow in correspondence with Sen, economists throughout this book emphasized that their models were *merely* models – stylized constructs, heuristic devices, tools for investigation. And yet, it was precisely such framing that allowed Solow's model to be employed in a variety of ways and unfold its suggestive power, irrespective of the modeler's intentions. Ultimately, it turned into a model of what it means to think like an economist.[5] The ambiguity it already featured on Solow's desk remained. "At any rate," Sen replied, "others have read much more into your 1956 model."[6] Perhaps in an attempt to control the model's openness, he added a footnote in the published anthology, quoting the modeler's own motivation that "the idea is to trace full employment paths, no more."[7]

A SIMPLE MODEL OF GROWTH

As one of several formulations of a "neoclassical growth model," Solow's model is most commonly credited with "explaining economic growth and the long-term effects of economic policy" and with "illuminating the importance of innovation and technological progress to society's increasing wealth."[8] In "A Contribution to the Theory of Economic Growth," published in the *Quarterly Journal of Economics* in 1956, specific notions of "explanation" were at play. In a nutshell, the "simple model" featured the relation between the growth rates of the variables "output," "capital," and "labor."[9] While labor was given outside and independently of the model, capital could vary and adapted flexibly to the given amount of labor in order to ensure the most efficient output. The result was a self-sustaining equilibrium expressed in the form of a linear differential equation: A state of growth determined only by output and saving, in which both capital and labor were fully employed. Consequently, population growth or capital investment were not enough to increase this optimal growth rate. Instead, it could only be changed through additional factors that were not part of the model, such as "technological change." The model's simple appearance provided a rather efficient view of economic growth, drawing a line between a clean, well-ordered inside and a messy outside of all kinds of things that were excluded from analysis. A year later, in 1957, the model figured as an instrument for measuring economic growth and its sources. It estimated that technical change was responsible for almost 90 per cent of growth since the turn of the century.[10]

Soon, the "Contribution" found its professional readership. In contrast to other economists' works in the 1950s, it was not likely to be read by lay readers. It was, as a commentator noted, one of the more "technical papers, not suitable for leisurely general reading."[11] Heavily discussed within the realm of economic theory, it was singled out as the "most important paper" that contributed to a "major revision" of contemporary growth theory.[12] It became a constitutive pillar of American mainstream economics that dominated the profession until the 1970s and frames economic knowledge, in academe as well as policy-related realms, to the present day. In 1987, it earned its constructor the highest accolade of the profession, the Swedish national bank's Prize in Economic Sciences in Memory of Alfred Nobel. Established proponents of economics enthusiastically celebrated "the Solow model" as being "at the back of all economists' minds in approaching growth theory." It was said to have provided not only "an engine of analysis" but nothing less than "the organizing structure" of a variety of disciplinary fields – from development economics to international trade and public finance.[13] At the same time that Solow's model experienced a striking success, it was confronted with the most fundamental criticism. In fact, if success means that it was received and discussed widely, it had an equally successful life in the eyes and hands of its critics. The model attracted criticism for the utter unrealism of its assumptions, the provision of tautological knowledge, and the ideological veiling of capitalist destruction. It was dismissed for failing to explain growth and to provide an understanding of why economic development was uneven. In this way, Solow's model also became a symbol for economists' disinterestedness in the economic world, and an exemplar for the discipline's shaky scientific foundations.

Indeed, what a curious world this model presented. It depicted the relation between capital and labor, yet it excluded questions of power between social formations. It spoke of a community, its production, and growth. Yet there were no workers on factory floors, no investment decisions by managers, no material transformations. There were no nonaugmentable things such as energy or land, no environmental depletion. There were no unpaid activities like the rearing of children. And there was no money. To interpret the mathematical equations in terms of a physical economy required a series of assumptions regarding its space and time. Most importantly, it presented a world of "perfect competition," in which the fully flexible working of a market ensured equilibrium. There were no failures to coordinate, no overproduction, no underproduction. At each moment in time, everything that was produced was immediately either consumed or saved and invested. The assumption of "perfect foresight" established that future developments of prices and interest rates were known in the present. There was no uncertainty, no risk. In this frictionless cosmos, nothing essential evolved. The mathematical economy changed only in scale, not in composition – a ceaseless cycle taking place at one point in time. Historical dynamics and contingency were excluded. This list of absences can of course be continued.[14]

What was it that made this utterly frictionless world so appealing to economists and soon to other academics, policy-makers, and professionals? In the eyes of its contemporary theorists, what set the model apart was not some novel idea. That growth was not entirely dependent on capital accumulation had already been theorized in different ways. What made this model so attractive was precisely its specific format. Sen's introduction lauded Solow's model for its "beautiful simplicity," adding to a long line of appraisals that denoted it "an ingeniously simple yet extremely useful model for the examination of various aspects of the problem of growth," which is how one of the early readers described it.[15] The trouble with statements like this is that the qualities of being "simple" and "useful" depended on their relation to other forms of growth knowledge that were around. How was the problem of growth formulated such that, both in the eyes of contemporaries and in retrospect, Solow's model could provide a simple and useful means to investigate it?

PROBLEMATIZING GROWTH AT MIDCENTURY

Solow's model equipped the postwar vocabulary of growth, development, and productivity with an efficient image of a manageable mechanism that led toward an ever more prosperous future. By 1956, growth had already become the center of American political economy, guiding both domestic policies and Cold War geopolitical strategy. The "eschatology of peaceful prosperity," as Charles Maier has framed it, formed the core of American identity as a liberal capitalist nation.[16] Transgressing party lines, private enterprise was seen as the very foundation for rising national output; government was assigned the status of a neutral arbiter deciding in the interest of growth. The politics of growth and productivity built on the rising importance of economic language and knowledge within government institutions since the beginning of the century. In the United States and elsewhere, it subjected policy-making to a primarily economic evaluation; public expenditures were mainly legitimized by their contribution to growth – a synonym of progress.[17] The expansion of the economy became the primary goal of national economic management, achievable through increasing efficiency and rising consumption and decoupled, for instance, from any limitations through natural resources.[18] The career of Solow's model went hand-in-hand with the "economic miracle" of the postwar golden age of growth that saw rising production and decreasing unemployment as well as a rise in carbon emissions and decreasing biodiversity. Much of the research surrounding it was financed by the notorious Cold War knowledge institutions. It fit a postwar climate of anti-communism as well as the forms and procedures of high modern bureaucracy. In the most straightforward "biographical" sense, it may have had its beginnings in Cold War culture. But it decisively related to earlier forms of economic knowledge as much as it contained various potentialities for future engagements with growth.

That Solow's system of mathematical equations was plausible as a "model of growth" depended on its fit with existing economic knowledge. First and foremost, its variables related to the statistical entity of the economy, a scientific-administrative object that already exhibited historical depth. Shaped by the rise of the nation state, the associated military planning, and early twentieth-century managerialism, governmental statistics gave new form to older visions of the economy. Since the seventeenth century, it had been presented as a closed and self-regulating system. Whether in encyclopedic, organic, mechanic, hydraulic, or bookkeeping form, portrayals of the economy not only made it intellectually manageable but also prompted action to realize that order.[19] Actualizing earlier displays of the economy, the postwar era established an intricate knowledge infrastructure based on metaphors of flows and cycles in which goods, capital, and work circulated.[20] While long-standing ideas about the flourishing of the whole (such as the growth of the wealth of nations or the improvement of productive techniques) remained central parts of governmental thought, the very objects of inquiry and intervention differed considerably.[21] It was still about the performance of a system as a whole, but now that system had the money-based form of an aggregated macroeconomy. The most prominent numbers in this regard were the national income and its reformulations, the gross national product (GNP), and the gross domestic product (GDP). These metrics featured the national economy as a closed entity of interdependent statistical parameters that was amenable to administrative action.[22] Drawing on longer-standing forms of economic knowledge, Solow's model bolstered the belief that stable growth could be created and sustained. Merging with other midcentury tools of governance, it gave the relations between the growth rates of national product, capital, and labor statistics.

When working on this book, I wanted to gain a better understanding of the knowledge that provided "growth" with its specific form. Genealogies of the economy have often focused on the broader problematizations of that entity as a central administrative–quantitative category. In a Foucauldian vein, they investigated the historical processes of how and why something previously unproblematic turned into a problem and became the object of social regulation – scientifically, ethically, and politically.[23] While these approaches emphasized the crucial role of economic knowledge tools for a liberal governmentality, the specifics of these instruments have rarely come to the fore. This book focuses on the characteristics of models and measurements of growth. It does so by investigating the problematization of the growing economy in economic *research*. This does not need to imply the perspective that economists' problems are autonomous from those outside their field's boundaries. There is no doubt, certainly not for the historical actors themselves, that their work intensively interacted with governmental interest. It was prompted and funded by governmental institutions; in turn, their renditions of the growing economy made the very phenomenon to be governed appear visible and amenable.[24] Looking at how different tools of modeling and measuring shaped the scientific problematic of growth, this book takes inspiration from a branch of history of science that has focused on how things (as diverse as dreams, the self, or atoms) gained scientific interest, how they turned into objects of scientific inquiry, and how they lost scientific attention. In the process, this literature has argued, phenomena became more or less real, depending on how "densely they are woven into scientific thought and practice."[25]

The measurers and modelers of the following pages were aware that their research was not in the first place dealing with some world out there but rather a matter of "phenomenotechnique."[26] Framed by Gaston Bachelard, the concept emphasizes the notorious difficulty to clearly differentiate between tools and phenomena when they are transformed into scientific problematics.[27] The growing economy that was assembled and scrutinized in the offices of national accountants, the mainframe computers of input–output researchers, and the notebooks of MIT's modelers was not a phenomenon of the life world. What economists denoted their "instruments" embodied theoretical ideas, conventions, normative judgments, beliefs, and imaginations, which all contributed to realizing the phenomenotechnical growing economy.[28] The problematics of growth research consisted of mathematical variables, correlation coefficients, and statistical parameters. In this sense, the growing economy that Solow's model depicted was already a scientific object that constituted a mesh of earlier and new threads, disregarding some and actualizing other elements of previous research objects.[29] Most importantly, it spoke to the variables in time series data of national product, capital, and labor. Built on similar assumptions, the model neatly fit the dominant empirical problematization of economic growth. It inscribed itself into an infrastructure of knowledge, in which models and data mutually stabilized each other.

In her review of works historicizing economic growth, historian Venus Bivar wondered whether the difficulty of merging the history of statistics with newer approaches to the history of capitalism came from a difficulty "to marry the material and the abstract."[30] While this book will not provide such warranted synthesis, it does seek to concretize the abstract in treating models and measurements of growth as deeply entrenched in research practices that were both discursive and material. The shaping and reshaping of the growing economy involved not only intellectual considerations but also practical requirements, institutional backing, and public financing. Paying attention to the nitty-gritty of the tedious phenomenotechnical work that went into the numbers of national accounts, productivity measurements, and input–output analysis allows me to feature Solow's model as part of a process of giving form to the problem of growth and thereby reframing that problem in a specific way. From this perspective, Solow's model contributed a further leap in both abstraction and concretization. Presenting growth as a simple mechanism, it carried the objectification of the economy to extremes. The model was used as a highly efficient gauge, detached from previous attempts to get closer to the material realities of production, separated from the intricate work of making numbers, and ignoring the contexts and weaknesses of the underlying empirical material. It fortified the idea of the economy as a separate sphere that was independent of all things social, cultural, political, and temporal. Doing so, it eased the perception of growth numbers as a glimpse into a world *out there*. This somewhat paradoxical effect was not simply a matter of continuities and breaks from earlier instantiations of the growing economy. Rather, it derived from a decisive transformation: The reformulation of economic growth in terms of a model and its embedding into a practice of modeling.

MODELS AS MULTIFARIOUS ARTIFACTS

"Modeling is an age-old business," an operations researcher noted, thinking of the "clay models of the great pyramids at Giza or a wooden model of Noah's ark."[31] Indeed, practices of modeling, designing, blueprinting, planning, and sketching have a long history. But the history of mathematical modeling as an epistemic practice is decisively shorter, the history of mathematical modeling in the social sciences even shorter, and the history of talking about mathematical economic models in terms of material objects shorter still. Only in the middle of the twentieth century were mathematical models rather than mechanical analogies widely seen as the stuff of modern science. Only then did it become customary in fields of applied mathematics to use the term "model" and speak of "modeling" as the prime scientific activity.[32] In the aftermath of wartime planning, a larger movement of social scientists, among them economists, also adopted the language of modeling. Their use of the term "model" was characterized by a diversity in practices stretching from cybernetics to information theory, from systems analysis to game theory, from operations research to systems engineering.[33] The 1960s saw a veritable boom of the use of the term for a whole variety of things: Mechanical models, theoretical constructs, pictures, diagrams, computational models, hypothetical models, copies, prototypes, mental constructs, material models in museums and for teaching as well as logical models that had no reference outside language. What the contemporary observer Wartofsky called a "model muddle" was not only semantic but also ontological. It related to both the status of whatever was labeled a model and the status of the things it was said to represent – encapsulating the exchange between Sen and Solow above.[34]

Scholarship in the history of science has shown how larger postwar developments made it easy and attractive for social scientists to problematize their objects in terms of mathematical systems and dispense with other approaches. As part of these shifts, one instantiation of "the economy" was a perfectly efficient, optimizable system of simultaneous equations, which provided postwar economics with one of its major research objects. Historians have given particular attention to to game theory, general equilibrium theory, operations research, Cold-War interdisciplinary rationalities, mathematical economists' flashy cybernetic imaginaries, and the puzzling emphasis they put on the epistemic virtues of mathematical beauty and elegance.[35] This book also relates to the analytical frameworks of formalist economics and the impact of the digital computer, involves a partly similar personnel, and sometimes sets the storyline at overlapping institutions. At the center, however, is a specific practice and language of modeling that aimed to draw on quantitative knowledge, related more strongly to prewar economics, adapted a more antiquated kind of mathematics, and connected "simplicity" with empirical and political "usefulness" rather than formal "elegance." Distancing their projects from the abstract aesthetics and intricate makeup of axiomatic systems of general equilibrium theory, the mathematical economists in this book thought that their models promised to make economic theory more realistic and closer to empirical relevance. And in contrast to some of their contemporaries, whose enthusiasm for the computer fed into a matching penchant for complexity, they wanted to keep the complexity of their models to a minimum. Their views testified to a multiplicity of model understandings in the sciences, in particular when it came to the varying status of mathematical models between concrete objects and abstract entities.[36]

The modelers in the following pages adhered to the view that mathematics was the "language of modern science," which only made it natural for them to turn to the archive of mathematical formalisms. In the first place, to put it very bluntly, making economics "scientific" to them meant something like reframing ill-defined problems by using the abstract and precise language of mathematics and making the underlying presumptions explicit. The clear-eyed scientific economist explicitly stated assumptions and definitions. These set up a logically consistent mathematical formulation. Conclusions were clear-cut. Utterings in this vein, however, made up only one layer of economists' model talk. When they went into what they were *doing* in their research, it often came across as a concrete activity of working toward and with some kind of artifacts. In this vein, historian of science Mary S. Morgan has described economic modeling as a "style of reasoning" that consists in constructing and manipulating "small mathematical, statistical, graphical, diagrammatic, and even physical objects." Models, in this sense, are not abstract structures but concrete artifacts that are deliberately made in a process that involves articulated as well as craft-based knowledge.[37] In the following chapters, economists, especially Solow, will indeed refer to their modeling work as an art and handicraft. Such statements, often made in a fairly casual way and rarely part of a formalized methodology, make up a second layer of model talk. Here, modeling appears as a concrete activity of making something new and artificial and of tinkering and toying with it. The relation of the resulting knowledge to a world outside the confines of models was rather informal. Model knowledge was not supposed to be true or lead to exact forecasts or precise statements about probabilities. The two layers of model talk did not necessarily agree with one another. But they both belonged to a practice of modeling that is understood here as involving the *work* as well as the *performance* of economics as a modeling science.

Taking seriously economists' model talk as a part (and not simply as a description) of their modeling work opens the possibility to investigate how the power of economic abstractions derived from the way they were built and used as artifacts. For one, it highlights models' difficult relation to a reality outside their confines. Solow's "Contribution" did not present any empirical study – its results merely derived from the constructed model, and neither the model nor its assumptions were "tested." The growth rate it presented was derived from a mathematical equilibrium system, rather than calculated from numbers of the past. When the model was used as an instrument of measurement, it served as a means to interpret given data as if the numbers resulted from a world that looked like the model. Whatever was not part of the clean cosmos (the ever-extendable list of absences I sketched in the first section) was stashed away in a "residual," which now captured the messy outside of the model in a separate error-term. From a methodologist's standpoint, Marcel Boumans has noted that it is through the process of creating new objects from already existing bits and pieces of knowledge (metaphors, analogies, mathematical concepts and techniques, data, and policy views) that the "justification" for models is "built in." They do not have to satisfy some disconnected, external criteria but have to be adequate for their very specific purpose.[38] Seen in this way, the model was a successive form, picking up on what was there, integrating justification from the start.

When it came to the making of his model, Solow hinted at its being a side-product of a different modeling endeavor in the context of teaching. It then, however, turned out to have a different purpose as a contribution to economic theory and, in the ensuing years, created several new purposes, revealing a stimulative character. As an artifact, Solow's model was not simply a transparent representation of some facets of the economic world. Its specific material and medial characteristics both restricted what could be thought, seen, and done with its help and afforded various uses and interpretations. Depending on the specific engagements with the model, it was able to actualize different capacities. In this sense, it was not simply a passive instrument.[39] The reader of the "Contribution" above who enthused over the model's ingenious simplicity highlighted that it was also "extremely useful." In various ways, Solow's model prompted its use as a practical "tool," realizing several of its instrumental and pedagogical functions. As a working object, it offered the opportunity to learn something about the (ever so parsimoniously defined) problem of growth. As an instrument of measurement, it formatted data in a way that economists deemed productive for further inquiry. Understood as a "prototype," it laid a foundation for both building larger-scale models and for integrating more factors into its small world. As a miniature, it provided the minimally efficient scale to investigate the growth dynamics of bigger models. As a teaching device, it served as an entry point to the practice of modeling and becoming an economist. In all these engagements, the simple artifact provided a first step. It was seen as tentative because its makeup was too sketchy, in need of further work. At the same time, it provided the rules for subsequent models. Being adaptable and extendable, the simple model, for instance, allowed for the accommodation of various other factors, but only if they were first formatted in a suitable way. Its clean-cut form did not allow for contaminations. In this sense, the model was something preliminary and provocative, realizing its active potential.[40]

The introduction of models in economics, as the mentioned scholarship emphasized, did not merely translate verbal study into the more precise and efficient language of mathematics. Models are not simply texts to be read; they not only repackage but format theoretical ideas. Modeling transformed the very objects of investigation and thereby changed the problems economists deemed relevant and, not least, the ways they thought were appropriate to approach these questions.[41] As in any other science, economists distanced their knowledge from mere opinion. From midcentury onwards, they did so primarily through reference to mathematical models. While the practice of modeling was indeed personal and drew on the skills and qualities of the modeler, it was still seen as providing privileged, depersonalized knowledge – not necessarily in the sense of scientificity relating to some specific rules and criteria (for instance, Popperian ones) but in the sense of a counterpart to subjective, irrational opinion that distinguished itself through asking the "right" questions. In effect, modeling provided economists with scientific appeal and public authority on a diverse range of questions. After all, the discipline was stylized as the most scientific of the social sciences – a status that has been claimed and challenged ever since. This book focuses on one model in particular, which makes it possible to not only think about modeling as a way of reasoning more generally but to investigate a specific instantiation of a modeling practice within American postwar economics. The practice came with a situated meaning of "technical economics" that related to both the work of modeling and the application of the knowledge thereby gained within the realm of economic expertise.[42]

THE POLITICS OF A MODEL

"The basic neoliberal model of growth is the Solow model. Like all neoliberal thinking, the Solow model is based on the assumption of pervasiveness and efficiency of markets."[43] The ambiguity broached by Sen on the eve of his publication continued to accompany the model. In this case, it was almost sixty years later in 2012 that the Ethiopian Prime Minister (and former President) excoriated "development" policies and their phantasmatic belief in the power of markets. That Solow's model, developed in relation to national statistics and postwar interventionism, could turn into a symbol of market fundamentalism was due to its specific ambivalence and openness as a "model." Was it an image of the world as it was, an imaginary of what it should look like, or a vision of a world yet to come? The model carried these possibilities into its different engagements, to an extent that makes it hard to speak of the same model.[44] From the perspective taken here, its specific politics pertained not only to the (necessarily political, value-laden) imagery of the growing economy and what it turned (in)visible. It also consisted in its efficient format, which made it easy to repurpose and to tell clean-cut stories about growth and its sources.[45] The historical actors in this book related the epistemic and the political in a more confined way, above all, with regard to the sphere of economic expertise and policy-making. It was especially in these situations that the model could unfold its suggestive power – the world it portrayed was to be established. And since it did not provide any hints at how to do so, it was adaptable to a variety of political strategies. In this sense, the story of Solow's model provides a further angle on a history of market thinking that is not restricted to the circulation of neoliberal ideas. Instead, it points to the persistence of knowledge artifacts and infrastructures that are intended to manage the macroeconomy across the twentieth century.[46]

When it came to the economy Solow's model portrayed, it was indeed a world of fully competitive markets that constituted what most of its critics saw as its ideological content. This was a world that certainly did not exist in the 1950s. But it could be understood as a nostalgic reference to an imagined nineteenth-century in which a large number of entrepreneurs competed rationally in order to maximize profit. After all, it was called "neoclassical," a label that, in the postwar United States, denoted approaches loosely affiliated with a heritage of the previous century in the form of marginal productivity theory. Marginal productivity theory provided an explanation of how returns of national wealth were allocated to the various "factors" involved in its production. While economists had previously cast this question in terms of rivalling social groups who participated in creating wealth (capital and labor in particular), neoclassical theory at the turbulent turn of the century answered it through the workings of competitive markets.[47] Value accrued from utility rather than, for instance, labor cost. In this way, production and distribution became analytically separated; within that analytical frame, no statement relating to justice of distribution was viable. Everyone was assumed to gain exactly the fair share of what they had contributed to production. Mathematical renditions of neoclassical theory formulated systems of supply and demand equations; their solution provided equilibrium prices. In such a framing, income distribution appeared independent of institutions, social relations, and history – which would also become one of the main arguments against neoclassical theory in the second half of the twentieth century, the Solow model in particular.[48]

Already in the nineteenth century, neoclassicism was not easily mapped onto political preferences. Some marginalist thinkers (such as Carl

Menger) actively pursued anti-socialist campaigns and offered forceful apologias of the status quo against the booming workers' movement. Others (such as Léon Walras) focused on the compatibilities of marginalist theory with models of a moneyless planned economy and socialist politics.[49] This political indeterminacy carried into post–Second World War economics as it picked up on optimization techniques from the context of war planning and the computer metaphors that came with the mainframe. Equilibrium systems presented mechanisms that ensured the efficient "allocation" of resources. Akin to other kinds of postwar structuralist reasoning, these systems were interpreted as fitting different kinds of institutional setups, ranging from "centrally planned" to "free market" economies. In any case, such models were intended to transform economic theory in order to make it more useful for governmental purposes.

Conceptualizing models as interventionist tools was also not specific to the postwar era. The creation of macroeconomics as a separate field in the 1930s, for instance, had been intrinsically related to the ideas and practices of interwar economic governance. In the view of early econometric modelers such as the Dutch economist Jan Tinbergen and the Norwegian Ragnar Frisch, economics was a means to fight unemployment and inequality. Because of the existence of crises, frictions, and depressions, they argued for a decidedly scientific approach to policy-making, which essentially meant that models should provide the basis for economic planning, for monetary as well as fiscal policies.[50] These early econometricians provided new analytical tools that distinguished between the economics of individual action (the micro-level of economic analysis) and the large-number-phenomena of economic statistics (the macro-level).[51] Tinbergen pushed the notion of a mathematical "model" as a representation of an economic mechanism. As early as 1942, he constructed and implemented a neoclassical growth model.[52] Other early models that explored long-term growth possibilities were built in the context of the design of five-year-plans: The Soviet economist G. A. Fel'dman developed, among several others in the 1920s, mathematical formulations of Marxian schemes of expanded reproduction, and the Indian planner Prasanta C. Mahalanobis sought to maximize long-run growth by calculating the optimal allocation of investment among sectors in the early 1950s.[53]

MIT's Department of Economics and Social Science took a particular place in American postwar economics in that it linked the "usability" of mathematical forms to their fit with "economic" meaning and their practicality for intervention. Solow's model was not intended to directly provide knowledge for policy-making. However, MIT's "neoclassical synthesis," the theoretical label to which the model is usually subsumed, did have a distinctly governmental character. It was based on the notion that integrating neoclassical ideas of a self-regulating market in a Keynesian framework allowed for more effective policy designs. In the midcentury US, interventionist policies under the label of "Keynesianism" directed attention at what has been called "the mixed economy," a shifting mixture of private and public ownership, free enterprise, and planning.[54] The new economics held that national economic management required a scientific apparatus and propped up the idea of macroeconomic stabilization by *using* markets.[55] The government's job was to establish high employment, set up an equitable distribution of income, control the business cycle, and enhance growth whenever wages and prices did not adjust quickly enough to bring markets into equilibrium.[56] MIT's mathematical economics came with an overtly self-conscious "middle of the road" political positioning between libertarian and radical economists, both of whom, to MIT's protagonists, lacked intellectual rigor and mathematical competency.[57] They reconciled "left-liberal statist impulses with imperatives to repudiate socialism," as the historian Philip Mirowski has put it. "Keynesian macroeconomics was seen as the epitome of the 'middle way'."[58]

The essential "moral" of the model, as Solow and other neoclassical modelers in the 1950s and 1960s agreed, was that if government took the right steps, the model, in the long-run, would come into its own. In this imagined world of manageable growth, the product of (industrial) economies would grow at approximately the same rate as capital accumulation. The possibility came from an intervening government; judicious fine-tuning would balance saving and investment so that everything saved was invested. Or, as Trevor Swan, who constructed a neoclassical growth model the same year as Solow, put it, either "the Authorities have read the *General Theory* or . . . they are socialists who don't need to."[59] Seen as one element in a toolkit of governmental technologies of postwar liberalism, Solow's model visualized the bright promises of a messianism of affluence, based on the possibilities of balancing the whole and establishing full employment to link an expanding mass-consumption society with increasing wealth and welfare. For Solow and his colleagues, the fact that the model portrayed a world of free markets did not imply that what they saw as real-world markets worked best without government regulations or organized labor. The model itself, however, left open how the world it portrayed could be achieved, for it excluded any interaction between the micro- and macro-level (through the assumption of perfect competition) and between the short- and long-run (through the assumption of perfect foresight). This was one of the facets of the model's ambiguity that opened it up to various political uses and made it compatible with different political ideologies.

The stimulating effects of models often disappointed their own constructors. A recurring theme in this book is the frustration and sometimes even regret that economists uttered when they saw how their artifacts stabilized.[60] In their own work, phenomenotechnical toolmakers shifted between a language of inquiry (being frank and careful about possible shortcomings and problems with a certain technique, model, or measure) and a language of advocacy that came with the authoritative economic expert.[61] As a corollary of dealing in clean and closed worlds, they seemed, at least at times, uncomfortably aware of the limits of their approach outside of those worlds. This is why this book pays attention to the messiness, the disarrays, and nagging doubts that accompanied models from the very outset. At times, modelers worried about the absences that made their models "deceivingly exact," conceded that the practice of modeling created "in some cunning way ... a substitute for reality itself," and bemoaned that economists were often "too taken with technique and theory" and did not care enough "about the practical meaning" of what they were doing.[62] They also admitted disciplinary blind spots: "No doubt we are all too prone to deal in closed systems because they are neat and aesthetically satisfying, and we forget how intimately economic variables are enmeshed in psychological and social and political forces."[63] But such utterings did not change the fact that, as policy experts, for instance as "growthmen," they did act as the providers of "determinate" and "trustworthy" knowledge. Both types of performance, this book argues, came along with the active potential of models and the muddles they created.

OUTLINE

The book begins with the 1956 publication of Solow's model, though its storyline does not proceed sequentially from there. Rather than following a chronological narrative, each chapter constructs different trajectories that – moving back and forth in time – embed the model in practices of modeling and measuring the economy and its growth between the 1930s and the 1960s. Most episodes in the following pages relate to the making of phenomenotechnical instruments that visualized the growing economy. I use them to think through the particular features of Solow's model, the knowledge it generated, and the epistemic virtues and scientific personae that came with this kind of modeling. In historicizing the model from different angles, the trajectories feature different characteristics of the model as they were realized in specific engagements and in relation to other forms of knowledge. Neither of the research episodes that follow were necessary or determinate for Solow's model achieving its eventual form.[64] It could very well have come together in different ways. In fact, as indicated, Solow was neither the only one nor the first to publish a neoclassical model of growth. Such simultaneity is a common theme in the history of science that points to the difficulties of when a history of a model starts (and where it ends, for that matter). Priority is not at issue here. What are of issue are the forms of research into the growing economy as well as the stakes, hopes, and disappointments that came with it. To get at these, this book draws on archival material (such as private correspondence, research reports, and lecture notes) as well as on close readings of published sources.

Chapter 1 focuses on the narratological strategies that turned a set of mathematical equations into an economic model in the "Contribution," the article behind the classic reference "Solow 1956." In the first place, the "Contribution" was all about the setup and behavior of a smoothly working neoclassical growing economy. The whole paper revolved around this artifact, made (up) by the narrator figure and, at the same time, to be used and experimented with by others, independently of its construction history. While denoting the artifact "a model" throughout, references to a world beyond its narrow boundaries were vague; there was no explicit link to any quantitatively measured entity. Its function as an exemplar for how economic reasoning should look and how the new "art of theorizing" was to be done was straightforward. The text presented its model as improving a so-called precursor, the "Harrod-Domar model." In this way, it canonized earlier dynamic theory with its focus on instability and crisis by turning it into a special case of steadily growing equilibrium systems. Pulling readers into its realm, the model set the course for an angled historiography of growth theory that downplays the differences in approaches and objects until the present day.

Chapter 2 highlights a further displacement brought about by Solow's model – the introduction of the so-called "Solow residual" that came with its use as an instrument of measurement. This episode relates the model to the postwar politics of growth and productivity and a line of inquiry that sought to gauge the national whole in terms of monetary units. Existing measurement practices at the National Bureau of Economic Research (NBER) involved the activities of collecting, compiling, and processing data; its researchers complemented and qualified their numbers with descriptive, verbal accounts about how the data had been made and how different measurement procedures led to different results. Here, the model reordered knowledge and nonknowledge about productivity. While commentators were shocked by its utter constructivism and disregard for the ways data were made, it offered a seemingly clean-cut method of measurement that turned statistical inference into a technical procedure. Whatever the model's neoclassical reading of numbers did not account for was efficiently stashed away in a residual term labeled "technical change." While Solow explicitly noted that the rest captured all kinds of (relevant) things, both the technique and the label remained.

That Solow's model actually had little to say about productivity growth was a major point of contention and made it a prime example for the intellectual weaknesses and the lack of usefulness of econometric knowledge for policy-making. The disengagement that came with mathematical models is central to Chapter 3. The 1940s saw the reconciliation of a panoply of mathematical wartime techniques with social scientific theorizing. I examine how the economy was depicted as a huge optimization problem that would be solvable by electronic computers. Investigating input–output analysis as it was done at the Harvard Economic Research Project (HERP) under the directorship of Wassily Leontief illustrates the difficulties of making an economic abstraction work in measurement practice. The chapter draws a trajectory from the HERP to the Conference of Activity Analysis of 1949, where mathematical economists combined new techniques of linear programming with what they saw as conventional neoclassical economics. The move from planning tools to devices for theoretical speculation came along with a shift in modeling philosophies and notions of realism. Focusing entirely on mathematical formalisms and abandoning the concern with measurement brought about the main research object of the economics profession in the subsequent years: The economy as a fully flexible and efficient system of production in the form of a system of simultaneous equations. This was the economy that provided the primary point of reference for Solow's model.

Against the background of mathematical techniques spreading in postwar social science, Chapter 4 situates Solow's model in the heterogenous landscape of mathematical economics in the early 1950s. Here, Solow enters as a historical actor who got acquainted with different strands of structuralist and mathematical reasoning before he devised the model more or less incidentally in the context of teaching engineering students at MIT. On the trajectory from the linear economy at the Conference on Activity Analysis to Solow and Samuelson's joint modeling work,

I describe Solow's model as a miniature – not of the world but of other models. Its smaller scale and reduced mathematical form fit older mathematical economics while, at the same time, it related to the more sophisticated systems of proof and proposition characteristic of general equilibrium theory. Rigor and axiomatization also played a role in the construction of the miniature. The related style of modeling, however, did not revolve around the austere beauty of proposition and proof. Rather, it centered on creating simple and manageable artifacts that upheld the promise of being useful tools for economic governance. In the actors' understanding, this meant finding the minimum efficient scale that allowed for a workable model that could still be provided with economic (here, "neoclassical") meaning. The efficient shape of Solow's model made it a particularly talkative artifact. Not least, it provided a starting point for a number of stories, including what economists themselves called "fables" or "parables" about growth.

Throughout the book, we see economic modelers distancing themselves from any explanatory power or realist intentions of their artifacts. Chapter 5 takes a closer look at such utterings as a specific kind of model talk that accompanied modeling as a practice. Economists struggled with both the epistemological status of their small-scale artifacts and the ontological status of the things they were (ever so loosely) supposed to represent. Frequently, such talk related to the power of mathematics as a language, centering on the greater "virility" of their transparent and unambiguous mathematical methods compared to their verbal counterparts and predecessors. In contrast, I focus on instances in which economists grappled with their tricky artifacts and their messy practices. Specifically in the late 1960s, equipping unrealistic assumptions and technical narrowness with political appeal and scientific legitimacy was as much methodological reflection as it was part of struggles for authority in academe and institutions of economic expertise. The talk surrounding Solow's model presented it as a didactic device, a prototype for larger-scale planning models, an imagery of a world that macroeconomic management was capable of creating, and a part of a toolbox that equipped economists as "little thinkers" with technically sound and rationally appropriate knowledge. While model talk in the first place emphasized the epistemic and political tentativeness of models, Solow's turned into the epitome of what graduates called the "MIT style of modeling."

In the course of the 1960s, mathematical modeling gradually stabilized as the primary mode of academic economic research. The Epilogue sketches the fate of "the Solow model" as it consolidated as an epistemic standard for an intellectual practice that focused on refining mathematical artifacts and using them to estimate model-relationships in any given data sets. Building on the idea that it already developed a life of its own at Solow's desk, the Epilogue inquires into the movements and transformations of the multifarious artifact. It was adapted, extended, and reduced in relation to specific local, institutional, and strategic arrangements in planning offices, universities, and research institutions. Sketching some of its trajectories in the field of growth accounting and macroeconomic management, I wonder how the model sedimented into knowledge infrastructures and how the model's knowledge, as precarious as it might have been, was equipped with computability, prognostic potential, and policy effectiveness.

***

Moving away from a primary focus on people and their ideas and focusing on knowledge artifacts, this book seeks to contribute to a literature that investigates continuities between the 1930s and 1980s. The tenacity of Solow's model defies all-too clean narratives about the succession of theoretical schools in that it cut across different paradigms over the decades. While broader political dynamics are beyond this book's purview, the transformations the model underwent – from a personal toy model to an epistemic standard, from model talk to disciplinary language – speak both to the sedimentation of a specific kind of economic reasoning and to the continuities in governmental knowledge.[65] In what follows, I argue that it was the combination of market imaginaries and the compactness and practical capabilities of economic abstractions that led to their enduring dominance. That models could combine these qualities relied as much on their treatment as artifacts as on their suggestive power – often independently of their modelers' intentions. Ambiguity was at the core of Solow's model, even in that one paper in which it was first published. It is here that Chapter 1 begins.

Notes

1   Amartya Sen, *Growth Economics: Selected Readings* (Harmondsworth, Middlesex: Penguin Books, 1970), 9.
2   Amartya Sen to Robert Solow, January 1, 1970, Solow papers, box 2, Correspondence, January–August 1970 (1 of 2). I am grateful to Michaël Assous for sharing this material.
3   Robert Solow to Amartya Sen, January 14, 1970, Solow papers, box 2, Correspondence, January–August 1970 (1 of 2).

4 Marx W. Wartofsky, "The Model Muddle. Proposals for an Immodest Realism (1966)," in *Models: Representation and the Scientific Understanding*, edited by Marx W. Wartofsky (Dordrecht: D. Reidel Publishing, 1979), 1–11, 6.

5 On the shifts in what constituted proper economic rationale in both academe and politics, see Marion Fourcade, *Economists and Societies: Discipline and Profession in the United States, Britain, and France, 1890s to 1990s* (Princeton: Princeton University Press, 2009); Mary S. Morgan, *The World in the Model: How Economists Work and Think* (Cambridge: Cambridge University Press, 2012); Elizabeth Popp Berman, *Thinking like an Economist: How Efficiency Replaced Equality in U.S. Public Policy* (Princeton: Princeton University Press, 2022).

6 Sen to Solow, January 1, 1970, Solow papers, box 2, Correspondence, January–August 1970 (1 of 2).

7 Sen, *Growth Economics*, 24, n15.

8 This is what the AI "Bearly" replies to the question "What is the Solow model?"

9 Robert M. Solow, "A Contribution to the Theory of Economic Growth," *Quarterly Journal of Economics* 70, no. 1 (1956): 65–94, 91.

10 Robert M. Solow, "Technical Change and the Aggregate Production Function," *Review of Economics and Statistics* 39, no. 3 (1957): 312–20.

11 Vernon L. Smith, "The Theory of Capital," *American Economic Review* 52, no. 3 (1962): 481–91, 488.

12 F. H. Hahn, "The Stability of Growth Equilibrium," *Quarterly Journal of Economics* 74, no. 2 (1960): 206–26, 206, n1.

13 R. C. O. Matthews, "The Work of Robert M. Solow," *Scandinavian Journal of Economics* 90, no. 1 (1988): 13–16, 13; Avinash Dixit, "Growth Theory after Thirty Years," in *Growth/Productivity/Unemployment: Essays to Celebrate Bob Solow's Birthday*, edited by Peter Diamond (Cambridge, MA: MIT Press, 1990), 3–22, 3; Edward C. Prescott, "Robert M. Solow's Neoclassical Growth Model: An Influential Contribution to Economics," *The Scandinavian Journal of Economics* 90, no. 1 (1988): 7–12, 11.

14 More specifically on the vagaries of capturing "capital," see, for instance, Emma Rothschild, "Where Is Capital?," *Capitalism: A Journal of History and Economics* 2, no. 2 (2021): 291–371; Mary A. O'Sullivan, "A Confusion of Capital in the United States," in *The Contradictions of Capital in the Twenty-First Century: The Piketty Opportunity*, edited by Pat Hudson and Keith Tribe, 131–66 (Newcastle: Agenda Publishing, 2016).

15 Sen, *Growth Economics*, 21; John Buttrick, "A Note on Professor Solow's Growth Model," *Quarterly Journal of Economics* 72, no. 4 (1958): 633–36, 633.

16 Charles S. Maier, "The Politics of Productivity: Foundations of American International Economic Policy after World War II," *International Organization* 31, no. 4 (1977): 607–33, 609.

17 On the politics of growth in the US, see Lizabeth Cohen, *A Consumers' Republic: The Politics of Mass Consumption in Postwar America* (New York: Vintage Books, 2004); Robert M. Collins, *More: The Politics of Economic Growth in Postwar America* (Oxford: Oxford University Press, 2000); Andrew L. Yarrow, *Measuring America: How Economic Growth Came to Define American Greatness in the Late Twentieth Century* (Amherst: University of Massachusetts Press, 2010). On the harmonizing of national growth discourses in the OECD's "growth paradigm," see

Matthias Schmelzer, *The Hegemony of Growth: The OECD and the Making of the Economics Growth Paradigm* (Cambridge: Cambridge University Press, 2016). On the politics of growth in other national contexts, see, for instance, Alexander Nützenadel, *Stunde der Ökonomen: Wissenschaft, Politik und Expertenkultur in der Bundesrepublik 1949–1974*, Kritische Studien zur Geschichtswissenschaft, Bd. 166 (Göttingen: Vandenhoeck & Ruprecht, 2005); Scott O'Bryan, *The Growth Idea: Purpose and Prosperity in Postwar Japan* (Honolulu: University of Hawaii Press, 2009); Eric Hirsch, *Acts of Growth: Development and the Politics of Abundance in Peru* (Stanford, CA: Stanford University Press, 2022). On the intersection of growth and development discourses, see Stephen Macekura, "Development and Economic Growth: An Intellectual History," in *History of the Future of Economic Growth: Historical Roots of Current Debates on Sustainable Degrowth*, edited by Iris Borowy and Matthias Schmelzer (New York: Routledge, 2017), 120–8.

18 See, for instance, David E. Nye, *Consuming Power: A Social History of American Energies*, 3. print (Cambridge, MA: MIT Press, 2001). On the history of growth and its discontents, see Stephen J. Macekura, *The Mismeasure of Progress: Economic Growth and Its Critics* (Chicago: University of Chicago Press, 2020); Matthias Schmelzer, Andrea Vetter, and Aaron Vansintjan, *The Future Is Degrowth: A Guide to a World beyond Capitalism* (New York: Verso, 2022), chapter 3.

19 Genealogies of the economy have provided the object of the economy with a long and divergent history, multiple sites of emergence, diverse threads, and different periodizations. See, for instance, Susan Buck-Morss, "Envisioning Capital: Political Economy on Display," *Critical Inquiry* 21, no. 2 (1995): 434–67, 439; Margaret Schabas, *The Natural Origins of Economics* (Chicago: University of Chicago Press, 2006); Joseph Vogl, *The Specter of Capital* (Stanford, CA: Stanford University Press, 2015); Ute Tellmann, *Life & Money: The Genealogy of the Liberal Economy and the Displacement of Politics* (New York: Columbia University Press, 2018).

20 For a discussion of the notion of "knowledge infrastructures" and the relevant literature, see Paul N. Edwards, Lisa Gitelman, Gabrielle Hecht, Adrian Johns, Brian Larkin, and Neil Safier, "AHR *Conversation: Historical Perspectives on the Circulation of Information*," *The American Historical Review* 116, no. 5 (2011): 1392–435, in particular 1421–4. Daniel Hirschman has made the concept productive for the historical analysis of economic knowledge, "Rediscovering the 1%: Knowledge Infrastructures and the Stylized Facts of Inequality," *American Journal of Sociology* 127, no. 3 (2021): 739–86.

21 Historians and historical actors alike linked the GDP to the *political arithmetick* of seventeenth-century Elizabethan and Cromwellian England. See, for instance, Philipp Lepenies, *The Power of a Single Number: A Political History of GDP* (New York: Columbia University Press, 2016), chapter 2 and Richard Stone, "Review of *Commodity Flow and Capital Formation* by S. Kuznets," *The Economic Journal* 49, no. 194 (1939): 308–9. On the pitfalls of equating the objects of these early metrics and today's money-based measures, see Eli Cook, *The Pricing of Progress: Economic Indicators and the Capitalization of American Life* (Cambridge: Harvard University Press, 2017).

22 On the historical novelty of this economy, see, for instance, Timothy Mitchell, "Fixing the Economy," *Cultural Studies* 12, no. 1 (1998): 82–101; Daniel Breslau, "Economics Invents the Economy: Mathematics, Statistics, and Models in the

Work of Irving Fisher and Wesley Mitchell," *Theory and Society* 32 (2003): 379–411; Peter Miller and Nikolas Rose, "Governing Economic Life," *Economy and Society* 19, no. 1 (1990): 1–31; Tomo Suzuki, "The Epistemology of Macroeconomic Reality: The Keynesian Revolution from an Accounting Point of View," *Accounting, Organizations and Society* 28, no. 5 (2003): 471–517; Adam Tooze, "Imagining National Economies: National and International Economic Statistics, 1900–1950," in *Imagining Nations*, edited by Geoffrey Cubitt (Manchester: Manchester University Press, 1998), 212–84; Alain Desrosières, "Managing the Economy," in: *The Cambridge History of Science, VII: The Modern Social Sciences*, edited by Theodore M. Porter and Dorothy Ross (Cambridge: Cambridge University Press, 2003), 553–64.

23 This book takes Foucault's notion of problematization to heart in that it does not provide a history of ideas of growth, analyzing the development of a specific concept in relation to other ideas but instead aims at shedding light on the practical, material, and institutional entanglements of growth research, which eventually contributes to a "history of the way people begin to take care of something [growth], of the way they become anxious about this or that [growth]," Michael Foucault, *Fearless Speech*, edited by Joseph Pearson (Los Angeles: Semiotext(e), 2001), 74.

24 On political action and statistics transforming each other, see Emmanuel Didier, *America by the Numbers: Quantification, Democracy, and the Birth of National Statistics*, translated by Priya Vari Sen (Cambridge, MA: MIT Press, 2020), in particular p. 342. My investigation aligns with the history of statistics that has investigated how quantitative tools gained increasing political relevance as instruments of state control, providing numerical images of the objects to be governed from the early nineteenth century on. See, for instance, Alain Desrosières, *The Politics of Large Numbers: A History of Statistical Reasoning* (Cambridge, MA: Harvard University Press, 1998); Theodore Porter, *Trust in Numbers: The Pursuit of Objectivity in Science and Public Life* (Princeton: Princeton University Press, 1996); Thomas Stapleford, *The Cost of Living in America: A Political History of Economic Statistics* (Cambridge: Cambridge University Press, 2009). For a critical discussion of the literature's prime focus on the role of quantification in the making of the modern state, see William Deringer's epilogue of *Calculated Values: Finance, Politics, and the Quantitative Age* (Cambridge, MA: Harvard University Press, 2018).

25 Lorraine Daston, "The Coming into Being of Scientific Objects," in *Biographies of Scientific Objects*, edited by Lorraine Daston (Chicago: University of Chicago Press, 2000), 1–14, 1.

26 Gaston Bachelard, *The New Scientific Spirit*, translated by Arthur Goldhammer (Boston, MA: Beacon Press, 1984 [1934]), 12.

27 On Bachelard's notion of "problematic," its difference from the Heideggerian focus on the life world as the site for fundamental questioning, and its foundation for Foucault's problematization, see Patrice Maniglier, "What Is a Problematic?," *Radical Philosophy* 173: 21–23. On Bachelard's wider epistemology, see Monika Wulz, *Erkenntnisagenten: Gaston Bachelard und die Reorganisation des Wissens*, Kaleidogramme 61 (Berlin: Kulturverl. Kadmos, 2010). For a discussion of phenomenotechnique in the history of economic knowledge, see Thomas Stapleford,

"Historical Epistemology and the History of Economics: Views through the Lens of Practice," *Research in the History of Economic Thought and Methodology* 35A (2017): 113–45.

28 For the relevant work of national income accounting, see Mary S. Morgan, "Making Measuring Instruments," in *The Age of Economic Measurement* (supplement to *History of Political Economy* 33), edited by Judy L. Klein and Mary S. Morgan (Durham, NC: Duke University Press, 2001), 235–51, 236.

29 Cf. Hans-Jörg Rheinberger, "Gaston Bachelard and the Notion of 'Phenomenotechnique'," *Perspectives on Science* 13, no. 3 (2005): 313–28, 325.

30 Venus Bivar, "Historicizing Economic Growth: An Overview of Recent Works," *The Historical Journal* 65, no. 5 (2022): 1470–89, 1475.

31 Saul I. Gass, "Model World: A Model Is a Model Is a Model Is a Model," *Interfaces* 19, no. 3 (1989): 58–60, 58.

32 On the development of the idea and understanding of a "mathematical model" as an actors' category, see Moritz Epple, "'Analogien', 'Interpretationen', 'Bilder', 'Systeme' und 'Modelle': Bemerkungen zur Geschichte abstrakter Repräsentationen in den Naturwissenschaften seit dem 19. Jahrhundert," edited by Eva Axer, Eva Geulen, and Alexandra Heimes, *Forum Begriffsgeschichte* 5, no. 1 (2016): 11–30.

33 See, for instance, Ronald Kline, *The Cybernetics Moment, or, Why We Call Our Age the Information Age* (Baltimore: Johns Hopkins University Press, 2015), 190–5.

34 Wartofsky, "Model Muddle," 3.

35 See, for instance, Philip Mirowski and Edward M. Nik-Khah, *The Knowledge We Have Lost in Information: The History of Information in Modern Economics* (Oxford: Oxford University Press, 2017); Hunter Heyck, *Age of System: Understanding the Development of Modern Social Science* (Baltimore: Johns Hopkins University Press, 2015); Till Düppe and E. Roy Weintraub, *Finding Equilibrium: Arrow, Debreu, McKenzie and the Problem of Scientific Credit* (Princeton: Princeton University Press, 2014); Paul Erickson, Judy L. Klein, Lorraine Daston, Rebecca Lemov, Thomas Sturm, and Michael D. Gordin, *How Reason Almost Lost Its Mind: The Strange Career of Cold War Rationality* (Chicago: The University of Chicago Press, 2013); Joel Isaac, "Tool Shock: Technique and Epistemology in the Postwar Social Sciences," in *The Unsocial Social Science? Economics and Neighboring Disciplines since 1945* (supplement to *History of Political Economy* 42), edited by Roger E. Backhouse and Philippe Fontaine (Durham, NC: Duke University Press, 2010): 133–64; William Thomas, *Rational Action: The Sciences of Policy in Britain and America, 1940–1960* (Cambridge, MA: MIT Press, 2015).

36 In the sciences, the shift from material analogues to mathematical models between the mid-nineteenth and the mid-twentieth century equipped the term "model" with varied meanings, from the theoretical realizations of formal axiomatic systems in formal logic to mathematical abstractions of complex processes in the applied mathematics of physics or mathematical biology. See Michel Friedman and Karin Krauthausen, "How to Grasp an Abstraction: Mathematical Models and Their Vicissitudes between 1850 and 1950. Introduction," in *Model and Mathematics: From the 19th to the 21st Century*, edited by Michael Friedman and Karin Krauthausen (Cham: Springer International Publishing, 2022), 1–49. On the

variability of modeling criteria in economics, in particular of what economists mean by "tractable," see Béatrice Cherrier, "The Price of Virtue: Some Hypotheses on How Tractability Has Shaped Economic Models," *OEconomia* 13, no. 1 (2023): 23–48. On three different images of mathematics as a science that guided different mathematization practices in economics, see Marcel Boumans, "The History of Mathematisation in Economics" (manuscript submitted to the elements series in the history of economics, Cambridge University Press, October 2023).

37 Morgan, *World in the Model*, 25. Cf. Marx W. Wartofsky, "Introduction," in *Models: Representation and the Scientific Understanding*, edited by Marx W. Wartofsky (Dordrecht: D. Reidel Publishing Company, 1979), xiii–xxvi, xviii. On models as "epistemic artifacts" and the argument that representational views are restricted to "finished science," see Tarja Knuuttila, *Models as Epistemic Artefacts: Toward a Non-Representationalist Account of Scientific Representation*, Philosophical Studies from the University of Helsinki 8 (Helsinki: Department of Philosophy, 2005). On the related notion of models as "cultural artifacts," see Jarosław Boruszewski and Krzysztof Nowak-Posadzy, "Economic Models as Cultural Artifacts: A Philosophical Primer," *Filozofia Nauki (The Philosophy of Science)* 29, no. 3 (2021): 63–87. For my initial thoughts on economic models as artifacts, on which this book builds, see Verena Halsmayer, "Following Artifacts," *History of Political Economy* 50, no. 3 (2018): 629–34. For a survey of the broader literature on economic modeling, see Tarja T. Knuuttila and Mary S. Morgan, "Models and Modelling in Economics," in *Philosophy of Economics*, edited by Uskali Mäki, vol. 13, Handbook of the Philosophy of Science (Amsterdam: Elsevier Scientific, 2012), 49–87.

38 Marcel Boumans, *How Economists Model the World into Numbers* (New York: Routledge, 2005), 3.

39 For a discussion of the "active potential" that models share across the sciences and the arts, see Reinhard Wendler, *Das Modell zwischen Kunst und Wissenschaft* (Munich: Wilhelm Fink Verlag, 2013). For economic models, see Morgan, *World in the Model*, chapter 10. On a model being "often much richer than its intended character," see Tarja Knuuttila, "Imagination Extended and Embedded: Artifactual versus Fictional Accounts of Models," *Synthese* 198, no. S21 (2021): 5077–97, 5092. For a related framework focusing on the "agency" of models, see the sociologists of science Daniel Breslau and Yuval Yonay's "Beyond Metaphor: Mathematical Models in Economics as Empirical Research," *Science in Context* 12 (1999): 317–32.

40 Despite its modest appearance, a model, as Wartofsky argues, is a "normative construction" in that it embodies both specific beliefs and a willingness to act in a specific way. The model demands: "This is how it ought to be done; this is what needs to be understood; this is how one ought to operate." Marx W. Wartofsky, "Telos and Technique: Models as Modes of Action (1968)," in *Models: Representation and the Scientific Understanding*, edited by Marx W. Wartofsky (Dordrecht: D. Reidel Publishing Company, 1979), 140–53, 143. See also Wendler, *Das Modell*, 41–43. I previously discussed the model as a prototype and design, though without fully realizing the intricacies of the interplay of practice and discourse: Verena Halsmayer, "From Exploratory Modeling to Technical Expertise: Solow's Growth Model as a Multi-Purpose Design," in *MIT and the*

Transformation of American Economics (supplement to *History of Political Economy* 46), edited by E. Roy Weintraub (Durham, NC: Duke University Press, 2014), 229–51.

41 Morgan, *World in the Model*, 2–3; Boumans, *How Economists Model the World into Numbers*, 14; Fourcade, *Economists and Societies*, 110. On the related story of how economics was mathematized, see E. Roy Weintraub, *How Economics Became a Mathematical Science* (Durham, NC: Duke University Press, 2002).

42 See Mary S. Morgan, "Technocratic Economics: An Afterword," in *Economics and Engineering: Institutions, Practices, and Cultures* (supplement to *History of Political Economy* 52), edited by Yann Giraud and Pedro Garcia Duarte (Durham, NC: Duke University Press, 2020), 294–304, 295–96. On the performance of technical expertise, see, for instance, Harro Maas, "Making Things Technical: Samuelson at MIT," in *MIT and the Transformation of American Economics* (supplement to *History of Political Economy* 46), edited by E. Roy Weintraub (Durham, NC: Duke University Press, 2014): 272–94.

43 Meles Zenawi, "States and Markets: Neoliberal Limitations and the Case for a Developmental State," in *Good Growth and Governance in Africa: Rethinking Development Strategies*, edited by Akbar Noman, Kwesi Botchwey, Howard Stein, and Joseph E. Stiglitz (Oxford: Oxford University Press, 2012), 140–74, 149.

44 On the productivity of mathematical models deriving from a surplus in meaning, see Sebastian Giacovelli and Andreas Langenohl, "Temporalitäten in der wirtschaftswissenschaftlichen Modellbildung: Die Multiplikation von Zeitlichkeit in der Neoklassik," in *Die Innenwelt der Ökonomie: Wissen, Macht und Performativität in der Wirtschaftswissenschaft*, edited by Jens Maeße, Hanno Pahl, and Jan Sparsam (Wiesbaden: Springer VS, 2017), 33–53.

45 Here, my approach aligns with attempts to account for the intricate relationships between the epistemic and the political that go beyond the role of expertise in modern policy-making. For the idea that the epistemic frames the space of the political, see Kijan Espahangizi and Monika Wulz, "The Political and the Epistemic in the Twentieth Century: Historical Perspectives," *KNOW: A Journal for the Formation of Knowledge* 4, no. 2 (2020): 161–74.

46 For a related argument on the persistence of the discretionary management of the macroeconomy from the age of Roosevelt to the age of Reagan, see Timothy Shenk, "Taking Off the Neoliberal Lens: The Politics of the Economy, the MIT School of Economics, and the Strange Career of Lawrence Klein," *Modern Intellectual History* 20, no. 4 (2023): 1194–218. On one of the modelers who professed to work in the "MIT style," Paul Krugman, and Neo-Keynesians of his generation "policing . . . the boundary of actually existing neoliberalism," see Adam Tooze, "The Gatekeeper," *London Review of Books*, April 22, 2021, available at: www.lrb.co.uk/the-paper/v43/n08/adam-tooze/the-gatekeeper, last accessed April 11, 2024.

47 See Charles Camic, *Veblen: The Making of an Economist Who Unmade Economics* (Cambridge, MA: Harvard University Press, 2020), 10–11. On the coinage of the term "neoclassical" by Thorstein Veblen, see also Tony Aspromourgos, "On the Origins of the Term 'Neoclassical'," *Cambridge Journal of Economics* 10, no. 3 (1986): 265–70.

48 An instance is Maurice Dobb, *Theories of Value and Distribution since Adam Smith: Ideology and Economic Theory* (Cambridge: Cambridge University Press, 1973), 35.

49 See Mischa Suter, *Geld an der Grenze: Souveränität und Wertmaßstäbe im Zeitalter des Imperialismus 1871–1923* (Berlin: Matthes & Seitz, 2024), chapter 2. See also Johanna Bockman, *Markets in the Name of Socialism: The Left-Wing Origins of Neoliberalism* (Stanford, CA: Stanford University Press, 2011), chapter 1; Ian Steedman, ed., Socialism & Marginalism in Economics 1870–1930 (London: Routledge, 1995).

50 See Francisco Louçã, *The Years of High Econometrics: A Short Story of the Generation that Reinvented Economics* (London: Routledge, 2007), 192. On the history of econometrics, see Mary S. Morgan, *The History of Econometric Ideas* (Cambridge: Cambridge University Press, 1990) and the contributions to Marcel Boumans and Ariane Dupont-Kieffer, eds. *Histories of Econometrics*, supplement *History of Political Economy* 43 (Durham, NC: Duke University Press, 2011).

51 See Kevin D. Hoover, "Microfoundational Programs," in *Microfoundations Reconsidered: The Relationship of Micro and Macroeoconomics in Historical Perspective*, edited by Pedro Garcia Duarte and Gilberto Tadeu Lima (Cheltenham, UK: Elgar, 2012), 19–61, 22–25.

52 See Boumans, *How Economists Model the World into Numbers*, 21–2. Tinbergen's growth model was published in "Zur Theorie der langfristigen Wirtschaftsentwicklung," *Weltwirtschaftliches Archiv* 55 (1942): 511–49, translated in "On the Theory of Trend Movements," in *Jan Tinbergen: Selected Papers*, edited by L. H. Klaassen, L. M. Koyck, and H. J. Witteveen (Amsterdam: North-Holland, 1959), 182–221. On the models of macrodynamists and their attempts to integrate them with economic policy-making, see Michaël Assous and Vincent Carret, *Modeling Economic Instability: A History of Early Macroeconomics* (Cham: Springer, 2022).

53 The English translation of Grigorij A. Fel'dman's work on growth was published in Nicholas Spulber, ed., *Foundations of Soviet Strategy for Economic Growth, Selected Short Soviet Essays 1924–1930* (Bloomington, IN: Indiana University Press, 1964); Prasanta C. Mahalanobis, "Some Observations on the Process of Growth of National Income," *Sankhyā: The Indian Journal of Statistics* 12, no. 4 (1953): 307–12. On the whole, this book concentrates more on economists' with the artifacts they constructed than on the theoretical contributions they wanted to make. On Solow's model in the context of a history of growth theory, see, for instance, the contributions to Mauro Boianovsky and Kevin D. Hoover, eds., *Robert Solow and the Development of Growth Economics*, supplement to *History of Political Economy* 41 (Durham, NC: Duke University Press, 2009); Stephen A. Marglin, *Raising Keynes: A Twenty-First-Century General Theory* (Cambridge, MA: Harvard University Press, 2021), chapter 17. More specifically on what has been called the "Cambridge Capital Controversy," see Geoffrey C. Harcourt, *Some Cambridge Controversies in the Theory of Capital* (Cambridge: Cambridge University Press, 1972).

54 On the "functioning of a 'mixed' capitalistic enterprise system," see Paul A. Samuelson, *Economics: An Introductory Analysis* (New York: McGraw-Hill Book Company, Inc., 1948). Amy Offner recently highlighted the mixed economy's reliance "on the imagined dichotomy between public and private while systematically conjoining the two," Amy C. Offner, *Sorting out the Mixed Economy: The Rise and Fall of Welfare and Developmental States in the Americas* (Princeton: Princeton University Press, 2019), 17.

55 MIT economists such as Lawrence Klein, Paul Samuelson, Franco Modigliani, and Don Patinkin were crucial in framing a Keynesian economics in terms of mathematical models, denoted by its critics as "bastard Keynesianism." On Keynes himself "enunciating the Bastard Keynesian doctrine," see the interview with Joan Robinson in Soma Golden, "Economist Joan Robinson, 72, Is Full of Fight," *New York Times*, March 23, 1976, available at www.nytimes.com/1976/03/23/archives/economist-joan-robinson-72-is-full-of-fight-economist-joan-robinson.html, last accessed April 11, 2024. On American Keynesianism as essentially a postwar theory of income analysis, see Roger E. Backhouse, *Founder of Modern Economics: Paul A. Samuelson, Vol. 1: Becoming Samuelson* (New York: Oxford University Press, 2017). On the related models and diagrams, see, for instance, Michel De Vroey and Kevin D. Hoover, eds., *The IS–LM Model: Its Rise, Fall, and Strange Persistence*, supplement to *History of Political Economy* 36 (Duke, NC: Duke University Press, 2004).

56 See, for instance, its most iconic expression in Samuelson, *Economics*. On the central threads of Samuelson's soon best-selling economic textbook, see Backhouse, *Becoming Samuelson*, chapter 25.

57 See Yann Giraud, "Negotiating the "Middle-of-the-Road" Position: Paul Samuelson, MIT, and the Politics of Textbook Writing, 1945–55," in *MIT and the Transformation of American Economics* (supplement to *History of Political Economy* 46), edited by E. Roy Weintraub (Durham, NC: Duke University Press, 2014), 134–52.

58 Philip Mirowski, "Twelve Theses Concerning the History of Postwar Neoclassical Price Theory," in *Agreement on Demand: Consumer Theory in the Twentieth Century* (supplement to *History of Political Economy* 38), edited by Philip Mirowski and Wade D. Hands (Durham, NC: Duke University Press, 2006), 343–79, 355.

59 Trevor W. Swan, "Growth Models: Of Golden Ages and Production Functions," in *Economic Development with Special Reference to East Asia*, edited by Kenneth Berrill (London: Palgrave Macmillan UK, 1964), 3–18, republished in Sen, *Growth Economics*, 203–18, 205. Swan's growth model was published in T. W. Swan, "Economic Growth and Capital Accumulation," *Economic Record* 32, no. 2 (1956): 334–61. When he eventually encountered Swan's work, Solow was intrigued: "I must tell you that I can't remember when I've enjoyed a piece of economics so much. It was sheer pleasure." Robert Solow to Trevor Swan, April 1, 1957, Solow papers, box 60, file S: 2 of 7. On the occasion of receiving the Nobel Memorial Prize, he highlighted the simultaneous construction and supported the naming of the "Solow–Swan model."

60 This goes especially for Solow, who became a frequently cited authority figure both when it came to the advantages and dangers of mathematical modeling and (probably as a counterpart to versions of his model) against conservative or neoliberal policies.

61 Jeff Biddle has made a similar observation in Paul Douglas's writings on production in Jeff Biddle, *Progress through Regression: The Life Story of Empirical Cobb-Douglas Production Function* (Cambridge: Cambridge University Press, 2021), 306–10.

62 Robert M. Solow, "Review of the Failures of Economics: A Diagnostic Study by Sidney Schoeffler," *Review of Economics and Statistics* 39, no. 1 (1957): 96–98, 96;

Evsey D. Domar, "Economic Growth: An Econometric Approach," *American Economic Review* 42, no. 2 (1952): 479–95, 481 and 484; Robert Solow to Holland Hunter, October 26, 1955, Solow papers, box 55, file H: 2 of 3.

63 Solow, "Review of the Failures of Economics," 97.

64 On this notion of "research episode" highlighting that different research practices might lead to the same (formal) outcome, see Moritz Epple, "Between Timelessness and Historiality: On the Dynamics of the Epistemic Objects of Mathematics," *Isis* 102, no. 3 (2011): 481–93, 487–8.

65 For three recent contributions in that vein, see Hirschman, "Rediscovering the 1%"; Berman, *Thinking Like an Economist*; Shenk, "Taking Off the Neoliberal Lens."

1

The Artifact and the Experimental Report

All theory depends on assumptions which are not quite true. That is what makes it theory. The art of successful theorizing is to make the inevitable simplifying assumptions in such a way that the final results are not very sensitive. A "crucial" assumption is one on which the conclusions do depend sensitively, and it is important that crucial assumptions be reasonably realistic. When the results of a theory seem to flow specifically from a special crucial assumption, then if the assumption is dubious, the results are suspect.[1]

The "Contribution to the Theory of Economic Growth" started with a methodological preamble. While this introductory statement may sound casual, it self-confidently laid the groundwork for both dismissing the prevalent approach to theorizing about economic growth and opposing one of the best-known treatments of economic methodology at the time. In a widely read essay, Chicago's Milton Friedman had suggested that the "more significant the theory, the more unrealistic the assumptions."[2] According to the conventional reading of Friedman's odd mixture of positivist and instrumentalist rhetoric, if the predictions deduced from a theory were true, then it was possible to proceed *as if* the assumptions were true. In contrast, the "Contribution" was part of a research endeavor that was more invested in models. The preamble introduced the paper of a young, not particularly well-known economist who had been hired by the Department of Economics and Social Science at MIT seven years earlier. It directed the reader's attention, right from the outset, to a specific way of *doing* economics, an "art of theorizing." The explicit focus on theorizing as an activity contrasted decisively with the differentiation between a positive science of economic theory and a normative art of economic policy-making that had been common in the 1930s. The introductory statement hinted at a very specific conception of economics as a craft that was based on a particular set of techniques and skills and imparted a certain practical knowledge. The article did not contain any further methodological explications about "successful theorizing," how to make the "inevitable simplifying assumptions," or about which assumptions might be "reasonably realistic." It performed it.

Edited at Harvard University's Department of Economics since 1886, the prestigious *Quarterly Journal of Economics* published a diversity of contributions both in terms of topics and approaches. The issues before Spring 1956 reflected the varied state of the midcentury economics discipline: An essayistic treatment of the "Soviet capital controversy"; discussions of the American reception of Keynes's theories of interest; an account of "the problem of 'underdevelopment'" from a history of economic thought perspective; a behavioral model of rational choice; new formulations of nineteenth-century mathematical economics; an analysis of bank mergers in the United States in the early 1950s; an investigation of the consequences of David Riesman's *The Lonely Crowd* for the common framing of a rational economic man; and a statistical examination of the problem of raiding among American Unions.[3] The articles ranged over many forms of knowledge – literary descriptions, historical case studies, econometric arguments, anecdotes, algebraic equations, descriptive statistics, numerical examples, geometric reasoning, and thought experiments. Unlike most of the articles published in the *Quarterly Journal*, the "Contribution" contained a significant number of diagrams and algebraic equations in the main text. This setup conformed with what was increasingly taken as economic science. Earlier renditions of economics as a theoretical and scientific enterprise that was distinct from the nonacademic sphere did involve algebraic and diagrammatic formulations but most commonly relegated them to footnotes and appendices.[4] In contrast, the "Contribution" revolved around a mathematical model – its construction, operation, and how it reacted to a series of small experiments. Describing how the model worked and contemplating its interpretation constituted the sole focus of inquiry.

Paying attention to the forms and aesthetics of the 1956 article, this chapter showcases what it means to conceive of mathematical economic models as artifacts. The prime focus of my reading is not the paper's theoretical content or the specifics of the mathematical formulations but rather its particular combination of mathematical equations, prosaic passages, and diagrams. Only this combination constituted the "model," something that, in principle, stood for more than itself. In this sense, the following pages explore what exactly the "Contribution" presented as a model and in which way it did so. The first section analyzes the article's order of events, the specific presence of a narrative authority, and its references to objects beyond the text. It is here that the model appeared as an artifact that was constructed and at the same time attributed an autonomous existence. The second section delineates the ways in which the mathematical system of equations was presented as an economy, in particular how the assumptions of perfect competition and perfect foresight gave economic meaning to the mathematics. Most importantly, the third section concludes, this model world had to function. It was all about the making of a well-working system that could be experimented with. What the introductory preamble called "reasonably realistic" related primarily to the functioning of the model and had only loose ties to the world of economic practices. In the first place, it was about securing the very purpose of the model: Establishing and analyzing a full-employment growth equilibrium. On the whole, the "Contribution" looked straight *at* the model (constructing, setting up, and qualifying an artifact). It did not look at the world *through* the model. That there was a relation between the model and a world beyond, as tenuous as it might have been, was merely suggested by lowering any expectation that it could be practical for policy-making on its own.

Other chapters in this book ponder the power of models to angle reasoning with regard to economic measurement and policy-making. This chapter zooms in on the intriguing developments at play in processes of what is commonly called "formalization." There was one instance in which the "Contribution" looked straight *through* the model, namely when it came to presenting it as an improvement to existing economic theory. The article took up wider discussions among postwar modelers who considered much of the predominantly narrative, nonmathematical economics to be obscure and logically flawed. In the work of institutionalist economics, some modelers saw merely descriptive accounts, bordering on the non- or even anti-theoretical. Restricting proper "theory" to mathematical models, a similar verdict met the (otherwise much admired) John Maynard Keynes. His *General Theory* was widely seen to represent incomplete and vague reasoning in need of clarification. American Keynesians, as they came to be called, transformed his work into a collection of small-scale mathematical and geometrical working objects.[5] The "Contribution" treated the British Keynesian Roy F. Harrod's dynamic theory, published at the end of the 1930s, in a similar vein, presented it *as* if it was a postwar model, and turned it into a special case of the neoclassical approach. The fourth section argues that such histories of formalization fundamentally underestimate the formatting of knowledge in terms of models and the serious losses it involved.[6] The concern with sustained capitalist instability was not easily modeled through a closed system of differential or difference equations; it was first caricatured in the so-called Harrod–Domar literature and then vanished from a growth theory that constituted itself in terms of equilibrium models and, for some time, was regarded as the modeling endeavor *par excellence*. In this way, the "Contribution" was a major step both in marginalizing a different way of economic reasoning and in converting interwar thinking about dynamics, frictions, and crisis into equilibrium models of stable growth.

NARRATOLOGICAL DIMENSIONS

The narrative structure of the "Contribution" was akin to that of an experimental report. Even if readers skipped over the explicit wordings of "experiment" and "experimentation," they could not escape being taken on a tour through the model on which they encountered an object that could be manipulated with some surprising results.[7] In the first section, the article introduced the reader to the "model of long-run growth."[8] It laid out its specific assumptions, defined the variables, and put them in relation to each other. In a further step, it described the model's workings and demonstrated how it reacted to various changes of parameters. The next section extended the system of equations by adding new variables showing how this would affect its fundamental outcomes. In this way, the article familiarized the reader with constructing and manipulating a mathematical model – the "art of theorizing," which the preamble pushed so emphatically. All verbal formulations served to describe, demonstrate, and explain what happened with the model in the course of experimenting. References to any phenomena or knowledge extraneous to the system's austere architecture were scarce. Only a short last section, under the heading "qualifications," discussed differences between what happened in the mathematical model and the realm of economic policy-making (Figure 1.1).

The text contained a strong narrator who directly addressed the readers, especially when it came to investigating the model's "behavior." It encouraged them, for instance, to play with the parameters ("The reader can work out still other possibilities"[9]) or to manipulate the graphs ("The reader can draw a diagram . . . in which the growth paths pass to steeper and steeper or to flatter and flatter rays"[10]). During model experiments, the narrator shifted to the pronoun "we": "inserting (2) in (1) we get . . .," "we see that . . .," "we know that . . .," "these conclusions are . . . just what we should expect."[11] These instructions, guidelines, and commentaries turned

A CONTRIBUTION TO THE THEORY OF
ECONOMIC GROWTH

By Robert M. Solow

I. Introduction, 65. — II. A model of long-run growth, 66. — III. Possible growth patterns, 68. — IV. Examples, 73. — V. Behavior of interest and wage rates, 78. — VI. Extensions, 85. — VII. Qualifications, 91.

I. Introduction

All theory depends on assumptions which are not quite true. That is what makes it theory. The art of successful theorizing is to make the inevitable simplifying assumptions in such a way that the final results are not very sensitive.[1] A "crucial" assumption is one on which the conclusions do depend sensitively, and it is important that crucial assumptions be reasonably realistic. When the results of a theory seem to flow specifically from a special crucial assumption, then if the assumption is dubious, the results are suspect.

Figure 1.1 Title page of the "Contribution." The table of contents conveys the paper's narrative structure.
(Solow, "Contribution," 65)

the mathematical system into an autonomous object that could be used and manipulated – independently of its construction history, by others aside from the modeler. At the same time, the narrator appeared as the model constructor ("the way I have drawn," "I have elsewhere discussed").[12] At least at some points in the article, the model appeared as an economist's personal product. But it already took the first steps into autonomy, open to manipulations and other usages by, in principle, anyone. Those not familiar enough with the algebra could focus on the sections dealing with the basic outline of the model and try to work out the diagrams.

Diagrams did not only make the model visible in a different, perhaps more accessible form than algebraic equations, they played a major role when the paper unfurled as a series of experiments. In fact, the relevant equations were only given in footnotes or were not given at all. The article's central diagram (Figure 1.2) visualized the algebraic equilibrium graphically as the point where two curves intersect in Cartesian space. By drawing variants of this first diagram, the narrator investigated the specific properties of the model, asked what happened if the curves were formed differently, and illustrated the specific properties of the model as they unfolded in the course of experimenting.

By drawing different shapes, the diagrams in Figure 1.3 showed that the stability of equilibrium depended on very particular assumptions about production. The model experiments depicted in Figure 1.4 consisted of making small changes *ceteris paribus* (that is, leaving everything else unchanged) in order to see whether the economy still found its way to the equilibrium growth path.

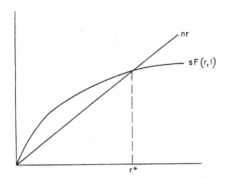

Figure 1.2 The central visualization of the model. r*, the point where the two curves intersect, signifies the equilibrium growth rate.
(Solow, "Contribution," 70)

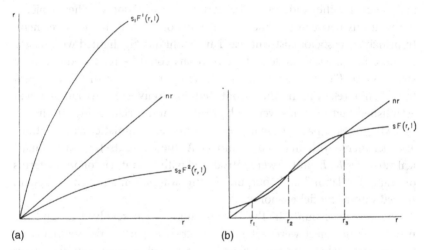

(a)   (b)

Figure 1.3 Drawing different shapes.
(Solow, "Contribution," 71 and 72)

Beyond simply illustrating the equilibrium mechanism, the diagrams fostered a different level of understanding than did the mathematical equations. They were essential in capturing the workings of the mathematical artifact – in an almost literal sense. Readers were not only told how the model worked, they also had the chance to turn into model manipulators themselves and experience the sensual character of formal operations.[13]

To really get a full grasp of the model, the reader had to combine algebraic, graphic, and verbal elements.[14] Diagrams included labels for axes and graphs in symbolic form, which referred to the model's

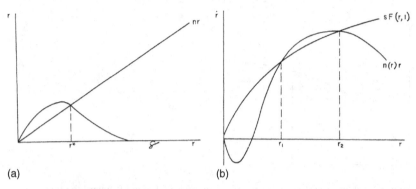

Figure 1.4 Experimenting with variables.
(Solow, "Contribution," 89 and 90)

parameters (or they did not, as the axes in Figure 1.2 show). They depicted
the relations between parameters but did not further characterize them.
In principle, as sociologist Andreas Langenohl has highlighted with regard
to static neoclassical models, these relations could be read as depicting a
synchronous ("to the same extent as"), temporal ("given that"), or causal
("if, then") relation. In the "Contribution," only the surrounding text
established that relations were to be read as causal relationships in time.[15]
Likewise, prosaic passages made sense of the diagrammatic manipulations
as experiments with an *economic* model. At the very outset, the mathematical variables K, L, and Y were introduced with the rather colloquial terms
of "capital," "labor," and "output." In this way, the mathematical system
turned into a "model economy."[16]

The verbal accounts in the "Contribution" that revolved around the
mathematical object were not just a descriptive part of the mathematics
but qualified what was happening in the model. In this way, they were
central in making mathematical economic modeling seem like the construction of new artifacts. In contrast to contemporary publications in
game theory or the emerging general equilibrium theory that devised more
sophisticated formal systems, here mathematical proofs occupied only very
little space. Instead, there were substantial blocks of text that contained no
symbols but explicated in plain language the economic rationale of what
was going on. Statements such as the following made sure that mathematical equations had economic content:

Alternatively (4) $[L = L_0 e^{nt}]$ can be looked at as a supply curve of labor. It says that
the exponentially growing labor force is offered for employment completely
inelastically. The labor supply curve is a vertical line which shifts to the right in
time as the labor force grows according to (4). Then the real wage rate adjusts so

that all available labor is employed, and the marginal productivity equation determines the wage rate which will actually rule.[17]

In this way, the mathematical equation turned into the behavior of the supply of labor over time. This also meant to redefine verbal terms in a very specific way: "labor force" was a vertical line, a mathematical concept. The verbal account detached everyday terms from their common meanings and filled them with new conceptual content in relation to the mathematical object. Moreover, it ensured that the system of equations made sense as a highly specific economy in which, for instance, an "exponentially growing labor force" existed. From this perspective, the ominous "assumptions" (for instance, that labor was supplied inelastically) that necessarily belonged to any model did not so much simplify, abstract, or idealize "the real world." Rather, they were crucial in providing the constructed mathematical system with some economic meaning (however detached from the world of economic practices).

Despite its formal precision, a model can still be indeterminate in the sense that it is open to various interpretations. The central component of the growth model, for instance, was a production function: $Y = F(K, L)$. The mathematical formalism spoke of some variables, homogenous somethings called "output" (Y), "capital" (K), and "labor" (L). The verbal account explicated: "There is only one commodity, output as a whole."[18] The production of aggregate output was like the production of one good. Ambiguities remained, as the article left open whether the variables were to be thought of as aggregate measures, composite numbers (comprising the production processes of several firms), or hypothetical figures of one singular firm producing one good. The model's polyvalent equations were open to different textual explications: Was K, the composite capital, to be read as the result of the actions of rational economic agents, was it more like a summary statistic, or both? This ambiguity would become central in the life of the model after it was published, both as a focal point of critique and as a major driver for the model's manifold adaptations. In the years to come, even the modeler himself looked at the model from different points of view, interpreting the its variables as being based on individual businesses' behavior in a general equilibrium in some instances and as observable aggregate entities in others.[19]

A VERY SPECIFIC ECONOMY

Taking mathematical system, verbal accounts, and diagrams together, the model in the "Contribution" portrayed a particularly smooth-running and manageable world, which later became the dominant image of growth in economic reasoning. The inputs of production (capital and labor) were both "homogenous," meaning that there was no difference, say, between manual and intellectual work or between variable or fixed capital. Moreover, there were no such things as energy, land, or any other non-augmentable resources. Output equaled the "community's" real income.[20] At every instant in time, part of the output was consumed while the rest was saved and immediately invested. This meant that savings equaled investment in new capital at every instant.

The equations for production were encapsulated by the quintessentially neoclassical assumption of *perfect competition*.[21] In this way, the model relied on the presumption of fully competitive markets in which flexible prices and wages kept supply and demand (for capital and labor) in equilibrium. The so-called marginal conditions applied, meaning that prices straightforwardly reflected relative productivity: Capital and labor could just be substituted for one another whenever relative prices changed. Consequently, there was constant full employment of both labor and capital. The rationale for this assumption was that it provided a story of why the rate of interest and the wage rate could be directly derived from the production function. Thus, money was excluded from the model, and production turned into a mechanical combination of physical inputs and physical output.

These assumptions about perfectly flexible production laid the foundation for investigating growth – in the very specific sense of a self-sustaining growth equilibrium. The relevant expression took the form of a linear differential equation. It determined "the time path of capital accumulation" by the movements of output and saving.[22] Labor was given exogenously, which meant that it was given outside the model through a constant rate of population growth. All available labor was employed: Whenever the supply of labor changed, the relative prices of capital and labor changed. Capital reacted flexibly to these changes; whatever the necessary relation to ensure efficient production, capital adapted in the appropriate way. There was "always a capital accumulation path consistent with any growth rate of the labor force."[23]

To make sense of the notion of time that came with the linear differential equation, the "Contribution" assumed *perfect foresight*. Essentially, this meant that the future development of interest rates was known in the present and allowed for perfect arbitrage over time. Differences in prices and interest rates in the future were efficiently utilized today. Plans were always realized: There was no risk, no uncertainty. Speaking with Deirdre McCloskey, a solvable linear differential equation implied "a rather brute form of time, a mere chronology." The equilibrium growth path was independent of initial conditions. The system already started to run in equilibrium. "Behind a differential equation lies the idea of a timeless process."[24] Historical dynamics, frictions, and contingency were thus excluded. The central characteristic of the time path of the growing economy was that it was, in a specific sense, mathematically clear-cut and tractable.[25]

The wondrously smooth world of perfect competition and perfect foresight featured a growth equilibrium in which capital and labor were always fully employed in an unchanging relationship.[26] This long-run equilibrium, the "balanced growth path," was proven to be stable, "whatever the initial value ..., the system will develop *toward* a state of balanced growth."[27] If the growth rate of labor increased, the system adjusted and asymptotically "approach[ed] a state of steady proportional expansion."[28] In this economy nothing essential evolved or transformed during the growth "process." The use of a composite commodity made sure that the growing economy only changed in scale but not in composition. Accordingly, the growth rate of output could be permanently increased only through exogenous factors that were not part of the inner workings of the model: Alterations of the model government's policy, demographic changes, or "technological change."[29] All these changes came from the outside and did not modify anything inside the efficient, timeless system of physical relations.

The main purpose of the "Contribution" was to lay out the conditions that enabled the mathematical possibility of a stable equilibrium growth rate. For such a mathematical equilibrium to exist, the strict differentiation between effortlessly working production on the inside and all kinds of actual dynamics on the outside was essential. Internally consistent and manipulable, the model appeared as a small-scale mathematical object. It demonstrated a stable growth equilibrium, which came with a neat storyline about a smoothly working economy in which everything just added up. As we will see, things became messier once the narrator dared to move away from the realm of the model.

WEAK KNOWLEDGE

The epistemological conundrums of such a parsimonious model were at stake in the last section of the paper. They appeared as rather casual, seemingly mundane comments from the vantage point of the practitioner. These comments dealt with those differences between the model and the world that the modeler deemed obvious. They gave an impression of what "reasonably realistic" might mean and conjectured about the (non)uses of such a simple model for thinking about policy. While the better part of the "Contribution" was about presenting and highlighting the model's characteristics, the final paragraphs emphasized it was merely a model and hinted at the fragile character of what it had termed "experimental" knowledge in the previous pages.

Today, economic papers circling around a model usually end with a section of conclusions or policy prescriptions. This article ended with "Qualifications," a section that was quite outspoken: Neither was the economy the paper presented even approximately believed to be real, nor was the model of any use for directly drawing policy conclusions. Here, the narrator most evidently appeared as the model constructor: "I have been deliberately as neoclassical as you can get." Compared to today's standards of economic writing, this modeler was rather careful about drawing conclusions from the model that related to something beyond its confines. The absences they emphasized as relevant belonged to another realm of economic theory dealing with so-called Keynesian income analysis."[30] Clearly, the model eclipsed all kinds of "difficulties and rigidities," but it was "not [the modeler's] contention that these problems don't exist, nor that they are of no significance in the long run."[31] There was no assertion of the real-world-existence of a market creating spontaneous order as a self-regulating system. Quite in contrast to the model, which always adapted to equilibrium, the qualifying remarks highlighted that it "may take deliberate action to maintain full employment ... via tax, expenditure, and monetary policies."[32] "Economic stabilization" relating to the ups and downs of the business cycle or high unemployment rates would require different models. One could discuss how the short-run features of such "Keynesian" models might impinge on the neoclassical long-run world of growth and investigate what would happen if the conditions chosen in the paper did not apply.[33]

When it came to the relation between the artifact and policy questions, it was all too obvious that the portrayed economy was so tremendously specific that any relation to a world outside the model had to remain rather vague. This, however, did not mean that the "Contribution" was silent on economic governance. On the contrary, it situated the model within the context of short-run policies that determined, among others, the extent to which an economy was imagined to be able to achieve full employment. The advantage of such "highly abstract analysis" was that it provided a "theoretical counterpart" to "practical possibilities."[34] If short-run policies worked out, the smoothly running neoclassical world of perfect competition, this "land of the margin," provided a framework for discussing the relationship between investment and consumption, between present and future consumption, as well as the various factors that would affect that relationship.[35] In the parallel publication of another neoclassical growth model, the Australian economist Trevor Swan made explicit the belief that would become central for the so-called neoclassical synthesis and highly relevant for macroeconomic planning: "When Keynes solved 'the great puzzle of Effective Demand,' he made it possible for economists once more to study the progress of society in long-run classical terms – with a clear conscience."[36] In neither of the models was the assumption of full employment an expression of a belief that the free market would eliminate unemployment. They complemented the vision of a patchwork of models rather than one overarching mathematical framework, which could integrate all kinds of aspects (such as the short- and long-run, individual actions, and macro dynamics). What one model could not handle might be depicted in another one. However, such statements were ambiguous, as models were open to several interpretations. The catchy point that the growth model was the "neoclassical side of the coin" could easily be interpreted in different ways.[37] It could promote, for instance, the idea of an overarching framework integrating both sides of the coin, which was exactly what happened in the revival of neoclassical growth theory from the 1980s on. Another way to read the statement was that it strictly separated between the factors that were seen to promote long-run development and those that contributed to short-run issues like full employment.[38]

In an equally loose manner, the "Contribution" elaborated on the central argument of the introductory paragraph, that assumptions needed to be "reasonably realistic." In the first place, the argument was a side blow against what it called the "Harrod–Domar line of thought," the dominating strand in economic growth theory at the time.[39] Overturning its "dubious" assumption of a fixed relation between capital and labor, the article built on the alternative assumption that inputs could be substituted flexibly. What made it reasonably realistic, in the modeler's reasoning, was that in the long run it was just not reasonable that the relation of inputs was fixed. The underlying notion of what was realistic was a matter of plausibility rather than of econometric testing, empirical falsifiability, or predictive accuracy. The "Contribution" did not contain any empirical support of the model's realism; neither did it try to maintain that any of the other assumptions was particularly close to a reality. In the end, the "Qualifications" underlined that what was reasonably realistic depended on the specific purpose a model was thought to fulfill. The purpose of this model was not to present a "credible theory of investment" but to investigate a stable long-run growth equilibrium.[40] This involved the model's ability to check how the growth process worked without the assumption of flexible inputs. Before this background, reasonably realistic meant something like *as long as it does not endanger the workability of the model.* When legitimizing the chosen shape for the production function (Cobb-Douglas), for instance, the modeler argued frankly that it was "tractable" and avoided the complications of a more general shape.[41] The more practical shape involved the assumption that innovations came from changes in relative prices, happening exactly when they were due.

My reading of the "Contribution" in the preceding pages illustrated how modelers, more generally, see the key quality of their working objects not in their truthfulness but in their ability to effectively pose a problem. For the case for model organisms, it has been argued that they offered opportunities for interaction and experience because they could not be entirely controlled.[42] For mathematical models, their main quality was some kind of efficiency in expression. Or as the mathematician Marc Kac has put it: their "main role ... is not so much to explain and predict ... as to polarize thinking and to pose sharp questions."[43] What economists presented as "simple" models made it possible to raise precise questions due to their specific form, which imposed constraints on reasoning. The "Contribution" demonstrated the restricting and opening effects of such models, as they have been analyzed in the literature on modeling as a scientific practice. On the one hand, models determined the readers' "freedom to maneuver," as philosopher of economics Marcel Boumans has framed it: What they could do with the curves in the diagrams, how they thought with and through the model.[44] Reasoning with the neoclassical growth model was restricted to the confines of a mathematical equilibrium in a "frictionless, competitive, causal system."[45] On the other hand, despite all the strategic simplifications on which it was based, a model is more than just a well-defined version of modelers' pre-existing ideas. Even though it conforms to some extent to the modeler's intentions, she does not necessarily know the results of her investigations in advance. In model experiments, the modeler–economist and the model are, to use Mary Morgan's words, "jointly active participants."[46] She has argued that experiments just as the ones in the "Contribution" did not actually confound the modeler; the results might be unexpected but were still explicable given existing knowledge.[47] Yet playing with the model still prompted new ideas and coined new concepts. Retrospectively, Robert M. Solow, the modeler of the "Contribution" at least claimed he had been surprised that the model's steady-state rate of growth was independent of the savings rate: "I thought it was a real shocker. It is not what I expected at all."[48]

Compared to its strong presentation of the model as an experimental artifact, the article's reference to any real growing economy was rather feeble. There was no explicit attempt to show the mathematical system as a representation of some quantitatively measured entity. There was no empirical test, no reference to empirical studies. The "Contribution" can be read as making a case for much looser and more informal knowledge. Its major achievement was to separate out a smoothly running mathematical system: On the inside was a mechanism of steadily increasing physical production; on the outside were all the factors that were able to impact but never to disturb the sheltered sphere. When readers accepted the invitation to engage with the model, they ventured on an undertaking that, at least for the moment, suspended all kinds of complications and uncertainties. The many difficulties of linking the model to a real world were not simply shortcomings. They contributed decisively to the model's productivity. Proponents and critics alike built on its blunt portrayal, sought to deal with its shortcomings, provided it with different meanings, or used it as a comparative foil to build alternative worlds. The following chapters will demonstrate various interpretations and uses the model provoked. Moreover, the model lured reasoning into its narrow confines when it came to past theorizations of growth. It is here that the following section locates the suggestive power of models.

A MODEL STORY OF FORMALIZATION

For the professional readership, which the "Contribution" found rather quickly, the article signified a substantial contribution to modern growth theory and capital theory, most often mentioned alongside Trevor Swan's and James Tobin's similar models.[49] Sometimes it was singled out as the "most important paper" that contributed to a "major revision" of the widely held "Harrod–Domar" belief.[50] Such readings conformed with the article's own presentation of the neoclassical growth model as a remedy to the pitfalls of existing growth theory. The story went something like this: The conventional, so-called Harrod–Domar model dubiously assumed that the relation between capital and labor never changed (a fixed capital coefficient). Due to this assumption, it portrayed a peculiar "knife-edge," the suspicious "tightrope view of economic growth."[51] In this world, any step away from the equilibrium growth rate led inexorably to mass unemployment and depression. Against the foil of the pervasive Harrod instability, the "Contribution" assumed that, due to perfect competition, inputs were substitutable. This neoclassical angle guaranteed that deviations from the equilibrium would be self-correcting. Having corrected the problematic assumption, the model now featured stable growth instead of crisis.

Until today, the history of growth theory as it is usually told by economists – critics and supporters of neoclassical growth theory alike – follows this narrative.[52] In a joint paper with Kevin Hoover, I have argued that review essays, textbook accounts, and historical introductions to economic articles have told and retold some version of how the field progressed from a deficient first model to the neoclassical one that laid the foundation for modern growth theory.[53] One particularly widely read version of this narrative is found in one of today's major mainstream textbooks on economic growth theory. It states that Harrod "used production functions with little substitutability among the inputs to argue that the capitalist system is inherently unstable. Since [he] wrote during or immediately after the Great Depression, these arguments were received sympathetically by many economists. Although these contributions triggered a good deal of research at the time, very little of this analysis plays a role in today's thinking."[54] Likewise, historians of other fields, when they tapped into the history of economics, reverted to such potted histories.[55]

Ironically, the primary target of the "Contribution," Harrod's "Essay in Dynamic Theory" (1939), did not subscribe to the image of economic growth that it was said to uphold. Most notably, it dealt with a different time horizon focused on capitalist instabilities and was preoccupied with the question of stabilization policies.[56] It did not even contain a model in terms of a small-scale and manipulable mathematical object. Published in 1939, Harrod's essay adhered to the style and form of British Keynesian and Marshallian economics before the Second World War. It used mathematics in a limited way. The reading of Harrod's work in the "Contribution" in terms of a mathematical model meant imposing a different way of reasoning, which decisively transformed the essay's contents. Looking through the lens of mathematical modelers, the essay amounted to utterly vague thinking in need of being clarified – through a proper model.

When reading the "Contribution" and Harrod's essay side-by-side, it is difficult not to see neoclassical economics appropriating older-style Keynesian argument, providing it with a new form, and hereby substantially changing its content. The growth equations in the "Essay" provided specific reasoning tools; it even included the terminology of "tool of analysis."[57] It did present a couple of algebraic equations, which, not unlike the "Contribution," related the growth of output with capital accumulation. But neither were the variables part of a well-defined mathematical system nor was it based on any specific assumptions about the growth of labor, the conditions of production, or the factors that might influence the development of the cycle. It did mention all these aspects and wove them into verbal explanations of the cycle, but they were not part of the growth equations. Paired with some numerical examples to exemplify the argument, the essay's equations offered a loose framework for discussion of what might happen if various factors in economic life led to other circumstances than those expected by entrepreneurs. These reflections were exclusively verbal; the equations themselves were not touched in the process.[58] Due to the obvious differences, many critical readers have pointed out the crucial "misunderstandings," "misinterpretations," and "misrepresentations" in the modelers' reception of Harrod's essay.[59] The soon dominant approach to economics came with blind spots and angled historiographies as part of a larger postwar culture of reading prewar works that had made do without mathematical models as central working objects.

The specific reading of Harrod's 1939 article in terms of a growth model developed within an extensive literature on macrodynamics and growth in the immediate postwar period. During the Second World War, the resources of economics had changed decisively: New data had become available, among them national income accounts that presented coherent and clean figures of "the whole economy" (which will be central to Chapter 2), and the new mathematical techniques of wartime planning started to trickle into economic analysis and were about to fundamentally change the idea of economic dynamics (as will be discussed in Chapters 3 and 4). Most readers expressed some kind of doubt as to "what Harrod actually meant." Thomas C. Schelling, at the time a teaching fellow in economics at Harvard University, for example, wondered "whether [Harrod] meant to imply that [investment] actually would be proportionate to income, or only meant to give it formal expression."[60] They wondered about the status of the equations, criticized supposedly unclear notations, and struggled with apparently incomplete definitions.[61] Also Solow, in a letter to a colleague in Cambridge, England, spoke of his "uneasiness in this Harrod maybe–maybe land of equilibrium growth, in which one never knows anything about the behavior–dynamics of the system."[62] Akin to the way in which modelers transformed Keynes's *General Theory* into a collection of small-scale mathematical and geometrical working objects, mathematical economists brought Harrod's work into the form of a system of equations.[63]

Reinterpreters, such as William Baumol, were convinced they would merely make implicit assumptions explicit and "Mr. Harrod's system work the way he says it does."[64] A particular strategy was to use the "clearer" notations and formalisms of Evsey D. Domar's "Capital Expansion, Rate of Growth, and Employment," published in 1946 in *Econometrica*, the main outlet of the new mathematical economics.[65] In that paper, Domar had investigated capitalist difficulties in creating and maintaining full employment via a mathematical system that portrayed the relation between capital accumulation and employment.[66] In contrast to Harrod's essay, here the primary category of reasoning was an equilibrium growth rate that would ensure full employment.[67] On their clarifying, mathematical economists formulated a "complete model" with a specified production function and merged it with Domar's model.[68] In this way, Harrod's work turned into a system of difference equations. Many hands constructed the new Harrod–Domar model, which became one of economists' predominant working objects in the postwar period. Already at the end of the 1950s there was the complaint that "countless craftsmen" had turned the Harrod–Domar model into the "most over-worked tool in economics," and it continued to be widely-used.[69] Providing crucial argumentative material for justifying catch-up development policies in the 1960s, it would remain ubiquitous in development economics for the following decades.

The formalization of Harrod's work crucially changed the meaning of some of his concepts. Only in the form it was provided by postwar modelers, it featured the very implications they so vigorously rebutted. They introduced the assumption of a constant capital coefficient, readily referred to as the "constant capital coefficient as employed by Domar and Harrod,"[70] which led to the "straight and narrow paths from which the slightest deviation spells disaster," the "Hiccup" dynamic and its "dismal," "gloomy," and "masochistic" prophecies.[71] That literature's assumption of a constant capital coefficient was the very assumption that the "Contribution" took issue with and, as a neoclassical contribution, replaced it with a flexible capital coefficient. Harrod himself vigorously rejected the interpretation of his work as an equilibrium model of growth throughout his life. His ideas about the instability of capitalist economies were fixed into a mathematical equilibrium system, subsumed as a special case in a more general neoclassical model. "I found myself in the position of Le Bourgeois Gentilhomme who had been speaking prose all his life without knowing it. I had been fabricating 'models' without knowing it."[72]

Harrod's protest aptly captured the irony of having been turned into a precursor figure, someone who seemed to have invented the current state of affairs in earlier times – yet with some crucial flaws. Precursors have been criticized by historical epistemologists as essential figures in the "triumphal epic" of scientific progress.[73] As a "false historical object," the precursor results from replacing "the historical time" of scientific inventions with their "logical time."[74] The figure of the precursor makes it seem that concepts, objects, and techniques, which are particular to time and place, were the same all along and just became more and more refined.[75] Notably, also modeler-economists referred to *Le Bourgeois gentilhomme*, but in the affirmative, claiming that economics had always been a modeling endeavor. "Like Molière's M. Jourdain and his prose, economists have been doing linear economics for more than forty years without being conscious of it."[76] This was a quite natural assumption for economists, who were interested in modeling whatever they conceived as their object. Absorbing different kinds of knowledge in model form meant a process of highlighting and neglecting, valuing and devaluing, translating and passing over what seemed to be incomprehensible, a process that was guided by the specific requirements of mathematical systems to ensure the existence and uniqueness of equilibria.

While the implicit metanarratives might be problematic from the historian's point of view, such reinterpretations and reappropriations are integral features of research. Research, as Gaston Bachelard has emphasized, advances not by rejecting its past but rather by devising something new that cultivates a connection with its past.[77] The received history of growth theory adopts the perspective of economic research and directs its major interest at the object of "economic growth," not the contingent ways in which economists have shaped and reshaped that object. There are no losses in such narratives, just gains – more clarity, more rigor, more science. The past is recounted as a series of steps toward a *status quo*, in which "Harrod" – as personification of his deficient approach to model growth – is made out to be a precursor of "Solow" and, subsequently, of what is now conceived as modern growth theory. (The same, for that matter, happened to "Solow" in the revival of neoclassical growth theory from the 1990s onwards, as recounted in the Epilogue.) In popular accounts, the now canonical story turned into a heroic tale of the young economist Robert M. Solow who was dissatisfied with existing accounts of a crisis-prone capitalism and revolutionized the subject by creating a model that showed the stable long-run progress of economies.[78]

POWERFUL INSTRUMENTS OF MISEDUCATION

Economists like Solow or Domar pushed model-based reasoning primarily on economical grounds. Precisely because growth was "determined by the very essence of a society," including the "physical environment, political structure, incentives, educational methods, legal framework, attitude to science, to changes, to accumulation," the economist needed "highly simplified symbolic models." In addition to more general treatises, Domar argued at the beginning of the 1950s, these models provided "extremely useful instruments" to eventually arrive at a "workable theory of growth." Such focus on usefulness and workability did not fully legitimize all kinds of assumptions. In fact, Domar maintained, deciding which factors to include and leave out was "the very essence of theorizing."[79] That the design choices in the process of modeling were not merely practical ones but had profound political character is one of the most persistent strands of criticism – in particular when it came to the ideological underpinnings of neoclassical theories of production and distribution.

Soon the most famous critique of neoclassical modeling in this vein was uttered by Joan Robinson, lecturer at the University of Cambridge, England. Already world-renowned for her contributions to the economics of imperfect competition and the further development and exposition of Keynes's *General Theory*, she went on to translate Marx into academic economics. Robinson's was not a general criticism that models were unrealistic because they simplified a more complex reality. She was not opposed to modeling or mathematical reasoning in economics per se. In *The Accumulation of Capital*, she presented a formalized account of economic growth in a 1930s British economics style. As common for Marshallian economics, diagrams and formulae were safely stashed away in the appendix. While the book was received widely, several reviewers emphasized that it was a "book written for economists," which made "no concessions to the ordinary reader," relied on "equational thinking," and basically consisted of a "model," an "ideal abstraction" warranting the question of whether it was even "supposed to correspond to reality."[80] The book extended the Keynesian concept of effective demand into the long-run and investigated capital accumulation and its instabilities. Most importantly, Robinson emphasized the determining role of both historical configurations as well as political processes, which she posited against the notion of a self-sufficient economic mechanism given in definite laws. This was also one of her main arguments in an article, which, in a sweeping blow, contested the use of a homogeneous capital substance in conventional production functions.[81] Both the mathematical production functions of neoclassical theory and contemporary measurements of capital within the framework of national income accounting utterly disregarded the material realities of production. Assuming perfect competition, theoretical and empirical production functions constructed a singular entity called "capital," measurable in terms of monetary values. In contrast, Robinson's argument went, capital goods in production were physically heterogeneous and precisely not to be confused with the (money-)value of capital. That value varied with the rate of profit, which in turn was given by the rate of capital accumulation and therefore depended on social institutions (such as private property or the existence of different classes). From this perspective, excluding the social and political embeddedness of economic processes from neoclassical imaginaries made them effective instruments for obscuring political–economic realities.

The basic argument at the time for introducing mathematical models was that it equipped economic reasoning with more precision, the formalization of Harrod's work being just one example. Robinson, in contrast, argued that neoclassical models were logically inconsistent. They did not include a reasonable determination of the rate of profit, of income distribution, and the role of saving. Against the proponents of formalization she made the case that the neoclassical treatment of production was indefinite, somewhat lazy, and beset with serious intellectual flaws – precisely because it was so clear-cut and easy-going.

The production function has been ⬥ powerful instrument of miseducation. The student of economic theory is taught to write $O = f(L, C)$ where L is a quantity of labor, C a quantity of capital and O a rate of output of commodities. He is instructed to assume all workers alike, and to measure L in man-hours of labor; he is told something about the index-number problem in choosing a unit of output; and then he is hurried on to the next question, in the hope that he will forget to ask in what units C is measured. Before he ever does ask, he has become a professor, and so sloppy habits of thought are handed on from one generation to the next.[82]

Robinson's foreboding became reality when mathematical models were widely accepted as the new epistemic standard. Ironically, as highlighted in the Epilogue, the modelers who had brought them into the world also bemoaned the restrictive thought of later generations of economists, who had, from their first steps as economics students, been drawn into model worlds.

In the mid-1950s, neoclassical economics was not yet the new mainstream, mathematical models were not yet the primary form of economic argument, and Solow was still a junior professor preoccupied with bringing together new mathematical techniques with what he thought of as conventional economic theory (Chapter 4). He seems to have already identified with a new neoclassicism and felt part of a group of modelers who he thought were entirely misunderstood. Against that background, he engaged with the more prestigious scholar's criticism. Robinson's article and Solow's riposte retrospectively turned into early episodes of what came to be known as the "Cambridge Capital Controversies." There is no reason to recount the enfolding exchange between Cambridge scholars on the two sides of the Atlantic; others have accounted for its theoretical stakes and the boundary work it contained.[83] The point here is simply to highlight the intrinsic entanglement of epistemic and political argument.

After reading Robinson's critique, Solow wrote to one of her colleagues: "I am not at all epaté by the political propaganda; but I am a little put off by the withering attacks on what may be neo-classical stinking fish in England, but bears no visible relation to any doctrine taught on this side of the Atlantic."[84] An article sought to set the record straight. In a manner that foreshadowed his argumentative style in later exchanges about the politics and ideology of economics, Solow made a case for the tool-like character of mathematical models: He defended the assumption of a one-commodity economy not by arguing that it was somewhat realistic but that it was simply "useful" to assume only one kind of physically homogeneous capital good.[85] Then output and capital could be measured "in the *same* units." He agreed with Robinson that, when measuring production processes, there was only a small range of examples for which the different capital inputs could be captured by a single index-figure of capital-in-general. But this kind of realism was not what his modeling and measuring work was about. He emphasized the difference between concepts related to the model (like the return to capital) and concepts he related to "the real world" (like the income of capitalists).[86] Similar to his idea of an assumption being "realistic enough," as discussed in the previous sections, he emphasized that the most important question was whether an assumption suited the concrete purpose of a model. With the special focus on optimality in long-run equilibrium modeling, he argued, it made no difference whether there was specific treatment of heterogenous capital or not. (A couple of years after the exchange with Robinson, Solow and Samuelson argued by way of mathematical propositions and proofs that the dynamics of a model accounting for heterogeneous capital goods could be shown in a simpler model that only dealt with one abstract capital good.[87])

Solow's reply indicates some of the main themes of neoclassical modeling that will be treated in the next chapters. Whenever the assumptions of perfect markets or an intertemporal invisible hand were questioned, modelers' main counterargument pushed their "usefulness."[88] It was the workability of the model that counted. This was as central thread of this kind of reasoning that extended to the model's applications as an instrument of measurement (Chapter 2), highlighted its practicality in comparison to more extensive empirical work (Chapter 3), nurtured its very emergence from postwar techniques of linear modeling (Chapter 4), and produced a variety of model talk (Chapter 5). Merging both treatments of capital that Robinson had criticized (national income accounts and mathematical production functions), the model of the "Contribution" became more than simply a contribution to economic theory. Chapter 2 will deal with empirical measurements of the economy and its overall productivity. On this trajectory, the model depicted stable economies for which crises did not play any major role – prophetic images that would be crucial for the politics of growth in the decades to come. Conceived as a tool to measure the sources of growth, it turned into an essential part of the interventionist toolkit. Compared to existing approaches to measurement, the model appeared as the more efficient gauge, turning them unclear, imprecise, and confusing (not unlike Harrod's work in the preceding pages). The new style turned them into something that needed to be rectified, hereby confining all kinds of uncertainty and nonknowledge to a realm outside of the model. When Solow first used his model as an instrument for measuring growth and its sources, he referred in a footnote to Robinson's critique that hardly any "precise meaning" could be given to "capital." He alleged that he was fully aware of the artificiality of the procedure and, in the same breath, denied the necessity of discussing his modeling approach: "I would not try to justify what follows by calling on fancy theorems on aggregation and index numbers. Either this kind of aggregate economics appeals or it doesn't."[89]

Notes

1 Robert M. Solow, "A Contribution to the Theory of Economic Growth," *Quarterly Journal of Economics* 70, no. 1 (1956): 65–94, 65.

2 Milton Friedman, *Essays in Positive Economics* (Chicago: University of Chicago Press, 1953), 14. For a set of diverging interpretations of Friedman's methodological stance, see the contributions to Uskali Mäki, *The Methodology of Positive Economics: Reflections on the Milton Friedman Legacy* (Cambridge, UK: Cambridge University Press, 2009) in particular that of Kevin D. Hoover, which departs from the following conventional reading of Friedman.

3   Alfred Zauberman, "A Note on Soviet Capital Controversy," *Quarterly Journal of Economics* 69, no. 3 (1955): 445–51; Edward Nevin, "Professor Hansen and Keynesian Interest Theory," *Quarterly Journal of Economics* 69, no. 4 (1955): 637–41; Erskine McKinley, "The Problem of 'Underdevelopment' in the English Classical School," *Quarterly Journal of Economics* 69, no. 2 (1955): 235–52; Herbert A. Simon, "A Behavioral Model of Rational Choice," *Quarterly Journal of Economics* 69, no. 1 (1955): 99–118; James M. Henderson and Richard E. Quandt, "Walras, Leontief, and the Interdependence of Economic Activities: Comment," *Quarterly Journal of Economics* 69, no. 4 (1955): 626–31; Charlotte P. Alhadeff and David A. Alhadeff, "Recent Bank Mergers," *Quarterly Journal of Economics* 69, no. 4 (1955): 503–32; Theodore Levitt, "The Lonely Crowd and the Economic Man," *Quarterly Journal of Economics* 70, no. 1 (1956): 95–116; Joseph Krislov, "The Extent and Trends of Raiding among American Unions," *Quarterly Journal of Economics* 69, no. 1 (1955): 145–52.

4   See Roger E. Backhouse, *The Ordinary Business of Life: A History of Economics from the Ancient World to the Twenty-First Century* (Princeton: Princeton University Press, 2004), 178–82; E. Roy Weintraub, *How Economics Became a Mathematical Science* (Durham, NC: Duke University Press, 2002), 22.

5   See Solow's retroactive views of Keynes in his widely-read Robert M. Solow, "How Did Economics Get That Way and What Way Did It Get," *Daedalus* 126 (2005): 87–100, as well as his associations with Schumpeter's book on business cycles: Echoing Cowles criticism leveled in 1947 in relation to the institutionalist empirical work of Mitchell, Schumpeter's book was "more like a map on the scale of one foot equals two feet: you see the potholes, but you do not learn much about the scenery," Robert M. Solow, "Heavy Thinker. Review of *Prophet of Innovation: Joseph Schumpeter and Creative Destruction* by Thomas K. McCraw," *New Republic*, May 21, 2007, available at www.newrepublic.com/article/heavy-thinker, last accessed April 12, 2024. Though Samuelson could also see "theory" from the older institutionalist perspective and credited Keynes as having created a general theory, he also described the latter's work as an "indoor guessing game", "random notes", or "obscure book", see Roger E. Backhouse, *Founder of Modern Economics: Paul A. Samuelson, Vol 1: Becoming Samuelson, 1915–1948* (Oxford: Oxford University Press, 2017), 526–9.

6   See Marcel Boumans, *How Economists Model the World into Numbers* (New York: Routledge, 2005), 14.

7   Solow, "Contribution," 88 and 80.

8   Solow, "Contribution," 65.

9   Solow, "Contribution," 91.

10 Solow, "Contribution," 82.

11 For instance, Solow, "Contribution," 67, 70, 82, and 84.

12 Solow, "Contribution," 83.

13 On the sensual character of formal operations, see Sybille Krämer, "Mathematizing Power, Formalization, and the Diagrammatical Mind or: What Does 'Computation' Mean?," *Philosophy & Technology* 27, no. 3 (2014): 345–57. On diagrams in economic reasoning, see the special issue *Thinking and Acting with Diagrams* in the *East Asian Science, Technology and Society: An International Journal* 14, no. 2 (2020), edited by Hsiang-Ke Chao and Harro Maas; Mark Blaug and Peter Lloyd,

eds., *Famous Figures and Diagrams in Economics* (Cheltenham, UK: Edward Elgar, 2010). For a case study, see Yann Giraud, "Legitimizing Napkin Drawing: The Curious Dispersion of Laffer Curves, 1978–2008," in *Representation in Scientific Practice Revisited*, edited by Catelijne Coopmans, Janet Vertesi, Michael E. Lynch, and Steve Woolgar (Cambridge, MA: MIT Press, 2014), 269–90.

14 See also Mark Blaug and Peter Lloyd, "Introduction," in *Famous Figures and Diagrams in Economics*, edited by Mark Blaug and Peter Lloyd (Cheltenham, UK: Edward Elgar, 2010).

15 Andreas Langenohl has argued that the temporal ambiguity of static neoclassical models (their ability to be interpreted statically or dynamically) created a symbolic surplus – a surplus of meaning in the sense of temporal options and potentialities: Andreas Langenohl, "Neoklassische Polychronie. Die Temporalitäten algebraischer Modelle bei Alfred Marshall," in *Forum interdisziplinäre Begriffsgeschichte* 5, no. 1, edited by Eva Axer, Eva Geulen, and Alexandra Heimes, (2016), 102–14.

16 Solow, "Contribution," 78.

17 Solow, "Contribution," 67–8. The rationale of this paragraph relies on joint work with Roger E. Backhouse; Roger E. Backhouse and Verena Halsmayer, "Mathematics and the Language of Economics" (paper presented at the Workshop "Language(s) and Language Practices in Business and the Economy," Vienna University of Economics and Business, October 23–25, 2014).

18 Solow, "Contribution," 66.

19 Cf. Matthieu Ballandonne and Goulven Rubin, "Robert Solow's Non-Walrasian Conception of Economics," *History of Political Economy* 52, no. 5 (2020): 827–61.

20 Solow, "Contribution," 66.

21 The article did add a more specific portrayal of market behavior but these "causal dynamics" that linked the equilibrium conditions for price and output were simply plugged in. In principle, the model worked without integrating the price–interest dynamics, as it was simply assumed that "the real wage and the real rental of capital adjusting instantaneously so as to clear the market" (Solow, "Contribution," 78–9).

22 Solow, "Contribution," 67.

23 Solow, "Contribution," 68.

24 Deirdre N. McCloskey, "History, Differential Equations, and the Problem of Narration," *History and Theory* 30 (1991): 21–36, 22.

25 On the varying ways economists have dealt with the trade-off between what they understood as tractability and realism, see Béatrice Cherrier, "The Price of Virtue: Some Hypotheses on How Tractability Has Shaped Economic Models," *Œconomia* 13, no. 1 (2023): 23–48.

26 The "fundamental equation" showed the change in the capital–labor ratio as the difference between two terms. The first term indicated the amount of investment (equal to savings), while the second term indicated the amount of investment needed to maintain the work force. The difference between them (the amount of capital surplus to requirement) gave the rate at which the capital–labor ratio changed.

27 Solow, "Contribution," emphasis in original.

28 Solow, "Contribution," 73.

29 Solow, "Contribution," 90. For those interested in the details: The linear differential equation was analytically solved for three different cases, the Harrod–Domar case

(exhibiting fixed proportions and therefore the "knife-edge" property), the Cobb–Douglas function (where the natural rate of growth equals the warranted rate as a consequence of demand–supply adjustments), and the whole family of constant-returns-to-scale production functions (differing from the Cobb–Douglas case in that production is possible with only one factor). In order to see the effects of specific changes (introduction of technological change, a personal income tax, variable population growth, etc.) on the model economy, Solow used the Cobb–Douglas case.

30 Both: Solow, "Contribution," 93.

31 Solow, "Contribution," 91.

32 All: Solow, "Contribution," 93. The relation between Keynesian policies and neo-classical growth model had been equally addressed in Evsey D. Domar, "Capital Expansion, Rate of Growth, and Employment," *Econometrica* 14, no. 2 (1946): 137–47, 145. Domar similarly argued that he offered "a theoretical point of view, without considering the numerous practical questions that the income guarantee would raise."

33 Two examples (rigid wages and liquidity preference) were given. One worked out nicely, the other identified limitations of the model and delineated a space in which other models would lead to different conclusions.

34 Solow, "Contribution," 93.

35 Solow, "Contribution," 66. Cf. Robert M. Solow, "Growth Theory and After," *American Economic Review* 78, no. 3 (1988): 307–17, 309–10.

36 On the multiple meanings of the neoclassical synthesis, see Michel De Vroey and Pedro Garcia Duarte, "In Search of Lost Time: The Neoclassical Synthesis," *The B.E. Journal of Macroeconomics* 13, no. 1 (2013): 1–31, 20–1. They also cite Solow, who kept to the conviction that "one can be a Keynesian for the short run and a neoclassical for the long run." Robert M. Solow, "Swan, Trevor W.," in *An Encyclopedia of Keynesian Economics*, edited by Thomas Cate (Northampton, MA: Edward Elgar, 2013), 594–97, 594. In fact, his theoretical work over the decades focused on the combination of the short- and long-run, in particular, the question of deviations from an equilibrium growth path. On Solow and his colleagues' attempts to bridge Keynesian and neoclassical modeling, Michaël Assous, "Solow's Struggle with Medium-Run Macroeconomics, 1956–95," *History of Political Economy* 47, no. 3 (2015): 395–417. On macroeconomic planning, see the Epilogue.

37 Solow, "Contribution," 91.

38 This is what evolutionary economist Richard R. Nelson, for instance, has argued in "Numbers and Math Are Nice, But . . .," *Biological Theory* 10, no. 3 (2015): 246–52.

39 Solow, "Contribution," 65.

40 Solow, "Contribution," 93.

41 Solow, "Contribution," 86.

42 See Reinhard Wendler on Georges Canghuilem's view that it is precisely the uncontrollability that makes a model productive: Reinhard Wendler, *Das Modellz wischen Kunst und Wissenschaft* (Munich: Wilhelm Fink, 2013), 12.

43 Marc Kac, "Some Mathematical Models in Science," *Science* 166, no. 3906 (1969): 695–9, 699, quoted in Saul Gass, "Model World: A Model Is a Model Is a Model," *Interfaces* 19, no. 3 (1989): 58–60, 60.

44 Boumans, *How Economists Model the World into Numbers*, 13.

45 Solow, "Contribution," 91. A second set of rules, according to Morgan, is determined by the subject matter, for instance, that manipulations have to be in a certain order for them to make economic sense, Mary S. Morgan, *World in the Model: How Economists Work and Think* (Cambridge: Cambridge University Press, 2012), 26. In the case of the neoclassical growth model, an example for such rules was that production could not be negative.

46 Morgan, *The World in the Model*, 256. On "epistemic artifacts" opening up new ways of thinking, see also Tarja Knuuttila, *Models as Epistemic Artefacts: Toward a Non-Representationalist Account of Scientific Representation* (Helsinki: Department of Philosophy, 2005).

47 See Morgan, *World in the Model*, 296: In contrast to laboratory experiments, model experiments are of a different materiality vis-à-vis the world they are supposed to represent. Therefore, the "surprising results of model experiments lead not to the discovery of new phenomena in the real world, but to the recognition of new things in the small world of the model, and thence to the development of new categories of things and new concepts and ideas in economics."

48 Robert Solow, quoted in Brian Snowdon and Howard R. Vane, *Conversations with Leading Economists: Interpreting Modern Macroeconomics* (Cheltenham: Elgar, 1999), 275.

49 See, for instance, I. M. D. Little, "Classical Growth," *Oxford Economic Papers* 9, no. 2 (1957): 152–77, 152, n3; H. A. John Green, "Growth Models, Capital and Stability," *The Economic Journal* 70, no. 277 (1960): 57–73, 57; Hirofumi Uzawa, "On a Two-Sector Model of Economic Growth," *The Review of Economic Studies* 29, no. 1 (1961): 40–7, 40. Swan published his model in Trevor W. Swan, "Economic Growth and Capital Accumulation," *Economic Record* 32, no. 63 (1956): 334–61, Tobin in James Tobin, "A Dynamic Aggregative Model," *Journal of Political Economy* 62, no. 2 (1955): 103–15.

50 Frank H. Hahn, "The Stability of Growth Equilibrium," *Quarterly Journal of Economics* 74, no. 2 (1960): 206–26, 206. Others spoke of "the well-known neoclassical growth model by Professor Solow," Ronald Findlay, "Economic Growth and the Distributive Shares," *The Review of Economic Studies* 27, no. 3 (1960): 167–78, 175.

51 Solow, "Contribution," 73, 91.

52 From the perspective of post-Keynesian economics, Harrod was seen to have assumed a constant savings rate, and Joan V. Robinson and Nicholas Kaldor were the ones to correct the mistake. See Daniele Besomi, "Harrod's Dynamics and the Theory of Growth: The Story of a Mistaken Attribution," *Cambridge Journal of Economics* 25 (2001): 79–96.

53 This section builds on Verena Halsmayer and Kevin D. Hoover, "Solow's Harrod: Transforming Macroeconomics Dynamics into a Model of Long-Run Growth," *European Journal for the History of Economic Theory* 23 (2016): 71–97, in particular on section 2.

54 Robert J. Barro and Xavier Sala-i-Martín, *Economic Growth* (Cambridge, MA: MIT Press, 2003), 17. Another example is found in an article by the well-known growth theorist Olivier La Grandville, "The 1956 Contribution to Economic Growth Theory by Robert Solow: A Major Landmark and Some of Its Undiscovered Riches," *Oxford Review of Economic Policy* 23, no. 1 (2007): 15–24, 16.

55 See, for instance, Alexander Nützenadel, *Stunde der Ökonomen: Wissenschaft, Politik und Expertenkultur in der Bundesrepublik 1949–1974*, Kritische Studien zur Geschichtswissenschaft, Bd. 166 (Göttingen: Vandenhoeck & Ruprecht, 2005), 77; Stephen Macekura, "Development and Economic Growth: An Intellectual History," in *History of the Future of Economic Growth: Historical Roots of Current Debates on Sustainable Degrowth*, edited by Iris Borowy and Matthias Schmelzer (New York: Routledge, 2017), 110–28, 117.

56 R. F. Harrod, "An Essay in Dynamic Theory," *The Economic Journal* 49, no. 193 (1939), 14–33.

57 Harrod, "Essay," 33.

58 On Harrod's stance toward economics as a science and his use of mathematics, see Daniele Besomi, *The Making of Harrod's Dynamics* (London: Macmillan, 1999) and Warren Young, *Harrod and His Trade Cycle Group. The Origins and Development of the Growth Research Programme* (London: Macmillan, 1998).

59 Examples are Besomi, *Making of Harrod's Dynamics*; Athanasios Asimakopulos, "Harrod on Harrod: The Evolution of a Line of Steady Growth," *History of Political Economy* 17, no. 4 (1985), 619–35; Jan A. Kregel, "Economic Dynamics and the Theory of Steady Growth: An Historical Essay on Harrod's 'Knife Edge'," *History of Political Economy* 12, no. 1 (1980): 97–123.

60 Thomas C. Schelling, "Capital Growth and Equilibrium," *American Economic Review* 37, no. 5 (1947): 864–76, 867.

61 David Wright, a Harvard graduate, showed, for instance, that Harrod used six independent qualifications regarding the warranted rate of growth, David Wright, "Mr. Harrod and Growth Economics," *Review of Economics and Statistics* 31, no. 4 (1949): 322–8.

62 Robert Solow to Harry G. Johnson, September 28, 1953, Solow papers, box 56, file J: 1 of 2.

63 John Hicks's simple diagram reduced the *General Theory* to a relationship between output and interest rate. In the hands of Hansen, Hicks's diagram turned into the IS-LM model and became a central element of Keynesian textbooks of postwar economics. See Backhouse, *Ordinary Business of Life*, 233.

64 William J. Baumol, "Formalisation of Mr. Harrod's Model," *Economic Journal* 59, no. 236 (1949): 625–9, 629.

65 Using a strand of Marxist economics as a point of departure, Domar, who was completing a doctorate at Harvard, linked capital accumulation and employment in terms of a small-scale mathematical model.

66 Domar, "Capital Expansion, Rate of Growth, and Employment," 137. The stated idea was that, in contrast to dominating policy views at the time, the growth of the labor force and its productivity did not bring about income by itself – "the demand side of the equation [was] missing" (138). Later, Domar emphasized the enormous role played by early Soviet growth models, which were written in response to the immediate practical problems of planning. Among recent Western writers, Domar pointed among others to the works of Gustav Cassel, Michał Kalecki, Joan V. Robinson, Eric Lundberg, and Paul Sweezy. See Evsey D. Domar, "Economic Growth: An Econometric Approach," *American Economic Review* 42, no. 2 (1952): 479–95, 480, n4.

67 On Domar's understanding of the "mathematics of growth" and his modeling work, see Mauro Boianovsky, "Modeling Economic Growth: Domar on Moving

Equilibrium," *History of Political Economy* 49, no. 3 (2017): 405–36. Similar to Solow, Domar is predominantly remembered for his growth model. On Domar's specific way of narrativizing in his work on economic history, comparative economic systems, and Soviet economics, see Ibanca Anand, "Resisting Narrative Closure: The Comparative and Historical Imagination of Evsey Domar," in *Narrative in Economics: A New Turn on the Past* (supplement to *History of Political Economy* 55), edited by Mary S. Morgan and Thomas S. Stapleford (Durham, NC: Duke University Press, 2023), 497–521.

68 Baumol, "Formalisation of Mr. Harrod's Model," 625.

69 James Tobin to Robert Solow, March 19, 1959, Solow papers, box 61, file T: 2 of 2.

70 Harold Pilvin, "Full Capacity vs. Full Employment Growth," *Quarterly Journal of Economics* 67, no. 4 (1953): 545–52, 548.

71 Tobin, "Dynamic Aggregative Model"; Kenneth Boulding, "In Defense of Statics," *Quarterly Journal of Economics* 69, no. 4 (1955): 185–502, cited in Robert Eisner, "On Growth Models and the Neo-Classical Resurgence," *The Economic Journal* 68, no. 272 (1958): 707–21, 707.

72 Roy F. Harrod, "What Is a Model?," in *Value, Capital and Growth. Papers in Honour of Sir John Hicks*, edited by J. N. Wolfe (Edinburgh: Edinburgh University Press, 1968), 173–92.

73 Hélène Metzger, *Newton, Stahl, Boerhaave et la doctrine chimique* (Paris: Blanchard, 1974 [1930]), 6, cited in Cristina Chimisso and Nicholas Jardine, "Hélène Metzger on Precursors: A Historian and Philosopher of Science Confronts Her Evil Demon," *HOPOS: The Journal of the International Society for the History of Philosophy of Science* 11, no. 2 (2021): 331–53.

74 Georges Canguilhem, *Études d'Histoire et de Philosophie des Sciences*, 3rd ed. (Paris: Vrin, 1975), 22, cited and translated in Hans-Jörg Rheinberger, "Reassessing the Historical Epistemology of Georges Canguilhem," in *Continental Philosophy of Science*, edited by Gary Gutting (Malden, MA: Blackwell, 2005), 187–97, 191.

75 See Christoph Hoffmann, *Die Arbeit der Wissenschaften* (Zürich: diaphanes, 2013), 90–5.

76 Robert Dorfman, Paul Samuelson, and Robert M. Solow, *Linear Programming and Economic Analysis* (New York: McGraw-Hill, 1958), 1. Going one step further, the same reference was also used to suggest that the long history of economic thought had always already looked at the capitalist economy as a cybernetic self-regulating system: "Mr. Jourdain, a hero of one of Molière's comedies was surprised to be told by his teacher that he spoke in prose all his life. A similar situation exists in economics and cybernetics. From the very onset of the development of the political economy, economists were engaged in problems which we define today as cybernetic problems," Oskar Lange, *Introduction to Economic Cybernetics* (Oxford: Pergamon Press, 1970), 1.

77 See Cristina Chimisso, "Narrative and Epistemology: Georges Canguilhem's Concept of Scientific Ideology," *Studies in History and Philosophy of Science Part A* 54 (2015): 64–73, 65.

78 Douglas Clement, "Interview with Robert Solow," *The Region. Banking and Policy Issues Magazine* (September 1, 2002), available at www.minneapolisfed.org/article/2002/interview-with-robert-solow, last accessed May 6, 2024.

79 Domar, "Economic Growth," 481, 484.

80 H. A. V., "Economic Fact and Theory," *The Financial Times*, September 10, 1956, JVR/xv/9.5/1; John Strachey, "Dead and Dumb Sciences," *New Statesman and Nation*, August 4, 1956, JVR/vx/9.1/2; "Capital Issues," *The Times Literary Supplement*, October 5, 1956, JVR/ xv/9.6/2, all: Joan V. Robinson papers at King's College Archive Centre at the University of Cambridge. For intellectual biographies of Robinson, see Nahid Aslanbeigui and Guy Oakes, *The Provocative Joan Robinson: The Making of a Cambridge Economist* (Durham, NC: Duke University Press, 2009); Geoffrey C. Harcourt and Prue Kerr, *Joan Robinson* (Basingstoke: Palgrave Macmillan, 2009).

81 Joan V. Robinson, "The Production Function and the Theory of Capital," *Review of Economic Studies* 21, no. 2 (1953–54): 81–106.

82 Robinson, "Production Function," 81.

83 The Controversies encompassed a series of exchanges between economists from Cambridge, England and Cambridge, Massachusetts that stretched from the mid-1950s to the 1970s, filled with intricate theoretical arguments as well as full-blown polemics. The most prominent account, in a way only making the Controversies is Geoffrey C. Harcourt, *Some Cambridge Controversies in the Theory of Capital* (Cambridge: Cambridge University Press, 1972). Tiago Mata sheds light on the aftermath of the debate that saw the formation of a "Post-Keynesian" identity, Tiago Mata, "Constructing Identity: The Post Keynesians and the Capital Controversies," *Journal of the History of Economic Thought* 26, no. 2 (2004), 241–59. Avi J. Cohen and Harcourt discuss the relevance and importance of the Controversy from a contemporary economists' viewpoint, Avi J. Cohen and Geoffrey C. Harcourt, "Whatever Happened to the Cambridge Capital Theory Controversies?" *Journal of Economic Perspectives* 17, no. 1 (2003), 199–214. A more recent contribution that focuses on the perspective of Cambridge, MA is Roger Backhouse, "MIT and the Other Cambridge," in *MIT and the Transformation of American Economics* (supplement to *History of Political Economy* 46), edited by E. Roy Weintraub (Durham, NC: Duke University Press, 2014), 252–71.

84 Solow to Johnson, September 28, 1953, Solow papers, box 56, file J: 1 of 2.

85 Robert M. Solow, "The Production Function and the Theory of Capital." *Review of Economic Studies* 23, no. 2 (1955–56): 101–8, 101.

86 Both: Solow, "Production Function," 103.

87 The argument was that the necessary condition for optimality over time was identical and, therefore, the simple model had "great heuristic value" – "even though there is no such thing as a single abstract capital substance that transmutes itself from one machine form to another like a restless reincarnating soul," Paul A. Samuelson, and Robert Solow, "A Complete Capital Model Involving Heterogeneous Capital Goods," *Quarterly Journal of Economics* 70, no. 4 (1956), 537–62, 537–8. On the relation between modeling the path of capital, and Richard E. Bellman's dynamic programming, see Nancy Wulwick, "The Mathematics of Economic Growth" (Working Paper No. 38, Jerome Levy Institute, 1990), and Esther-Mirjam Sent, "Engineering Dynamic Economics," in *New Economics and Its History* (supplement to *History of Political Economy* 29), edited by John B. Davis (Durham, NC: Duke University Press, 1998), 41–62.

88 For the idea that "the most myopic vision on the part of market participants" leads to "efficiency over long periods of time," see the textbook on linear programming

that will be treated more extensively in Chapter 4: Dorfman et al., *Linear Programming and Economic Analysis*, 321. On Joan Robinson's most famous criticism of neoclassical time, see Joan Robinson, "History versus Equilibrium," Indian Economic Journal 21, no. 3 (1974): 202–13. See also Harvey Gram and G. C. Harcourt, "Joan Robinson and MIT," *History of Political Economy* 49, no. 3 (2017): 437–50.

89 Robert M. Solow, "Technical Change and the Aggregate Production Function," *Review of Economics and Statistics* 39, no. 3 (1957): 312–20, 312.

2

The Problematic of Growth and Productivity

Writing about growth mid-century was nothing innocuous, restricted to the realm of economic theory. Growth was already a dominant theme in national and international politics. Political and economic elites pushed the idea that an increasing gross national product (GNP) was the essential if not the only means to end poverty for all, raise standards of living everywhere, and secure American geopolitical interests. The politics of growth and productivity centered around the idea that a state was primarily responsible for a national economy. Through rational management, government created the right "environment" for business to perpetuate productivity increases and ensure future prosperity.[1] The neoclassical growth model was not only embedded in the discourse of growthism but also actively equipped it with a comparatively easy-to-use instrument for making empirical knowledge about growth and its sources. One year after publishing his version of a neoclassical growth model, Solow used it as a tool for measuring growth in the article "Technical Change and the Aggregate Production Function."[2] In contrast to the "Contribution," which focused entirely on the little cosmos of the model, this paper presented the growing economy as a real object, an object outside economic discourse. Eventually becoming a standard tool, Solow's model contributed to the idea of the economic being a sphere separate from social, ecological, and political concerns. Chapter 1 looked at the model as it was published in the 1956 "Contribution" and analyzed it primarily in terms of the article's textual features. This chapter brings out other facets of the small-scale artifact by situating it in a history of measurement, in particular of national growth and productivity.

It has widely been acknowledged that the problematization of growth in the 1950s built on the idea of "the economy," which had gained new contours as a quantitative entity with the first coherent large-scale national income accounts in the 1930s. The New Deal reorganized national identity around shared, albeit exclusive economic destiny.[3] Still, from the vantage point of the 1930s, it was all but self-evident that growth would turn into the primary goal of economic policy-making and the dominant category of economic analysis. Prior to the Second World War, the process of economic expansion was seen as inherently unstable and susceptible to crisis. Postwar research, in contrast, mostly ignored questions about how successive crises would develop from earlier ones. Over the course of the 1940s and 1950s, growth eclipsed the business cycle as the predominant object of economic research and policy. The shift was radical, in empirical as well as theoretical studies, in highly abstract academic work as well as in areas closer to policy-making.

As laid out in the Introduction, the following pages take indices and models as phenomenotechnical instruments. This makes it possible to focus on how they shaped and reshaped the object of the growing economy – a capacity that practitioners frankly acknowledged: "We are, in truth, transmuting actual experience in the workaday world into something new and strange."[4] What Arthur Burns and Wesley Mitchell wrote about the making of the business cycle hinted at the work involved in scientific problematization. Economic growth research did not simply take up everyday or governmental problems but created new problems and new phenomena in the form of mathematical coefficients, tables of numbers, and curves. The quantitative object of the growing economy provided the field of growth economics with its main explanandum and served as a major point of reference for policy-making. This chapter zooms in on the specific characteristics of the tools that economic statisticians and empirical economists developed to measure national output, its development over time, and its sources. Moving from quantitative accounts in the 1920s to the use of Solow's model as a gauge, the following sections show how the model built on and went beyond a specific line of measurement practice in both technical and political senses. The growing economy evolved from measurements in an institutionalist vein that put a prime on concrete empirical work and focused on questions of distribution.[5] While one might distinguish between different theoretical "schools" of institutionalism and neoclassicism, the story here highlights instead the continuities and differences in quantitative techniques from national income accounting to econometric methods. Against this background, Solow's model represented a further step in making the growing economy both more abstract and more concrete at the same time, now cast in a deliberately neoclassical light.

Solow's exercise in measurement did not bring about any surprising empirical results. Contemporary quantitative research into growth and productivity had already shown that it was not simply increases in capital or labor that pushed growth. What set the publication apart was that it used a different instrument of measurement. A colleague, after having read Solow's paper, congratulated him: "You challenge that unruly giant, the real world, with your skill in using the economist's sling. Three cheers for hitting him so hard."[6] The economist's sling, I will show in the following pages, was a neat device that brought neoclassical categories to bear on quantitative data. As an efficient tool for gauging growth, I argue, the model economized the empirical endeavor to get at the "sources" of rising output. It brought nonknowledge into an easily manageable format and turned "what we don't understand" into "what we cannot (yet) measure." In this sense, the model reified a new style of quantitative reasoning that also transformed the framing of previous approaches. Similar to how mathematical modelers in Chapter 1 reinterpreted earlier economic theory in terms of their models, measurement in terms of indices came to be seen through the lens of Solow's model. It was presented as clarifying the measurement procedure and making assumptions explicit. This chapter will focus on what was lost in such genealogy of the growing economy and its productivity.

THE ECONOMY AS A MATTER OF INDICES AND TRENDS

The neoclassical growth model gauged a phenomenon that was clearly circumscribed in terms of the GNP. Like other federal statistics, national accounting evolved from the mutual shaping of measurement practices and interventionist policies. As a "cultural hybrid," the historian of science Theodore M. Porter has argued, this economy was constituted by the quantitative tools of the state. At the same time, this reification gave "economists, planners, and engineers something to measure and direct."[7] While it was certainly federal governance and the associated, so-called Keynesian policies that pushed the GNP, the techniques needed to create the relevant numbers had a longer and politically more diverse history. Attending to the metric's history shows how the growing economy measured by Solow's model had evolved contingently in a series of inclusions, exclusions, and reassessments.

In the US, the first steps to measure a national income were undertaken in the early twentieth century in the interstices of academia, public data collection, and economic research institutions. Concern for the distribution of income and wealth, part of a larger debate over the social and cultural cohesion of modern industrial society, motivated such measurements. The relevant numbers were to feed into the design of social policy, not least to prevent social conflict and to contain organized labor.[8] Created by private experts and organizations, early empirical studies took the form of social and historical surveys.[9] Gaps in the data were so wide, however, that it was impossible to create comprehensive accounts. During the Great Depression and New Deal era, national income accounting turned into a large-scale, systematic measurement effort when the governmental endeavor to improve society increasingly focused on economic problems.[10]

In 1931, the Department of Commerce appointed the National Bureau of Economic Research (NBER) to prepare estimates of national income for the previous three years.[11] Linked to the rise of institutional economics, the Bureau was already an established nonteaching social science research institute. Its purpose was to provide empirical knowledge for social reform, representing an "empiricist" strand of economic knowledge that opposed theory-led inquiries.[12] Already its first project had been a study of national income, its size, industrial composition, growth, fluctuations, and distribution. The study provided time series for the years 1909–1919 for the analysis of business cycles. It made visible both the uses of the goods produced (investment, final consumption, intermediate consumption) and the incomes they generated.[13] To that effect, the numbers figured both as a means to make economic analysis more scientific and as a vital factor in national planning.

What set national income statistics apart from earlier depictions of the economy was that it visualized the whole in terms of a coherent system, which systematically linked its parts according to specified rules. An entry on "National Income" in the *Encyclopedia of the Social Sciences* of 1933 described the procedures of constructing a national income for the Department of Commerce.[14] In between Emil Lederer's article on "National Economic Planning" and an entry on "National Socialism, German," the NBER's principal investigator of national income, the economist and statistician Simon Kuznets provided insight into the making of numbers.[15] Despite being aimed at a lay public, the entry laid out methodological problems encountered in the practice of measurement. This makes it the perfect exemplary text to think about the commonalities and differences between the phenomenotechnical growing economy in the 1930s and that of Solow's model in 1956.

Kuznets critically discussed the new metric from the practitioner's perspective and gave insight into the many contingent aspects of the making of numbers. In particular, he put emphasis on the restrictions of the existing statistical material: National income was "not so much a theoretical choice of inclusion or exclusion"; its shape was "largely conditioned by the given data, and so by the prevailing accounting procedure, for instance in industries."[16] It was crucial to settle definitions in the initial stage of measurements; at the same time, these definitions were a matter of the availability of suitable data. In effect, Kuznets's entry provided an intricate reflection of how to make something that held together. "Made consistent (or objective) by measurement," as Alain Desrosières put it in his *The Politics of Large Numbers*, "a thing can be included in a . . . system of things that holds together independently of its constructor."[17] Creating such an entity was not straightforward.

The national income connected several kinds of measurement by aggregating, complementing, and estimating numbers. The basic problem researchers faced was how to bring together ideas of the economic system with available observations. In the words of Mary Morgan, who has provided a vocabulary to study practices of "observation" in the history of the social sciences, the making of national accounts resembled a "jigsaw puzzle," though with the complication that "one neither knows the size of the whole nor has a clear sight of the individual items."[18] National income researchers combined the materials at hand with the concept of the economy as a circular flow between three stages: Income produced (production), income received (distribution), and income consumed (consumption). The result was an accounting framework that made all the data from diverse sources – such as wages, dividends, or rents – fit together. Mirroring the rules of double entry bookkeeping, the income of the three stages of circulation had to "check."[19] The variables of the national figures thus related to each other in an unambiguous way, which provided a means to cross-check the consistency of the data and impute missing variables where the relevant microeconomic data did not exist in archives or almanacs. The underlying rationale was that the resulting data were more reliable if they were based on different sources that fitted the same framework.[20] Data on consumption and savings, for instance, were hardly available and were therefore used mainly as a "stop gap" when industrial or income statistics were "badly lacking."[21] Rather than observing an economy "out there," national income accounting generated a new entity by summing up existing numbers and triangulating missing data. And, since there was not yet a standardized procedure for measuring national income, different institutions came up with different calculations.[22]

In contrast to the almost exclusive focus on growth and productivity of the postwar era, of which Solow's model was a part, the 1930s national income measurements linked to wider ambitions. The new metric's prime purpose was to gauge and appraise a country's economic performance but also its "economic organization."[23] First, the data should enable comparison with other nations' performances. Second, transformed into a continuous series of annual estimates, the figures would suggest whether and at which pace the nation was growing richer or poorer. Observing the behavior of this new entity over time was thus part of the measurement of national income from the outset. However, economic growth was not the sole, nor even the most important criterion for assessing national economic performance. In the NBER's studies, more important than the measurement of the "mere total" was the allocation of national income to various constituents (among others, economic regions and industrial sources) as well as the distribution of income. From the outset, national income was thought to provide knowledge for intervening in the object it devised. Its major point of departure, however, was the cycle, not growth. The economic overview of the nation was about bringing the whole into balance and easing instabilities brought about by the business cycle.

Tying in with the Bureau's reputation of providing impartial knowledge, the object of the economy aligned with heterogenous political agendas. It served the goals of a business-driven philanthropy to stabilize corporate capitalism against popular opinion and the labor movement. It also fit the aims of corporate liberals, who pushed the need for social reform and argued for the making of statistical data on both economic growth and inequality. With its interest in income distribution, the NBER's prewar reports equally appealed to left-leaning technocrats, despite the somewhat embellished measurements.[24] Also, managers and bankers could, in principle, take account of the NBER's overview of the whole in order to avoid erroneous decision-making that was merely based on price signals.[25]

At the same time as its multivalent politics facilitated its further development, the national income was all but a neutral tool. The new object came with specific design choices, which involved specific valuations that also characterized the object of Solow's model. Most fundamentally, the national income was a monetary measure. This meant that it treated the market as a "unifying mechanism," which reduced heterogeneous actors to one single value entity through a common unit of measurement. It included activities that accrued market value and excluded those that did not. In his encyclopedia entry, Kuznets described this as a "natural" thing to do.[26] Nevertheless, he emphasized the pitfalls of such an identification: There were commodities and services for which there was no flow of money (for instance, those received in barter), just as there were money payments to which no commodity or service corresponded (for instance, gifts, charity, relief, and pensions). Most importantly, there were commodities and services that were produced and consumed within the household and therefore never came into contact with markets. With regard to the question of whether unpaid (female) reproduction work was to be included in the national income – one of the most widely used examples for the politics of GDP up to the present – Kuznets stated forthrightly that "the general agreement" at the time was to exclude "housewives' services" from the national income.[27] The paid services of a housekeeper, however, were included. Car accidents and environmental pollution increased national income if they involved repair work.

The size of national income was based on strictly and arbitrarily segregating economic from noneconomic activity, which made it a highly questionable measure of welfare. Kuznets's entry in the *Encyclopedia* warned readers of drawing "misleading inferences."[28] Since different ways of composing national accounts yielded different estimates and provoked different conclusions, the accounts only appeared to be precise. The "clear and unequivocal character of such estimates [was] deceptive."[29] In a later publication, as historian Timothy Mitchell has pointed out in his study of the failures of the modern understanding of the economy, Kuznets more specifically cautioned against the use of the national total as it "facilitate[d] the ascription of independent significance to that vague entity called the national economy."[30] When national accounts achieved the status of administrative statistics, however, this was precisely what happened. The Department of Commerce established a permanent national income section. From 1937 on, national income figures were issued monthly to be more useful for policy-making.[31] In the process of its institutionalization and professionalization, national income became embedded into the federal bureaucracy as the dominant depiction of the economy as a whole.

In the 1940s, the GNP took the national income's place as the central metric of the economy – the one that Solow's model gauged. With the entry of the United States into the Second World War and the rise of what was broadly labeled "Keynesianism," Kuznets's students at the Department of Commerce gave the national total the major role to play.[32] The GNP was the sum of three components of the final uses of production: Consumption, investment, and government expenditure on goods and services. The new income and product statistics proved highly useful for wartime planning. They enabled the War Production Board (WPB) to design programs for optimizing production and reducing consumer demand, which were more efficient than the military's own production plans.[33] Economists were soon to pride themselves for having won the war. "It has been said that the last war was the chemist's war and that this one is the physicist's. It might equally be said that this is an economists' war," Paul Samuelson (in)famously noted.[34]

The prestige that national accounting accrued during wartime carried over to the dawn of the Cold War and ultimately strengthened the militarization of the national economy. The National Income and Product Accounts (NIPA), first published in 1947, merged the measurement procedures of the GNP with the first attempts to harmonize national accounting to improve international comparability.[35] The NIPA stabilized the emphasis on national productive capacities and the inclusion of the state as a central economic actor. In contrast to the national income's focus on markets, the NIPA made visible the decisive role of the state in not only distributing but also generating income. Government expenditure could now more easily be legitimized as increasing the national total, even if it did not provide goods for consumption by end consumers (such as was the case with armament, infrastructure, or transport).[36] One of the postwar repercussions of capturing the economy in terms of the NIPA was the legitimization of peacetime military spending: When national security policy-makers included the overarching aim of economic growth into Cold War strategy, the accounts helped argue for the *economic* benefits of national defense. "Before the making of the economy," Timothy Mitchell has put it in a nutshell, "it was difficult to imagine how the decision to build a permanently militarized society after 1947–48 was not somehow at the expense of improvements in welfare and wages for the majority."[37]

The specific problematization of the economy in terms of the GDP laid the essential groundwork for economic growth to become the central goal and vehicle of postwar policy. The metric was implemented as a knowledge infrastructure that enabled the continuous tracking of the economy, as sociologist Dan Hirschman has recently framed it.[38] In a similar vein, economic sociologist Onur Özgöde has shown how the accounted money flow served as the basis for assessing the productive capacity of the whole, intervening into imbalances, and monitoring the behavior of the economy over time. The associated governmental framework narrowed political outlook. Public spending became subsumed to an economic realm in which increasing national production was the one and only measure of success.[39] Other characteristics of the national aggregate that more directly related to social welfare such as the distribution of income, so crucial to early national income measurements, were now subordinated to increasing productive capacity. This was not lost on Kuznets, who became a fervent critic of national accounting. He not only took issue with the focus on increasing production rather than consumption needs. He also objected that the accounts would in the first place register macroeconomic constructs, whereas his design of national income did not rely on an underlying theoretical framework.[40] The result was an arsenal of tools that provided interventionist knowledge directed at the economy as framed by national accounts and hereby privileging economist and productivist agendas.

AN OBJECT OF POLITICS AND RESEARCH

Given the expectation of a postwar slump and massive unemployment, the success of the problematization of growth as a measurable and manageable phenomenon hinged on the promise of national accounts to be useful for planning a peacetime economy. An abundance of reports and pamphlets by the National Resources Planning Board (NRPB) detailed concrete, mostly confidential programs to ensure that the US economy retained its wartime activity. Alongside government officials and business leaders, NRPB economists – among them the Harvard Keynesian Alvin Hansen and MIT's Paul Samuelson – argued that the times of scarcity were over. The US stood "on the threshold of an economy of abundance."[41] Eventually, the expected new affluence would allow not only for establishing full employment but also wider social measures such as a "minimum standard of security," which involved both a minimum level of income and the public provision of health, education, and welfare.[42] The associated notion of planning relied heavily on macroeconomic categories. National accounts presented an integrated system of several building blocks depicting the parts of the macroeconomy. In the form of macroeconomic models, the relations between these blocks could be investigated, for instance, to derive the relationship between consumer demand and employment levels.

The NRPB's reports alluded to corporatist groupings within a picture of the economy that would only fully crystallize after the war.[43] The postwar partnership of public and private – in concert with scientific management, business planning, and industrial cooperation – came, however, with a different notion of planning and a different relation between economic expertise and decision-making than the NRPB reports might have envisioned. The years 1945–1946 saw the largest wave of worker strikes in US history, which could only be defeated by the federal government's deployment of armed forces.[44] In a series of unfavorable decisions on questions important to the liberal social policy planners of the late New Deal and early war periods, the Senate seriously weakened the Full Employment Act. Compared to NRPB's suggestions, the act had already been watered down in focusing simply on the economic right to full-time employment instead of wider social and economic rights and freedoms.[45] The Employment Act of 1946 further watered down the bill to stating that government was to "promote maximum employment, production and purchasing power."[46] High – not full – employment and stability were now formally recognized as the main macroeconomic objectives. And the basis for creating high employment was not public expenditures but rather the support of private business. The National Planning Association (NPA) now reported that the "basis of America's post-war economy should be private enterprise, with the Government acting as impartial referee."[47]

As an impartial referee, government demanded the technical expertise of economists. The Employment Act implemented the CEA as a body that would gather and disseminate economic information to public and private enterprise and advise the president on a regular basis.[48] At a time when the framework of macroeconomic analysis was not yet taken for granted, the CEA pushed its role in "integrat[ing] governmental and private thinking in a way that is essential for making rational decisions."[49] Economic experts were neither technocratic decision-makers as had been the case in the New Deal era, nor members of planning boards, as was their role in war- and peacetime planning. They would instead serve in a purely advisory capacity in an institution that had an educative purpose. While in the 1930s economists had more personal influence on decision-making (often in terms of emergency actions), following the Employment Act, the economics profession achieved unprecedented publicity. The number of economists working for the federal government increased from 600 at the end of the 1920s to 5,000–8,000 by the beginning of the 1950s.[50] Continuing the rise of importance of economic language and knowledge within government institutions since the beginning of the century, macroeconomic analysis and quantitative argument progressively supplanted ethical and rights-based styles of deliberation.[51]

Based on national income accounts and macroeconomic models, the new planning was crucially intertwined with the idea of economic growth. Under the leadership of Leon Keyserling, Harry Truman's CEA turned increasing aggregate economic performance into the predominant aim of postwar policy.[52] The new program subordinated redistribution to growth, which was now praised as the remedy for the "ancient conflict between social equity and economic incentives."[53] At the same time, many unions subscribed to the idea of growth and, as the historian Tom Stapleford has argued, rendered the labor movement a partner in the pursuit of prosperity (and its fairer distribution).[54] The CEA's 1949 "Economic Report of the President to the Congress" symbolized the new direction in national policy, suggesting that growth alone would allow the US to fulfill domestic social goals as well as geopolitical strategy. Its major point of reference was the "interests of the economy as a whole."[55] And it was the CEA that communicated the interests and needs of this economy.

Tantamount to a manifesto for growth, the 1949 report presented a program for realizing "our growth possibilities."[56] Its views related to the object of the economy in terms of the national accounts, which were included in the report in the form of "the nation's economic budget," a balance sheet. Accordingly, objectives for growth involved the balancing out of "production and consumption, income and investment, and prices, profits, and wages."[57] In that light, the report presented a growth rate of 3–4 percent for the economy as a whole as "reasonable."[58] The major means to achieve that goal was a rise in labor productivity of 2.5 percent per year. How to achieve productivity increases? For one, the report stressed the cooperation of government, labor, and management. It emphasized that government had a decisive role to play in that it promoted growth in private industry and hereby induced businesses' "confidence." In particular, it did so through the peacetime continuation of government-funded scientific research – already under the label of "research and development" that would gain prominence in growth and productivity calculations based on Solow's model from the 1960s onward.[59] The following years would see the making of theoretical and empirical accounts that demonstrated causal links between growth, productivity, and technology.

At the end of the 1940s, economic figures lacked the specific kind of causal knowledge that Solow's model, alongside other intellectual tools, came to provide. The CEA did argue that "the decisions ... which we make from year to year will be more intelligent if we take a longer look ahead."[60] Ideally, calculating technologies provided a glimpse into future possibilities, which was to form the basis for immediate practical action. In 1949, however, such utterances were primarily signaling a desire for such guiding devices. The growth figures presented in the report ended with the available data and did not include any kind of forecasting. The lack of more detailed visualizations of growth, prospective levels of output, and suggestions on how to achieve them was hardly surprising. While growth in the form of national accounts became the dominant aim of national policy at the end of the 1940s, there had been hardly any academic work on this specific problematization. The CEA's portrayals of the economy relied little on knowledge from economics as it was done at academic institutions; it built on the work of institutions such as the NBER, compiling large-scale, aggregate data sets. In the eyes of Washington, academic economists, working on what they considered to be the frontiers of economic theory, had barely any specialist knowledge on the growing economy to offer.[61]

In response to the importance of growth in the political arena in the late 1940s, academic economic theorists began to see it as an absorbing object of research. Kuznets, twenty years after the abovementioned reflections on the making of the national income, noted that the contemporary rise in academic concern for economic growth was "largely an aftermath of current events," as the "traditional corpus of economic theory" had unduly excluded the problem.[62] As one of the key figures in pushing growth as a research object, he somewhat left aside that the economy in terms of national accounts had only been in place for a rather short time. In the intervening years, economists focused on the business cycle and unemployment. Economic expansion was captured as part of counter-cyclical policies. Going further back into the history of economic thought, neoclassical theory focused on micro-level analysis, the behavior of individual agents; and classical political economy dealt with the growth of wealth, of population, of trade, and resources, but not with the growth of the economy in terms of national accounts. So even if there had been studies of the long run in the past, the object of research was different: there simply had not been any figures for national income or national product, and it was these entities to which the contemporary concept of "economic growth" referred.

The first larger academic conference focusing on growth was organized in 1948 by the Universities-National Bureau Committee with Kuznets as its chairperson. The Committee's main purpose was to stimulate topics of concern to both the NBER and university researchers. The first of these problem-defining conferences was held on the growth "of large aggregates such as nations or regions." Consequently, the focused on surveying the relevant state of knowledge in empirical research. The conference report, as Kuznets noted in his foreword, could only take the form of a "tentative and preliminary exploration" because of the "relative scarcity of sustained empirical work, and the absence of an agreed upon body of theoretical hypotheses concerning factors determining economic growth."[63] The report was a testimony to the paucity of expert knowledge on the new problematic, which the Committee thought needed to be compensated.

The problem of growth progressively made its way to the core of the discipline, even though there was still no clearly circumscribed object. The program of the 1952 Annual Meeting of the American Economic Association (AEA) featured three sections dedicated to growth: "The Theoretical Analysis of Economic Growth," "General Factors in Economic Growth in the United States," and "Growth in Underdeveloped Countries."[64] In the same year, an AEA survey of the state of the art of economics included "the economics of growth," though the editor felt uneasy trying to capture it as a separate field: its "boundaries ... have been difficult to define at all."[65] Indeed, the relevant chapter summarized diverse strands of work ranging from the theory of capital and savings to economic history and recent statistical work done at the NBER. The survey included aspects of classical political economy, of Marx and Marxist economics, the German historical school, American institutionalism, of Keynes and Keynesian economics as well as individual contributions from rather diverse intellectual backgrounds ranging from Max Weber, Thorstein Veblen, Wesley C. Mitchell, Joseph Schumpeter, and Alvin Hansen to Paul Baran, Joan Robinson, and Michał Kalecki.

While the sheer amount and heterogeneity of treatments of long-term economic developments might have provoked an analysis of the different problematizations, the surveyor, NBER researcher, and Stanford economist Moses Abramovitz, who had previously worked at the War Production Board, instead bemoaned the lack of "any organized and generally known body of doctrine."[66] In what followed, he synthesized the surveyed works as relating to a common research object and defined the essential purpose of the new field in a way that resonated with the politics of growth: trace and explain the growth of a given economy over time (read: US growth), of different economies with similar institutional frameworks (read: the growth of industrialized countries), and of economies with different institutions (read: the growth of so-called "backward," "preindustrial," or "under-developed," as well as communist countries).[67] When it came to the specific form such an "explanation" of growth should take, programmatic texts at the time spanned a variety of approaches. But they all shared the reference to statistical time trends, measurements, and visualizations of the economy's behavior over time, which built, again, on a series of specific phenomenotechnical maneuvers.

VISUALIZING GROWTH

The wartime making of the economy in terms of GNP not only had governmental and political effects. It also prompted a further profound epistemic transformation. As soon as economic statisticians started to extend the relevant data sets into the deeper past, their inscriptions displayed another dimension of the economy's behavior over time. The new tables and curves showed its short-run fluctuations merely as cyclical surface phenomena because at the very foundations of the economy there was a stronger, structural force: growth. The essential presumptions that went into such clean displays will be at the center of this section. They configured the growing economy that Solow's model accessed both with regard to the composition of the whole and its temporality. Tracing the characteristics of these data helps us understand how the model's link to empirical work relied on the similarity of its assumptions to those that already went into the numbers. The step to interpreting these data as stemming from a neoclassical world in a growth equilibrium was smaller than might be assumed.

The NBER turned into one of the major research sites of investigating economic growth from the late 1940s on. It referred to growth as "the pace of sustained change in the output of economic communities."[68] The terminology suggested a certain closeness to the rhythms of economic life, monitoring the activities of collectives. Indeed, NBER researchers typically spoke about their work in terms of "observing" specific characteristics of growth and building on "a wide survey of experience."[69] This is not to say that they took a naïve stance toward measurement. On the contrary, as practitioners involved in the intricate and time-consuming procedures of collecting and processing data, they were widely aware that measurement was not simply a matter of recording something "out there." As was the case for compiling an aggregate whole in terms of national accounts in the previous section, making growth visible in terms of intertemporal comparisons necessitated multiple design choices. The Bureau's publications commonly included voluminous appendices that elaborated on the assumptions, practical requirements, and conventional definitions that went into the numbers they presented. This was also the case in NBER's growth studies, which described how researchers found strategies to both rearrange past data and compile new data regularly.[70]

The "sustained change" that NBER's growth research set out to measure concerned the long-term developments of output figures. Interwar business cycle research had described short-term fluctuations as deviations from a secular trend. The essential problem had been to exclude the trend to get at the dynamics of oscillations (due to entrepreneurs' uncertain and erroneous projections about the future, or to a consequence of technical change). The new studies shifted interest to the trend itself. The problem was that national income and product accounts only covered about fifty years, which was not sufficient for investigating the secular, long-run development of the US economy. Kuznets, who had already worked on economic growth in his 1930 dissertation, promoted the compilation of long-run data to extend and improve the figures in place. Together with his assistants Lillian Epstein and Elizabeth Jenks, he pushed data series back as far as 1869, creating long-term accounts of output, the inputs of production (capital and labor), and population for the entire period.[71] To them, such time series made visible the very basic structural features of the economy, obscured by the ups and downs of the business cycle.

The extension of the observation period of the economy enabled the clean-cut visualization of the growing economy in the form of tables and curves and put long-standing notions of development in perspective. Early studies showed what economists at the time thought rather striking, namely the "outstanding finding" that there had been an enormous growth in output per capita between the turn of the century and the late 1930s.[72] A typical mode of visual representation of growth figures were tables that listed the relative changes of output over time. Figure 2.1 facilitated such relative comparisons, inviting the reader to trace the development of output, population, and output per worker across four decades.

The table in Figure 2.1 appeared in George Stigler's *Trends in Output and Employment* (1947), one of NBER's studies that visualized the growing aggregate and attempted to get at the sources of growth. Published in the year of the release of the first NIPA, the book presented time series of output and employment for a group of twelve major industries. Lumping the industries' output together, Stigler, who later became one of the central figures of Chicago economics together with Milton Friedman, suggested wider relevance of his study as it covered "four-tenths of the American

	1899	1909	1919	1929	1939
Output	100	146	195	283	289
Employment	100	129	153	150	130
Output per worker	100	113	127	189	222

Figure 2.1 Outstanding growth: Table featuring time trends of output, employment, and output per worker, 1899–1939.
(Stigler, *Trends in Output and Employment*, 3)

economy" as portrayed in national income figures.[73] Going through the table horizontally allowed the reader to compare the numbers for specific years between the turn of the century and the end of the 1930s. In fact, the numbers only made sense in temporal comparison; their absolute value remained hidden, as the base value, set to 100 for all quantities in 1899, was not given. The columns gave the percentage differences from the base in the series. For instance, output in 1939 was 2.89 times higher than in 1899, which meant that output nearly tripled during these four decades. As typical for statistical trends, the series related to a linear concept of time, depicting it as the difference between decade-average values.

These numbers involved a good deal of abstraction work. Such tables translated varied statistical materials into coherent entities whose development could easily be traced. The necessary steps of constructing such neat appearances (and the complexities lost on the way) vanished behind the clean surface. The table in Figure 2.1 reported "indexes," statistical measures of change in a scaled time series. As instruments of measurement, such indices provided the rules for both aggregating individual industries into a more compact whole and calculating the rate of change of that aggregate over time.[74] In this case, these rules were arithmetic formulae that determined how to lump together individual industries according to their contribution to total output. Tracing the aggregate over time came with further design choices. Given that Stigler's overall aim was to measure the growth of real, "physical output," the figures were specifically intended to abstract from fluctuations in the value of money. Accordingly, he constructed a price index to deflate the time series, which was not only difficult as data were scarce but also beset by the so-called index-number problem: The relations of industries had to stay constant over time. Otherwise, fluctuations between industries would show up in the aggregate number and could not be differentiated from variations in aggregate output as a whole. The resulting measures of total output combined somewhat unwieldy disaggregated data into one plain figure and disregarded both the movements of the single industries and alterations in the relation between industries.

CEA reports drew on empirical economic knowledge and its visualizations of the growing economy. The 1949 report that pushed growth as the dominant aim of policy included a chart showing economic growth as an overall increasing line for the whole economy between 1896 and 1948 (Figure 2.2). The figure was divided into two parts with the left-hand side providing decade estimates and the right-hand side annual estimates. The fine print noted that data prior to 1929 were not "exactly comparable" with

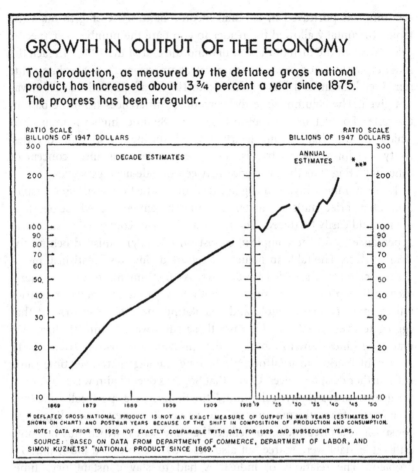

Figure 2.2 Growth in output of the economy, 1869–1948.
(CEA, "Economic Report 1949," 51)

subsequent years, but the report used the table despite its shortcomings. The graph's upward slope provided an easy-to-grasp image of the growing economy: "between the decade beginning in 1869 (earliest available estimates) and the decade ending in 1918, the gross output of the economy doubled about every 20 years."[75] Irrespective of all qualifications in the small print, the curve intimated a coherent past and possible further development of the economy.

Figure 2.2 illustrates how the object of the growing economy in research was not the same as in policy work. Practitioners in measurement emphasized the pitfalls of such clean-cut visualizations of aggregate numbers.

Kuznets, for instance, warned about using the quantitative concept of the economy as a quasi-natural and stable entity. In his *Encyclopedia* entry, he emphasized there was no clean line between the "area of the economic principle and the ways of life at large."[76] Instead, he talked about a plurality of economic systems framed by institutions and contingent with regard to time and place. Somewhat ironically, the visualization of the growing economy in Figure 2.2 drew on Kuznets's time series of national product. An instance where the cultural embedding of economic activity and particularity of measurement techniques became obvious in governmental practice was when British national accountants carried out an "experiment" in the early 1940s to check whether national income measures would fit nonwestern economies in Central Africa. Phyllis Deane, responsible for the project on the ground, sharply questioned the measurement rules that only counted monetary transactions and ignored subsistence production and barter trade, which, after all, largely dominated the kinds of exchange in her study.[77] Also Stigler pointed out how the cultural embedding of the economic affected the study of American growth: whether "men shave themselves or hire barbers" made a huge difference for the size of national output. Because growth trends omitted the declining share of household production, the rise of national output over time was necessarily exaggerated.[78] Had the CEA taken seriously the cautions against presenting the economy as a universal and separate category, the estimates in Figure 2.2 would have been combined with a narrative account of changes in the economic, social, and cultural institutions – as did some of the NBER's studies.

Most NBER studies of growth in the 1940s and early 1950s elucidated how their figures came about and did justice to the considerable efforts invested in constructing ever more sophisticated index numbers. Appendices elaborated on the making of data, discussed issues of coverage and classification, elaborated on the chosen index construction, and compared it with alternative methods by other agencies. Moreover, these studies abounded with verbal descriptions of, for instance, developments of individual industries and specific products.[79] While neat tables such as Stigler's in Figure 2.1 did have the purpose of making data more intelligible, the accompanying text was clearly directed at complicating the images' deceptively clean surfaces. The table appeared in the first chapter of a study that summarized its findings and gave perhaps all-too-simple impressions. Later chapters, however, provided ample discussion of the weaknesses of both the underlying data sets and the index construction. They included, for instance, additional time series such as the development of output in the individual industries.[80] The NBER's researchers were wary of letting the activities of collecting, compiling, and processing data slide into oblivion. When the tables moved into another realm uncoupled from their research milieu, they unfolded their suggestive power uninhibited – in the CEA's growth manifestos, for instance. The separation of the spheres of research and policy work, however, was notoriously porous, and most texts discussed in these pages made use of languages of both scrutiny and advocacy.[81] In particular, this was the case when it came to "explaining" growth that took the form of constructing productivity indices and directly related to political endeavors to foster higher growth rates.

THE QUEST FOR THE SOURCES OF PRODUCTIVITY

In the 1960s, Solow's model became one of the prime instruments for measuring the contribution of various factors to economic growth. Its measurement procedure consisted in what was seen as a more economical, practical way of dealing with data sets. The model was an agent of a specific style of econometric work that came with a different practice of dealing with numbers and a distinct understanding of knowledge and nonknowledge when it came to national productivity. As a GNP-related concept, "productivity" came into focus during the World Wars when the level of national output became a pressing concern for governments.[82] But empirical investigations of productivity had a longer history. It had been one of the quantitative critical concepts to think about all kinds of economic activities since the nineteenth century. In the 1920s, scientific management, business planning, and work efficiency studies aligned the notion more closely with a technical understanding of production. Denoting the relationship between physical inputs and output, this concept of productivity was applied to varying scales – from the shop floor to the firm, the industry, the sector, the region, and the economy as a whole.[83] A major motivation was fear of technological unemployment – the loss of skilled jobs in a time when production was rationalized and reorganized around new machinery. In the context of New Deal politics, productivity numbers were essential to questions of welfare. Providing empirical knowledge for governmental intervention, measurements were thought to support the central policy goal of creating sufficient demand, to counteract underconsumption, and to smooth cyclical depressions.

As was the case with national income research delineated in the first section, empirical studies of productivity in the 1920s and 1930s differed in method, scope, and focus from those in the late 1940s. As was common for statistical work in the 1920s, early studies consisted predominantly of verbal accounts of production methods and changes in technology. They drew on numerical data from the trade press, trade associations, voluntary company reports, questionnaires, and field trips to capture the panoply of changing production methods. Sometimes studies included photographs of specific innovations and detailed reflections on how these changed production practices – in particular, the amount of labor necessary for producing certain quantities of output. The numbers provided were largely descriptive and not based on statistical calculation.[84]

By the mid-1920s, the Bureau of Labor Statistics (BLS), one of the institutions that created reports on productivity, introduced the "productivity index."[85] The index represented a new empirical method and stabilized the notion of productivity as a statistical measure.[86] It came with both a different kind of numerical material and a different way of dealing with this material. The index related measures of output to measures of labor and used regularly collected data of the Census of Manufactures and the Chamber of Commerce. Instead of individual data embedded in narrative reports, "productivity" now related to a large body of census data captured through a numerical index. There was, however, no standardized technique of measuring productivity. Different approaches co-existed for several decades, and the BLS itself only started to calculate productivity indices routinely in the mid-1950s.[87]

Of the many approaches to studying productivity in the 1920s and 1930s, only a few took direct account of productivity as a source of economic growth, as the historian of economics Jeff Biddle has highlighted.[88] The BLS, for instance, combined the productivity index with the better-known cost-of-living index in order to delineate possible relations between productivity and wages and to establish how much labor was necessary to afford a certain standard of living. In this way, the productivity index took part in the larger movement toward a greater reliance on economic statistics in political discourse. In his work on the history of "cost of living," Tom Stapleford has laid out how, alongside the creation of legal protections for labor (often in exchange for stifling union action), objects such as wage rates increasingly turned from normative matters of fairness or of economic power into calculable and economically sound facts.[89] Already in the 1930s, reform objectives became aligned with national prosperity – which would become essential for the postwar politics of growth.

The few early productivity studies that did investigate growth pushed a new measure that provided "productivity" with new conceptual content, this time by linking it to technology. Existing metrics calculated labor productivity – the output per worker or work-hour. This helped thinking about how productivity increases changed the labor intensity of production, and how this affected wages and employment. But when it came to growth, labor productivity was only a starting point for taking account of, ideally, all kinds of factors that increased output. The rationale could also be found in discussions of Paul H. Douglas's and Charles Cobb's time series regressions from the late 1920s on.[90] The idea, as Douglas expressed it, was to find out which "forces affect[ed] the volume of production," in particular which part of growth was due to changes in what he called – with recourse to Adam Smith – "technical knowledge" and the "industrial arts."[91] In the early 1940s, the "Cobb-Douglas regression" was adjusted to attribute some part of growth to something other than growth in labor or growth in the capital stock.[92]

The argument that labor productivity was a deficient measure for what motivated growth was also essential for the NBER's researchers. By the end of the 1930s, the Bureau set up a research program to investigate the long-run trends of output, employment, and productivity for single industries but also for aggregates – groups of industries (such as manufacturing, electric and gas utilities, mining, transportation, and agriculture) and, ultimately, the economy as a whole.[93] Initially, publications reported in particular on the effects of productivity growth on employment and the distribution of income. This changed when, by the late 1940s, the governmental concern with fostering economic growth rose to wholly new prominence. Stigler's aforementioned *Trends in Output and Employment* was among the first studies that approached a measure of national productivity. Recall that Figure 2.1 showed that, while output per capita (as a measure for the growth of "national wealth") tripled, employment only rose by a third. Labor productivity more than doubled in the covered period.[94] Interpreting the numbers, Stigler echoed much of the reasoning of the existing literature on productivity. Changes in productivity, he figured, could simply be due to "factor substitution," meaning that capital had become cheaper than labor and was therefore used more in production. For this reason, he argued for the development of another index that was able to capture the suspected "great technological advance."[95] His "index of efficiency" measured the relation between output increases and increases in *total* inputs, of labor and capital jointly – now not only for manufacturing industries but for a group of twelve industries taken to stand for the economy as a whole.[96] In principle, measuring the productivity of all factors of production was rather straightforward: It was about comparing changes in total inputs with changes in total output. However, just as in the case of measuring national income and its growth over time discussed in the first two sections, the practice of actually constructing such a metric was intricate. Its design involved, for instance, indices for aggregating industries, which captured the changing relations of inputs and output over time, and it necessitated distinct price indices, which deflated both input and output measures in order to speak of physical entities. Accordingly, different studies, whether at the NBER or other institutions, came up with different index calculations.[97]

What different productivity indices shared were specific assumptions necessary for making intertemporal comparison work. These assumptions fundamentally framed the phenomenon of the growing economy and prompted, among others, the critique of Joan Robinson, as reported in Chapter 1. Index constructors assumed, for instance, that consumers of all periods had the same tastes as in the base-period and that all other crucial relationships in the economy were linear over time. Moreover, productivity indices rested on the implicit assumption of a circular flow of money. And they invoked marginal productivity theory already before there was "the neoclassical growth model." To construct a measure of output per unit of inputs, it was necessary to gauge the two classes of inputs, labor (measured either in "workers" or "work hours") and capital (measured in physical units), in a comparable way. The quantities of labor and capital were thus defined as flows during an equal period – labor-years and annual services of capital. Then, parallel to the way that diverse types of goods were combined in order to reach the index of national output, monetary value was chosen as a common base unit of measurement. But goods were heterogeneous on every other level, so weights had to be introduced to overcome the problem of averaging in a manner that would take account of both amounts and values. Attached to prices as if they were homogeneous entities, "capital" and "labor" were weighed by their relative contribution to national income in terms of their respective market values ("value-added" for capital, and wages for labor), which were then assumed to be constant over time.[98]

Index constructors sometimes presented the neoclassical framing of their numbers as a pragmatic matter of the craft of measurement, sometimes as a proper theoretical viewpoint relating to the purity of real-world competition. Stigler explicitly legitimized his estimation procedure through recourse to marginal productivity theory: "the entrepreneur adjusts quantities of various productive services so that at the margin he obtains equal product per dollar of expenditure on each."[99] This economist, who jarringly spoke of the nineteenth century as "the pleasant century that followed on the *Wealth of Nations*," interpreted his data as stemming from a neoclassical equilibrium in the world.[100] His notion of "efficiency" thus related to a static equilibrium allocation, which provided the distribution of income. Due to the equilibrating effects of a competitive market, each "factor" was paid its due product. Most NBER researchers, however, presented their assumptions not in terms of theory but as pragmatic design choices that enabled measurement in the first place. Some maintained that there was simply no plausible substitute for measuring productivity.[101] Others referred to accounting conventions, which identified the value of inputs with the value of outputs, and disregarded possible theoretical implications.[102] The related publications complemented metrics of aggregate productivity with discussions of how these numbers came about and compared them with production functions of singular industries. In these accounts, there could, in principle, be all sorts of reasons why aggregates behaved and correlated the way they did.

On the basis of the available, always scanty, always sketchy data, indices of joint productivity invited far-reaching inferences that went well beyond the data material – foreshadowing the conventions of measuring techniques based on Solow's model. Stigler, for instance, did not leave it at the rather descriptive conclusion that the large increases in output over the past four decades stemmed from increased efficiency either through improvements in labor ("better training, better minds, and better physiques") or capital ("increasing the quantity or improving the quality of cooperating resources").[103] Epitomizing a wider trend, he unabashedly denoted the index a measure for "economic progress."[104] An index that linked the development of production in monetary terms to numbers on efficiency turned into the basis for a celebratory account of the history of modernity: "We have extended our mastery over nature or over ignorance: we live better without working harder."[105] Stigler's formulation was just one example of how the agenda of growth and productivity could draw from easily manageable figures. Twelve industries turned into representatives for the economy as a whole, the economy as a whole into a representative for "us," higher production into the equivalent of a better life, and increased efficiency into a lesser need to work for apparently everybody. Equating "progress" with producing ever more output with ever less labor either simply ignored questions relating to a standard of living, the (global and domestic) distribution of the rising product, and wage levels, or assumed that these were nonissues with rising productivity.

Efficiency indices founded a whole new strand of empirical research devoted to finding the factors of increased national efficiency. In the 1950s, building on the national accounts, the NBER made the study of economic growth and national productivity its main focus. The numerical results and arguments of these studies were similar to the ones already discussed. While national income per capita had quadrupled over eight decades, total input per capita had risen by less than a fifth. Consequently, "the major source of our economic advance" had to lie in "vastly improved efficiency."[106] A 1956 interim report on the study of productivity trends linked gains in efficiency to "the process of technical advance" and "innovation," which in turn was, "of course," prompted by competition in a market economy." Very much in line with the contemporary political outlook, the report pushed that firms competing for profits and markets needed to be "creative" and that "investment in research and development activity" was crucial for them to succeed.[107] Having discovered efficiency, the NBER's statisticians embarked whole-heartedly on the project of finding out about its drivers and saw its main source in technology.

Continuing to emphasize the relevance of its numbers as inputs for national politics, the NBER started to position itself as the best institution to provide knowledge about growth and how to implement and sustain it. The 1954 report extolled the Bureau's statistical research, which got at the workings of long-term "forces pushing our national level of living upward."[108] With growth rates hardly found anywhere else, the US was looking into a promising future, *if* it kept fostering growth:

The average family in the United States had an income of somewhat over $5,000 in 1953. If we progress at as high and consistent a rate in the next eighty years as in the last, our grandchildren or great-grandchildren will have average family incomes of about $25,000 of 1953 purchasing power – a level now attained only by the top 1 per cent or so of the nation's families.[109]

Five years after the CEA's manifesto for economic growth as the primary aim of economic policy that would benefit all social classes, the NBER likewise held up the positive effects of economic growth for all members of society. The Bureau's public statements joined the broad postwar consensus on the politics of growth and productivity that extended from Eisenhower republicans and most of the business community to Keynesian liberals.[110] As the director of the research program on productivity trends, John W. Kendrick, reinforced in an 1956 interim report, productivity growth was of "paramount importance in raising levels of living, in strengthening potential national security, and in the provision for future economic growth."[111] In tying together metrics of output and inputs, productivity measurements gave more substance to the object of the economy and sought to provide access points for steering its growth. Or, as a review of the European Productivity Agency put it most directly: "The ultimate purpose of all measurements and research in the field of productivity is to find the answer to the question WHAT MAKES PRODUCTIVITY INCREASE?" Founded in 1953 as a branch of the Organization for European Economic Co-operation (OEEC), the agency's stated purpose was to raise "European standards of living" through stimulating productivity. "If we know the answer, we also know what action to take."[112] In line with the corporatist ideas surrounding the entity of the economy, the endeavor was not only to impact governments but also to make business and labor see the advantages of productivity and to cooperate to that effect.

There was an essential tension between such neat official presentations and research: However much actors emphasized the importance of raising productivity, their numbers said little about productivity growth. Measurements essentially compared two indices. Their difference contained whatever was not captured by conventionally defined measures of capital and labor and thus absorbed all kinds of things that went into production. The vagueness of what was actually measured was reflected in a number of different labels given to productivity indices over time. Most often, picking up on the 1930s literature, it was "innovation" and "technical change."[113] Kendrick's 1956 report eventually claimed to make the broadest effort to measure "total factor productivity," a term that was invented, as he noted, by a "movement to measure productivity in terms of all relevant inputs."[114] This rather technical expression would ultimately stick, and its acronym "TFP" became an essential part of economists' vocabulary. Regardless of its label, the interpretation of the index was contested from the outset. Proponents as well as critics listed a variety of factors that obviously went into the measurement but were not separately accounted for. Items on such lists ranged from qualitative characteristics of inputs, economies of scale, and imperfect competition to the organization of productive units, economic power, and working conditions.[115] List-like explanations of growth highlighted the incompleteness of the endeavor. Accordingly, Kendrick emphasized that studying the efficiency index was about continuously approximating "the 'missing' factor."[116] Abramovitz, who had surveyed the field of growth economics for the AEA, denounced efficiency studies on more fundamental grounds. Seeing growth as a social phenomenon, he took issue with the neglect of all kinds of nonquantifiable factors, which made them give "lopsided importance to productivity increase." In the end, as he famously noted, the index constituted "a measure of our ignorance about the causes of economic growth."[117]

Extensive lists of excluded factors did not mean that productivity measurements were to be abandoned. Researchers argued instead that such exclusions could be progressively integrated into index calculations. This involved extending the domain of the measurable by making ever more factors of production accountable – intangible knowledge and skills, habits of cooperation, the effectiveness of administration, or the quality of management. While early NBER studies had provided descriptive accounts of qualitative improvements of products in specific industries, postwar scholars deviated from the practice of combining quantitative and narrative investigation. Stigler, for instance, made the case for calculating an "over-all number." In "our statistically-minded age," he maintained, things that were not "subjected to general measurement," such as narrative accounts of improvements in the quality of products, were "easily forgotten."[118] Including ever more factors in growth measurement promised to make the object of the growing economy ever more substantial in that it got more tightly embedded in empirical research as well as in economic analysis. It is here that Solow's model enters my story of productivity measurements.

MANAGING IGNORANCE

"The intricate and ingenious mosaic of the index numbers . . . is described in great detail. But what the book lacks, oddly enough, is a simple model showing the implications of the basic assumptions on which it rests."[119] This is how the growth economist Evsey D. Domar reviewed a 1961 NBER study on productivity trends under the telling title "On Total Productivity and All That." Domar was one of the economists to whom the Harrod–Domar model, the major comparative foil for the neoclassical growth model, was attributed. In the mid-1940s, he translated a Keynesian concern for demand into a mathematical model of long-run growth, which, as outlined in Chapter 1, provided an exemplar for model-centered theorizing. Already in that paper, he criticized the use of the NBER's studies of growth and productivity for questions of political governance. In his view, they were "theoretically incomplete."[120] In a similar vein he also commented on Kuznets's research on capital formation. While the study did imply relations between economic categories, it lacked an "explicit model" to account for these relations in causal terms.[121] By the beginning of the

1960s, Domar could assume his modeler's perspective to be widely shared. The GNP had already turned into the universally accepted depiction of the economy and was about to become what has been called "the world's most powerful number."[122] Moreover, the idea that mathematical models, complementing large-scale economic measurement endeavors, could help economic governance fine-tune its parameters had been widely established. "Even if obvious to the index-number specialists, [index numbers] are worrisome to amateurs like myself."[123] Coquetry or not, Domar's review expressed the perspective of what in the 1960s became economists' dominant methodological conviction: Mathematical models were complete (containing enough relationships to explain all the variables) and determinate (each relationship had to be fully specified). As such they were widely thought to make their assumptions explicit and to provide clear-cut instructions for measurement. From such a view, the NBER's extensive verbal appendices appeared to hide the conceptual preliminaries of its numbers.

A model that compensated for the contested lack of a "proper explanation" in productivity research was the neoclassical growth model. One year after Abramovitz had denoted the efficiency index a measure of ignorance, Solow published "Technical Change and the Aggregate Production Function."[124] In that paper, the model figured as an instrument for measuring growth and its sources in NBER's aggregate time series for the US between 1909 and 1949. In a first step, the article related the variables of the mathematical model economy to empirical categories in the data sets. The abstract variable "output" equaled the measured number of total real product, while its "inputs" equaled aggregate measures of total real-factor input. After some algebraic reformulations ("intensive form"), the model provided a fully specified and complete aggregate production function as the essential measuring rod. Each point of the production function associated a level of the capital–labor ratio with a level of labor productivity (the output–labor ratio). Solow complemented the production function with a variable that included everything not measured by conventional metrics of labor and capital. It captured "slowdowns, speedups, improvements in the education of the labor force, and all sorts of things." Nevertheless, Solow denoted the variable simply "technical change."[125] The paper bluntly concluded that, for the US between 1909 and 1949, technical change accounted for 87.2 percent of growth of output per capita. Capital accumulation contributed only little to economic growth, and technical change was its real driver.

In the eyes of modeling economists, what set the model apart was that it offered a straightforward procedure of measurement. It efficiently

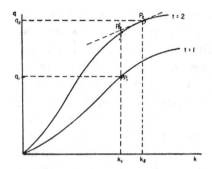

Figure 2.3 From the model . . .
(Solow, "Technical Change and the Aggregate Production Function," 313)

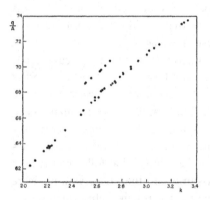

Figure 2.4 . . . to the data.
(Solow, "Technical Change and the Aggregate Production Function," 317)

differentiated between GNP growth that was due to rising inputs of capital
and labor (*movements along* the aggregate production function) and GNP
growth that was due to "technical change" (*shifts of* the production function).[126] The chart in Figure 2.3 provided a graphical representation of the
mathematical model. It showed how the production function shifted from
a lower to a higher level due to technical change. The scatter plot in
Figure 2.4 showed the interpretation of data in terms of the model. Each
point represented the relation between a level of the capital–labor ratio and
a level of labor productivity (with the outlying points being statistical
artifacts, which Solow excluded from analysis).

It can hardly be overstated that this kind of empirical work was not
supposed to provide a test of the model, to verify or falsify the production
function, or any of the model's assumptions. Rather, it was a way to

interpret given time-series data – assuming that they were brought about by a world that worked like the model.[127] Philosopher of measurement Marcel Boumans has noted that "confronting a model with phenomenological facts ... means comparing this instrument with another instrument that generated these facts."[128] Indeed, it was one of the major points of criticism against Solow's paper that its aggregate production function fit the data so well simply because it essentially regressed a national accounting identity.[129] Brought into the model's categories, the data served to specify the shape of the aggregate production. Here, the job of the modeler-measurer was to find the shape that best characterized the data in Figure 2.4. "Fitting a curve to the scatter," Solow experimented with five different parametric forms to estimate model parameters.[130] Probabilistic techniques helped to conduct "linear regressions" and conduct a "test of goodness of fit" – terms that related to econometric estimation and that would soon, in the course of the 1960s, find their way into economists' language.[131]

Solow's curve-fitting procedure amounted to choosing a particular reading of given data points. He applied specific formulae – statistical models with certain assumptions about the joint distribution of variables – to the data. The estimation technique, as Jeff Biddle and Marcel Boumans have pointed out, came along with a reinterpretation of time series in terms of a seemingly experimental logic. Econometric procedures treated time series data as observations brought about by a mechanism that followed the laws of probability. This involved the assumption that observations were random and that the world was governed through stable quantitative relationships that could be uncovered through a rather formal procedure of statistical inference.[132] In Solow's estimation, the semilogarithmic and the Cobb-Douglas function had the best results, but he could not "help feeling that little or nothing hangs on the choice of functional form."[133] The specific shape of the production function was clearly subordinate to the paper's principal contributions: First, using the aggregate production function as a tool to measure growth and its factors; second, introducing the blanket assumption that technical change was "neutral." This meant that technical change did not change the relations of production; it was an external factor outside the narrow confines of the model economy.

As was the case in the realm of economic theory (Chapter 1), the model unfolded a magnetic pull in the field of economic measurement. In the NBER's index number research, statistical inference relied on economists' knowledge of the specific data sets and how they came about. It also depended on their narrative accounts, which established relations that were not there in the data. In contrast, Solow's paper revolved around the model itself, its capacities, and its weaknesses. The model not only assumed a functional relation between aggregates, it also involved a straightforward interpretation of these relations. It presented the growing economy as a smooth-working system based on the assumption of a competitive long-run equilibrium. In its empirical application, everything excluded from the neoclassical economy but still there in the data went into a separate term outside the economy. The residual swallowed the whole lists of absences that productivity researchers in the past decades had emphasized. The feedback Solow received was accordingly:

> To end up analyzing what happened over so long a period, . . . as if 87.2% of the rise in gross output per man hour were manna from heaven, something that has come from nothing (some new twist of the invisible hand) – must be wrong. What you have in your box labeled 'technical change' is . . . not something exogenous given to us by some capricious God.[134]

In his paper, Solow qualified his model work, as he had done in the "Contribution." He did speak of a "crude application" and reflected on unwarranted implications of the model's setup. But still, statistical inference was based on this one specific tool, on this one particular set of rules. There was no consideration of other forms of knowledge.

On the trajectory I have drawn in this chapter, I pictured how productivity first turned into a statistical concept, then related to the economy as a whole, involved not only labor but also capital, and was now thoroughly cast in neoclassical terms. All measurement endeavors on the preceding pages shaped both knowledge and nonknowledge about growth and productivity, and thereby "selected, filtered, purified, shaped" these phenomena.[135] The Solow model doubled down on the construction of the economy as a separate sphere in that it provided a clean-cut instruction for a reproducible estimation procedure. Its great advantage was that it tidily reordered knowledge and ignorance about growth. Everything that went beyond the smooth neoclassical world was neatly tucked away in a residual, which therefore not only captured all kinds of measurement errors but also all kinds of factors and dynamics that might have had an effect on GNP. Philip Mirowski has talked about "the Revenge of the Repressed," as under the label of "technical change" all things social, cultural, and temporal made a reappearance in analysis.[136] It was not really a revenge, though. The paper's conclusion was not that the measurement procedure was silent regarding almost 90 percent of growth. The residual was not presented as an index for the detachedness of the model from the world of economic practices. Solow frankly acknowledged that the model had almost no explanatory power. But in his research endeavor this was not its job to begin with. It was actually about bringing order into empirical work, separating between an orderly inside and a messy outside.[137] In the NBER reports, it was the measured phenomena themselves that were intrinsically characterized by nonknowledge. The model cast the problem of nonknowledge in terms of a problem of inclusion and exclusion from the neoclassical cosmos. At a time when there were no stabilized measurement procedures in place, the neoclassical growth model offered the alluring opportunity to turn a measure of ignorance into an easily replicable measurement procedure. Hand in hand with econometric estimation becoming the dominant way of conducting empirical work, its particular rendering of nonknowledge made a sparkling career in the decades to come. Dominating a specific strand of empirical research into growth, the model came to fortify the view that numbers are easily treated like glances at a distant reality.

A WILLING SUSPENSION OF DISBELIEF

The Solow model's clean-cut procedure for measuring growth and its sources circulated widely. Already a year after its publication, discussions of technical change at the Conference on Research in Income and Wealth were to a large extent framed in terms of movements along and shifts of production functions.[138] With the model's use as an instrument of measurement, "technical change" turned into the common label of the error term, and the inference that it was neutral became a common conclusion. When the model was seen to be too coarse of a measuring instrument, it was not abandoned. In the field of "growth accounting," the challenge became to refine both understanding and measurement of the residual. In the realm of policy-making, the so-called Solow residual provided a straightforward yardstick to allocate resources "in the interests of economic growth."[139] In the first section of this chapter, national accounts captured the economic benefits of public expenditure and, at the same time, contributed to subjecting policy to a merely economic evaluation. The neoclassical growth model took part in this broader movement as it became one crucial instrument to measure how all kinds of factors contributed to the increase of national income and thus, so the argument commonly went, to progress. Integrating ever more things into the production function enlarged the realm of the economy at the same time as it deprived them of their special extra-economic characteristics – which I will discuss as "neoclassical growth in action" in the Epilogue. It testifies to the ability of artifacts to develop a life of their own that the late economist Solow urged the profession to do research as it was done by the NBER in the 1950s – the very research that the Solow model helped to eclipse. "I would try to do something like choose a fairly narrowly defined industry, and get a technological history of that industry over some years, so that what you were looking at were discrete, in a way, changes in productivity."[140]

The wide dissemination of the Solow residual fit with the standardization of econometric work in the 1960s and 1970s. The construction of a simple model and the insertion of figures into that model from a set of time-series or cross-section data in a curve-fitting procedure became the dominant form of empirical economics. The move to model-guided methods came, as the case of the neoclassical growth model illustrated, with a more detached relation to empirical data. NBER economists in this chapter were concerned with the pitfalls of measurement. They discussed and delineated the heterogenous and often informal ways they arrived at their numerical outcomes and laid open how they chose to interpret these numbers. Model-based measurement, in contrast, meant following rules and adhering to specified criteria for what made statistical inference reliable. The shift involved a different relation to the empirical material as modeler–economists stopped actively contributing to the creation of data – thereby constructing the world they would subsequently theorize – and became passive consumers of data found elsewhere. Personal judgment and skills were still an essential part of professional empirical work but became hidden behind formalized, rule-based inferential techniques.[141]

When the president of the American Economic Association, Wassily Leontief, noted in 1970 that the discipline rode "on the crest of intellectual respectability and popular acclaim," he referred to such practices of econometric measurement.[142] His target was in particular growth models with highly aggregative variables that, he argued, "can contribute very little to the understanding of processes of economic growth, and they cannot provide a useful theoretical basis for systematic empirical analysis."[143] In constructing aggregate models for interpreting data from secondary or tertiary sources, economists created objects that were far removed from actual economic practices.[144] As an outspoken critic of econometric practice, Leontief opposed aggregative models and negated their usefulness for policy-making.[145] Instead of concealing economic reality through aggregation, as he saw it, Leontief pushed research that purposefully collected data on a different scale in order to make underlying economic structures visible. Somewhat breezily, Solow and the economists who followed his use of the aggregate production function did away with the epistemic complications it entailed. "In this day of rationally designed econometric studies and super input–output tables, it takes something more than the usual 'willing suspension of disbelief' to talk seriously of the aggregate production function."[146] Solow had been an assistant to Leontief, and was, to a certain extent, familiar with detailed data work and its complexities. That he left all that behind and became famous with a model that stood for a new, detached relation to empirical work was part of a wider epistemic shift between the 1930s and the 1950s delineated in Chapters 3 and 4. Chapter 3 moves into the depths of measurement practices in input–output research. It shows how questions that the neoclassical growth model conveniently set aside posed serious problems and sometimes insurmountable obstacles at the very basis of the making of empirical knowledge.

Notes

1   Council of Economic Advisers, "Economic Report of the President: Transmitted to the Congress, January 28, 1954" (Washington, DC: GPO, 1954), iv. On the politics of growth in the US, see Robert M. Collins, *More: The Politics of Economic Growth in Postwar America* (Oxford: Oxford University Press, 2000); Andrew L. Yarrow, *Measuring America: How Economic Growth Came to Define American Greatness in the Late Twentieth Century* (Amherst: University of Massachusetts Press, 2010).

2   Robert M. Solow, "Technical Change and the Aggregate Production Function," *Review of Economics and Statistics* 39, no. 3 (1957): 312–20.

3   See Gary Gerstle, *American Crucible: Race and Nation in the Twentieth Century* (Princeton: Princeton University Press, 2016), chapter 4; Ira Katznelson, *Fear Itself: The New Deal and the Origins of Our Times* (New York: Liveright, 2013).

4   Arthur F. Burns and Wesley C. Mitchell, *Measuring Business Cycles* (New York: NBER, 1946), 17, cited in Jeff Biddle and Marcel Boumans, "Exploring the History of Statistical Inference in Economics: Introduction," in *Exploring the History of Statistical Inference in Economics* (supplement to *History of Political Economy* 53), edited by Jeff Biddle and Marcel Boumans (Durham, NC: Duke University Press, 2021), 1–24, 10.

5   From an institutionalist perspective, scientific economics focused on empirical inquiry rather than proceeding from axioms about human behavior. In this vein, statistical findings were not simply there to provide governmental knowledge but also to refine and check historical and economic theories as well as wider common notions about broader tendencies in capitalist development, the business cycle, or industrial evolution. See Malcolm Rutherford, *The Institutionalist Movement in American Economics, 1918–1947: Science and Social Control* (Cambridge: Cambridge University Press, 2011), 45.

6   Theodore W. Schultz to Robert Solow, May 29, 1957, Solow papers, box 56, file J: 1 of 2.

7   Theodore M. Porter, "Locating the Domain of Calculation," *Journal of Cultural Economy* 1, no. 1 (2008): 39–50, 43.

8 See Bradley W. Bateman, "Clearing the Ground: The Demise of the Social Gospel Movement and the Rise of Neoclassicism in American Economics," in *From Interwar Pluralism to Postwar Neoclassicism* (supplement to *History of Political Economy* 30), edited by Mary S. Morgan and Malcolm Rutherford (Durham, NC: Duke University Press, 1998), 29–52.

9 Willford I. King, *The Wealth and Income of the People of the United States* (New York: Macmillan, 1915). For earlier, rather isolated attempts to construct a national income, see Carol Carson, "The History of the United States National Income and Product Accounts: The Development of an Analytical Tool," *Review of Income & Wealth* 21 (1975): 153–81.

10 See, for instance, Charles Camic, "On Edge: Sociology during the Great Depression and the New Deal," in *Sociology in America: A History*, edited by Craig Calhoun (Chicago: University of Chicago Press, 2007), 225–80.

11 Carson, "History of the United States National Income and Product Accounts," 155.

12 The NBER was founded in 1919 to compensate for the lack of organized statistical information detected when the federal government sought to manage mobilization and the wartime economy during the First World War. On the Bureau's history, see Rutherford, *Institutionalist Movement*, chapter 9; Eli Cook, *The Pricing of Progress: Economic Indicators and the Capitalization of American Life* (Cambridge, MA: Harvard University Press, 2017), epilogue.

13 National Bureau of Economic Research, *Income in the United States: Its Amount and Distribution, 1909–1919, vols. 1 and 2* (New York: NBER, 1921 and 1922).

14 Funded by the Rockefeller Foundation, the Carnegie Foundation, and the Russell Sage Foundation, the *Encyclopedia* was first published in 1930 to go beyond disciplinary boundaries. See Edgar A. J. Johnson, "The Encyclopedia of the Social Sciences," *Quarterly Journal of Economics* 50, no. 2 (1936): 355–66, 355.

15 Born in the Russian Empire in 1901, Kuznets worked in the Ukrainian Bureau of Labor Statistics before he emigrated from the Soviet Union to the US in the early 1920s. There, he entered professional academia at Columbia University under Wesley Mitchell. After his graduation, Mitchell invited him to join the staff of the NBER, where he began a long career in the study of business cycles, national income, and capital accumulation. For biographical sketches of Kuznets, see Cristel Anne de Rouvray, "Economists Writing History: American and French Experience in the Mid 20th Century," PhD dissertation, London School of Economics and Political Science, 2005, 123–4; Rutherford, *Institutionalist Movement*; and Robert W. Fogel, Enid M. Fogel, Mark Guglielmo, and Nathaniel Grotte, *Political Arithmetic: Simon Kuznets and the Empirical Tradition in Economics* (Chicago: University of Chicago Press, 2013), chapter 2.

16 Simon Kuznets, "National Income," in *Encyclopedia of the Social Sciences*, vol. 11, edited by Edwin R. A. Seligman (New York: Macmillan, 1933), 205–44, 214.

17 Alain Desrosières, *The Politics of Large Numbers: A History of Statistical Reasoning* (Cambridge, MA: Harvard University Press, 1998), 30.

18 Mary S. Morgan, "Seeking Parts, Looking for Wholes," in: *Histories of Scientific Observation*, edited by Lorraine Daston and Elizabeth Lunbeck (Chicago: University of Chicago Press, 2011), 303–25, 305.

19 Kuznets, "National Income," 215.

20 For examples of triangulation as a strategy to increase trust in numbers, see Biddle and Boumans, "Exploring the History of Statistical Inference in Economics," 11–12.

21 Kuznets, "National Income," 214.

22 Both the Brookings Institution and the Federal Reserve developed alternative measures of a national income. See Carson, "History of the United States National Income and Product Accounts," 161–7.

23 Kuznets, "National Income," 205.

24 On the politics of the NBER, see Cook's epilogue "Towards GDP" to his account of money-based measures in *Pricing of Progress*. Emphasizing the crucial role of corporate capital in the founding of the NBER, he has pointed to the "smart" lumping of salaried management and wage labor, which allowed the report to include profits in the share of labor and to support "an age-old argument by pro-business thinkers" (261).

25 See Daniel Breslau, "Economics Invents the Economy: Mathematics, Statistics, and Models in the Work of Irving Fisher and Wesley Mitchell," *Theory and Society* 32, no. 3 (2003): 379–411, 405.

26 Both: Kuznets, "National Income," 208.

27 Kuznets, "National Income," 209. "Reproductive labor" pertains to the day-to-day housework, falling within a feminine-gendered sphere. The call for the recognition of unpaid reproductive labor has been part of feminist movements from their very beginning. From the mid-1970s onward, the government commissioned the measurement of the contribution of housework to GNP in dollar value. For a discussion, see Silvia Federici, "The Restructuring of Housework and Reproduction in the United States in the 1970s (1980)," in *Revolution at Point Zero: Housework, Reproduction, and Feminist Struggle*, edited by Silvia Federici (Oakland, CA: PM Press, 2012), 41–53.

28 Kuznets, "National Income," 219. To illustrate this point, Kuznets confronted the deviating results of different estimates he had undertaken.

29 Kuznets, "National Income," 206.

30 Simon Kuznets, *National Income and Its Composition, 1919–1939*, vol. 1 (New York: NBER, 1941), xxvi, cited in Timothy Mitchell, "Fixing the Economy," *Cultural Studies* 12, no. 1 (1998): 82–101, 89.

31 See Mark Perlman and Morgan Marietta, "The Politics of Social Accounting: Public Goals and the Evolution of the National Accounts in Germany, the United Kingdom and the United States," *Review of Political Economy* 17, vol. 2 (2005): 211–30, 220.

32 Milton Gilbert, Georg Jaszi, Charles F. Schwartz, and Edward F. Denison, "National Income and Product Statistics of the United States, 1929–1946," *Survey of Current Business* 27 (1947): 1–54.

33 See Paul Studenski, *The Income of Nations: Theory, Measurement, and Analysis* (New York: New York University Press, 1958), 149–54.

34 Paul A. Samuelson, "Unemployment Ahead," *The New Republic*, September 11 (1944): 297–9, 298. On the increased professional self-esteem of economists in the aftermath of the Second World War, see Mary S. Morgan and Malcolm Rutherford, "American Economics: The Character of the Transformation," in *From Interwar Pluralism to Postwar Neoclassicism* (supplement to *History of Political Economy* 30), edited by Mary S. Morgan and Malcolm Rutherford (Durham, NC: Duke University Press, 1998), 1–26, 12–13.

35 See Richard Stone, "The Use and Development of National Income and Expenditure Estimates," in *Lessons of the British War Economy*, edited by Daniel N. Chester (Cambridge: Cambridge University Press, 1951), 83–101. The NIPA aligned with the British design of national accounts as a double-entry production account for the entire economy with national income equal to national expenditure. The new framework was based on mathematical reinterpretations of Keynes's *General Theory*. See Gilles Dostaler, *Keynes and His Battles* (Cheltenham, UK: Edward Elgar, 2007), 201.

36 See Onur Özgöde, "Institutionalism in Action: Balancing the Substantive Imbalances of 'the Economy' through the Veil of Money," *History of Political Economy* 52, no. 2 (2020): 307–39, 325–6; cf. Philipp Lepenies, *The Power of a Single Number: A Political History of GDP* (New York: Columbia University Press, 2016), 76.

37 See Timothy Mitchell, "Econometality: How the Future Entered Government," *Critical Inquiry* 40, no 4 (2014): 479–507, 498.

38 Daniel Hirschman, "Rediscovering the 1%: Knowledge Infrastructures and the Stylized Facts of Inequality," *American Journal of Sociology* 127, no. 3 (2021): 739–86.

39 On the debates accompanying the new "Keynesian" policy focus, see Özgöde, "Institutionalism in Action," 308 and 331–3.

40 See Simon Kuznets, "Measurement: Measurement of Economic Growth," The *Journal of Economic History* 7 (1947): 10–34, 20–21. Cf. Daniel Speich Chassé, *Die Erfindung des Bruttosozialprodukts. Globale Ungleichheit in der Wissensgeschichte der Ökonomie* (Göttingen: Vandenhoeck & Ruprecht, 2013), 138–40.

41 US National Resources Planning Board, "National Resources Development: Report for 1943. Part I. Post-War Plan and Program" (Washington, DC, 1943), 4, cited in Collins, *More*, 14. The NRPB was originally set up as the National Planning Board (NPB) in 1933 as part of the Public Works Administration. As the center of New Deal planning, it was chaired by Frederic Delano; another member was the NBER's Wesley C. Mitchell. See Alan Brinkley, "The National Resources Planning Board and the Reconstruction of Planning," in *The American Planning Tradition: Culture and Policy*, edited by Robert Fishman (Baltimore: Johns Hopkins University Press, 2000), 173–91. On Hansen's and Samuelson's NRPB work see Roger Backhouse, *Founder of Modern Economics: Paul A. Samuelson. Vol. 1: Becoming Samuelson* (New York: Oxford University Press, 2017), chapter 19.

42 See Theda Skocpol, *Social Policy in the United States: Future Possibilities in Historical Perspective* (Princeton NJ: Princeton University Press, 1995), 168–74.

43 Charles S. Maier, "The Politics of Productivity: Foundations of American International Economic Policy after World War II," *International Organization* 31, no. 4 (1977): 607–33, 613.

44 Mitchell, "Econometality," 486.

45 Skocpol, *Social Policy in the United States*, 198. Overriding the veto of President Harry S. Truman, who had just assumed office, the US Senate passed the Labor Management Relations Act, better known as the "Taft-Hartley Act" in 1945. The act was designed to mitigate the influence that labor unions had won during the New Deal, for instance, by imposing limits on labor's ability to strike.

46 See Márcia L. Balisciano, "Hope for America: American Notions of Economic Planning between Pluralism and Neoclassicism, 1930–1950," in *From Interwar Pluralism to Postwar Neoclassicism* (supplement to *History of Political Economy* 30), edited by Mary S. Morgan and Malcolm Rutherford (Durham, NC: Duke University Press, 1998), 153–78, 174.

47 National Planning Association, *National Budgets for Full Employment* (Washington, DC: National Planning Association, 1945), cited in Balisciano, "Hope for America," 173–74. The report was published by the board of trustees; Hansen was a member of the board; Kuznets and Gerhard Colm helped prepare the report.

48 On the establishment of the CEA, see Michael A. Bernstein, *A Perilous Progress: Economists and Public Purpose in Twentieth-Century America* (Princeton: Princeton University Press, 2001), 104–11. Whereas Bernstein presents the Council as the "institutional zenith" of economists' influence, Mitchell has argued that the CEA was a means to keep economists out of government processes, "Economentality," 490–1.

49 CEA, "Economic Report 1949," 75.

50 Yarrow, *Measuring America*, 26–27.

51 See Elizabeth Popp Berman, *Thinking Like an Economist: How Efficiency Replaced Equality in U.S. Public Policy* (Princeton: Princeton University Press, 2022), chapter 2.

52 See Collins, *More*, 18.

53 Council of Economic Advisers, "Business and Government: Fourth Annual Report to the President" (Washington, DC: Government Printing Office, 1949), 6, cited in Collins, *More*, 20.

54 Thomas A. Stapleford, "Shaping Knowledge about American Labor: External Advising at the U.S. Bureau of Labor Statistics in the Twentieth Century," *Science in Context* 23, no. 2 (2010): 187–220, 207.

55 Council of Economic Advisers, "Economic Report of the President Transmitted to the Congress, January 7, 1949" (Washington: Government Printing Office, 1949), 38.

56 CEA, "Economic Report 1949," 9.

57 CEA, "Economic Report 1949," 8.

58 CEA, "Economic Report 1949," 36.

59 All: CEA, "Economic Report 1949," 63.

60 CEA, "Economic Report 1949," 50.

61 See Collins, *More*, 32.

62 Simon Kuznets, "Comment," in *A Survey of Contemporary Economics*, edited by Bernard F. Haley (Homewood, IL: Richard D. Irwin, Inc., 1952), 178–81, 180, cited in Collins, *More*, 31–32.

63 Universities–National Bureau Committee on Economic Research, "Problems in the Study of Economic Growth" (New York: NBER, 1949), ii.

64 "Program of the Sixty-Fourth Annual Meeting of the American Economic Association," *American Economic Review* 42, no. 2 (1952): viii–xi.

65 Bernard F. Haley, *A Survey of Contemporary Economics* (Homewood, IL: Richard D. Irwin, Inc., 1952), viii.

66 Moses Abramovitz, "Economics of Growth," in *Survey of Contemporary Economics*, edited by Bernard F. Haley (Homewood, IL: Richard D. Irwin, Inc., 1952), 132–78, 153.

67 Abramovitz, "Economics of Growth," 132–33.

68 Abramovitz, "Economics of Growth," 134.

69 Moses Abramovitz, *Thinking about Growth and Other Essays on Economic Growth and Welfare* (Cambridge: Cambridge University Press, 1989), 12.

70 See Jeff Biddle, *Progress through Regression: The Life Story of Empirical Cobb-Douglas Production Function* (Cambridge: Cambridge University Press, 2021), 218–21.

71 Simon Kuznets, *National Income: A Summary of Findings* (New York: NBER, 1946).

72 George J. Stigler, *Trends in Output and Employment* (New York: NBER, 1947), 3.

73 On Stigler, see Edward Nik-Khah, "George Stigler, the Graduate School of Business, and the Pillars of the Chicago School," in *Building Chicago Economics*, edited by Robert Van Horn, Philip Mirowski, and Thomas A. Stapleford (Cambridge: Cambridge University Press, 2011), 116–48.

74 For a discussion of indices and practices of index number construction, see Judy L. Klein, *Statistical Visions in Time: A History of Time Series Analysis, 1662-1938* (Cambridge: Cambridge University Press, 1997), 76; Morgan, "Seeking Parts, Looking for Wholes," 240–2.

75 CEA, "Economic Report 1949," 51.

76 Kuznets, "National Income," 209. He proceeds: "Being conditioned by the institutional set up of the family and of economic society, the line between economic and non-economic activity shifts from country to country and from time to time." See also the relevant discussion in Speich Chassé, *Die Erfindung des Bruttosozialprodukts*, 82–8.

77 See Daniel Speich Chassé, "When Economics Went Overseas: Epistemic Problems in the Macroeconomic Analysis of Late Colonial Africa," in *Science, Africa and Europe: Processing Information and Creating Knowledge*, edited by Martin Lengwiler, Nigel Penn, and Patrick Harries (London: Routledge, 2019), 237–55.

78 Stigler, *Trends in Output and Employment*, 32.

79 An example is Solomon Fabricant, *The Output of Manufacturing Industries, 1899-1937* (New York: NBER, 1940). Note that the appendices stretch over more than 300 pages.

80 Presenting disaggregated series allowed for investigating the variations of size and composition of individual outputs and therefore substantiated the interpretation of aggregate results.

81 Cf. Jeff Biddle's observation of Paul Douglas's different rhetorical styles, *Progress through Regression*, 306–8.

82 On the discursive shift in the United Kingdom, but equally applicable to the US, see Jim Tomlinson, "The Politics of Economic Measurement: The Rise of the 'Productivity Problem' in the 1940s," in *Accounting as Social and Institutional Practice*, edited by Anthony G. Hopwood and Peter Miller (Cambridge: Cambridge University Press, 1999), 168–89, 168.

83 See Peter-Paul Bänziger, Marcel Streng, and Mischa Suter, "Histories of Productivity: An Introduction," in *Histories of Productivity: Genealogical Perspectives on the Body and Modern Economy*, edited by Peter-Paul Bänziger and Mischa Suter (London: Routledge, 2018), 5–10.

84 See Corinna Schlombs, *Productivity Machines: German Appropriations of American Technology from Mass Production to Computer Automation* (Cambridge, MA: MIT Press, 2019), chapter 1; Biddle, *Progress through Regression*, 225–6.

85 Typical of the spread responsibility of US statistical bodies, there were other institutions developing indices for productivity: The National Industrial Conference Board investigated productivity trends in nonmanufacturing industries, the Bureau of Agricultural Economics of the Department of Agriculture directed measurement efforts of farm output and efficiency. For a contemporary overview, see Hiram S. Davis, *Productivity Accounting* (Philadelphia: University of Pennsylvania Press, 1955).

86 See Schlombs, *Productivity Machines*, 13ff. The study's author was Ewan Clague, who was essential in integrating productivity measurements into the Marshall Plan.

87 Stapleford, "Shaping Knowledge about American Labor," 208.

88 Biddle, *Progress through Regression*, 222.

89 See Thomas A. Stapleford, "Defining a 'Living Wage' in America: Transformations in Union Wage Theories, 1870–1930," *Labor History* 49, no. 1 (2018): 1–22, 11.

90 Douglas was one of the early empirical economists who not only reported numbers and percentages but were familiar with statistical theory. In 1928, together with the mathematician Charles Cobb, he estimated the relationship between quantities of output, capital, and labor with recent statistical techniques (least squares regression and correlation analysis). On the making and discussions of the Cobb-Douglas production function, see Biddle, *Progress through Regression*, part 1.

91 Paul H. Douglas, *The Theory of Wages* (New York: Macmillan, 1934), 18, 20.

92 This was done by adding a linear trend to the regression, which would not have worked with the Cobb–Douglas data because of multicollinearity. See Biddle, *Progress through Regression*, chapter 3.

93 Morris A. Copeland and E. M. Martin, "The Correction of Wealth and Income Estimates for Price Changes," in *Studies in Income and Wealth*, vol. 2, edited by Conference on Research in National Income and Wealth (New York: NBER, 1938), 85–135. On Copeland pushing the idea of using national income to measure growth and "technical change," see Biddle, *Progress through Regression*, 232–3.

94 Stigler, *Trends in Output and Employment*, 3.

95 Both: Stigler, *Trends in Output and Employment*, 5.

96 Stigler, *Trends in Output and Employment*, 52.

97 For an overview see Dale W. Jorgenson, "Productivity and Economic Growth," in *Fifty Years of Economic Measurement: The Jubilee of the Conference on Research in Income and Wealth*, edited by Ernst R. Berndt and Jack E. Triplett (Chicago: University of Chicago Press, 1991), 19–118.

98 Value-added was calculated by subtracting all costs of capital-inputs from the market value of output.

99 Stigler, *Trends in Output and Employment*, 51.

100 George J. Stigler, "The Division of Labor Is Limited by the Extent of the Market," *Journal of Political Economy* 59, no. 3. (1951): 185–93, 185. In *Trends in Output and Employment*, he maintained, for instance, that the data referred to years, "in which departures from equilibrium may have been large," 51.

101 See, for instance, retrospectively, Abramovitz, *Thinking about Growth*, 14.

102 See Biddle, *Progress through Regression*, 253–5 and 279–80.

103 Stigler, *Trends in Output and Employment*, 42.

104 Stigler, *Trends in Output and Employment*, 49. At the end of the 1950s, Stigler criticized the use of productivity indices as metrics of "economic progress." See Biddle, *Progress through Regression*, 253.

105 Stigler, *Trends in Output and Employment*, 42–5.

106 Solomon Fabricant, "Economic Progress and Economic Change: Thirty-Fourth Annual Report" (New York: NBER, 1954), 8, available at www.nber.org/books/ annu54-1, last accessed April 15, 2024.

107 All: John W. Kendrick, "Productivity Trends: Capital and Labor: NBER Interim Report 1956" (New York: NBER, 1956), 19, available at www.nber.org/chapters/ c5596, last accessed April 15, 2024.

108 All: Fabricant, "Economic Progress and Economic Change," 5.

109 Fabricant, "Economic Progress and Economic Change," 5.

110 Yarrow, *Measuring America*, 62.

111 Kendrick, "Productivity Trends," 1. Biddle has linked the NBER's postwar enthusiasm about growth with funding issues, *Progress through Regression*, 242.

112 Productivity Measurement Advisory Service of the European Productivity Agency, "In this Number," *Productivity Measurement Review* 16 (1959): 3–4, 3.

113 Jacob Schmookler, "The Changing Efficiency of the American Economy, 1869–1938," *Review of Economics and Statistics* 34, no.3 (1952): 214–31, 225.

114 Kendrick, "Productivity Trends," 2, n1.

115 Frederick C. Mills, *Productivity and Economic Progress*, NBER Occasional Paper 38 (New York: NBER, 1952), 31.

116 Kendrick, "Productivity Trends," 6.

117 Both: Moses Abramovitz, "Resource and Output Trends in the United States since 1870," *American Economic Review* 46, no. 2 (1956): 5–23, 11.

118 Stigler, *Trends in Output and Employment*, 13.

119 Evsey D. Domar, "On Total Productivity and All That," *Journal of Political Economy* 70, no. 6 (1962): 597–608, 597.

120 Evsey D. Domar, "Capital Expansion, Rate of Growth, and Employment," *Econometrica* 14, no. 2 (1946): 137–47, 138. On the making of the "Harrod–Domar model," see Chapter 1.

121 Evsey D. Domar, "Comment," in *Capital Formation and Economic Growth*, edited by Moses Abramovitz (Princeton: Princeton University Press, 1955), 107–11, 110. On Domar's methodological stances, see Mauro Boianovsky, "Modeling Economic Growth: Domar on Moving Equilibrium," *History of Political Economy* 49, no. 3 (2017): 405–36.

122 Lorenzo Fioramonti, *Gross Domestic Problem: The Politics behind the World's Most Powerful Number* (London: Zed Books, 2013).

123 Domar, "On Total Productivity and All That," 597.

124 Robert M. Solow, "Technical Change and the Aggregate Production Function," *Review of Economics and Statistics* 39, no. 3 (1957): 312–20.

125 Solow, "Technical Change and the Aggregate Production Function," 312, 320.

126 Solow, "Technical Change and the Aggregate Production Function," 320.

127 See E. Roy Weintraub, "Commentary on Learning Economic Method from the Invention of Vintage Models by Bert Hamminga," in *Post-Popperian Methodology of Economics: Recovering Practice*, edited by Neil De Marchi (Boston: Kluwer Academic Publishers, 1988), 355–73, 367.

128 Marcel Boumans, *How Economists Model the World into Numbers* (New York: Routledge, 2005), 121.

129 See, for instance, Warren P. Hogan, "Technical Progress and Production Functions," *Review of Economics and Statistics* 40 (1958): 407–11.

130 Among them a linear, a hyperbolic, a semilogarithmic, and a Cobb–Douglas function, see Solow, "Technical Change and the Aggregate Production Function," 318.

131 Solow, "Technical Change and the Aggregate Production Function," 319.

132 Regression techniques supported the assumption that "Nature" ejected observations of aggregates, and the model provided the "theory" to explain the behavior of these observations. See Biddle and Boumans, "Exploring the History of Statistical Inference in Economics," 16–17.

133 Solow, "Technical Change and the Aggregate Production Function," 318.

134 Schultz to Solow, May 29, 1957, Solow papers, box 56, file J 1 of 2.

135 Here I use the terminology of Gaston Bachelard, *The New Scientific Spirit*, translated by Arthur Goldhammer (Boston, MA: Beacon Press, 1984 [1934]), 12. See also the Introduction.

136 Philip Mirowski, *Science-Mart: Privatizing American Science* (Cambridge, MA: Harvard University Press, 2011), 71.

137 Cf. Mirowski's critique in *Science-Mart*, 72–3.

138 See Biddle, *Progress through Regression*, 254–5.

139 Robert M. Solow, "Technical Progress, Capital Formation and Economic Growth," *American Economic Review* 52, no. 2 (1962): 76–86, 86.

140 See Peter Dizikes, "The Productive Career of Robert Solow," December 27, 2019, available at www.technologyreview.com/2019/12/27/131259/the-productive-career-of-robert-solow/, last accessed April 15, 2024.

141 See Harro Maas and Mary S. Morgan, "Observation and Observing in Economics," in *Observing the Economy* (supplement to *History of Political Economy* 44), eds. Harro Maas and Mary S. Morgan (Durham, NC: Duke University Press, 2012), 1–24, 19; Biddle and Boumans, "Exploring the History of Statistical Inference in Economics," 202. "Passive observations" was a self-consciously chosen actors' term, see Chapter 3.

142 Wassily Leontief, "Theoretical Assumptions and Non-Observed Facts," *American Economic Review* 61 (1971): 1–7, 1.

143 Wassily Leontief, "Comment on Chipman, in *The Technology Factor in International Trade*, edited by Raymond Vernon (New York: Columbia University Press, 1970), 132–7, 132, cited in Mirowski, *Science-Mart*, 72.

144 In a later critique, this time addressing a larger audience outside economics, he maintained that the highly aggregative variables of regression analysis could hardly

"be identified with those directly observable in the real world," Wassily Leontief, "Academic Economics," *Science* 217 (1982), 104–5, 104.

145 On Leontief's scathing critique of dominant practices of aggregation and correlation, see also Vincent Carret, "Wassily Leontief's Research Program: Science, Beliefs, Institutions," *History of Political Economy* 56, no. 4 (2024): 653–84.

146 Solow, "Technical Change and the Aggregate Production Function," 312.

3

Modeling the Economic System

The Second World War brought about both new ways of modeling and the associated language of the economy as structure, system, and computer. One of the largest modeling projects at mid-century emerged with the endeavor to use wartime mathematical techniques in peacetime and the Cold War. Chapter 2 indicated, how, by the end of the 1940s, the NBER's numbers shaped aggregate visions of managing the national whole toward increasing growth rates through fiscal policies and investment programs. In addition, more detailed schemes under the label of "input–output analysis," at the center of this chapter, fortified belief in the possibility of managing economic processes more directly. In 1948, the *Christian Science Monitor* reported on the establishment of a new research project that had been founded by the Bureau of Labor Statistics the year before:

[A] question now before the military establishment, the Council of Economic Advisers, National Security Resources Board, Office of Naval Research, and the Bureau of Labor Statistics, is whether or not the government should spend military research dollars for developing an economic technique and an electronic computing machine to guide a war economy ... Advocates of the plan believe they can develop from the Leontief theories a supercomputer which would have built into it the whole complexity of interindustry relationships, plus data on national production capacity. One would merely tell such a machine what kind of war one wants to fight, and it would, in turn, give the most effective combinations of munitions, civilian goods, new plants, etc. In case you don't want to fight any kind of war, Professor Leontief says such a machine could conceivably tell you what kind and amount of public works were needed to pump-prime your way out a depression.[1]

Under the title "Electronic Economics," the article picked up on the plans, hopes, and doubts invoked by the Harvard Economic Research Project (HERP). The HERP was one of the first – if not *the* first – large-scale, computer-based research centers that created and processed scientific data.[2] The aim was to construct an all-encompassing input–output table of the United States' "national economy as a whole."[3] In this way, the project created a phenomenotechnical instrument essential to consolidating the object of the economy after 1945.

For sociologist and historian of statistical reason Alain Desrosières, input–output tables symbolized the language of technical rationality of the *État ingénieur*. Akin to the way in which a production manager in an individual firm was responsible for keeping production going, this state was thought to regulate the statistical entities of production and the circulation of goods and services.[4] Input–output analysis and the associated linear modeling came with a technical understanding of the economy. It was more strongly aligned with economic planning and portrayed the economy in greater detail than national accounting did (Chapter 2). It presented a system of industries, households, and the government sector and depicted their interconnections in terms of flows of goods and services. Through looking at the industrial structure and not simply the aggregate whole, the HERP offered a more fine-grained analysis of the effects of policies and thus a more comprehensive technique to deal with the "what-happens-if" problems of intervention. The procedures the HERP developed laid the foundation for the standardization of input–output analysis as a tool of economic governance. In the context of both indicative planning and more centralized planning, input–output turned into one essential component of the economist's toolkit for both European reconstruction and what came to be called "international development." Adaptable to Marxist and Socialist economics as well as to "Keynesian" management based on national accounting, input–output analysis diffused globally from the 1950s onward.[5]

This chapter situates Solow's model on a trajectory of different strategies to depict the economy in terms of linear models. It traces the phenomenotechnical economy from the HERP into the hands of economists gathered by the Cowles Commission in 1949. At a conference on "activity analysis," they merged techniques of linear programming with what they conceived as conventional neoclassical theory. Doing so, they dispensed with the HERP's concern for measurement. Detached from the goal to get closer to the material realities of production, the economy became a flexible mathematical system that turned into one of the major research objects in postwar economics – not least in the modeling work of the graduate student Solow, who worked part-time at the HERP.[6] The HERP was part of the larger trend toward big science, enabled by huge resource investments. Gathering and processing its large data-sets was not only cost-intensive but also tedious and time-consuming. It is against such a background of computer-driven empirical research that Solow's model and other such blackboard exercises appeared as a contrasting yet complementary epistemic form: A "simple model," a "pencil-and-paper object" that provided "speculative" and "qualitative" knowledge.[7] Tracing the object of the economy in different modeling projects, this chapter highlights different ways of using mathematical models in economic research and hereby different roles of economic abstractions.

The models presented in this chapter portrayed the national economy as a self-contained world of constant, unhampered circulation. All inputs could be used for production, and all outputs either went into production as inputs or were, for instance, consumed by households or used in private capital formation. In such a balanced system, there was no slack and no general over- or underproduction. A contemporary commentator described input–output as a system of "whirlpools and cross currents where goods flow back and forth between industries."[8] The imagery of flows of goods referred to older metaphors of exchange and circular flows: Money flowing like water, national wealth circulating like blood in the body.[9] The different uses and interpretations of the economy as a flow do not only concern the internal epistemic matters of the economics discipline. They link to the larger problem of making sense of economic processes with the help of abstractions and fictions. In his genealogy of flow metaphors, historian Augustine Sedgewick has raised the question "why the coded language of flows ... which is ultimately insufficient for capitalist production itself has been adopted by technocrats, scholars, and the broader public."[10] This chapter confronts the use of flow images within specific research projects. It illustrates how economic abstractions were effective not only as utopian designs or as figures of thought and their political aesthetics, they also had practical qualities that made them, at least to some, useful in capturing the economy as a quantitative entity. This was particularly relevant when research was geared to the needs of economic governance.

On the trajectory sketched in this chapter, one flow model of the economy turns from a tool of measurement into an independent economic abstraction. As such it became the basis of Solow's work, who (as I will argue in Chapter 4) miniaturized that flow model. As an empirical research institute, the HERP vigorously differentiated its work from the postwar centers of neoclassical theory as well as from "modern school statistical econometricians." Its proponents did not want to content themselves with the refinement of mathematical model worlds and the deductive use of these models to estimate model-relationships in any given data sets.

Similar to the practices at the NBER, input–output researchers were involved in gathering data and paid attention to its complexities. In contrast to the NBER's "radical empiricism," however, the HERP's aim was not to construct individual macroeconomic indices or time series.[11] The aim was to get at the structure of the economy, to measure the technical relations of production. This involved the portrayal of the economy as a system of material flows in which goods, capital, and labor circulated without frictions or losses. In a further step, linear programmers made the phenomenotechnical economy lose its anchoring in empirical data and become a perfectly efficient, optimizable system of flows.

Comparing the empirical with the mathematical research object, the depicted economy featured different characteristics. Rather than combining (empirical) knowledge of the parts to arrive at the whole, now the understandings of the parts came from disaggregating the whole. The HERP had realized the abstract object of the economy by bringing together a variety of concrete artifacts: Empirical material such as accounting books or, sometimes, notes from interviews with production engineers; an input–output scheme that facilitated the homogenization and organization of numbers into tables; and a model that could subject the numbers to various computational experiments. The HERP's mundane, rather unspectacular work of bringing together these different materials revealed the barriers to an empirical reality to which it wanted to provide access. Behind the phantasms of the capabilities of "electronic economics" hinted at in the *Christian Science Monitor* lurked the difficulties of empirical research – difficulties that mathematical theorists dispensed with and that were ultimately of no concern to the neoclassical growth model.

INPUT–OUTPUT KNOWLEDGE FOR INTERVENTION

The HERP was an institution in between public data centers and a university department. Its research linked to the interventionist endeavor of managing material production flows just as earlier renditions of input–output knowledge had done. In the US, parallel to early productivity measurements at the Bureau of Labor Statistics (BLS) in the mid-1920s (Chapter 2), the Bureau of Agricultural Economics conducted statistical studies on productivity in agriculture. Based on investigations of farm management, these studies investigated how variations in inputs changed output in farming. Such analysis already appeared under the label of "input–output analysis" and aimed at increasing agricultural productivity.[12] At the time, Leontief published on similar strategies of economic measurement in the Soviet Union.[13] He had just emigrated from the USSR to the Weimar Republic (as many Menshevik economists did), where the *Statistische Reichsamt* under Ernst Wagemann planned its first census of industrial production. Wagemann's census also portrayed input–output relations in terms of connections between industries by enumerating the raw materials used in production.[14] Familiar with various strategies to measure and theorize such economic structures, Leontief finished his dissertation (*Die Wirtschaft als Kreislauf*, 1928) with Werner Sombart and Ladislaus von Bortkiewicz. He continued his research on the circular flow of economic activity at the Institute of the World Economy in Kiel, one of many recently founded institutions to investigate the business cycle and the role of economic structures, and, after a year in China as an adviser at the Ministry of Railways, he emigrated to the US in 1931. On a short stay at the NBER in New York, he further developed his approach of input–output analysis.[15]

For Leontief, economics needed to be both empirical and theoretical, and input–output flows were the shape he sought to achieve this. In stark contrast to his new environment at the NBER, Leontief was very much in favor of using mathematics in economic measurement. In his view, economics was an empirical science that had to collect data. But, in order to organize these "facts," economists needed theoretical, mathematical frameworks. Leontief's idea aligned with previous input–output work in the US in that the relations between inputs and output were a matter of technology rather than economy. From this perspective, input–output ratios were "structural" parameters. Research into these technical relations provided numerical knowledge of the structure of the economy as a whole. In contrast, economists such as Theodore Schultz (who we have seen congratulate Solow for controlling his data with the "economist's sling") or some of the index number constructors in Chapter 2 pushed the role of entrepreneurs' decision-making, which were thought to depend on changing prices and expectations.[16] For Leontief, the concept of a circular flow helped make visible the causal interconnections of the economy as a whole, which, in turn, necessitated empirical research into technological relationships.

For such a large-scale measurement endeavor, funding was crucial. It was only after Leontief started to work at Harvard University in 1932 that he applied for a grant large enough to start serious empirical research. The amount he asked of the Harvard University Committee on Research in the Social Sciences was rather small compared to the budgets of the HERP ($1,500, adjusted for inflation about $30,500 in July 2023), but it still by far exceeded what the common, solitary thinker-economist required.[17] "The senior faculty," longtime HERP researcher Anne P. Carter recalled, was "puzzled and skeptical."[18] The Committee approved the funding, and the first input–output table of the US industry was finished in 1935.[19] It took ten years for Leontief's research to be financed by the government as one of many federal statistical services that would measure economic activity after the United States' entry into the Second World War. Input–output research would contribute, he claimed, to regulating the economy in war-time as well as to planning the strategic bombing of Nazi Germany. As a consultant at the US Office of Strategic Services and for the Department of Labor, Leontief supervised the compilation of a ninety-two-sector table for the organization of the war economy at the BLS. In a letter of December 1942, E. B. Wilson, a Harvard mathematician, protégé of the physicist and thermodynamics expert Josiah Willard Gibbs, and mentor to Paul Samuelson, tried to answer some questions about his colleague's high security research:

Leontief is working on a government project at Harvard ... [H]e acts as if he weren't very much at liberty [to talk about it] ... [I]t seems to me, however, that it is so much in line with the sort of thing the government should be trying to find out in connection with all this war rationing and regulation and all the post-war rationing and regulation that may become necessary that the government really ought to do it.[20]

Leontief pushed the use of his tables and models not only as tools for wartime but also for peacetime planning. Shortly before the end of the war, he began a paper with a question of interest to the BLS: "How will the cessation of war purchases of planes, guns, tanks, and ships – if not compensated by increased demand for other types of commodities – affect the national level of employment?"[21] Input–output research promised to provide the devices for investigating the economic consequences of disarmament and for designing stabilization policies during the demobilization period.[22] The Department of Labor created input–output numbers for the economy as a whole, and the Bureau of Economic Analysis, situated at the Department of Commerce, incorporated an input–output table in its national income calculations. Besides supporting government policy, input–output numbers were also queried by representatives of specific industries to help assess their prospects.[23]

With its big science setup and the associated needs, the HERP fit uneasily into the traditional departmental and disciplinary organization. Established with the help of a four-year grant from the Rockefeller Foundation in 1947, it was based on cooperation between Leontief, the Department of Labor, and the Census Bureau.[24] Though it emerged in a series of contexts during the interwar period and Depression, Leontief's input–output analysis only gained solid footing through its applicability to wartime and postwar industrial policy. In the immediate postwar era, the collaboration of universities with statistical offices and state institutions was already quite common. The mathematical and econometric research of the Cowles Commission, for instance, only existed thanks to such settings. Yet for the Department of Economics at Harvard University this kind of research was highly unusual and remained dubious in the eyes of department members.[25] They still pursued a whole variety of economic analyses stretching from traditional institutionalism to neoclassic theory, from Marxist, Socialist, and Keynesian approaches to the history of economic thought. The common research work of economists consisted of writing narratives and developing numerical examples. Research instruments were pens and paper and maybe card catalogs to capture excerpts from the many books that populated economists' libraries. In contrast, Leontief and his collaborators envisaged a large-scale measurement project with computer-based processing of the collected data.

As a division of the Bureau of Labor Statistics, the HERP's task was to create a comprehensive input–output table of the American economy. Under Elizabeth W. Gilboy, the HERP's associate director for many decades, a whole team of researchers from different academic fields (especially the engineering sciences), programmers, and administrative personnel was to handle the task with the help of the new mainframes, which had just been developed at Harvard and MIT.[26] At the dawn of the Cold War, a big part of the project's research was financed by a contract with the US Air Force, which thought it useful for avoiding possible obstructions to repeated wartime mobilization. The Air Force integrated input–output into an interagency project known as Project SCOOP (Project for the Scientific Computation of Optimum Programs), which focused on research on the mechanization of programming techniques for decision-making through the new electronic digital computers.[27]

The HERP's first big publication, *Studies in the Structure of the American Economy* (1953), presented input–output tables as a survey of the economic whole and its parts, which would reveal the "structural interrelations in the economy."[28] Its tables were to feed into forecasts and analyses of long-run "structural change" and assess the impact of rearmament.[29] The numbers supplied were intended to allow national economic management to ask more concrete questions than the existing macro data of national income accounting afforded, as Leontief had explained years earlier in a letter to the editor of the *Christian Science Monitor*:

What will happen to prices in the year 1949? What will the steel output be in the second half of 1948? By how much would the prices increase if industrial wages are raised by ten percent while industrial profits and agricultural incomes remain unchanged? How much additional output will various American industries have to supply and how many additional labor hours must they employ in order to supply Europe with increased American aid without cutting down on our own living standards at the same time?[30]

To answer these questions, input–output tables portrayed the economy as a whole. In contrast to contemporary macroeconomic models and the figures of national income accounting, they not only presented "end products" but also "intermediate products." The production of steel, for instance, included coal, iron ore, and transportation; the production of coal in turn included steel (which it also contributed to producing) and transportation; and transportation needed both coal and steel. The constituent sectors were thoroughly defined based on an industrial classification scheme and were included in the system through the inputs and outputs, which related them to one another.[31]

Basically, an input–output table was an accounting scheme that captured transactions between different sectors. In 1952, the HERP published the most comprehensive input–output table so far for the year 1947. In the first place, the table comprised 45 industries, the public sector, households, and "foreign countries" (Figure 3.1). The figures entered along any one horizontal row showed how the 1947 output of a particular industry was distributed among all the other industries, households, and the government. Total output was shown at the end of the row. If examined column-wise, the same figures show the 1947 input structure of the economy: The figures entered along any one vertical column contain the various annual inputs of each particular industry that had been provided by all other industries, households, and the government. For instance, the row for "Iron & Steel" (enhanced in Figure 3.2) said that six million dollars of this industry's output went into production of the sector "Agriculture & Fisheries," two million dollars went into the aggregated industry denoted "Food & Kindred Products," 33 million dollars into the industry "Nonferrous Metals," and so on. The production of iron and steel, in turn, necessitated six million dollars' worth of inputs from "Agriculture & Fisheries," two million from "Food & Kindred Products," 324 million from "Nonferrous Metals," and 3.982 million dollars of inputs from itself. The total money-value of these inputs ("Total Gross Outlays," last row in Figure 3.1) equaled the total output of the iron and steel industry, at the

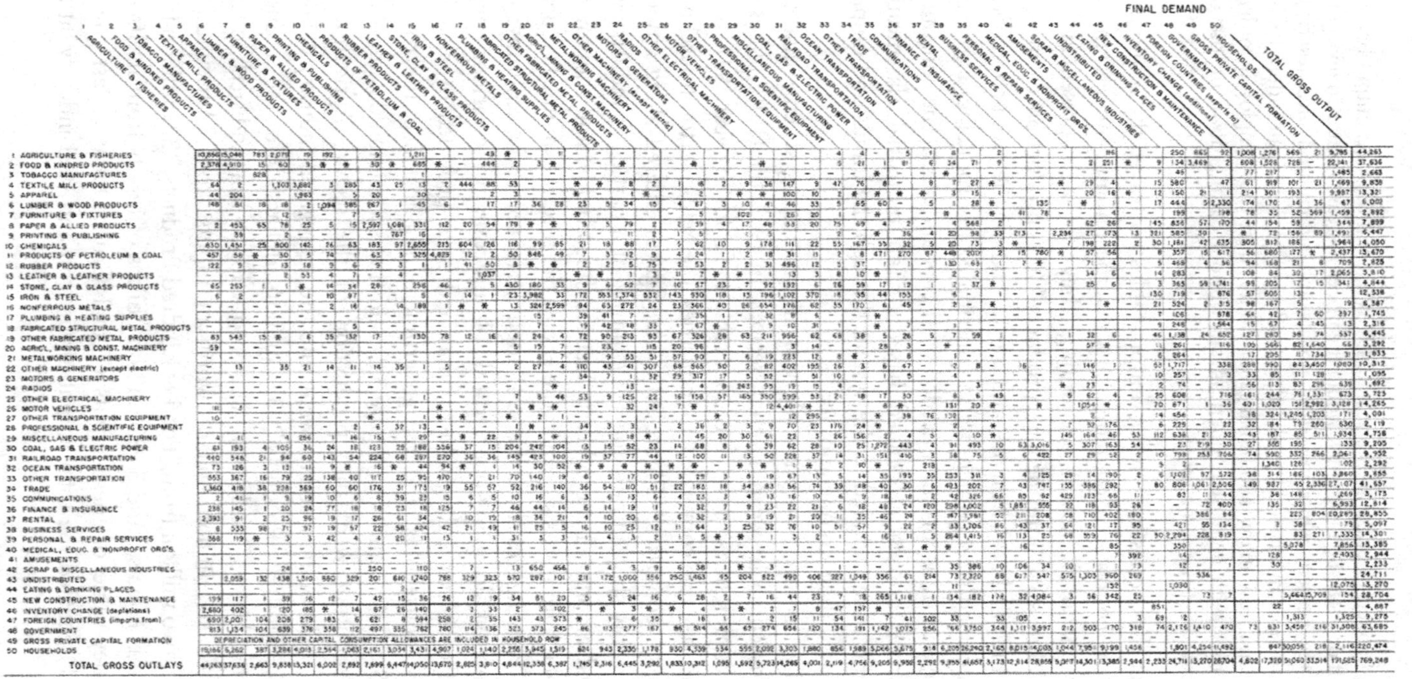

Figure 3.1 Input–output table, "Interindustry Flow of Goods and Services by Industry of Origin and Destination, 1947."
(W. Duane Evans and Marvin Hoffenberg, "The Interindustry Relations Study for 1947." *The Review of Economics and Statistics* 34, no. 2 (1952): 97–142, 143–4.)

	1 AGRICULTURE & FISHERIES	2 FOOD & KINDRED PRODUCTS	3 TOBACCO MANUFACTURES	4 TEXTILE MILL PRODUCTS	5 APPAREL	6 LUMBER & WOOD PRODUCTS	7 FURNITURE & FIXTURES	8 PAPER & ALLIED PRODUCTS	9 PRINTING & PUBLISHING	10 CHEMICALS	11 PRODUCTS OF PETROLEUM & COAL	12 RUBBER PRODUCTS	13 LEATHER & LEATHER PRODUCTS	14 STONE, CLAY & GLASS PRODUCTS	15 IRON & STEEL	16 NONFERROUS METALS	17 PLUMBING & HEATING SUPPLIES	18 FABRICATED STRUCTURAL METAL PRODUCTS	19 OTHER FABRICATED METAL PRODUCTS	20 AGRIC'L, MINING & CONST. MACHINE	21 METALWORKING MACHINE	22 OTHER MACHINE	23 MOTORS	24
1 AGRICULTURE & FISHERIES	10,856	15,048	783	2,079	19	192	–	9	–	1,211	–	–	49	*	–	11	–	–						
2 FOOD & KINDRED PRODUCTS	2,378	4,910	15	60	9	*	*	30	*	685	*	–	444	2	3	*	–	–						
3 TOBACCO MANUFACTURES	–	–	828	–	–	–	–	–	–	1	–	–	–	–	–	–	–	–						
4 TEXTILE MILL PRODUCTS	64	2	–	1,303	3,882	3	285	43	25	13	2	444	88	33	–	–	*	*						
5 APPAREL	44	204	–	–	1,963	–	5	20	–	30	–	–	2	3	–	–	*	–						
6 LUMBER & WOOD PRODUCTS	148	81	18	18	2	1,094	385	267	1	45	6	–	17	17	36	28	23	5						
7 FURNITURE & FIXTURES	–	–	–	12	–	–	7	5	–	–	–	–	–	–	–	–	*	–						
8 PAPER & ALLIED PRODUCTS	2	453	65	78	25	5	15	2,597	1,081	331	112	20	54	179	*	*	9	5						
9 PRINTING & PUBLISHING	–	39	–	2	–	–	–	–	767	16	–	–	–	–	–	–	1	–						
10 CHEMICALS	830	1,451	25	800	142	26	63	183	97	2,655	213	604	126	116	99	85	21	18						
11 PRODUCTS OF PETROLEUM & COAL	457	58	*	30	5	74	1	63	3	325	4,829	12	2	50	846	49	7	3						
12 RUBBER PRODUCTS	122	9	–	13	18	9	6	9	3	1	1	41	50	8	*	*	2	2						
13 LEATHER & LEATHER PRODUCTS	–	–	–	2	53	4	7	–	4	–	–	–	1,037	–	–	–	*	*						
14 STONE, CLAY & GLASS PRODUCTS	65	253	1	1	*	14	34	28	–	258	46	7	5	430	180	33	9	6						
15 IRON & STEEL	6	2	–	–	1	10	97	–	–	5	6	14	1	23	3,982	33	172	553	1,					

Figure 3.2 Close-up of Figure 3.1, entries in million dollars

right-hand margin of the table in Figure 3.1, and amounted to 12.338 million dollars. The sum of all inputs was equal to the sum of all outputs – this was valid for each sector and for this economy as a whole. In this way, an input–output table created a system of numerically precise relationships between clearly separated entities.

The shape of input–output tables related to a flow model that made national production accessible to mathematical treatment. The tables' entries could easily be presented in the form of a matrix – the "structural flow matrix or simply the flow structure of the corresponding economic system" –which could in turn be fitted into a system of simultaneous equations.[32] With this system, researchers calculated the maximum output possible through the efficient organization of production.[33] Also, the system could give the input quantities necessary for a specific desired output or describe the potentialities of production under "what-if" constraints. In this way, the tables not only suggested what would happen in the real economy in case of a change in specific parameters but also encouraged a belief in the possibility of optimizing the processes of the national economy as a whole. This is where the HERP situated the step "from description to explanation."[34] In the case of the NBER's work on productivity trends in Chapter 2, "explanation" was about comparing indices of output growth with indices of input growth. At the HERP, "explanation" meant the manipulation of a mathematical system with data-filled boxes. Such model experiments would provide insight into what would happen in the economy in case of a change in specific parameters.

A major factor for the establishment of the HERP was its promise to be directly useful for the rational organization of the national economy. Its overview of inputs and outputs afforded the possibility of balancing the whole, for instance via rerouting "labor" from a sector with little demand into one with higher demand. To that effect, the project needed to translate model experiments into numerical governmental knowledge. For this, new computational techniques and equipment were essential. When Leontief compiled the first US input–output table at the beginning of the 1930s, slide rules and electric calculators did the job.[35] His attempt to calculate a system of forty-four input–output equations, however, failed due to lacking computing capacities. In what followed, Leontief started to cooperate with his MIT colleague John B. Wilbur. The Wilbur Machine, a mechanical analogue computer that was the size of a small car and weighed half a ton, allowed a colleague from the department of civil engineering to calculate a system with ten sectors.[36]

Ten years later, in 1947, the same year in which the BLS and Leontief founded the HERP, a group of researchers around Howard Aiken and Grace Hopper finished the Harvard Mark II. Financed by and built for the US Navy, the electromechanical computer had built-in hardware for several mathematical functions (among them the logarithm, the square root, and the exponential). Leontief and Herb F. Mitchell, who was Aiken and Leontief's PhD student, used this large relay computer to solve a static system of thirty-eight simultaneous linear equations. The calculation obtained numerical results on an unprecedented scale. It did not only prove useful to economists but also to computer scientists as it helped in developing improved calculation methods.[37] Responding to the questions of the *Christian Science Monitor* in 1948, Leontief excitedly pushed the angle of technical tasks the projects involved:

To give you an idea about the magnitude of the computational job involved in inverting a 38 × 38 matrix, it is sufficient to state that in the process of this work, nearly 300,000 ten-digit numbers were punched into and read from tapes, and 1,500,000 digits were printed. Approximately 110,000 multiplications and 350,000 additions were performed. The whole process took 59½ hours of uninterrupted machine time. This time should be doubled to include the time for set-up, tape-checking, trouble-shooting, etc.[38]

At the end of the 1940s, these numbers were astonishing. (After all, even the census used a succeeding computer, the UNIVAC, only in 1951.)[39] In the mid-1950s, such operations had already become routine, and the same computation was repeated on the ENIAC in a computing time of only 45 minutes.[40] Yet while the processing of data worked ever faster, the HERP's whole procedure of building up tables still took about two years.[41] For input–output research to provide interventionist knowledge, researchers needed to bring together the flow model of the economy, the data, and the requirements of computing machines. In this sense, the HERP was a site for the mutual shaping of visions of the economy, a mathematical model, computing techniques, practical problems of measurement, and, not least, the desires of economic governance. Exciting new technology aside, the central research problem that took the most time and effort was the often cumbersome and costly creation of empirical data.

MAKING EMPIRICAL MATERIAL

For translating the manageability of the scheme of flows into the manageability of the economy itself, the HERP needed to make appropriate empirical material. Existing data often proved unsuitable for the portrayal of the economy as a system of production flows. Accordingly, what *Studies in the Structure* described as the most important job of postwar economics was "the task of widening radically and effectively its empirical basis."[42] HERP researchers argued that their investigation was more realistic than other contemporary treatments of production, in particular in comparison to conventional neoclassical theory. Neoclassical production functions postulated that producers simply reacted to changes in relative prices and adapted their use of inputs accordingly (Chapter 1). Underlying this view was the assumption that commodities could be produced in countless different ways and that producers could switch between different input compositions at any moment. In contrast, the HERP spoke of industrial production as a technological relationship. Instead of smoothly adapting to fluctuations in prices, the relationships between inputs and outputs were seen as resulting from the actual dynamics in production. This involved, for instance, the time needed to make decisions, reorganization of production processes, or accommodation to higher input prices when it was better (for whatever reasons) to stick with established methods.

The HERP's tables were intended to build on data gained from the level of the shop floor. *Studies in the Structure* emphasized the contrast to conventional econometrics, which looked at the economic structure "from above" by relating prices and total outputs. In contrast to such "indirect" measurement, the HERP's charts resulted from "direct observation of the actual stocks and flows," measured for individual industries through cross-section data.[43] Input–output ratios were taken to be given by the technical realities of production and entered tables as fixed entries, as "technical coefficients."[44] In economists' language, these technical production functions displayed "linear technologies," in the sense that a doubling of output would imply a doubling of all inputs. This, however, was not an assumption to simplify a theoretical system. Neither were production technologies thought to actually be linear and to disallow substitution. Instead, linearity related directly to the HERP's empirical focus: For each coefficient, only one number was available; possible alternative technologies at one point in time simply could not be measured. In the actors' eyes, it was this technical outlook that made the tables as realistic as economic research could be.

The frequent assertion of the specific realism of input–output numbers notwithstanding, the HERP's publications did not give any serious description of the material that the project's staff created and worked with. *Studies in the Structure*, for instance, hinted only vaguely at "technical" and "engineering data" as "a promising and accessible source."[45] Such empirical information, it seemed to suggest, could simply be collected and would then provide ample access to the structure of the national economy. In the course of his career, Leontief made it a habit to point to the different possible sources of knowledge he deemed fruitful for input–output work. In an article in the early 1940s, he mentioned engineering handbooks and other kinds of expert knowledge on production and consumption: "In analyzing the changing structure of the steel industry, we must get our information from the technical literature, from ironmasters and from rolling mill managers. To study the changing pattern of consumer behavior, we have to develop practical co-operation with psychologists and sociologists."[46] In an interview from 1998 he emphasized once more the importance of knowledge from practitioners: "The people who know the structure of the economy are not statisticians but technologists ... My idea was not to infer the structure indirectly from econometric or statistical techniques, but to go directly to technological and engineering sources."[47] From this point of view, deciphering the structure of the economy necessitated collecting data at the sites of production.

Beyond the sparse hints in the HERP's publications, there were meticulous efforts to compile empirical material. The project's progress reports, issued regularly to inform patrons about research advancements, illustrate that the related clerical work initially required a large proportion of the project's personal and financial resources. Most of the so-called technical and engineering data were gained from readily available compilations such as industry accounts in the form of balance-sheet data, corporation reports, papers in trade journals, and reports by government agencies. One of the HERP's progress reports listed the most important sources of capital data: The Bureau of Internal Revenue's statistics on income, Moody's company data, and the War Production Board's data on authorized war facilities. The rest of the data came from various administrative agencies such as the Bureau of Agricultural Economics and the Surplus Property Administrator and magazines such as *Aviation Facts and Figures* and the *Minerals Yearbook*.[48]

Apart from the reuse of already existing data as input–output research material, it was interviews with consulting production officials, engineers, and technicians that would shed light on technical relationships in production. Interviews were not a new addition to the economic researcher's repertoire. One earlier example were interviews with entrepreneurs in the 1930s, who were asked about their decision-making practices.[49] The HERP's work did not involve conducting personal and comprehensive interviews; it was not about capturing the embodied or tacit knowledge of capitalist actors or the skills and experience of experts. Engineers, technicians, or distributors should in the first place provide information about the quantitative relationships in production. These numbers could simply be transmitted by phone: "When I constructed the first input–output table ... I often used the telephone. I called up industries, particularly firms which were engaged in the distribution of commodities and got the data from them."[50] The HERP collected a variety of empirical material consisting of notes from interviews, newspaper excerpts, telephone notes, and balance sheets of firms as well as tables with accounting data as compiled by the BLS. Yet the available sources leave it unclear how the process of data collection worked. Was the content of telephone conversations with production engineers recorded in standardized forms? Were interviews recorded on the ground? Which questions were asked? Did interviewers rely on experts' utterings, or did they get insight into production records? How did all of these and other circumstances in the making of empirical knowledge about production shape the material with which HERP staff continued to work? Leontief's remarks suggest a rather easygoing flow of information from experts of production and consumption to the HERP, which somewhat mirrors the circulation of commodities in input–output tables.

In 1950, after only two years of empirical research, the above-mentioned progress report granted that the HERP's endeavor was in fact a "new departure for economics." It also had to concede that the project entailed several unexpected difficulties, in particular when it came to the question of data availability and their trustworthiness. Under the (almost accusatory) heading "We need to know," the report registered the problems of creating research material and mentioned all the categories of the input–output scheme for which no sources could be found. Not only was little information gained from experts in production, but some of the numbers had also been shown to be unreliable. The goal of making comprehensive technical datasets for the economy as a whole was now deemed "utopian." In the end, the report still noted confidently that this was not a serious issue: "It is felt that in spite of the many limitations of these data the important coefficients are of the right order of magnitude." The HERP wanted to remedy lacking numbers with techniques of estimation and extrapolation. In order to estimate the capital structure for investigating war mobilization, it would be good enough to have the coefficients for the ten most important industries: "It is felt that a fair degree of accuracy was obtained in the measurement of those coefficients." Here, the project waived the collection of technical data from the shop floor. The report compromised by saying that the remaining funds should be used to make the most of existing data from accounting sources. Eventually, its main work relied on statistical and econometric techniques and focused on numerical experiments on the basis of the new dynamic models.[51]

FILLING TABLES

It is customary, as historian Theodore Porter has noted on the practices of measurement, that the heterogeneity and ambiguity of the measured objects are ignored or buried in footnotes, that "quantitative social information typically advertises a degree of precision that goes beyond its capacity to represent the real state of things."[52] Also the HERP's published tables hid all the work, practical decisions, and both the conventional and spontaneous valuations that went into its numbers. Input–output's prime epistemic maxim was precision. This eventually invited its reception in terms of an abstract framework that also grounded the research object that Solow dealt with. In the HERP's research, accuracy in the sense of a correct empirical observation of the material movements between industries became subordinate.[53] Its research priority was not to get the most accurate data sets but to portray the economy "from above," to see the whole, its parts, and what moved from one sector to the other. Whatever data the HERP collected, it had to be made to fit the object of research (the structure of the US economy), its specific problematization within a theoretical frame (input–output flows between sectors), and the requirements of the research infrastructure (mathematical models, computing techniques). Precision relates to following a rule – in this case the balancing rule of the mathematical model. The data had to be integrated into the input–output system with the help of an accounting scheme. With the goal of providing techniques for intervening in the economic whole, input–output research committed itself to precision rather than accuracy, measuring the circular flow of the economy as a system of production.

The HERP's data came from various sources and had been created for different purposes and questions, with varied instruments of measurement, and under contingent circumstances. To create coherent input–output tables from such diverse data was all but straightforward. It took, as Anne Carter reminisces, decades to develop "meaningful and consistent conventions," that is, the very rules of classification and definition that would later turn into a standard procedure: "Should transactions be measured in producers' or purchasers' prices? What about transportation costs? How should inconsistencies in reporting best be treated?"[54] For one, to bring the collected data in the form of an input–output table it was necessary to provide sector classifications. Industries were subdivided into several sub-industries, such that the detailed data gathered on sub-industries could be "collapsed" into a single aggregate industry, "so as to reduce the amount of necessary computations."[55] The choice of how to divide the economy into sectors depended on a trade-off between computability (given by the capacities of computing machines) and complexity (provided by the empirical material at hand). The more sectors taken into account, the more detailed the analysis, but also the more complex the required computation. One of the four fold-out tables inserted in the back of *Studies in the Structure* contained a comparison of eight different schemes of industrial classifications that had been used. About 50 percent of the classified industrial groups were based on complete coverage. Whether the collected data were sufficient to count for the remaining industries was a matter of researchers' judgment. The progress report of 1950, for instance, mentioned that the available data for those industries with only a minor coverage of their plants "were *felt* to be typical of the industries which they represented."[56]

Another necessary task in creating tables that likewise involved the researchers' judgment were the techniques and procedures of data homogenization. From different kinds of empirical material, HERP researchers extracted "information" – data on various capital goods, work, and credit that went into production. Here, the mathematical flow model had a very concrete, practical function – it provided specific accounting rules to shape the collected material. An input–output table was basically a double-entry table charting the "transactions" between different industries. For a specific year, the table tracked what each sector supplied to every other industrial sector and to final demand (households, government, "foreign countries," and gross private capital formation). Accordingly, statistical workers brought the data into an annual balance. Similar to the procedures of national income accounting, the BLS and the HERP's staff extrapolated data of individual firms to aggregated industries as given in industrial classifications and triangulated missing numbers. Commonly, analysts were responsible for a set of industries, so that for each given cell in an input–output table there were two different numbers calculated – one by the analyst of the producing industry, one by the analyst of the using industry. "The two analysts got together and resolved the differences."[57] Similar judgement-based compromises were necessary at other points in the laborious tasks of amassing, organizing, and computing statistical data, each having an impact on the results of input–output analysis.[58]

Despite the allusions to "technical" production functions, the HERP's main scientific object was a money economy. The overarching aim of presenting a coherent whole in which all lines and columns summed up to the same amount required bringing all data into the same unit of measurement. Practitioners and experts, the supposed main source for data, talked about production in terms of physical units such as tons, bushels, ton miles, or man-hours. A "manager of a steel plant or a metallurgical expert," as Leontief emphasized, could hardly give information on the size of parameters of a theoretical production function.[59] The question was how to value the bits and pieces of the material realities of production that the HERP sought to describe. In the end, input–output researchers followed the accounting convention of measuring in monetary values. Similar to the practices of national accountants in Chapter 2, treating prices as the main measuring rod meant combining heterogeneous things into one single value entity. The HERP turned different measuring units into the monetary quantities of their wholesale prices. Thus, input–output tables did not present the desired "technical" prices, representing technical relations in production, but implicitly assumed that prices represented the relations between products. This meant omitting all kinds of factors relevant to market prices, such as oligopolies and monopolies, cartels, dumping, subsidies, and controls. Ultimately, it was not so much about the realities of production but about the reality of the system of flows that was amenable to computer experiments and therefore essential for the making of macroeconomic interventionist knowledge.

ELECTRONIC ECONOMICS

Computational techniques and equipment were not simply neutral calculation devices. For one, they brought about a decisive change in the character of economic research as they essentially restructured the practices of empirical research. Apart from working with pen and paper, the HERP's many assistants – as usual for statistical workers and computing personnel at the time predominantly female – operated mainframes, used electric calculators and punching equipment to prepare cards, and waited for results.[60] The computational routines also determined the composition, the division of labor, and the skills required for the HERP's staff, which, in addition to many full- and part-time researchers, included a professional computer programmer, a librarian, and secretarial personnel.[61] In the late 1950s, the HERP had relocated to a spot close to Harvard's computing center. Its assistants' work consisted mainly in the handling of punch cards and working with smaller and larger computing machines:

One room was set aside for electric calculating machines and for card punching equipment. The Harvard mainframe computer, first an IBM 7094 then upgraded to an IBM 360, was housed nearby, about a block and a half away, and researchers and programmers carried their boxes of cards back and forth for submissions, corrections and resubmissions.[62]

In addition to these very concrete effects on the daily life of researchers, the introduction of computing techniques encouraged belief in the capabilities of planning. Visions of an "electronic economics" (to which the *Christian Science Monitor* alluded at the outset of this chapter) related to the ability to precisely calculate the reaction of the economy to certain changes and to act accordingly. "Mechanical Calculators Eject Right Answers Quicker'n a Flash," "Robot Works Problems Never Before Solved."[63] Press clippings spoke of Harvard's "huge calculator," the "25-ton 'mechanical brain'," "wizard work," and of "statistics [that] could be pumped into the machine and out would come the answer."[64] Several journalists readily adopted the angle that technological innovation pushed the capabilities of economic management. "Suppose that in an economic depression precise information was desired on the effect of a program of public works – not just supposition and hope but an exact factual look into the next chapter." The HERP, so the partly excited, partly skeptical tenor, was able to provide detailed what-happens-if knowledge, "say, how a postoffice-building program would affect the apricot industry in California."[65]

Against such technofuturistic enthusiasm that envisioned input–output as the timely driver of interventionist policies, the HERP's researchers had to wait. Not only for the computing procedures to be finished but also to get data from a group of economists and statisticians at the BLS, which continuously compiled them from accounting sources. This posed a problem for an economic statistics intended to act as the metronome of national management.[66] The tables in *Studies in the Structure of the American Economy* in 1953, for instance, referred to the year 1947, and it had to be assumed that no essential, that is structural, change had happened in the meantime. "The future of this work," Leontief remarked on the potential of input–output research at the end of the 1940s, "will depend to a large extent on our ability to secure a sufficient flow of up-to-date information."[67] As a kind of basin, so the idea went, the HERP received continuously actualized streams of data, which it then steadied and fixed as "flows of information" between sectors in input–output tables.

Project Cybersyn in early 1970s Chile pursued such a vision of a computing center that processed information directly from industries in real time. Developed by the cybernetician Stafford Beer, "Santiago's electrical brain" connected to all industries via data cables in order to get information on the state of national production on a day-to-day basis. In an "operations room," the data were represented graphically on a desktop, which also offered suggestions for actions to decision-makers who pushed buttons as representatives of the Chilean population.[68] In contrast to such later revolutionary high-tech design and other cybernetic utopias of governance, the HERP's research was circumscribed to the more humdrum fashioning of accounting systems and concrete numbers in the boxes of the industrial matrix.

The computer was a welcome machine for solving concrete calculation problems. At the same time as it devalued earlier manual calculation techniques, it afforded the solution of large-scale input–output systems. The computer necessitated bringing the data in a form it could process. The input–output economy consisted of a system of simultaneous equations, reminiscent of the proverbial "black box": Tables did not show what happened in individual industries, they only presented flows of inputs and outputs between them. The depiction of the economy as a functional information schema resembled structuralist conceptions of all kinds of things in terms of systems, as an anecdote about the structuralist linguist and literary theorist Roman Jakobson illustrates:

[Jakobson] entered a Harvard lecture hall one day to discover that the economist Vassily Leontief, who had just finished using the room, had left an economic diagram of production on the blackboard. As Jakobson's students moved to erase the board, he declared, "Stop, I will lecture with this scheme." As he explained, "the problems of output and input in linguistics and economics are exactly the same."[69]

The framing of the economy as a system of information flows came with a rich use of computer metaphors. Leontief, in his appreciation of the Soviet economist Leonid Kantorovich's development of linear programming, pointed out that this technique afforded a perspective on the "entire national economy as a kind of gigantic computer," which, as he added a few years later, "tirelessly grinds out the solutions of an unending stream of quantitative problems."[70] In contrast to other uses of the computer metaphor, Leontief did not imply that markets would automatically bring about equilibrium.[71] The economy needed maintenance and often enough repair work, as Leontief emphasized in 1974, at a time when such a technical interventionist perspective got increasingly unpopular. "[A]nybody who has had practical experience with large automatic computers knows that these complex mechanisms break down a couple of times a day and that you must have repairmen standing around all the time fixing up this and fixing up that." From such a perspective, input–output analysis belonged to the toolkit of the "repair crew," who needed to "know exactly how an engine is constructed and how it operates."[72] In this vein, Leontief promoted an interventionist economics that did not differentiate between a macro- and microlevel. In contrast to common formulations for monetary and fiscal policy-making, he argued that if one was to study the likely effects of policies, it was of the essence to account for the entire industrial structure and not simply a national aggregate.[73]

Leontief's was a specific conception of computers, one that strictly separated a black box and whatever was inside from an outside. This view contrasted with conceptions of cybernetics (like Norbert Wiener's) that looked at the whole circuit, which consisted of the system, its environment, and, not least, the observer herself. Accordingly, Gregory Bateson, social scientist, cybernetician, and one of the key figures at the Macy Conferences, now remembered as a watershed moment in the history of cybernetics, argued against the behavioral scientists' interpretation of cybernetics as input–output systems: "The whole thinking that goes with the words 'input' and 'output' is monstrously bad. It draws a line across the systemic structure. Here there's input and there's output, and it's me against the universe at once, the moment you draw that line."[74] An input–output economy had no possibility of feedback. Such disregard was even more pronounced with the portrayal of the economy as a purely mathematical system that built on input–output models, which would become Solow's major research object after his work with the HERP.

With the change of the Administration in 1952, Air Force grants were discontinued, and the HERP had to maintain its work with a lower level of funding from the Ford Foundation and the National Science Foundation. The associate director of the project, Elizabeth W. Gilboy, conjectured that the "reason for the government's lack of enthusiasm" was "a general fear of 'centralized planning'."[75] Ironically, at the same time the HERP lost federal funding for its association with the shunned planning, the Council for United States Aid (CUSA), supported by the United Nations (UN), implemented input–output analysis in Taiwan, one of the Cold War frontlines, in order to organize and analyze political-economic decision-making, as historian of technology Honghong Tinn has shown.[76] On an international scale, input–output analysis started to become a widely accepted tool for policy-making. The HERP regained funding during the Kennedy presidency, and input–output tables were integrated in the National Income and Product Accounts (NIPA).[77] In 1968 the UN incorporated input–output tables into its system of national accounts by making "social accounting matrices" an integral part of national accounting strategies.[78]

While input–output became a component of the infrastructure of economic governance, it fell out of favor of the economics profession. The HERP eventually dissolved in the mid-1970s. Against the background of an economics discipline that counted human capital theory, rational choice theory, and game theory among its most cherished approaches, input–output analysis, with its emphasis on direct empirical research, had lost its sheen. In its empirical form, as it was done at the HERP, input–output research essentially vanished from academic research.[79] What now dominated were approaches that built on the reception of the input–output structure as an abstract framework that had already been underway three decades prior. In the late 1940s, highlighting the power of models as economic abstractions, the complicated relationship between mathematical techniques and the collection of data was solved or, better, set aside. In the context of a wider endeavor to reconcile the panoply of mathematical wartime techniques with conventional neoclassical theory, the whole economy was depicted as a huge optimization problem solvable by recently developed computers. This depiction of the economy developed in direct relation to military planning, and it was the one that Solow picked up when he was constructing his growth model in the first half of the 1950s.

ABANDONING THE CONCERN WITH MEASUREMENT

Mathematical programming, as developed during the Second World War, provided a rich repertoire of methods and techniques for a variety of fields, in particular management and organizational science but also economic research.[80] In 1949, Tjalling C. Koopmans, recently appointed Research Director of the Cowles Commission, organized the "Conference on Activity Analysis of Production and Allocation." By 1949, the Cowles Commission had already established itself as *the* site for reconstructing economic theory through the use of mathematical methods in empirical analysis.[81] Now, it explicitly targeted an approach to provide knowledge for state intervention and economic policy-making. The conference brought together over fifty economists, mathematicians, statisticians, and administrators from academic, governmental, and military backgrounds, whose compatibility had already been demonstrated during the Second World War through a shared recourse to mathematical techniques.

On analytical, personal, and institutional levels, there were various overlaps between strategies of military planning and strategies of organizing national production. Participants in the Conference on Activity Analysis built on these intersections when they presented linear programming as a technique for generalizing input–output models.

The overall goal of the conference was to solve what the participants saw as "the economic problem" per se, described as "the best allocation of limited means toward desired ends."[82] They depicted the economy in terms of a system of simultaneous equations, a structure that from their perspective had already been present in a variety of approaches.[83] One of these was "the input–output models by Leontief and the Bureau of Labor Statistics," mentioned at the outset of nearly every article in the conference proceedings. Leontief had been part of the group that put forward the idea for the conference (with Koopmans, Dantzig, Oskar Morgenstern, Harold Kuhn, and Albert Tucker) but was absent due to illness.[84] The reference to his large-scale project of economic measurement, however, was rather ambivalent: Its most prominent concern of how to gather and deal with data on production was almost absent. The HERP's preoccupation was with measurement, the specific characteristics of engineering data, and the practical problems of aggregation. All of this took a back seat at the Conference on Activity Analysis. This episode illustrates how the input–output system provided one facet of a new research object: The economy as a purified mathematical, perfectly optimizable system that, in contrast to the HERP's work, related to a concept of "choice" rather than "technology." The transformation not only came with particular gains and losses of the technophenomenon but also brought about specific epistemic values and scientific personae that framed Solow's modeling work, as discussed in Chapter 4.

The major technique of activity analysis was linear programming, which basically comprised a set of optimization techniques – mathematical procedures for calculating the most efficient ways of achieving particular objectives. An early formulation in economics, which was only later reframed as a linear programming problem, was approached during the Second World War. Stigler, one of the researchers working on productivity measurements in Chapter 2, had conducted mathematical and statistical investigations for the Manhattan Project. He set out to find the "most economical diet ... in August 1939 and 1944 for an active economist (weighing 70 kilograms) who lives in a large city."[85] The study illustrated the problems of cost-minimization: How could the necessary amount of calories be achieved most economically, meaning, at the lowest cost? Stigler's model was a system of nine equations in seventy-seven unknowns capturing all kinds of available alternatives in order to calculate an optimal solution.[86] Lacking the required computational capacities, his and other such problems were solved more efficiently by the "simplex algorithm." This iterative algorithmic procedure to find the optimal combination from a range of scenarios was developed at the Pentagon Project SCOOP, through which the Air Force also financed the HERP. It computed the solution for a system of linear inequalities in such a way that the costs of activities were minimized (or that the outputs of activities were maximized), subject to particular restraints on resources or technology.[87] Such linear programming made a whole class of models solvable and, therefore, as linear programmers put it, "worth building."[88] The framing hints at the understanding of such mathematical models as tools. Their construction was goal-oriented, usually directed at the solution of something that was framed as a technical problem. Indeed, it was very concrete problems and practical work in the relevant fields that nurtured the development of linear programming. Soon after the war ended, however, these techniques were transferred into the abstract realms of mathematical economic theory.[89]

Relating to the HERP's work, the conference presented a new research object. The whole economy was cast as an "efficient combination of activities" in the form of a system of linear equations, where commodities were transformed into each other.[90] However, whereas input–output research presented the economy as a quantitative object, here it turned up as a purely mathematical entity. By focusing on "the theoretical concepts underlying" input–output work, the conference abandoned the relation to data work and moved mathematical modeling, freed from the restrictions of measurement practice, to its center.[91] The input–output tables of the HERP defined production as a technological datum (to describe the capital structure of the economy and to investigate the feasibility of production plans). The reason for this procedure was, as highlighted in the section on the HERP's making of empirical material, that there was no data for alternative production possibilities available. Production coefficients, giving the relation between inputs and outputs, were therefore fixed. This meant that production technologies were fixed, there was no choice for producers. In contrast, the conference participants portrayed the economy as being confronted with a linear programming problem as a whole. With the whole system optimized from a menu of different (linear) technologies, there was a choice between alternative processes to produce the same good. This turned into the general case of production, while the HERP's system was framed as a special case, thereby subsuming it under the conference's approach.

The conference's special-casing ignored that the HERP's research purposefully failed to account for alternative technologies because they could not be measured.[92] Only one contribution to the conference volume, a three-page essay, discussed the empirical limitations of the mathematical economy. In a logical empiricist vein, Oskar Morgenstern argued that the data that linear programming was supposed to process were subject to various measurement errors.[93] While Norbert Wiener's *Cybernetics*, uttering a similar critique, concluded that cybernetic techniques such as mathematical prediction theory should probably not be applied to the social sciences at all, Morgenstern urged his colleagues to better engage with the way in which data came about and to pay attention to the relevant idiosyncratic circumstances.[94] If linear programmers did not develop a serious treatment of data that conformed to the intricacy of their computations, Morgenstern warned, all their modeling would lose its meaning. Such a view, however, was not shared by the other participants. Irrespective of whether the neglect was strategic or accidental, the working object that resulted was a purely mathematical economy, which laid the foundation for research that further dispensed with empirics.

The mathematical object retained a certain openness in economic meaning. In fact, for linear programmers, it was a decisive feature of the economy as a system of linear equations that it could but did not need to refer to the concept of a market.[95] They picked up on what they saw as conventional economic theory: Neoclassical framings of the economic as the interaction of rational agents that might lead to an efficient allocation of resources – the (in)famous economic equilibrium. Now, the new mathematics of linear programming got rid of the formal assumption of competitive markets. In a system of simultaneous equations, the values of goods and services derived from the workings of an efficient productive system rather than the smooth workings of supply and demand. There was no room for any kind of optimizing behavior on behalf of individual firms.[96] It was the economy as a whole that achieved the optimal allocation of productive resources in its shape as a large-scale optimization problem, a vast, efficient system of production. Accordingly, the conference participants used the term "prices" as a synonym for "shadow prices," "efficiency prices," or "accounting prices," concepts that were bound to technical efficiency rather than competitive behavior. The

interpretational openness of the mathematical object allowed linear programmers to boldly envisage the applicability of their techniques to a
"variety of possible institutional arrangements – centrally-planned socialist economy, a Western managed capitalistic economy, or a hypothetical
free market economy."[97]

Linear programmers fostered a polysemous politics of formalization, in
particular when it came to its notion of "planning." On the one hand, the
conference proceedings pushed the generalization of neoclassical economic
theory from a theory of competitive processes to one that would also
incorporate planning. In this way, activity analysis continued a project
that had been underway in some parts of mathematical neoclassicism for a
long time.[98] In the eyes of linear programmers, their technique held the
promise to make neoclassical theory more explicit, more realistic, and
closer to empirical relevance.[99] This might seem paradoxical, given its
difference from the HERP's empirical work. But in the proceeding's comparison to older-school neoclassical theory, the conference's categories
were to a large extent, at least in principle, quantifiable. (The volume did
not contain any references to quantifications of neoclassical production
theory such as Paul Douglas's work in Chapter 2 or interwar research on
statistical supply and demand curves.) On the other hand, the proceedings
sought to show how mathematical techniques associated with planning
were compatible with free-market systems. The technically efficient system
was in the first place interpreted as a hypothetical market economy, even
though the economic equilibrium was not explicitly modeled. In this way,
the HERP's technical coefficients turned into equilibrium positions: "[A]ll
desirable substitutions have already been made by the competitive
market."[100] The proceedings steered clear of any links with political programs of planning. A conference contribution on the application of linear
models to the Soviet economy was not even included in the published
volume.[101]

Planning here was an organizational necessity that had nothing to do
with an institutional setting of centralized decision-making, a grand political vision, or even specific policy measures.[102] This is illustrated in the
conference volume's uptake of what has been coined the "socialist calculation debates." In the early 1930s – when Leontief remembered having
arrived at the idea of using a large-scale computing machine in economics –
European scholars discussed the possibilities of socialist planning. The
reference to the calculation debates played a major role in Koopman's
introduction to the conference proceedings: "To von Mises' arguments

regarding the unmanageability of the computation problems of centralized allocation, the authors oppose the new possibilities opened by modern electronic computing equipment."[103] The reference fulfilled the purpose of posing a problem for which the technique of linear programming and the new computing capacities provided a technical solution. In Koopman's encapsulation, Ludwig von Mises had argued that planning was impossible as there was no way of valuing goods and services in an economy without a market. He built on the reply from Oskar Lange (who had in the meantime joined Cowles' staff) that planners could come up with a substitute procedure that calculated the same prices as brought about by the price system through an iterative trial-and-error scheme. The arguments of others such as Otto Neurath, who argued for planning in kind and emphasized a variety of tasks for planners beyond calculation, played no role. The Conference on Activity Analysis excluded all aspects of the calculation debates that related to the real-life mobilizations of decentralizing production and all of its complexities.[104] At the onset of McCarthyism, describing the technically efficient economy as a market system also proved helpful to deal with the suspicious similarity of "programming" and "planning." To avoid this vocabulary, the conference advocated the technical term "allocation." The framing also overlapped with the special focus of the RAND corporation, which financed the conference through funding from the Air Force.[105]

In its various adaptations, the conference's rendition of the economy as a system of simultaneous equations eventually turned into one of the central research objects of postwar economics.[106] Theorists at the Cowles Commission developed mathematical instantiations of so-called Walrasian general equilibrium systems.[107] Game theoretic formulations in turn dispensed with Walrasian competitive worlds but equally sought to link the parts and the whole. In contrast to both activity analysis and research at the HERP, where problems of individual decision-making played hardly any role, this research explicitly proceeded from the interaction of individual elements at the micro-level in an attempt to model the whole. It did so in a highly formalistic manner, constructing axiomatic systems of proof and proposition. The economy of the Conference on Activity Analysis already featured the major characteristics of the economy in the Solow model: The efficient productive system smoothly optimized production as a whole, fully dispensed with the role of demand, and disregarded the behavior of the parts. Everything beyond the efficient workings of production – the distribution of income, changes in technology, demand, or whatever else – were excluded from the system.

FROM QUANTITATIVE PLANNING TO
QUALITATIVE EXPERIMENTS

In 1952, a few years after assisting Leontief at the HERP, Solow sent his former dissertation adviser a draft paper on "Interest and Prices in Dynamical Input–Output Models." They had remained in close contact, and the archived correspondences give the impression of a rather well-balanced relationship with both economists asking the other for feedback through letters and in person. In this one exchange, they discussed problems of dynamic input–output analysis. Here, "dynamic" meant that future states of the system depended on past ones. At the HERP, Leontief and Nicholas Georgescu-Roegen engaged in dynamic analysis in order to derive an "empirical law of change" from the structural characteristics of the economy.[108] The paper Solow sent to Leontief included what he already denoted a "neo-classical model," a small-scale mathematical model of growth in the long run. As will be detailed in Chapter 4, this model came from an endeavor (in the vein of the Conference on Activity Analysis) to merge dynamic input–output modeling with what Solow conceived of as conventional neoclassical theory. The exchange highlighted the specific characteristics of small-scale modeling, which contrasted starkly with Leontief's big science.

In the otherwise affectionate exchange between Leontief and Solow, two different ways of modeling collided. Among other points of contention, Leontief was irritated by the latter's assumption of perfect foresight, the "*correct anticipation* by all individual capital goods' owners of the entire future course of price movements and changes in the rate of interest." Perplexed, he urged Solow to make his formulation "more realist" by replacing the "infinite expectational horizon" with a limited, very short one.[109] This was the time span of real-world decision-making practices ("conventional standards of behavior"; rules-of-thumb in business, industrial, and financial institutions).[110] Solow countered in a manner that he would retain in later exchanges on models and modeling. He was well aware that the assumption of perfect foresight was not a proper basis for a "realistic theory of price movements over time." But this was not the kind of realism Solow was after. Playing with the mathematical formalism that Leontief had suggested, he argued that it was simply "the finite approximation to my differential equations": The assumption of finite, very short periods in which capital goods owners capitalized their expected income certainly fit decision-making in economic practice better than Solow's own assumption. When it came to the smooth, long-run mathematical world, however, Leontief's reformulation did not alter the "qualitative properties of the solution."[111] In a further reply, Solow insisted on the superiority of his formulation: "It remains my opinion that the neo-classical model I used is the appropriate one."[112] This was a perspective that focused entirely on mathematical formalism and was tightly linked to the aim of constructing relatively simple, neat, and tractable mathematical artifacts.

Solow's reasoning was not about the empirical material, computing capacities, and the practicalities of compiling data. Instead, it focused on mathematical formalism and its most efficient expression. The resulting model provided what Solow called a "qualitative" impression of how growth worked. Here, the structural matrix of the HERP transformed into a different object. Instead of the interactions between the parts of a whole, it only displayed the whole. Rather than seeing the relations between capital and output as fixed, it described a fully flexible system in which inputs changed in accordance with changes in prices and wages. But not only was the portrayed world different, the portrayal itself had a different role to play. This model was not thought to be a direct instrument for planning but rather, using Leontief's words for his own dynamic approach, a tool for conducting theoretical "small-scale experiments."[113] The endeavor came with a different understanding of realism, as illustrated in a truly excited letter, which Solow wrote after reading with "delight" the published version of Leontief's Josiah Willard Gibbs Lecture. Thanking Leontief "for the treat," Solow expressed the fundamental differences between their approaches to modeling.

I am not so optimistic as you are about the success of direct empirical analysis. In fact, I am not so sure that there is any such thing as "direct" empirical analysis. You may throw statistical inference out the window; it has a way of sneaking back in with tomorrow's groceries. Also, I think I would rate the marginal productivity of pure theoretical speculation somewhat higher than you would, and that of extensive empirical work somewhat lower. But this reflects a difference in what we expect of economic theory. Scorn not the four or five variable aggregate model, and its accompanying vague and almost qualitative statistical clothing. I may be kidding myself, but I *feel* more secure in my understanding of the world because I am pretty sure the marginal propensity to consume is "about" .7.[114]

Only reading the first four sentences of the paragraph, it is easy to detect the contemporary ruptures between the HERP's "direct" empirical work and the "indirect" measurement procedures of econometricians. Associated primarily with the Cowles Commission, the latter reduced "statistical inference" to a technical procedure. At the time, mathematical modelers were about to make it state-of-the-art to use parameters from mathematical models and estimate them with given data sets instead of at least trying to come closer to the numerical reality of production in tedious empirical research.[115] This provided the background to Solow's emphasis of the "difference in what we expect from economic theory."

So far, the letter underlined the common fault lines in the history of postwar economics. More interesting are the following sentences in which Solow talked about the perks of small-scale models. Their advantages were not due to some "scientific method" or some other elaborate, objectifying, rationalizing procedure. The statistics of aggregative econometric models were "vague and almost qualitative," and yet they made Solow *"feel* more secure in my understanding of the world." Leontief advocated an empirical approach that built on the transformation of empirical material from bits and pieces taken from the material realities of production to the ready-made input–output table. There was an understanding of something that remained from the empirical world throughout the sequence of shaping and reshaping. Solow, in contrast, embraced the irreconcilable difference between the world of economic practices and the mathematical worlds of economists. In the cosmos of "theoretical speculation," as he put it, quantified theoretical categories like the marginal propensity to consume for an economy as a whole did give some purchase on the world. Chapter 4 will give more space to Solow as a historical actor and show what he was working on in the first half of the 1950s, which ultimately opened out into what is still known as "the neoclassical growth model." Against the heterogenous landscape of mathematical economics in the postwar US, Chapter 4 will portray the model as a miniature of larger-scale systems of linear equations, which not only reduced them in scale but also intensified their economic content. Chapter 5 will then take into account the many ways in which modelers made sense of their small-scale worlds combining epistemological, political, and social argument.

Notes

1 "Electronic Economics," in *Christian Science Monitor*, 4. November 1948, Leontief papers, HUG 4517.5, box 5, correspondence general 1948–1950, file C, Courtesy of the Harvard University Archives.

2 At least Leontief argued that the number of numerical operations exceeded that of previous "economic and statistical studies, or even in the natural sciences." Wassily Leontief, "Recent Developments in the Study of Interindustrial Relationships," *American Economic Review* 39, no. 3 (1949): 211–25, 215.

3 Wassily Leontief, Hollis B. Chenery, Paul G. Clark, James S. Duesenberry, Allen R. Ferguson, Anne P. Grosse, Robert N. Grosse, Mathilda Holzman, Walter Isard, and Helen Kistin, *Studies in the Structure of the American Economy: Theoretical*

and Empirical Explorations in Input–Output Analysis (New York: Oxford University Press, 1953), 11.

4 Alain Desrosières, "Managing the Economy," in *The Cambridge History of Science, VII: The Modern Social Sciences*, edited by. Theodore M. Porter and Dorothy Ross (Cambridge: Cambridge University Press, 2003), 553–64, 554.

5 For a survey of the European developments of input–output analysis, see Amanar Akhabbar, Gabrielle Antille, Emilio Fontela, and Antonio Pulido, "Input–Output in Europe: Trends in Research and Applications," *OEconomia* 1, no. 1 (2011): 73–98. On Turkey, see Erwin Dekker, *Jan Tinbergen (1903–1994) and the Rise of Economic Expertise* (Cambridge: Cambridge University Press, 2021), chapter 14. On Japan, see Shuntaro Shishido, "Japan's Economic Growth and Policy-Making in the Context of Input–Output Models," in *Wassily Leontief and Input–Output Economics*, edited by Michael L. Lahr and Erik Dietzenbacher (Cambridge: Cambridge University Press, 2004), 294–310. On Taiwan, see Honghong Tinn, "Modeling Computers and Computer Models: Manufacturing Economic-Planning Projects in Cold War Taiwan, 1959–1968," *Technology and Culture* 59, no. 4 (2018): 66–99.

6 In the preface of Leontief et al., *Studies in the Structure of the American Economy*, Solow is acknowledged "for his part in the basic empirical research on the capital structure" (vii).

7 These are all Solow and his colleagues' expressions, which make appearances throughout this book. See in particular Chapter 4. On my use of Gaston Bachelard's concept of "phenomenotechnology," see the Introduction.

8 Evsey D. Domar, "Economic Growth: An Econometric Approach," *American Economic Review* 42, no. 2 (1952): 479–95, 488–9.

9 On contemporary uses of the liquid metaphor, particularly in the context of the Newlyn–Phillips machine, see Mary S. Morgan, *The World in the Model: How Economists Work and Think* (Cambridge: Cambridge University Press, 2012), chapter 5. The HERP's 1948 research program included the reference to the prime example of visualizing an economic reality in terms of a flow from the mid-eighteenth century. It spoke of its aim to develop a *tableau économique*. See the preface of Wassily Leontief et al., *Studies in the Structure of the American Economy*, v.

10 Augustine Sedgewick, "Against Flows," *History of the Present: A Journal of Critical History* 4, no. 2 (2014): 143–70, 161–2.

11 Both: Leontief et al., *Studies in the Structure of the American Economy*, 5.

12 Amanar Akhabbar, "The Case against 'Indirect' Statistical Inference: Wassily Leontief's 'Direct Induction' and *The Structure of American Economy, 1919–29*," in *Exploring the History of Statistical Inference in Economics* (supplement to *History of Political Economy* 53), edited by Jeff Biddle and Marcel Boumans (Durham, NC: Duke University Press, 2021), 259–92, 283.

13 Wassily Leontief, "Die Bilanz der russischen Volkswirtschaft. Eine Methodologische Untersuchung," *Weltwirtschaftliches Archiv* 22, no. 2 (1925): 338–44; English translation: Wassily Leontief, "The Balance of the Economy of the USSR," in *Foundations of Soviet Strategy for Economic Growth, Selected Short Soviet Essays 1924–1930*, edited by Nicolas Spulber (Bloomington, IN: Indiana University Press, 1964), 88–94.

14 The census was eventually put on hold because of the Great Depression. On economic statistics in Weimar and Nazi Germany, see Adam Tooze, *Statistics*

and the German State, 1900–1945: The Making of Modern Economic Knowledge (Cambridge: Cambridge University Press, 2001).

15 On Leontief's early work, see Harald Hagemann, "Leontief and his German Period," *Russian Journal of Economics* 7 (2021): 67–90; Olav Bjerkholt, "Wassily Leontief and the Discovery of the Input–Output Approach" (Memorandum, No. 18, Oslo University, Department of Economics, 2016), available at https://EconPapers.repec.org/RePEc:hhs:osloec:2016_018, last accessed April 18, 2024.

16 Cf. "Case against 'Indirect' Statistical Inference," 285–6.

17 Wassily Leontief to Clifford Harvey, editor of the *Christian Science Monitor*, May 6, 1948, Leontief Papers, HUG 4517.5, box 5, file C, Courtesy of the Harvard University Archives.

18 Anne P. Carter, "Leontief's 'Stuff': An Archeology of Input–Output Material," *OEconomia* 1, no. 1 (2012): 51–9, 54.

19 For a conceptual comparison of Leontief's and other formulations of input–output systems, see the special issue of *Economic Systems Research* 18, no. 4 (2006), edited by Olav Bjerkholt and Heinz D. Kurz.

20 Edwin Bidwell Wilson to R. T. Crane, December 30, 1942, Wilson Papers, HUG 4878.207, Social Science Research Council Correspondence, 1929–38 (2 of 2), Courtesy of the Harvard University Archives. I am grateful to Roger Backhouse for sharing this material.

21 Wassily Leontief, "Output, Employment, Consumption and Investment," *Quarterly Journal of Economics* 58, no. 2 (1944): 290–313, 290.

22 Two decades later, Leontief published a widely discussed paper that would instigate a new field of "disarmament economics." See Olav Bjerkholt, "When Input–Output Analysis Came to Norway," *Structural Change and Economic Dynamics* 6 (1995): 319–30, 329.

23 Duncan K. Foley, "An Interview with Wassily Leontief," *Macroeconomic Dynamics* 2, no. 1 (1998): 116–40, 121–22.

24 Martin C. Kohli, "Leontief and the U.S. Bureau of Labor Statistics, 1941–1954: Developing a Framework for Measurement," in *The Age of Economic Measurement* (supplement to *History of Political Economy* 30), edited by Judy L. Klein and Mary S. Morgan (Durham, NC: Duke University Press, 2001), 190–212, 191.

25 Leontief to Harvey, May 6, 1948, Leontief Papers; cf. Robert Dorfman, "In Appreciation of Wassily Leontief," *Structural Change and Economic Dynamics* 6 (1995): 305–8, 307. A comparative case in sociology was Jacques Barzun's critique of what had become of the university in relation to the establishment of the Bureau of Applied Social Research at Columbia University. See Eric T. Hounshell, "A Feel for the Data: Paul F. Lazarsfeld and the Columbia University Bureau of Applied Social Research" (dissertation, UCLA Los Angeles, 2017), 464–76.

26 Carter, "Leontief's 'Stuff,'" 55. Before joining the HERP, Gilboy (1903–73) worked at the Harvard Committee on Economic Research, in particular on business cycle analysis and the estimation of demand curves. See Mary S. Morgan, *The History of Econometric Ideas* (Cambridge: Cambridge University Press, 1990), 154.

27 See Kohli, "Leontief and the U.S. Bureau of Labor Statistics," 204. On Project SCOOP, see Paul Erickson, Judy L. Klein, Lorraine Daston, Rebecca Lemov, Thomas Sturm, and Michael D. Gordin, *How Reason Almost Lost Its Mind: The*

Strange Career of Cold War Rationality. Chicago: University of Chicago Press, 58–61.

28 Leontief et al., *Studies in the Structure of the American Economy*, v.

29 Harvard Economic Research Project, "Preliminary Report of the Final Progress Report," 1950, Leontief Papers, HUG 4517.5, box 8, folder: Progress Reports – A.F., Courtesy of the Harvard University Archives.

30 Leontief to Harvey, May 6, 1948, Leontief Papers.

31 As an analytical framework, production has been described in such a way several times. The most prominent renditions are Marx's Schemes of Reproduction in the second volume of *Capital* and Quesnay's *tableau économique*.

32 Leontief et al., *Studies in the Structure of the American Economy*, 19.

33 They constructed the "inverse" of the matrix to calculate the production coefficients necessary to ensure a specified set of final outputs. This calculation was doable by humans. The larger the matrices, the more difficult the linear equations system was to solve.

34 Leontief et al., *Studies in the Structure of the American Economy*, 10.

35 Carter, "Leontief's 'Stuff,'" 54. For an outline of the history of the computer in economics, see Roger E. Backhouse and Béatrice Cherrier, "'It's Computers, Stupid!' The Spread of Computers and the Changing Roles of Theoretical and Applied Economics," in *The Age of the Applied Economist: The Transformation of Economics Since the 1970s* (supplement to *History of Political Economy* 49), edited by Roger E. Backhouse and Béatrice Cherrier (Durham, NC: Duke University Press, 2017), 103–26.

36 Wassily Leontief, "Interrelation of Prices, Output, Savings, and Investment," *Review of Economics and Statistics* 19, no. 3 (1937): 109–32, 109.

37 Mitchell's research was published in his doctoral dissertation (Herb F. Mitchell, "The Machine Solution of Simultaneous Linear Systems," Doctoral Thesis, Harvard University, 1948) and was continued by Kenneth E. Iverson, who, also under Leontief and Aiken, used the Mark IV for solving a dynamic economic model: Kenneth E. Iverson, "Machine Solutions of Linear Differential Equations to a Dynamic Economic Model" (doctoral thesis, Harvard University, January 1954).

38 Leontief to Harvey, May 6, 1948, Leontief Papers.

39 Edwin L. Dale, Jr., "Electronic Calculator Delivered to Bureau of Census: Science and Industry are Aided by New Electronic Calculators," *New York Herald Tribune*, 5 August 1951, Grace Murray Hopper Collection, Press Clippings, box 5, folder 24 (https://sova.si.edu/details/NMAH.AC.0324?s=0&n=10&t=C&q=&i=0#ref400).

40 Oskar Morgenstern, "Experiment and Large Scale Computation in Economics," in *Economic Activity Analysis*, edited by Oskar Morgenstern (New York: John Wiley & Sons, 1954), 484–549, 495–96.

41 Soma S. Golden, "Leontief Relates Economic Theory to Fact. Professor's Research Project Perfects Input–Output Analysis," *The Harvard Crimson*, December 17, 1959, available at www.thecrimson.com/article/1959/12/17/loentief-relates-economic-theory-to-fact, last accessed April 18, 2024.

42 Leontief et al., *Studies in the Structure of the American Economy*, 5.

43 Leontief et al., *Studies in the Structure of the American Economy*, 13. See Amanar Akhabbar, "Wassily Leontief as an Econometrician, and the Expansion of the Field of Direct Observation" (Working paper, August 2022), who also provides a

historical and analytical account of Leontief's differentiation between "direct" and "indirect" observation.

44 Leontief et al., *Studies in the Structure of the American Economy*, 13–14.

45 Leontief et al., *Studies in the Structure of the American Economy*, 14.

46 Leontief, "Recent Developments in the Study of Interindustrial Relationships," 225, cited in Marcel Boumans, "Logical Positivism and Leontief" (Working paper, University of Amsterdam, 2012), 4.

47 Foley, "Interview with Wassily Leontief," 122–3.

48 "Preliminary Report," 1950, Leontief Papers.

49 Economists at the Oxford Research Institute, for instance, conducted group discussions with business people on the basis of questionnaires to find out about their decision-making processes. See Robert L. Hall and Charles J. Hitch, "Price Theory and Business Behaviour," *Oxford Economic Papers* 2, no. 1 (1939): 12–45.

50 Foley, "Interview with Wassily Leontief," 121.

51 All: "Preliminary Report," 1950, Leontief Papers.

52 Theodore M. Porter, "Speaking Precision to Power: The Modern Political Role of Social Science," *Social Research* 73, no. 4 (2006): 1273–94, 1280.

53 On the distinction with regard to national income accounting see Mary S. Morgan, "Seeking Parts, Looking for Wholes," in *Histories of Scientific Observation*, edited by Lorraine Daston and Elizabeth Lunbeck (Chicago: University of Chicago Press, 2011), 303–25, 307–8.

54 Carter, "Leontief's 'Stuff,'" 54.

55 "Preliminary Report," 1950, Leontief Papers.

56 "Preliminary Report," 1950, Leontief Papers.

57 See Joseph W. Duncan and William C. Shelton, *Revolution in United States Government Statistics 1926-1976* (US Department of Commerce, Office of Federal Statistical Policy and Standards, 1978), 111.

58 See also Tinn, "Modeling Computers and Computer Models" on the practices of Taiwanese input–output work.

59 Wassily Leontief, "Academic Economics," *Science* 217 (1982): 104–7, 104.

60 Apart from the HERP's associate director Gilboy, Solow, and Benjamin Handler, who all received special acknowledgement from the ten co-authors, the preface of the *Studies in the Structure of the American Economy* mentioned the following names: Robert L. Allen, Judith Balderston, Otto Bird, Nancy Bromberger, Carol Cameron, William Capron, Sara Clark, Bernadette Drolette, Fay Greenwald, Ruth Kahn, Lora Katz, Robert Kavesh, Elaine Kazanowski, Mary Kazanowski, Lohn Lansing, Irwin Leff, Richard Levitan, Dolores McJilton, Leon Moses, M. Janice Murphy, Margaret Oliver, Myer Rashish, Richard Rosenthal, Ira Scott, Martha Shoesmith, Burton Singer, Edith Soodak, Raya Spiegel, Carl Stevens, Tun Thin, and Ruth Winer.

61 Carter, "Leontief's 'Stuff,'" 55–6.

62 Carter, "Leontief's 'Stuff,'" 56.

63 Herbert B. Nichols, "Mechanical Calculators Eject Right Answers Quicker'n a Flash," *The Christian Science Monitor* October 14, 1947 (https://sova.si.edu/details/NMAH.AC.0324#ref385) box 5, folder 24; "Robot Works Problems Never Before Solved," *Popular Mechanics Magazine*, October 1944; box 5, folder 22; both: Grace Murray Hopper Collection, Press Clippings.

64 Dorothy G. Wayman, "Harvard Gets Huge Calculator: 51-Foot Machine Costs $250,000, Took Six Years," *The Boston Daily Globe*, 7 August 1944, box 5, folder 11 (https://edan.si.edu/slideshow/viewer/?eadrefid=NMAH.AC.0324_ref356);   "25-Ton 'Mechanical Brain' Built at Harvard for Navy," *Boston Sunday Globe*, 7 March 1948, box 5, folder 24 (https://edan.si.edu/slideshow/viewer/?eadrefid= NMAH.AC.0324_ref374); "New Giant 'Brain' does Wizard Work," *New York Times*, 25 August 194?, box 5, folder 24 (https://edan.si.edu/slideshow/viewer/? eadrefid=NMAH.AC.0324_ref391); all: Grace Murray Hopper Collection, Press Clippings.

65 Both: "Forecast of the Future," editorial *Herald Tribune*, 12 January 1947, box 5, folder   25   (https://edan.si.edu/slideshow/viewer/?eadrefid=NMAH.AC.0324_ ref412), Grace Murray Hopper Collection, Press Clippings.

66 The term is borrowed from Adam Tooze, "Die Vermessung der Welt. Ansätze zu einer Kulturgeschichte der Wirtschaftsstatistik," in *Wirtschaftsgeschichte als Kulturgeschichte. Dimensionen eines Perspektivenwechsels*, edited by Hartmut Berghoff and Jakob Vogel (Frankfurt am Main: Campus Verlag, 2004), 325–51, 341.

67 Leontief to Harvey, May 6, 1948, Leontief Papers.

68 See Eden Medina, *Cybernetic Revolutionaries: Technology and Politics in Allende's Chile* (Cambridge, MA: MIT Press, 2011).

69 Bernard Dionysius Geoghegan, "From Information Theory to French Theory: Jakobson, Lévi-Strauss, and the Cybernetic Apparatus," *Critical Inquiry* 38 (2011): 96–126, 116. For Jakobson's quote see Slava Gerovitch, "Roman Jakobson und die Kybernetisierung der Linguistik in der Sowjetunion," in *Die Transformationen des Humanen: Beiträge zur Kulturgeschichte der Kybernetik*, edited by Michael Hagner and Erich Hörl (Frankfurt: Suhrkamp, 2008), 229–74, 243f. On system-thinking in the social sciences, see Hunter Heyck, *Age of System: Understanding the Development of Modern Social Science* (Baltimore: Johns Hopkins University Press, 2015).

70 Wassily Leontief, "The Problems of Quality and Quantity in Economics," *Daedalus* 88, no. 4 (1959): 622–32, 629; Wassily Leontief, *Essays in Economics* (New York: Routledge, 1966), 237, cited in Philip Mirowski, *Machine Dreams: How Economics became a Cyborg Science* (Cambridge: Cambridge University Press, 2002), 539.

71 In his well-known "The Use of Knowledge in Society," *American Economic Review* 35, no. 4 (1945): 519–30, Friedrich Hayek presented the market not as allocating material resources but as solving the epistemic problem of bringing together and processing the necessary knowledge – an operation not achievable through a central planning authority. For relating Hayek's text to what they see as the main shift of postwar economics, namely, that the "economic problem" no longer consisted in the allocation of material resources but in the collection and processing of information, see Philip Mirowski and Edward Nik-Khah, *The Knowledge We Have Lost in Information: The History of Information in Modern Economics* (Oxford: Oxford University Press, 2017), 63–4.

72 Wassily Leontief, "What an Economic Planning Board Should Do," *Challenge* 17, no. 3 (1974): 35–40, 37.

73 See also Vincent Carret, "Wassily Leontief's Research Program: Science, Beliefs, Institutions," *History of Political Economy* 56, no. 4 (2024): 653–84, 658. While in

theoretical debate, Leontief criticized the likes of Tinbergen, these planner-econometricians also opposed Keynesian frameworks like the multiplier from an input–output perspective, see Dekker, *Jan Tinbergen*, 22, n33.

74 Stewart Brand, "Both Sides of the Necessary Paradox," 1973, reprinted in Stewart Brand, *II Cybernetic Frontiers* (New York: Random House, 1974), 9–33, 28, cited in Ronald Kline, "How Disunity Matters to the History of Cybernetics in the Human Sciences in the United States, 1940–80," *History of the Human Sciences* 33, no. 1 (2020): 12–35, 23–24.

75 Golden, "Leontief Relates Economic Theory to Fact"; Kohli, "Leontief and the Bureau of Labor Statistics," 191, 207–8. See also Karen R. Polenske, "Leontief's 'Magnificent Machine' and Other Contributions to Applied Economics," in *Wassily Leontief and Input–Output Economics*, edited by Michael L. Lahr and Erik Dietzenbacher (Cambridge: Cambridge University Press, 2004), 9–29, 12.

76 Tinn, "Modeling Computers and Computer Models."

77 See Duncan and Shelton, *Revolution in United States Government Statistics*, 114. On NIPA, see Chapter 2.

78 See André Vanoli, *A History of National Accounting* (Amsterdam: IOS Press, 2005), 90–95, 149.

79 From the mid-1970s on, input–output also lost momentum as a primary policy tool and only today regains importance in the context of ecological planning and attempts to restructure economies toward lower emissions. On input–output morphing into computable general equilibrium models, see Charles L. Ballard and Marianne Johnson, "Applied General Equilibrium Analysis," in *Becoming Applied: The Transformation of Economics after 1970* (supplement to *History of Political Economy* 49), edited by Roger E. Backhouse und Béatrice Cherrier (Durham, NC: Duke University Press, 2017), 78–102.

80 See, for instance, Paul Erickson, *The World the Game Theorists Made* (Chicago: University of Chicago Press, 2015), chapters 3 and 4.

81 On Cowles' history, see the relevant chapters in Erickson et al., *How Reason Almost Lost Its Mind*, who look at Cowles' role as one of the primary fora that brought Cold War "action intellectuals" together; Till Düppe and E. Roy Weintraub, *Finding Equilibrium: Arrow, Debreu, McKenzie and the Problem of Scientific Credit* (Princeton: Princeton University Press, 2014), who introduce Cowles as one of the important enabling conditions of the construction of general equilibrium theory; Mirowski and Nik-Khah, *Knowledge We Have Lost in Information*, who focus on its role in fostering the imagery of the market as a computer (rather than a mechanical conveyor belt); Mirowski, *Machine Dreams*, who emphasizes the role of military patronage.

82 Tjalling C. Koopmans, ed. *Activity Analysis of Production and Allocation*. Cowles Commission Monograph 3 (New York: John Wiley and Sons, 1951).

83 Koopmans, *Activity Analysis*, 3. The approaches mentioned stretched from various formulations of a mathematical general equilibrium in the 1930s (formulating the behavior of supply, demand, and prices in an economic system), to recent game theoretic formulations of equilibrium; from technical discussions of the possibilities of economic planning in so-called welfare models to the linear modeling methods used in input–output analysis.

84 See Roger E. Backhouse, "Paul Samuelson, RAND and the Cowles Commission Activity Analysis Conference, 1947–1949" (working paper, version 2, October 2012), 35. Backhouse has also noted that the pre-circulated conference program did emphasize problems associated with data.

85 George J. Stigler, "The Cost of Subsistence," *Journal of Farm Economics* 27, no. 2 (1949): 303–14, 303. Other examples are transportation models as, for instance, in Frank L. Hitchcock, "The Distribution of a Product from Several Sources to Numerous Localities," *Journal of Mathematics and Physics* 20 (1941): 224–30.

86 See Erickson et al., *How Reason Almost Lost Its Mind*, 64–5.

87 See Erickson et al., *How Reason Almost Lost Its Mind*, 202, n.18.

88 Frederic H. Murphy and Venkat Panchanadam, "Understanding Linear Programming Modeling through an Examination of the Early Papers on Model Formulation," *Operations Research* 45, no. 3 (1997): 341–56, 345.

89 See Erickson et al., *How Reason Almost Lost Its Mind*, chapters 2 and 3.

90 Tjalling C. Koopmans, "Analysis of Production as an Efficient Combination of Activities," in *Activity Analysis of Production and Allocation*, edited by Tjalling C. Koopmans. Cowles Commission Monograph 3 (New York: John Wiley and Sons, 1951), 33–97, 33.

91 Koopmans, *Activity Analysis*, 3. Koopmans, true to his Cowles background, conceived of a particular "natural order" of economic work that the contributions of the volume followed: First theory, then application, and last, tools (7).

92 The proceedings contained a number of (non-)"substitution theorems," which provided mathematical demonstrations that alternative technologies would not be used and thereby justified their exclusion from analysis. In this way, they showed the (restrictive) conditions necessary to portray the efficient productive system as a neoclassical economy. Essentially, the theorems proved that the linear programming method for describing dynamics (finite differences with inequalities) was comparable to the mathematics that economists were used to applying (differential calculus with marginal conditions). The linear model could be reformulated as a system of continuously differentiable production functions (based on the smooth substitution of factor inputs according to relative prices). At the center of the mathematical maneuver was the redefinition of technical coefficients as equilibrium positions. See Paul A. Samuelson, "Abstract of a Theorem Concerning Substitutability in Open Leontief Models," in *Activity Analysis of Production and Allocation*, edited by Tjalling C. Koopmans. Cowles Commission Monograph 3 (New York: John Wiley and Sons, 1951), 142–46. Alternative proofs were provided by Georgescu-Roegen, who devised a similar theorem, Koopmans, who gave a proof for the case of a three-commodity economy, and Kenneth Arrow, who proved the theorem generally. On the logic of the theorems in the context of the conference, see Backhouse, "Paul Samuelson, RAND and the Cowles Commission Activity Analysis Conference."

93 A version of Morgenstern's conference paper, *On the Accuracy of Economic Observations* was published as a monograph in 1950. See Marcel Boumans, "Observations in a Hostile Environment: Morgenstern on the Accuracy of Economic Observations," in *Observing the Economy: Historical Perspectives* (supplement to *History of Political Economy* 44), edited by Harro Maas and Mary S. Morgan (Durham, NC: Duke University Press, 2012), 114–36.

94 On Wiener's skeptical stance when it came to cybernetic social sciences, see Kline, "How Disunity Matters to the History of Cybernetics," 15–16.

95 See Koopmans, *Activity Analysis*, 7.

96 Accordingly, the conference proceedings were "received with some astonishment by authors working in the neoclassical tradition" for their neglect of demand, see Heinz D. Kurz and Neri Salvadori, *Theory of Production: A Long-Period Analysis* (Cambridge: Cambridge University Press, 1995), 26.

97 Koopmans, *Activity Analysis*, 7.

98 Earlier neoclassical formulations of a mathematical equilibrium were equally seen as fitting different kinds of institutional set-ups. In general, there was no coherent politics of neoclassicism. See the Introduction.

99 Tjalling Koopmans to Robert Solow, April 18, 1952, Solow papers, box 57, file K: 1 of 4. Cf. Roger E. Backhouse, "Paul Samuelson, RAND and the Cowles Commission Activity Analysis Conference, 1947–1949," Version 2. October 2012, 1.

100 Samuelson, "Abstract of a Theorem," 143.

101 See Backhouse, "Paul Samuelson, RAND and the Cowles Commission Activity Analysis Conference," 32.

102 Cf. Till Düppe and E. Roy Weintraub, "Siting the New Economic Science: The Cowles Commission's Activity Analysis Conference of June 1949," *Science in Context* 27, no. 3 (2014): 453–83, 467; Mirowski, *Machine Dreams*, 243.

103 Koopmans, *Activity Analysis*, 7.

104 On the various ways that socialist planners anticipated the computer and the most recent ideas to get rid of markets by way of advanced forms of programming, see Aaron Benanav, "How to Make a Pencil," *Logic*, December 20, 2020, available at https://logicmag.io/commons/how-to-make-a-pencil, last accessed April 18, 2024.

105 See Erickson et al., *How Reason Almost Lost Its Mind*, 63. On RAND (short for "research and development"), soon the quintessential Cold War research think tank, and its involvement in building up postwar economics, see the relevant chapters in Düppe and Weintraub, *Finding Equilibrium*; Robert Leonard, *Von Neumann, Morgenstern, and the Creation of Game Theory. From Chess to Social Science, 1900–1960* (Cambridge: Cambridge University Press, 2010); Sonja M. Amadae, *Rationalizing Capitalist Democracy: The Cold War Origins of Rational Choice Liberalism* (Chicago: University of Chicago Press, 2003); Mirowski, *Machine Dreams*.

106 On the role of the conference for an emerging community of mathematical economists, see Düppe and Weintraub, "Siting the New Economic Science."

107 Already John von Neumann and Oskar Morgenstern's *Theory of Games and Economic Behavior* (Princeton: Princeton University Press, 1944) had presented a new concept of economic equilibrium that built on strategic rather than competitive behavior. While their fixed point theorems were picked up at the conference, their critique of competitive analysis as well as their game theoretic approach was ignored, see Mirowski, *Machine Dreams*, chapter 5.

108 These characteristics were determined from stock-flow relationships at one point in time. The underlying logic contrasted dynamic input–output analysis from the empiricist work of the NBER, which, in Leontief's eyes, could not *explain* long-run development because it could not account for structural change. See Leontief et al., *Studies in the Structure of the American Economy*, 53. Georgescu-Roegen later

became one of the intellectual references for various strands of an ecological economics, in particular for his critique of neoclassical production functions such as Solow's. In the above-mentioned conference volume he presented an aggregate production function based on dynamic input–output models as "analogous to the classical concept of the production function." See Nicholas Georgescu-Roegen, "The Aggregate Linear Production Function and Its Applications to von Neumann's Economic Model," in *Activity Analysis of Production and Allocation: Proceedings of a Conference*, edited by Tjalling C. Koopmans (New York: John Wiley & Sons, 1951), 98–116, 99.

109 All: Wassily Leontief to Robert Solow, October 29, 1952, Solow papers, box 57, file L: 2 of 2. The suggestion built on earlier exchanges and intended to reduce Solow's formulation to theorems of macroeconomic stability as developed by Georgescu-Roegen or Herbert Simon and David Hawkins. Solow thought the suggestion was ill-founded. On his work on stability, see Chapter 4. For a discussion of difference vs. differential equations in dynamic economics by Leontief, see Leontief et al., *Studies in the Structure of the American Economy*, 82–3.

110 Leontief et al., *Studies in the Structure of the American Economy*, 54–5.

111 Robert Solow to Wassily Leontief, November 6, 1952, Solow papers, box 57, file L: 2 of 2.

112 Robert Solow to Wassily Leontief, November 12, 1952, Solow papers, box 57, file L: 2 of 2.

113 Leontief et al., *Studies in the Structure of the American Economy*, 62.

114 Robert Solow to Wassily Leontief, January 27, 1954, Solow papers, box 57, file L: 2 of 2.

115 On econometrics at the Cowles Commission and Solow's growth model, see Chapter 2. On the heterogenous approaches to statistical inference in the twentieth century, see Biddle and Boumans, *Exploring the History of Statistical Inference in Economics*.

4

Growth in Miniature

In January 1954, the journalist and writer Godfrey Blunden sent a letter to a member of the department of political science at the Massachusetts Institute of Technology (MIT). He asked for help with a novel he planned to write "about some New York and Connecticut people, among them a mathematician." The idea was that "in a highly mechanised society the 'pure' mathematician is pretty much under pressure from the physicists, economists and statisticians to produce new theorems which may be of practical use in the applied fields." Hinting at the Manhattan project and the alluring opportunities of the new IBM calculators, Blunden wondered how mathematical economics could keep up: "I am thinking of a theorem, or a calculus, as fundamental to the analysis of our social economy as the Archimedean geometry was to the great builders, the infinitesimal calculus to the age of motion, the theory of relativity to the atomic physicists."[1] During the Second World War, mathematical methods had acquired enormous prestige when applied to national defense decision-making and military strategy. Against this background, the writer imagined his protagonist to be a mathematics whiz kid who developed a heroic scientific formula solving all kinds of social and economic problems. Indeed, an interdisciplinary community of decision-makers and social scientists at the time pushed the idea that the optimizing algorithms afforded rational decision-making more generally. When Blunden wrote the letter, these mathematical techniques were just about to turn into particular models in rational choice theory, utility theory, and systems analysis. Not least through the work of incubators such as the RAND Corporation and other research institutions financed by the Air Force, their spread brought about a shared, new meaning of rationality. Historians of science have coined the term "Cold War Rationality" not least to describe the profound change in character of social scientific knowledge that came with it in the second half of the twentieth century.[2]

Blunden's inquiry, however, did not find its way to a Thomas Schelling, Oskar Morgenstern, Herbert Simon, or any of the later Cold War "action intellectuals."[3] Instead, the letter was forwarded to Robert Solow, a recent hire at the Department of Economics and Social Science. Quite contrary to Blunden's plans for his novel, Solow was not an afficionado of pure mathematics. "It seems unlikely," he countered the writer's vision, "that any purely mathematical discovery would set economics on its ear." While it was indeed "very convenient ... to describe and formulate complicated economic systems in mathematical terms," the real difficulty of economic research was neither any gaps in mathematical knowledge nor any lack of large-scale computing machinery. "The bottleneck is that the functions and relationships that make up a theoretical model have to be given some empirical form and content."[4] Solow did not further specify what he meant by "empirical form and content." While the omission might have been accidental, it was symptomatic of the vagueness of what kind of epistemic practice mathematical modeling was in the mid-1950s. Apparently, for practitioners themselves, mathematical models had to be juxtaposed with a highly formalist economics such as general equilibrium theory and game theory, which rested on axiomatic systems of propositions and proofs.[5] But how exactly models related to a nonmathematical, "empirical," realm was less straightforward. Two years after the exchange with Blunden, Solow published his neoclassical growth model with its smooth equilibrium world of perfect competition and perfect foresight.[6] This chapter situates the making of the model within various branches of mathematical reasoning that took hold in the postwar era. I will argue that the small-scale artifact worked as a "miniature" – not of the world but of other models – and highlight how it accorded with a specific way of giving "economic" meaning to mathematical forms.

The story takes off where Chapter 3 ended, with the linear programming techniques presented to economists at the Conference on Activity Analysis in 1949. After the war, economists used the tools of mathematical programming to restructure what they saw as conventional theory. This not only changed their research styles but also the very problems they dealt with. Solow picked up on the central research object of the conference – the economy as a system of simultaneous equations – and started to investigate its dynamics. Model construction rarely equals a deliberate process of carefully picking components from a wide variety of different materials. After all, "science is often about constructing doable problems and taking the material at hand," according to a central argument of science studies.[7] Sometimes, new models just happen. They might be thought to be practical for a specific purpose and then surprisingly turn out to be useful for different endeavors. In the case of Solow's model, it came about as a more or less incidental side product of teaching or, at least, it was plausible to introduce it as such. Solow tried to make dynamic multi-good models as presented at the conference intelligible to MIT's students. In a paper, he mentioned that the job turned out to be tougher than expected, which prompted him to further simplify the model, to make a "desperate step to a one-commodity economy."[8] Doing so, he used a mathematical formalism that not only fitted the setting of the class but also conformed to an approach with which a larger part of economists were already familiar. Historians have emphasized the importance of the Conference on Activity Analysis as the site where a new identity for mathematical economists emerged, which essentially hinged on the epistemic virtue of axiomatic rigor.[9] The value of rigorous and elegant mathematical forms will also play its due role in the story that follows here. However, despite developing in close proximity (regarding the sites, people, and technical frameworks), the specific epistemologies and practices of mathematical economics were more fragmented than it is tempting to assume.

The following pages narrate the coming-into-being of Solow's model in a most local way. This brings about the entrance of Solow, not only as the narrator figure in the "Contribution" and occasional commentator as in the previous chapters but as the historical actor who constructed the version of the neoclassical growth model that is prominent until today. That he was able to do so depended on a variety of circumstances making him, to use the words of Ludwik Fleck, the "personified intersection of various thought collectives as well as of various lines of development of ideas and as a personal center of new ideas."[10] Indeed familiar with highly formalized approaches of mathematical economics, he nevertheless adhered to linear programming as a "useful theoretical tool."[11] The attitude is illustrated in a textbook on linear programming published together with Paul Samuelson and Robert Dorfman in 1958.[12] The textbook avoided higher mathematics and refrained from the mathematical complexities present at the Conference on Activity Analysis. Linear programming was presented as a simpler technique than general equilibrium analysis to model the economy as a whole. The construction of an equilibrium model served the purpose of raising questions such as "What would happen to the price of commodity *A* if the supply of factor *T* shifts to the right?" While general equilibrium theory could only reply "That depends," linear programming models, they argued, could give definite answers.[13] The assumption of an equilibrium (and all the exclusions that came with it) appeared as a practical necessity that guaranteed the system-character of economic knowledge and thus its ability to raise clear-cut questions and provide clear-cut answers.

By localizing the model's construction I spotlight one of its situated meanings, namely that of a "miniature." For one, Solow constructed the teaching model with a reduced number of equations as a "tool" to find out about the growth dynamics of linear programming models. These had provided the conception of "the economy" as a system of simultaneous equations. Making this economy grow, the miniature afforded small-scale manipulations to raise and answer what-happens-if questions with regard to the movements of variables and the directions of changes.[14] Moreover, it presented the minimum efficient scale that allowed not only for a workable growth model but also for providing it with "economic meaning."[15] In his reply to Blunden, Solow was realistic about the practical challenges of economic measurement, thanks perhaps to his knowledge of empirical practices in input–output analysis (Chapter 3):

It takes a year to get a year's figures on consumption and investment and inventories and so forth. And it takes many years' figures before any statistical sense can be made: the irregular, non-systematic element in economic life is far from trivial. And by the time the years have passed, the quantities and relations one is trying to estimate will probably have changed in some substantial but unknown way.[16]

In his miniature modeling project, he candidly followed the Conference of Activity Analysis in dispensing with empirical work. Providing "economic meaning" to mathematical forms meant interpreting them in terms of a neoclassical framework of fully competitive markets. Yet, as with the phenomenotechnical objects of Chapter 3, this economy was a perfectly efficient system of production; there was no choice, no individual action, no demand. The relation of the resulting model knowledge to the world of economic practices, the modeler emphasized, was akin to literary miniatures like fables or parables.

BECOMING A MATHEMATICAL ECONOMIST AROUND 1950

In the teaching scene mentioned by Solow, he taught dynamic programming and linear modeling techniques. These techniques were part of an applied mathematics that had been devised to deal with rather practical problems of wartime planning and was just about to diffuse into various fields in science, management, and planning.[17] Under the labels of operations research, control engineering, statistical decision theory, or information theory, the new modeling techniques reformulated research problems and nurtured new practices and self-understandings. In economics, the Conference on Activity Analysis, discussed in Chapter 3, was one of the crucial events that presented a new kind of mathematical economic theory. Linear programming started to trickle into the discipline of economics at a time when the mastery of mathematical tools was still uncommon. Solow actively promoted the new kind of mathematical economics. "Like all things good for body and soul, this book is going to hurt," he wrote in an early review of the conference proceedings. Himself just a newly hired professor, he addressed the fact that the majority of his colleagues did not have the necessary mathematical background to understand the kind of mathematics discussed. Yet he recommended that "everyone seriously interested in economic theory ought to keep a stiff upper lip and attempt to read it."[18] This was, at the beginning of the 1950s, a case for linear programming to be one of the waves of the future as much as it was a case for a serious engagement with mathematical techniques more generally.

Solow's plea was typical of the midcentury mathematical social sciences in the United States. "Even with the greater interest in mathematics of today," the editor of the *Review of Economics and Statistics* observed, "it is going to be a long time before one half of the economists are competent to understand the economics published in (say) *Econometrica*."[19] It was a small but zealous group of mathematical economists who pushed for the use of mathematics in the realm of economic theory. In the spirit of the technical interdisciplinarity of the postwar years, they were, at least on paper, involved with other mathematical social scientists.[20] Books such as *Mathematical Thinking in the Social Sciences*, published by the sociologist Paul Lazarsfeld in 1954, or *Rudimentary Mathematics for Economists and Statisticians* by mathematician and statistician William L. Crum and the mathematics-enthusiast Joseph A. Schumpeter sought to popularize mathematical reasoning across the social sciences. The endeavor was not only to reform graduate students' curricula but to promote mathematical training more generally and to swap tools across the individual disciplines.[21]

A subtext that frequently accompanied mathematization was the separation between the few who mastered the mathematical tools and those who could and should merely get the gist of mathematical economic argument. Even some advocates of the new methods could only be hopeful to understand the basics of mathematical economic theory: "The Cowles Commission materials, at least in abstract form, are too difficult for me at present," admitted cybernetician Gregory Bateson. "I look forward, therefore, to the appearance of the book in which I hope that there will be a sufficient admixture of words so that the weaker brethren may get a pretty clear idea of what the mathematics is about."[22] General equilibrium analysis as developed at Cowles was seen as top-notch mathematical social science, which came with such masculine rhetoric of success and failure (Chapter 5). The broader community was not expected to get a grip on its topological arguments and fixed-point-theorems. Linear programming took its place as a simpler alternative that did not require outstanding mathematical proficiency and, moreover, was easier to combine with quantitative economic data (Chapter 3). Books and workshops introducing mathematical reasoning to social scientists typically contained an elaboration of the problems, techniques, and applications of linear programming. As the reviewer of the proceedings of the Conference on Activity Analysis, Solow took a clear and self-confident stance that economists should adapt the technique. He did so against the background of training in a variety of approaches to economics and the social sciences more generally.

Solow was part of a transitional generation of economists who gained experience with various traditions of economic analysis before embracing and further elaborating the technical mathematical toolkit that would later become the core of economics education and practice. Several economists had contributed to remaking the discipline through their wartime work while serving as mathematicians, statisticians, or economists, applying mathematical methods to national defense decision-making. In contrast to what has been called "action" or "defense" intellectuals, who contributed to the war effort from offices and laboratories, Solow enlisted as a soldier in the US Army at the end of 1942.[23] He adjourned his BA studies in the interdisciplinary social science program at Harvard College. The program had introduced him to the major streams of social science that just started to develop its behavioralist, structural-functionalist foundations. Among his professors had been the sociologist Talcott Parsons and the social anthropologist Clyde Kluckhohn, both of whom became central figures in the postwar project of creating a cross-disciplinary social science with the overall goal of managing society in order to maintain social equilibrium.[24] Concurrently, Solow learned German, enabling him to study the German economics literature that, in the 1930s, played an important role in theorizing and measuring production. And he had started to read

European social science at a time when only a few American scholars were aware of works like *Die Arbeitslosen von Marienthal* by Marie Jahoda, Paul Lazarsfeld, and Hans Zeisel.[25] After returning from the Second World War, he enrolled together with a large number of veterans who received public funding for tuition and living expenses under the social policy of the G. I. Bill (the Servicemen's Readjustment Act).[26] In the meantime, Harvard's curriculum had been restructured toward a "general education" and increased cross-disciplinary exchange.[27]

Solow completed all of his higher education at Harvard, where studies in economics contained "a substantial dose of mathematics" but it was still "impossible to obtain anything beyond an elementary education in mathematical statistics."[28] During his studies, the teaching of economics was still rather broad, with no particular focus on any school of thought. It cut across ideas, theories, and analyses of American institutionalism, neoclassical economic theory, Marxist economics, the history of economic doctrines, as well as Keynesian economic theory.[29] While economics students were encouraged to read mathematical economics, it was not obligatory to take classes that imparted mathematical skills. The *Economics 103a* syllabus of Joseph Schumpeter, who covered several of the classes in Solow's curriculum and would subsequently become his undergraduate supervisor, illustrates the modest extent to which mathematical economics was taught at the time. Schumpeter "expected all members of this course to be, or to make themselves, familiar with [the] classics," a selection of European, mostly British, economic theory from the 1920s and 1930s that had used mathematics in a rather limited way.[30] It became common for US economists to recall the times this canon was formed as the most important period in the history of economics, the "years of high theory."[31] Simultaneously, they used these works as a contrasting foil from which their own mathematical formulations departed with regard to their clearer structure, logical consistency, and mathematical rigor. This was exactly the fate that met "Harrod" in Chapter 1: In the postwar era, he figured as the *grand seigneur* of growth theory while, at the same time, his work was condemned for being nebulously unclear and in need of formalization.

Not surprising for an elementary undergraduate class, books that required knowledge beyond simple algebra were recommended but not obligatory.[32] Learning how to construct and manipulate a mathematical model was certainly not part of Schumpeter's course. The major focus was on economic interpretation and discussion of mathematical theory, not on the mathematics itself, as illustrated by a problem set in the final exam of one of the follow-up courses:

"What is meant by Mixed Strategy (of duopolists) in Morgenstern and Neumann's argument and what is the advantage of introducing this concept?" ... Assume an otherwise stationary state of society, in which, however, population increases slowly. Will this interfere with the stability of the process? ... Explain and criticize.[33]

Being introduced to highbrow mathematical economic theory, students were not asked to demonstrate the paper's proofs but to explain the logics of the mathematical system. Courses like this were intended to train students in "the art of conceptualizing salient features of the economic process" – the salient features being specific mathematical characteristics ascribed to economic phenomena. *Economics 203a*, for instance, included "fundamental notions, especially determinateness and stability" and "the general dynamics of economic aggregates."[34] As a young academic, Solow would later embark on this field of economic inquiry.

While some of the essential lectures and seminars explicitly excluded the available research literature that made heavier use of mathematics, there were also more technical courses that Harvard students could take. "Technical" here referred not only to a larger amount of mathematical forms of reasoning but more specifically to the new techniques of mathematical programming and input–output modeling. These courses were taught, for instance, by Richard Goodwin, mathematician, economist, and self-acclaimed "lifelong but wayward" Marxist or by Solow's first dissertation adviser, Leontief.[35] Yet another form of technical engagement with economic analysis at the time came from teachers who had switched from engineering or science to economics in the aftermath of the Great Depression. Committed to the aim of preventing a further economic crisis and improving material living conditions through economic planning, these engineer-economists imported techniques to economics that they had learned and developed in their previous studies. An example is Solow's second dissertation adviser, former electrical engineer Guy H. Orcutt, who had constructed an early version of the regression analyzer, an electromechanical analogue computer that could deal with several differential equations at the same time and thereby laid the foundation for what he called "microsimulation."[36] Like Leontief, Orcutt dealt with detailed empirical schemes and assumed a critical position to what was the dominant approach to econometrics, the Cowles Commissions' focus on simultaneous equation modeling and on validating "theory" with aggregative data by way of ever more sophisticated statistical methodologies. Solow earned his BA in economics in 1947 and, having become acquainted with a large part of contemporary economics, subsequently enrolled in MA and PhD studies.

When the Conference on Activity Analysis took place, Solow was a PhD student and spent the academic year 1949–50 at Columbia University following his affinities for the more mathematical kinds of economic analysis. At Harvard, apart from Frederick Mosteller at the Department of Social Relations, the budding PhD student had not found the necessary background for his dissertation project. To improve his knowledge on probability models, stochastic processes, and statistical inference, Solow had applied for and was granted one of the competitive Social Science Research Council Pre-Doctoral Fellowships to study with the Statistical Research Group at Columbia.[37] His dissertation, "On the Dynamics of the Income Distribution," made ample use of stochastic techniques, which came with a specific, at the time still rather unconventional way of seeing economic phenomena. The thesis studied the size distribution of personal incomes using Markov processes, a stochastic tool to model the probabilities of future events, which was hardly used by economists. Accordingly, Solow opened his study by clarifying the purpose of mathematical-statistical analysis. True to the new social sciences, which distanced their endeavor from what they saw as merely observing and describing, the dissertation aimed at "explanation."[38] By this, he meant that the aim of the study was precisely *not* about trying to explain how and why incomes were distributed in a specific way among people. Such an inquiry, he argued, required the expertise of other professions – doctors, lawyers, psychologists, and sociologists. His view of the purpose and goodness of explanation related not to the income of individuals, which was simply "too fractious a thing to be studied." Instead, it was the purpose of economic *science* to investigate the "incomes of many individuals," which "behave collectively in a much more orderly manner."[39] The reference to the law of large numbers opened an investigation of the statistical properties of the generation, development, and stability of the frequency distributions of incomes.

The use of stochastic processes links Solow's dissertation with the broader history of structuralist reasoning and information theory. His work fit the larger midcentury movement to depict all kinds of things in terms of a mathematical system and to derive its temporal development from its structural characteristics. The thesis modeled the dynamics of income distribution in a way that its future size and growth was determined by the structure of a matrix of interdependent relationships. This meant that, in order to estimate the probability of future scenarios, only the last system state, given by the matrix, counted. Each event only depended on one or several preceding events; prior events were forever suspended and without repercussions.[40] Solow's notion of what made a proper explanation related to Markov chains, which came from a kind of mathematics that was committed to propositions and proofs. They were named after the Russian mathematician Andrey Markov who, in 1913, had developed his theory of probabilistic chains by investigating the alternation of vowels and consonants in Pushkin's novel Eugene Onegin.[41] While Markov adhered to nineteenth-century ways of doing pure mathematics, Markov chains achieved relevance through a variety of applications in fields stretching from linguistics, genetics, psychology, and psychoanalysis to fine arts.[42] Eventually, they became standard formulae used to problematize different phenomena in terms of a series of signs, communication systems whose probabilistic characteristics could be laid bare. Just like the simplex algorithm at the center of the Conference on Activity Analysis, this kind of work was about optimization according to technical criteria, about finding heuristic simplifications of calculation procedures. In 1950, when Solow started to work at MIT, he was already steeped in a line of reasoning that used mathematical forms from other fields as tools to design "economic" systems.[43] The goal was to find the most efficient formulation of mathematical problems without considering their semantics, their specific meaning in scientific fields. In contrast to purely mathematical endeavors, however, the research Solow embarked on was also guided by the concern to attach economic meaning to the newly imported mathematical forms.

INTUITIVE MATHEMATICS

Notions in the history of science such as "the age of system" emphasize the common features of thinking in terms of systems from information theory to systems theory to cybernetics.[44] Yet there were decisive differences in the kinds of mathematics used, in the way mathematics was used, and in the meaning attached to mathematical forms. In this regard, MIT took a specific place in the landscape of postwar economics that linked the usability of mathematical forms to their practicality for interventionist questions. Indeed, the Department of Economics and Social Science at MIT was a rising center for mathematical economics. Paul Samuelson had started to build a community of economists who were either mathematically-inclined, or, at any rate, not dismissive of mathematical analysis. That the department was able to attract strong economists was in part a consequence of the Institute's relative openness to hiring Jewish faculty compared to other universities, especially the Ivy League, where anti-Semitism was still strong.[45] Also in Solow's case, "no effective finger was lifted on his behalf" at Harvard.[46] MIT was not yet a particularly prestigious place in economics but, as a result of its involvement in national defense during the Second World War, it was a well-funded engineering school that housed several "big science" national research laboratories.[47] "For someone committed to the idea that economics was a science, it was a natural place to be," Roger Backhouse has noted in his biography of Samuelson.[48]

When Solow started to work at MIT, he entered a specific amalgam of social sciences, engineering, and military research, which enabled him to work with particular mathematical forms and to use them in a specific way. He moved into an office adjoining Samuelson's and the statistician Harold Freeman's and began to collaborate with the former on optimization in linear modeling and share teaching statistics with the latter.[49] In 1951, Samuelson introduced him to Charles J. Hitch, head of RAND's Economics Division in Santa Monica and one of the central Cold War defense intellectuals. Hitch (who later formulated the strategy of mutually assured destruction together with Robert McNamara) spurred Solow to read the RAND report "A Study of Project SCOOP Linear Programming" and invited him to spend some time in Santa Monica to work on "problems connected with dynamics of input/output models."[50] These problems preoccupied Solow's research in the years to come: Linear and dynamic programming techniques applied to the economy as a whole composed of different sectors, in particular what he called "optimal capital programming over time."[51] His research was co-funded by extra-university institutions like RAND and the Air Force from the outset – as was the case for many researchers who were simultaneously employed by national laboratories (largely engaged in national defense research) while obtaining NSF funding for their university departments.[52]

Solow's research in the early 1950s unfolded amidst broader concern with the stability of dynamic systems. This brought him into contact with a number of concepts circulating between control engineering, applied mathematics, and the social sciences.[53] While MIT was among the main institutions of information theory in the immediate postwar period, there was apparently no serious, if any, engagement between economists and cyberneticians such as Norbert Wiener. In general, members of the Department of Economics and Social Science worked in physical proximity to scientists and engineers, but contacts seem to have been rather loose and apparently did not exceed rather casual encounters.[54] They prepared, for instance, a series of reviews of current economic literature affecting engineering for the journal *Mechanical Engineering* at the request of the

Management Division of The American Society of Mechanical Engineers.[55] Other exchanges with colleagues in the engineering departments included Solow coming across the work of an electrical engineer who used linear graphs as flow diagrams to study simple networks – a technique that Solow carried over to inter-sector trading systems and which he sought to use as "a good expository device for reasonably small systems."[56] He was equally excited about an engineering thesis on "simplest feedback mechanisms" and "circuit theory," which "inevitably suggest [ed]" a series of analogies across fields of economic research.[57] These were not radically new associations. Solow, as did many other mathematical modelers, recycled mathematical forms that he encountered beyond the boundaries of his field for thinking about disciplinary issues. In the first place, his goal was to address structural similarities *within* economic theory. In one of his first papers, "A Note on Dynamic Multipliers," for instance, Solow harked back to an article on integral equations in the theory of electrons from the beginning of the century in order to demonstrate formal analogies between input–output models and what has been called "multiplier theory." In this way, he brought different economic problems into the same mathematical form in order to investigate their dynamic properties without having to go into the details of the individual fields.[58]

Solow's work, from which he developed his growth model, was part of a vogue of formalization that was just about to stabilize a specific notion of "dynamic" in a structuralist vein. In the very paper in which he stated a formal analogy between input–output and multiplier theory, he argued that the stability of the dynamic system depended on the *pattern* of time lags and thus on its *structural* characteristics.[59] This definition of dynamic stability decisively built on a definition of static stability that his friend, mentor, and intellectual collaborator Samuelson had presented some years earlier in 1947. Samuelson's *Foundations of Economic Analysis* was one of the first books in economics to place models at the center of both economic theory and empirical work.[60] Though he had done wartime work on ballistics at MIT's Radiation Laboratory, the book's roots went back to the intellectual background of 1930s Harvard. It related to the older mathematics of thermodynamic equilibrium and struck a chord with the evolving community of mathematical social scientists.[61] Samuelson's modeling built on the differential calculus (and its notion of continuity), mathematics that had been used in economics for some time, yet paid attention to discrete cases (finite changes, time-series, and statistical concepts) where the calculus was not applicable. Already in 1946, the

PhD student Solow inquired from across town whether "Professor Samuelson" would send him reprints of two of his papers on the stability of equilibrium.[62] In what followed, Solow participated in Samuelson's larger project to ground economics on what he saw as a modern and scientific epistemic basis.

The endeavor to turn economics into a "science" came with specific epistemic ideals and scientific *personae*, which will come to the fore in Chapter 5. Here, it is about what the relevant economists meant when they talked about making economics a science and how the resultant procedures shaped Solow's very research object. For one, Samuelson's *Foundations* alluded to shared analytical techniques in all fields and a common mathematical structure of scientific problems.[63] The *Foundations'* main point of reference was a mathematical concept from classical thermodynamics, the Le Chatelier principle formulated in 1884, that had already undergone a zigzagging history between different fields of scientific knowledge, accounting, and industrial organization.[64] Initially, the principle was a qualitative theorem in an experimental context that described a static notion of equilibrium as a balance of forces. It then turned into a general principle stating that if a system in equilibrium was exposed to changes (in pressure, temperature, or volume), then the system would readjust to counteract the disturbance and thereby establish a new equilibrium state. What constituted an *economic* equilibrium in this sense? Based on the work of physicist-mathematician E. B. Wilson, the *Foundations'* crucial assumption was that economic agents (consumers and firms) maximized their utility and profit, respectively.[65] Given departures from the equilibrium state *ceteris paribus* (when nothing else changed), a new equilibrium state could be determined. Leaving aside any notions of randomness or probabilistic limit theorems, time was reduced to comparative statics, comparing one snapshot of an equilibrium to another and disregarding what happened between the two equilibria. As in the case of Markov chains, these processes were decoupled from history: The values of a system's variables only depended on the system's relevant physical state, "independently of the particular path that led the system to its present state."[66]

Adopting Samuelson's definition of stability, Solow's dynamic equilibrium remained within the comfortable confines of comparative statics, skirting all kinds of dynamic problems. The practice of modeling consisted of both "giving form to ideas and making them formally rule-bound," as Mary Morgan has delineated.[67] Once a mathematical form is considered practical for the problem at hand, its rules determine what can be done with the model, opening up some lines of inquiry and closing off others. Solow's dynamic equilibrium, for instance, disallowed examination of how the system achieved its structure or how it interacted with its environment. Its "dynamics" consisted of a long-run equilibrium and disregarded short-run fluctuations of a business cycle, which had been at the center of economic studies of dynamics in previous decades. Once this dynamic research object was established, Solow delved deeper into the analysis of its mathematical structures. He turned his concept of dynamic stability into a topological problem, following the problematizations at the Conference on Activity Analysis (Chapter 3).[68] The underlying rationale was that the growth properties of a dynamic system could be derived from its topological structure. This meant that the way coefficients were connected was more important than their individual values.[69] A theorem named after the nineteenth-century mathematician Ferdinand G. Frobenius provided a complete mathematical foundation that afforded the application of Markov chains, with which Solow had worked in his dissertation. At the time, such a procedure was quite original, and still a few years later Solow bragged in a letter to a colleague that the related mathematical concepts were "first applied to Leontief models by little old me."[70]

Solow's concept of dynamic stability fulfilled both functional and aesthetic requirements of a new formal economics. It was based on an axiomatic system of propositions and proofs, and it was considered more elegant than existing approaches as it applied the more efficient algebra to solve a mathematical problem.[71] In contrast to the main lines of highly formalized economics, however, Solow placed a premium on the economic meaning of the mathematical system. The difference is illustrated in the correspondence between Solow and his mathematician colleagues Gerard Debreu and Israel N. Herstein. Right after the publication of Solow's article, Herstein, at the time Assistant Professor in Mathematics and Economics at the University of Chicago, suggested a yet "simpler, more elegant" way of proving one of Solow's lemmas.[72] Solow appreciated the reduced mathematical formulation and thanked him enthusiastically, alluding to the epistemic virtue of Ockham's razor, reducing complexity and constructing parsimonious models ("a tremendous improvement over my laborious method. Thanks for showing it to me").[73] But he did not approve of the detachedness that came with the work of his more formally inclined colleagues. In the same correspondence, he took issue with Debreu's work on formulating an intertemporal general equilibrium, which would later become formative for postwar American general equilibrium theory.[74] "For a man whose mathematics is as primitive as mine, this is not easy going ... I was also disturbed by the artificiality of the game-construction." Solow's playful humility aside, his major concern was just not the detached construction of mathematical systems. He juxtaposed Debreu's formal virtuosity with his own endeavor to make economic sense of mathematical forms, which he also broached in his correspondence with Blunden quoted at the outset of this chapter: "Lately I have been doing some work on the dynamical input–output system ... At the moment I am stuck; but the difficulty is economic rather than mathematical."[75]

What Solow understood as the "economic meaning" of mathematical forms is probably underwhelming for noneconomists: It simply meant integrating a neoclassical view of "prices" and "interest rates" into the model. And yet, this move was decisive in later making the growth model plausible as some kind of miniature and denoting it a "model." When Solow strained to characterize the dynamics of the systems of activity analysis in an "economically meaningful way," he was describing them as systems of competitive markets.[76] Here, "economic" and "neoclassical," as a view of the economy in terms of fully competitive markets, appeared as synonymous terms – so much so that it made sense to Solow to speak of his "economic intuition," or, retroactively, "in terms of the inherited instincts of economists."[77] But that did not mean that the market mechanisms (the price dynamics) were written out in full. Just as the economy in Samuelson's *Foundations*, Solow's system of equations did not demonstrate any relation between the equilibrium of consumers and firms (building on maximization techniques) and the equilibrium of the economy as a whole (which was kept in equilibrium through external constraints).[78] This absence accounted for much of the openness of Solow's model that invited different interpretations and reformulations, as I will trace in the Epilogue. It also points to the distance between the economists' mathematical models and the specific meanings their forms had in their previous research contexts.

In their transfer of mathematical forms from the sciences, Samuelson and Solow treated them as convenient tools, stripping them of all semantic analogies. As in the case of the Le Chatelier principle in *Foundations*, neither its chemical or physical meaning nor its initial experimental context played any role.[79] Thermodynamic systems were in a state of stable equilibrium because of the relations between their component parts. Applied to economics, the mathematical form was imported as an instrument and not taken seriously as a theoretical concept; the book included no discussion of thermodynamics or its uses in other scientific fields.[80] Whatever epistemological conundrums carried by mathematical forms did not matter to economic modelers as long as they fulfilled their very specific purposes in the construction of a new mathematical artifact. Much later, Solow was very frank about his attitude toward mathematical forms: "It will occasionally turn out that some piece of economics is mathematically identical to some piece of utterly unrelated physics. (This has actually happened to me, although I know absolutely nothing about physics.) I think this has no methodological significance but arises merely because everyone playing this sort of game tends to follow the line of least mathematical resistance."[81] This specific use of mathematics also characterized Solow and Samuelson's collaborative modeling of economic growth. The growing economy they constructed was the one later miniaturized by Solow.

MATHEMATICAL FORMS TO MAKE THE ECONOMY GROW

In early 1950s political discourse, steeped in Cold War anxieties, achieving and maintaining "balanced growth" was widely seen as the dominant task of economic policy. As delineated in Chapter 2, policy discussion presented balanced growth not simply as a means to prevent another great depression and to ameliorate the ups and downs of the business cycle. It carried the great promise of lifting society out of poverty – domestically as well as internationally. However, what precisely such growth involved was more ambiguous. In the language of the CEA reports to the president, balanced growth meant several things:

Business income and investment should be large enough to make full use of our technology, ... and our labor force, but not so large as to result in subsequent overproduction in relation to the absorptive capacity of markets. The income and spending of consumers should be sufficient to clear the markets of goods and to provide incentives for still more business enterprise, but not so large as to cause inflation. The expenditures of government should be large enough to provide those services which our resources permit, ... and which cannot so effectively be provided in any other way, but not so large as ... to dampen the incentives of free enterprise or alter the essential character of our economy.[82]

To make the economy grow was not only a goal per se, it also had the very specific purpose of bringing about arrangements that motivated businesses and consumers – the groups that figured as the main actors of this economy – *just to the right extent*. In the economics literature the concept unfolded further layers of meaning. In particular, when it came to "development," the common wisdom was that balanced growth was to keep emerging nations from converting into Communism in the context of a liberal trading order. The field of development economics was preoccupied with raging debates about the question of whether balanced or unbalanced growth were worth pursuing.[83] Here, the term "balanced growth" signified the joint actions of a system of sectors and industries creating its own demand. Disregarding country- or region-specific features of economic life, such a notion of development amounted to the vision that large-scale programs for industrialization could provide a "big push" of capital investment, which kick-started the entire economy into self-sustaining growth. Critics attacked the concept as an ideal of even development that bluntly ignored the complex and bewildering processes involved. "The temptation is strong," wrote Albert Hirschman, making a case for imbalances, "to leave all this backwardness alone and to dream of an entirely new type of economy where, in the words of the poet, '*tout est ordre et beauté*'."[84] All order and beauty – it was such a world of growth that mathematical economists were devising in the extreme.

Solow and Samuelson's collaborative work on growth built on one of the iconic models of formalist economics. The model had been used to introduce topological methods to economics at the Conference on Activity Analysis. It bore hardly any resemblance to the realms of policy-making. Published by the Germanophone mathematician John von Neumann in 1937 and translated into English in 1945, this growth model was not even developed as a contribution to economic theory. Rather, it was conceived as a mathematical framework for all kinds of systems, the economy being but one example. The concern was with mathematical conceptualization: Defining mathematical objects and then exploring their characteristics, notably via Brouwer's fixed-point-theorem. The article did, however, use familiar economic language ("goods," "factors of production," "processes of production") for "a typical equation system."[85] Though Neumann was solving a problem that originated in economics, his conclusions were mathematical. The article's formal style was so unfamiliar to economists at the time that the English translation was accompanied by a commentary. The economist's commentary explained what the model was about, provided it with economic meaning, and deplored the lack of illustrative example that would help in imagining the mathematical as an economic system.[86] The commentary was perplexed by the oddities that came from bluntly denoting mathematical variables with economic terms: "Wage costs are not considered as such, for labourers are not separately considered any more than are farm animals."[87] In Neumann's article, verbal analysis played no essential role other than as part of the mathematics.[88] In contrast, Solow and Samuelson set out to align its mathematical system with ideas familiar to economists. As Solow had done in his earlier modeling work outlined in the previous section, they sought to present the linear model of an expanding economy in "intuitive terms" and emphasized that it was in accord with "economic meaning."[89] This did not mean, however, that each mathematical term had to have economic meaning. Moreover, their approach came with a specific meaning of "economic."

The referents of the policy notion of "balanced growth" were essentially statistical objects such as the aggregated measure of the GDP. Balanced growth, for Solow and Samuelson, in contrast, did not relate to statistical entities but to propositions and proofs. Growth was described in terms of a stable equilibrium. Brouwer's theorem helped prove the existence of this kind of balanced growth. Straining to make the axiomatic system somehow economically meaningful, Solow and Samuelson denoted their research object an "economic sausage grinder": "We do not question what happens inside the economic sausage grinder; we simply observe that inputs flow into the economy and outputs appear."[90] They presented national production as a *black box* of flows of inputs and outputs. As in the linear models of the Conference on Activity Analysis, resources were allocated efficiently. Everything produced went into production in the next period. In contrast to the models so far, here Samuelson and Solow assumed inputs to be substituted continuously. The modelers had no interest in how the sausage was made; processes inside the grinder had no relevance for long-run development. This growing economy featured only changes in scale but not in composition; everything was assumed to grow at the same, balanced rate. Most aspects crucially related to growth processes, such as changes in institutions, population, or technology, figured merely as exogenous constraints to which the sausage grinder smoothly adjusted as a whole.

The interpretation of the sausage grinder in terms of an economic equilibrium was not straightforward – not even to other mathematical economists using linear programming techniques for economic analysis. Soon after the model's publication, Koopmans, director of the Cowles Commission, was puzzled by the supposedly economic meaning of the model. In a letter he asserted that he was impressed by their "skillful as well as economical [efficient]" way of using mathematics. He took issue, however, with the formulation of a sausage grinder that left no room for choices of economic agents (other than the proportions of inputs within the productive system) and certain principles according to which these choices were exercised.[91] In what seems to be a draft for a reply to Koopmans's criticism, Solow realized that their paper did not strike a chord with the mathematical economists at Cowles, even though they could easily understand their mathematics: "We did say that we were talking about a system consisting of a single production process; but we certainly did not warn the reader emphatically enough about what we were not doing."[92] What they were not doing was a lot. But the sausage grinder did provide an efficient model for a very specific purpose: To see how balance and stability of a growing productive system as a whole were mathematically possible.

The specific setup of this kind of balanced growth built on a longer history of describing growth processes in terms of topological properties in a variety of fields stretching from physics to chemistry to genetics and biology. Referring to articles on probability theory published in the *Annals of Mathematical Statistics*, Solow and Samuelson picked up on so-called renewal theory and branching processes, essentially special cases of Markov processes, which Solow had used in another context in his dissertation. The basic idea in that literature was to create a mathematical object, a "population," whose development was subject to the laws of chance. Such a population consisted of several members (whether neutrons, genes, animals, humans, microbes, or cosmic rays) who died and reproduced in a way that depended on their specific characteristics (age, energy, position, etc.).[93] More specifically, Solow and Samuelson used what was commonly termed the Lotka–Volterra equations to formulate particular laws of growth wholly derived from a population's structure and independent of both initial conditions and varying circumstances. As was the case for the Le Chatelier principle and Markov chains in the previous two sections, the modelers did not explain the formal analogy, elaborate on the meaning of these equations in other fields, or compare their vision of the growing economy with other phenomena.

Treating mathematical forms as practical devices differentiated Solow and Samuelson's modeling work from the universalist aspirations of companions such as Alfred Lotka, who had made Samuelson aware of population dynamics. The academic outsider, a statistician at the Metropolitan Life Insurance Company, was invested in thinking in terms of large numbers. He approached biological systems mathematically through the concepts of early twentieth-century energetics. Life, here, was defined as quantifiable energy exchanges. In that sense, all systems were living systems, and so, in some kind of energetic holism, the laws that applied to biological systems could equally apply to chemical aggregates as well as social and economic realms.[94] At the end of the 1930s, Marion Samuelson and her husband sought to solve a statistical problem by generalizing one of Lotka's functions. Drawing on electric circuit theory, they derived two theorems that would apply to the development of stocks of industrial equipment. They did not aim at a holistic theory, in which a few basic principles synthesized various disciplines. They were interested in business cycle theory and adapted Lotka's formalism accordingly. The contrast manifested in an exchange when Lotka, who was continuously involved in their work, took issue with the assumption that someone who died was immediately succeeded by a newborn baby. But the Samuelsons did not care about the development of human populations in this particular project; their assumption was specific to industrial production. When it came to capital investments, they thought that an exhausted capital good could indeed be immediately replaced with a new one.[95] More than a decade later, Solow and Samuelson referred the reader of their article on "balanced growth" to Lotka's *Théorie analytique des association biologiques* (1939). The book presented Lotka's "general demology" based on a thermodynamic vision of evolution as a physical law. While referring to the book with a wider outlook, the economic modelers used the Lotka–Volterra equations as a tool without baggage, a mathematical form that fit their specific modeling problem at hand.[96] They did not present any larger argument – neither about a unity of the sciences nor about a similarity of phenomena.

At the end of the nineteenth century, Alfred Marshall had famously suggested that economists should draw inspiration from biology. Ironically, as historian of economics Judy Klein has noted, twentieth-century economists thought it productive to make use of biometric tools rather than thinking in terms of organic growth and evolution, as Marshall had done.[97] The difference is illustrated in comparison to the work of Nicolas Georgescu-Roegen in the 1960s and 1970s. Georgescu-Roegen, encountered at the Conference of Activity Analysis in Chapter 3, built on Lotka's broader approach as he conceived of economic processes as intrinsically biological evolutionary processes. Accordingly, he thought to replace neoclassical production functions (like Solow's) that employed classical mechanics. His fund-flow model built on approaches in thermodynamics and evolutionary biology, taking into account qualitative and stochastic features because of what he argued in terms of an ontological similarity of the relevant phenomena.[98] In contrast, back in the 1950s, Solow and Samuelson extended, reworked, and combined mathematical forms from biology without discussing possible intersections and differences of the relevant phenomena. In this sense, the transfer of mathematical forms from the domain of biology by Solow and Samuelson was "limited."[99] Arguing for similarities in the mathematical structure might have freed the economists from a need to handle the metaphorical surplus that came with mathematical forms from other domains. Such surplus, however, contributed to the openness of models, which, in one way or another, led to a variety of uses, interpretations, and attempts of understanding both models and the practice of modeling (see Chapter 5).

Alongside the forms delineated, Solow and Samuelson built on population models, initially developed by biologists at the Bureau of Animal Population in Oxford. The so-called Leslie matrix showed the age structure of a population divided into different classes in terms of birth and survival rates (between age classes) just as the matrices in linear models showed the capital structure of an economy.[100] The underlying logic was that, once the stable distribution of capital (age distribution) had been achieved, the economy (population) underwent exponential growth, meaning it grew at a constant percentage. Irrespective of its initial size or distribution within, the object modeled tended to a steady-state growth rate. This portrayal of growth, parallel to Solow's previous topological treatment of dynamics, collapsed the future into the present and stripped production of historical time. As a phenomenotechnical instrument, this mathematical model presented a smoothly and continuously growing economy, which was the very object that Solow presented to his students.

MINIATURE MODELING

"In the course of simplifying this work for exposition to students I found that even when limited to two commodities the arithmetic rapidly became forbidding without matrix methods."[101] We return to the teaching scene that Solow recounted in "A Note on the Price Level and Interest Rate in a Growth Model." The article presented the basic formulation that would in 1956 become his neoclassical growth model.[102] In the first place, MIT had recruited Solow for instructing undergraduate engineering students. It was the primary task of the Department of Economics and Social Science to meet the increased demand for teaching social sciences to scientists and engineers.[103] Invoking the topos of engineers securing human progress, MIT argued that students ought to properly serve the needs of modern American democracy. To this end they were to complement their technical skillset by "devoting sufficient time to reflective thinking or to desirable social pursuits."[104] As part of the new curriculum in the social sciences, after English and modern history, engineering students were introduced to economics. Solow was assigned to teach statistics, probability, input–

output modeling, and econometrics. Classes were indeed predominantly taken by engineering students. And the curriculum for those who wanted to primarily study economics conformed with the requirements of an engineering school. It therefore contained a significant course load in science and engineering. Economics teachers could expect students to be adept in differential calculus, convex set theory, and basic statistics.[105] The matrix methods used in dynamic linear modeling, however, were too advanced, which is why Solow retreated to the simpler mathematics of a differential equation to get across the basic idea of dynamic economic systems. But even in this form, modeling two, not to mention several, goods was still too complicated. Perhaps somewhat out of desperation, Solow constructed a one-commodity economy.[106]

Irrespective of whether the teaching scene conformed with a real event or not, it demonstrated the standing of the new model *in relation* to the models with which Solow had been working in the preceding years. Its central feature was that it evolved from "the passage from a many-commodity to a one-commodity world."[107] Compared to the "economic sausage grinder" in the last section, the new model was a scaled-down version with a reduced number of equations. Due to its smaller scale, it figured as some kind of miniature model. The new mathematical economy produced only one good, but it *stood for* mathematical economies that produced many goods. Solow called its one good a "composite commodity," a bundle of goods whose relative prices did not vary and which could therefore be treated as one.[108] To assume one good only was not a big step: The sausage grinder, this smoothly working many-commodity system delineated in the previous section, already behaved as if it was one single production process. Speaking to the active potential of models, it essentially invited the reduction to a one-commodity economy. Carrying the traces of the linear modeling projects it emerged from, the miniature included neither a demand function nor individual action.

The miniature model served a specific purpose that legitimized its specific scaling. Its purpose was to devise the long-run equilibrium time paths of the general price level and interest rate for the dynamic many-commodity-models that preceded it.[109] For this endeavor it presented the smallest scale possible to feature a growth mechanism of the economy as a whole. It built on the demonstration at the Conference on Activity Analysis that the linear programming method for describing dynamics (finite differences with inequalities) was comparable to the mathematics that economists were used to applying (differential calculus with marginal conditions). For Solow, the miniature's major contribution was that it depicted a "more complete causal dynamics of the kind usual in business cycle theory." Whereas business cycle models portrayed short-run deviations from the long-run trend, the miniature presented the dynamics of that long-run trend, the balanced growth path. With the assumption of "perfect foresight" it remained within the confines of comparative statics. It established that the value of output in any period was – invested and reinvested – always enough to buy back current output. Or, in Solow's rather poetic wording, "the future is implicit in the present, a seed literally is its own future stream of net outputs of fruit, and must be worth the present value of its own future."[110] Future developments were accounted for in optimizing current production.

It is here in the cosmos of the miniaturized model that the connection between a material concept of capital and the marginalist concept of value, which would centrally characterize the 1956 model (as discussed in Chapter 1), became most obvious: A fraction of total output was consumed. What was not consumed was saved and invested. In this sense, capital was restraint from consumption and, as physical good, reused in production where it earned its marginal income. Since it entered the model in the form of one coefficient for the economy as a whole, the price level was "freed of all its allocative functions." There was no need for money in the short run, but in the "dynamics" of the long run the price level acted "as an intertemporal exchange ratio," measuring "the future value of present goods." In its long-run equilibrium, the performance of the economy was entirely given by the behavior of the interest rate that established equilibrium in the capital "market," balancing out savings and investment. The price level itself had "no functions to perform and hence stays where it is put."[111] Given that the miniature only featured one good, these price–interest dynamics could only be plugged in rather than actually modeled. But the plug-in provided the model with its neat appearance, which made it appropriate for telling clear-cut stories about neoclassical causalities of growth. With its help, "questions beginning 'What would happen if' would have exact answers."[112]

Solow's growth model published in 1956 essentially worked along the same lines as the miniature model. It showed a microcosmos of material production with marginalist values, in which time proceeded in terms of a differential equation. It also worked without actually integrating the price–interest dynamics. The difference was that now the miniature itself had become the working object. It turned from a tool (to investigate the price–interest dynamics in multi-sector models) into the object of inquiry (studied in terms of the properties of its equilibrium behavior): What would happen if some parameter was changed, an additional variable introduced, or relations between parameters modified?

The miniature's specific power derived from its ability to formulate existing model knowledge in a more intelligible way. Its reduced scale did not mean increased abstractness. After all, its algebraic form kept to a kind of mathematics to which engineering students and most economists at the time were accustomed. The resulting oddly simple cosmos spoke to existing economic theory. "I soon realised that what was left was nothing but the Harrod model thinly disguised."[113] The miniature allowed Solow to perceive a pattern that he recognized from the contemporary literature on growth. True to the structuralist perspective that pervaded economists' methodological comments in this chapter, Solow suggested that his model provided the perspective of a "man from Mars observing a Harrod economy in operation, [who was] ignorant of the social organisation underlying it."[114] Seeing in the miniaturized linear programming model the contours of "the Harrod model" implied a very specific reading of economic theory. For one, this view from above only saw mathematical forms and disregarded the texts accompanying them. Very much in line with the unification endeavors at the Conference on Activity Analysis, it turned disparate approaches into different cases of the same mathematical structure. Such a reading ignored, as Chapter 1 has pointed out, the fact that Harrod's work was directed at instability and crises rather than stability and growth. In any case, based on what he saw as a structural resemblance, Solow presented his new model as a link between existing economic theory and the new mathematical techniques.

Due to its reduced scale, the miniature exhibited a specific kind of *Anschaulichkeit* (visible clarity, concrete visuality), not only with regard to Solow's own framing of existing economic theory. Moreover, its "composite" variables resembled the newly acquired aggregate data on macroeconomic trends (Chapter 2). Calling on these empirical categories, the miniaturization made it possible to tell stories about growth that fit the contemporary discourse. In a sense, it provided the economic sausage grinder of previous models with empirical form and content, as Solow might have had it in his exchange with Blunden at the beginning of the chapter. *Anschaulichkeit* in this sense is an affordance, both a property of the model as well as an inclination of those who interact with it to see the mathematical system as a model for something else and not only for the models that preceded it.[115] It became common for neoclassical modelers to compare their small-scale models with literary miniatures, as Solow did on the very first page of his widely-read book, *Growth Theory*, published in 1970:

Please keep in mind that we are dealing with a drastically simplified story, a "parable," which my dictionary defines as "a fictitious narrative or allegory … by which moral or spiritual relations are typically set forth." If moral or spiritual relations, why not economic? You ask of a parable not if it is literally true, but if it is well told.[116]

Solow's model provided the cosmos for a well-told story, meaning that it provided a neatly organized world that allowed for a well-ordered and intelligible narrative.[117] The miniature about economic growth fit existing time-series data of GNP growth, harmonized with the contemporary impression that the industrialized economies were on a path to ever more affluence, and picked up on conventional wisdom about growth in economic theory. As he did with regard to his model as a tool, Solow emphasized that "even a well-told parable" should only be used in relation "to the domain in which it is not actually misleading."[118] Critics, in contrast, warned about the capability of parables to be taken as "profound truths."[119]

TROUBLESOME TOOLS

In the eyes of economists sympathetic to the use of neoclassical models, the 1956 growth model was a useful means for specific purposes: A device for teaching, a conceptual gadget for framing "the problem of growth," an instrument for interpreting data sets, and a narrative device for telling plain stories about growth and its sources. Perceived as tools, such models figured as working systems, which in the first place needed to function and fulfil the relevant purposes. Only rarely were they explicitly framed as representations of some real-world phenomena. The papers mentioned in this chapter put everyday terms like "capital," "labor," or "industries" in quotes, emphasizing that these were technical concepts relating to the microcosmos of the model and not to some alleged real world. An equally distancing gesture were the quotes around "about," when Solow noted in 1952 that "theories … are 'about' different things."[120] More outspoken when it came to the one-good production function, he emphasized that it was not about "any observed or observable path."[121] Such a reserved attitude cohered with the line between the model and the world that Solow, Samuelson, and Dorfman drew in their linear programming textbook:

If there is anything clear about the real economic world, it is that it exists, it functions ... But to reason this way is to miss the point. In the first place, it is not so clear that the ever-changing, imperfect, oligopolistic world has a statically timeless, frictionless, perfectly competitive equilibrium. In the second place, we can't blithely attribute properties of the real world to an abstract model. It is the *model* we are analyzing, not the world.[122]

These modelers were confidently aware of the difference between their models and the phenomena they wanted to think about. Still, there were apparently moments in their modeling work that made them see more in their artifacts than just mathematical systems. From this perspective, economic modelers' warnings about taking the model at face value were a corollary of their research work that, temporarily at least, did rely on the deceptive representative quality of equilibrium models.[123] This was particularly the case for a practice of modeling that came from the coalescence of the tools of governance with economic theory. Even a small-scale model suggested its use and implementation not only in economic theory but also in policy-making.

Chapter 5 asks how this ambiguity and suggestive power of models gave rise to discord and confusion about their intellectual worth, political purposes, and practical exploits. What made one model acceptable and another one not? What made a model a good model? These were highly contested questions, not only between those who pushed mathematical modeling as the proper way of doing economics and those who rejected it, but also among modelers themselves. Troublesome was not only the indeterminacy that models created when it came to relating their clean-cut appearance to questions of economic policy. Troublesome were also the difficulties of making a clean sweep in methodological debate. Economists were not alone in their struggle to get on top of the mushrooming multitude of models. In what Marx Wartofsky, in the introduction to this book, has denoted a "model muddle," a whole variety of scientific, technical, intellectual, and artistic fields created a vast number of accounts aimed at clarifying what models were all about.[124]

Notes

1 Godfrey Blunden to Harold Isaacs, January 10, 1954, Solow papers, box 53, file B: 7 of 7. See also Verena Halsmayer, "From Exploratory Modeling to Technical Expertise: Solow's Growth Model as a Multi-Purpose Design," in *MIT and the Transformation of American Economics* (supplement to *History of Political Economy* 46), edited by E. Roy Weintraub (Durham, NC: Duke University Press, 2014), 229–51, 229–30.

2 Once confined to the realms of engineering and the economy, the new rationality was meant to replace mindful deliberation, in particular to contain human

fallibility in the age of nuclear deadlock: Paul Erickson, Judy L. Klein, Lorraine Daston, Rebecca Lemov, Thomas Sturm, and Michael D. Gordin, *How Reason Almost Lost Its Mind: The Strange Career of Cold War Rationality* (Chicago: University of Chicago Press, 2013), 57–8.

3 Becoming popular in the mid-1960s, these labels referred to a "silent club" of illustrious social scientists who provided ideas and advice for governance, from foreign policy to defense to city planning. See Erickson et al., *How Reason Almost Lost its Mind*, 10–17; Daniel Bessner, *Democracy in Exile: Hans Speier and the Rise of the Defense Intellectual* (Ithaca: Cornell University Press, 2018).

4 All: Robert Solow to Godfrey Blunden, January 26, 1954, Solow papers, box 53, file B: 7 of 7.

5 "Axioms" were defined as mathematical statements that served as starting points from which other statements were logically derived. While late-nineteenth-century mathematics considered "rigor" and "axiomatization" antithetical, since only empirical research could be considered rigorous, in the second half of the twentieth century, rigor and axiomatization became virtually indistinguishable. On "rigor" as a historical concept, see Bruna Ingrao and Giorgio Israel, *The Invisible Hand: Economic Equilibrium in the History of Science* (Cambridge, MA: MIT Press, 1990); E. Roy Weintraub, *How Economics Became a Mathematical Science* (Durham, NC: Duke University Press, 2002).

6 Robert M. Solow, "A Contribution to the Theory of Economic Growth," *Quarterly Journal of Economics* 70, no. 1 (1956): 65–94.

7 The pointed formulation can be found in Amade M'charek, "Race, Time and Folded Objects: The HeLa Error," *Theory, Culture & Society* 31, no. 6 (2014): 29–56, 40. For a related view that emphasizes the role of selection in economic modeling, see Marcel Boumans, "Materials Selection in Economic Modeling," *Synthese* 201, no. 4 (2023): 125.

8 Robert M. Solow, "A Note on the Price Level and Interest Rate in a Growth Model," *Review of Economic Studies* 21, no. 1 (1953–54), 74–79, 75.

9 Till Düppe and E. Roy Weintraub have argued that the "conference defined, more than any other single event, the emergence of a new kind of economic theory." See Till Düppe and E. Roy Weintraub, "Siting the New Economic Science: The Cowles Commission's Activity Analysis Conference of June 1949," *Science in Context* 27, no. 3 (2014): 453–83, 455.

10 Ludwik Fleck, *Genesis and Development of a Scientific Fact* (Chicago: University of Chicago Press, 1979), 118.

11 Robert Dorfman, Paul Samuelson, and Robert Solow, *Linear Programming and Economic Analysis* (New York: McGraw-Hill, 1958), 346. In a similar vein, Solow mentioned in correspondence that he had been preoccupied with Wald's 1935 theorem on the existence of an equilibrium for a Walras–Cassel general equilibrium system. "My approach is much less general than what Ken Arrow and Gerard Debreu have been doing. I go back to Wald's specific problem and think I can solve it fairly simply using the duality theorem in linear programming," Robert Solow to Lawrence Klein, October 10, 1953, Solow papers, box 57, file K: 1 of 4.

12 Robert Dorfman was professor of political economy at Harvard and a former operations researcher in the US Air Force, who had studied at Columbia with the

above-mentioned mathematical statistician Hotelling. On the making of the textbook, see Roger E. Backhouse, "Linear Programming and Economic Analysis: The Collaboration between Samuelson, Dorfman and Solow, 1949–1958," September 1, 2012.

13 Dorfman et al., *Linear Programming and Economic Analysis*, 349.

14 In contrast to my narrative, Solow himself sometimes cast his model as a miniature of general equilibrium theory. The problem with Solow's self-description is that so-called Walrasian theory derived an overall equilibrium of the economy from the relations between rational economic agents. In contrast, Solow's model did not involve microlevel activities. Testifying to the ambiguities of mathematical models, several economists picked up on the linkage to general equilibrium models, as I will discuss in the Epilogue. Solow retrospectively regretted having made the link. See Robert M. Solow, "The State of Macroeconomics," *Journal of Economic Perspectives* 22, no. 1 (2008): 243–6, 244.

15 I owe the expression of "minimum efficient scale" to an exchange with Mary Morgan.

16 All: Robert Solow to Godfrey Blunden, January 26, 1954, Solow Papers, box 53, file B: 7 of 7.

17 See Chapter 3. For the development of linear programming and its early diffusion in economics, see Erickson et al., *How Reason Almost Lost Its Mind*, chapters 2 and 3.

18 Robert M. Solow, "Review Koopmans Activity Analysis of Production and Allocation," *American Economic Review* 42, no. 3 (1952): 424–9, 424.

19 Seymor Harris, "A Postscript of the Editor," *The Review of Economics and Statistics* 36, no. 4 (1954), 382–86, 383.

20 On mathematics as a new interdisciplinary language, see Roger E. Backhouse, "Economics," in *The History of the Social Sciences since 1945*, edited by Roger E. Backhouse and Philippe Fontaine (Cambridge: Cambridge University Press, 2010), 38–70; Joel Isaac, "Tool Shock: Technique and Epistemology in the Postwar Social Sciences," in *The Unsocial Social Science? Economics and Neighboring Disciplines since 1945* (supplement to *History of Political Economy* 42), edited by Roger E. Backhouse and Philippe Fontaine (Durham, NC: Duke University Press, 2010), 133–64. On the role of (federal) funding schemes in the reorganization of postwar social sciences, see Hunter Crowther-Heyck, "Patrons of the Revolution: Ideals and Institutions in Post-War Behavioral Science," *Isis* 97, no.3 (2006): 420–46.

21 Cf. Eric T. Hounshell, A Feel for the Data: Paul F. Lazarsfeld and the Columbia University Bureau of Applied Social Research (dissertation, UCLA Los Angeles, 2017), section 9.7.

22 Gregory Bateson to Jacob Marschak, January 8, 1947, Marschak Papers, box 97, folder No name, cited in Camila Orozco Espinel, "How Mathematical Economics Became (Simply) Economics: The Mathematical Training of Economists during the 1940s, 1950s and 1960s in the United States" (Center for the History of Political Economy at Duke University Working Paper Series, No. 2020-11, November 16, 2020), 19, available at https://papers.ssrn.com/sol3/papers.cfm?abstract_id= 3731733, last accessed April 29, 2024.

23 Retroactively, Solow stated that he went to war "simply because I wanted to fight Hitler," Richard Swedberg, *Economics and Sociology: Redefining Their Boundaries: Conversations with Economists and Sociologists* (New Jersey: Princeton University Press, 1990), 271. In the first years of his deployment, Solow served in North Africa and Sicily; from 1943 to the end of the war he served in Italy as a "private-tech. sgt." (Application for a NSF senior postdoctoral fellowship October 10, 1962, Solow papers, box 58, file N: 1 of 2.). Since he knew both Morse code (Harvard's psychology department had a contract with the Air Force) and German, he became part of the US Army Signal Corps from March 1943 onward and was honorably discharged in September 1945. See Solow's Personnel Security Questionnaire for Defense Industrial Security Clearance Office, which he had to fill out to work at the RAND Corporation, Solow papers, box 60, file Rand Corporation: 3 of 3.

24 On winning a book prize after getting top grades during his freshman year, Solow chose Parson's *Structure of Social Action*. He also took courses with George Homans in sociology, with Henry Murray in psychology, and with Carlton Coon in anthropology, see the interview in Swedberg, *Economics and Sociology*, 269.

25 See Robert M. Solow, "Unemployment as a Social Problem," In *Choice, Welfare, and Development. A Festschrift in Honour of Amartya K. Sen*, edited by K. P. Pattanaik Basu and K. Suzumura (Oxford: Clarendon Press, 1995), 313–22, 313–14.

26 The G. I. Bill was one of the most extensive social policy legislations in the second half of the twentieth century. It consumed 15 percent of the 1948 federal budget, which was more than the Marshall Plan. The bill was designed and implemented in a way that it benefitted mostly white middle-class men. See Kathleen J. Frydl, *The GI Bill* (New York: Cambridge University Press, 2009); Margot Canaday, "Building a Straight State: Sexuality and Social Citizenship under the 1944 G. I. Bill," *Journal of American History* 90, no. 3 (2003): 935–57.

27 The changes followed the baseline of suggestions in the so-called Red Book, a report commissioned in 1943 by Harvard's president James Bryan Conant. See Jamie Cohen-Cole, *The Open Mind: Cold War Politics and the Sciences of Human Nature* (Chicago: Chicago University Press, 2014), chapter 1.

28 Application for a NSF senior postdoctoral fellowship October 10, 1962, Solow papers, box 58, file N: 1 of 2.

29 Sometimes Harvard economics is described as the center of American Keynesianism. However, at the beginning of the 1940s, while some scholars among the younger staff were indeed Keynes enthusiasts, some among the senior staff, such as Harold H. Burbank, were critical and occasionally even hostile toward Keynesian theory. See Roger Backhouse, *Founder of Modern Economics: Paul A. Samuelson*, vol. 1: Becoming Samuelson (New York: Oxford University Press, 2017), part II. The textbooks Solow himself mentioned as having introduced him to the discipline were indeed Keynesian: The *Principles of Economics* by Frederic Garver and Alvin Hansen, one of the main figures bringing Keynes to the United States. Another textbook was the standard introduction to economics, *Modern Economic Society* by one of the most well-known contemporary economists

Sumner Slichter (Robert M. Solow, "How Did Economics Get That Way and What Way Did It Get," *Daedalus* 126 (2005): 87–100, 87–8).

30 The mentioned classics were Alfred Marshall's *Principles*, Knut Wicksell's *Lectures*, Edward H. Chamberlin's *Monopolistic Competition*, John M. Keynes's *General Theory*, and John R. Hicks' *Value and Capital* (Outline course Economics 103a, Fall Term of the academic year 1946–1947, Schumpeter papers, HUG (FP) – 4.62, box 7, file: Lecture Notes, Courtesy of the Harvard University Archives). I am grateful to Roger Backhouse for sharing this archival material.

31 On the structuring of autobiographical memories and its role in the collective imagination of the "years of high theory," see E. Roy Weintraub, "Autobiographical Memory and the Historiography of Economics," in *A Contemporary Historiography of Economics*, edited by Till Düppe and E. Roy Weintraub (London: Routledge, 2018), 9–21, 17–18.

32 Irving Fisher's *Theory of Interest*, Arthur C. Pigou's *Employment and Equilibrium*, Oskar Lange's *Price Flexibility and Employment*. As a last reading suggestion, Schumpeter mentioned the rather technical *General Equilibrium Theory* by Jacob L. Mosak but emphasized that the book was only recommended to students "in mathematical training." In a list of readings, papers that "required command of *advanced* mathematics" were specifically highlighted with an asterisk. Among them were two articles, to which Solow referred in his research a few years later: Metzler's "Stability of Multiple Markets" (1945) and Klein's "Macrodynamics and the Theory of Rational Behavior" (1946) (Outline course Economics 103a, Fall Term of the academic year 1946–1947, Schumpeter papers).

33 Economics 103b, Schumpeter papers, HUG (FP) – 4.62, box 7, file: Lecture Notes, Courtesy of the Harvard University Archives.

34 The reading assignments might represent Solow's knowledge of economic dynamics as a student, in particular Erik Lundberg's *Studies in the Theory of Economic Expansion*, and, again only for students with adequate mathematical knowledge, Samuelson's *Foundations* (Outline Economics 203a, fall term 1948–1949; Schumpeter papers, HUG (FP) – 4.62, box 7, file: Lecture Notes, Courtesy of the Harvard University Archives). Additional reading assignments were, among others, Samuelson "Dynamics, Statics, and the Stationary State" (1943), Tinbergen, "Suggestions on Quantitative Business Cycle Theory" (1935), and Modigliani "Liquidity Preferences, Interest, and Money" (1944).

35 Leontief also employed Solow as a part-time assistant at the Harvard Economic Research Project, one of the largest institutions for gathering social scientific measurements (Chapter 3). Goodwin worked on the interaction between long-run growth and business cycles; his work on the "matrix multiplier" was essential for Solow's early research.

36 Orcutt brought together Jan Tinbergen's modeling with designing an electric calculation machine. He saw his work as an alternative to the, in his view, methodologically weak approach of the Cowles Commission. See Chung-Tang Cheng, "Guy H. Orcutt's Engineering Microsimulation to Reengineer Society," in *Economics and Engineering: Institutions, Practices, and Cultures* (supplement to *History of Political Economy* 52), edited by Pedro Garcia Duarte and Yann Giraud (Durham: Duke University Press, 2020): 191–217.

37 The Statistical Research Group was led by Harold Hotelling with Allen Wallis. It consisted of Abraham Wald, J. Wolfowitz, Friedman, Jimmie Savage, Abe Girschick, Frederick Mosteller, and George Stigler.

38 Robert M. Solow, "On the Dynamics of the Income Distribution" (A Thesis Presented in Partial Fulfillment of the Requirements for the Degree of Doctor of Philosophy in the Department of Economics, Harvard University, 1951), microfilm Duke University, 1. The dissertation won Harvard's David Wells Prize 1951. Although the prize came with funds to cover publication with Harvard University Press, Solow never followed through with preparing the book (Robert Solow to John Kenneth Galbraith, December 10, 1953, Solow papers, box 55, file G, 1 of 3).

39 Solow, "On the Dynamics of the Income Distribution," 1.

40 In this way and in contrast to what is sometimes asserted, Markov chains are not "memoryless" but rather memory-afflicted. See Henning Schmidgen, "Figuren des Zerebralen in der Psychologie von Gilles Deleuze," in *Ecce Cortex: Zur Geschichte des modernen Gehirns*, edited by Michael Hagner (Göttingen: Wallstein, 1999), 317–49, 333.

41 Markov took issue with probability theory's restriction to independent random variables. Questioning the hypothetical experiments with ballot boxes and dices, as were common in probability calculus, he extended the validity of the law of large numbers for variables that exhibited dependencies. See Philipp von Hilgers, "Zur Einleitung: Eine Epoche der Markovketten," in *Andrej A. Markov: Berechenbare Künste*, edited by Philipp von Hilgers and Wladimir Velminski (Zürich: diaphanes, 2007), 9–27, 15.

42 The use of Markov chains in a variety of fields of research prefigured a shared notion of information that would come to fruition after the Second World War, pushed in particular by Claude E. Shannon's information theory. Roman Jakobson – encountered in Leontief's classroom in Chapter 3 – proclaimed, for instance, that natural language was to be understood as a Markov process.

43 MIT offered Solow an assistant professorship of statistics in 1949. Solow accepted but negotiated a leave of absence in his first year for the fellowship at Columbia.

44 Hunter Heyck, *Age of System: Understanding the Development of Modern Social Science* (Baltimore: Johns Hopkins University Press, 2015).

45 See E. Roy Weintraub, "MIT's Openness to Jewish Economists," in *MIT and the Transformation of American Economics* (supplement to *History of Political Economy* 46), edited by E. Roy Weintraub (Durham, NC: Duke University Press, 2014), 45–59. Solow emphasized Harvard's anti-Semitism in blocking Samuelson from a post: "You could be disqualified for a job if you were either smart or Jewish or Keynesian. So what chance did this smart, Jewish Keynesian have?" Allison Hoffman, "Economist Paul Samuelson Dead at 94: Smart, Jewish Keynesian Somehow Succeeded," *Tablet*, December 14, 2009, available at https://tabletmag .com/scroll/22290/economist-paul-samuelson-dead-at-94, last accessed April 19, 2024. Samuelson, in contrast, argued that he moved to MIT simply because he received a better offer – despite Harvard's anti-Semitism. See Backhouse, *Becoming Samuelson*, chapter 15.

46 Paul A. Samuelson, "Robert Solow: An Affectionate Portrait," *The Journal of Economic Perspectives* 3, no. 3 (1989): 91–7, 93. Solow was born in 1924 to a

Jewish family of second-generation European immigrants in Brooklyn, New York. His scarce autobiographical comments tell a story of upward social mobility. He spent his childhood and youth in Jewish Brooklyn, often described as an incubator of the postwar intelligentsia, heavily leaning on their immigrant backgrounds and Marxist-inspired youth; see Russell Jacoby, *The Last Intellectuals: American Culture in the Age of Academe* (New York: Basic Books, 1987), 78. Attending the neighborhood public schools ("I'm your basic Jewish boy from Brooklyn"), Solow found a mentor in his literature teacher, who encouraged him to apply to Ivy League universities rather than registering for the local college. Eventually, he won a scholarship to Harvard – at the age of sixteen, as one of the first of the family to attend a university. See Barnaby J. Feder, "Man in the News: Robert Merton Solow; Tackling Everyday Economic Problems," *The New York Times*, October 22, 1987, available at www.nytimes.com/1987/10/22/business/man-in-the-news-robert-merton-solow-tackling-everyday-economic-problems.html, last accessed April 19, 2024; Robert M. Solow, "Robert M. Solow – Biographical," NobelPrize.Org. Nobel Prize Outreach AB 2023, November 28, 2023, available at www.nobelprize.org/prizes/economic-sciences/1987/solow/biographical, last accessed April 19, 2024.

47 By the mid-1950s, the department was one of the most distinguished economic research departments in the US, and by the end of the 1960s it had become the most prestigious worldwide. On MIT and its role in transforming American economics, see the contributions to Weintraub, *MIT and the Transformation of American Economics*, in particular Béatrice Cherrier, "A History of Economics at MIT," in *MIT and the Transformation of American Economics* (supplement to *History of Political Economy* 46), edited by E. Roy Weintraub (Durham, NC: Duke University Press, 2014), 15–44.

48 Backhouse, *Becoming Samuelson*, 620.

49 Robert Solow to Tjalling Koopmans, April 24, 1952, Solow papers, box 57, file K: 1 of 4.

50 Mildred Herr to Robert Solow, April 25, 1951; Solow papers, box 59, file Rand Corporation: 2 of 3.

51 Robert Solow to Milton Friedman, October 25, 1954, Solow papers, box 55, file F: 3 of 3.

52 In an Air Force final report on the HERP, Solow listed several articles as well as "the work I did with Samuelson on optimization over time in Leontief and other dynamic models," Robert Solow to Elizabeth Gilboy, December 10, 1953, Solow papers, box 55, file: G: 1 of 3.

53 See Judy L. Klein, "Shotgun Weddings in Control Engineering and Postwar Economics, 1940–72," in *Economics and Engineering: Institutions, Practices, and Cultures* (supplement to *History of Political Economy* 52), edited by Pedro Garcia Duarte and Yann Giraud (Durham: Duke University Press, 2020), 115–42.

54 Cf. Philip Mirowski and Edward Nik-Khah, *The Knowledge We Have Lost in Information: The History of Information in Modern Economics* (Oxford: Oxford University Press, 2017), 98. On one failed attempt to produce such an encounter, see Roger E. Backhouse and Harro Maas: "Marginalizing Maclaurin: The Attempt to Develop an Economics of Technological Progress at MIT, 1940–50," *History of Political Economy* 48, no. 3 (2016): 423–47.

55 Solow's first publication, a review of macroeconometric modeler Lawrence Klein's *Economic Fluctuations in the U.S., 1921–1941*, was part of that series: Robert M. Solow, "Economic Model-Building: Review of Klein, L. R. (1950) *Economic Fluctuations in the United States*, 1921–1941. New York: John Wiley," *Mechanical Engineering* 72, no. 12 (1950): 990–1.

56 Robert Solow to Ronald Shephard, June 25, 1951, Solow papers, box 59, file Rand Corporation, 1 of 3.

57 "Even the familiar Kahn geometric series is there. Even further, the … 'two-node circuit' inevitably suggests the two-country foreign-trade multiplier of Machlup and others. Carried to greater generality, it appears that his type of circuit theory is analogous to the Goodwin–Chipman matrix multiplier and the Leontief input–output scheme," Robert Solow to Adolph Lowe, October 27, 1954, Solow papers, box 57, file L: 2 of 2.

58 Robert M. Solow, "A Note on Dynamic Multipliers," *Econometrica* 19, no. 3 (1951): 306–16. The purpose of the paper was to provide "a slightly more general model" than contemporary theory had to offer, which in this context meant John R. Hicks' 1950 version of a "Keynes-Kahn multiplier model in which the consumption function has an arbitrary lag pattern," 307.

59 Solow, "Note on Dynamic Multipliers." On the history of economic dynamics, see E. Roy Weintraub, *Stabilizing Dynamics: Constructing Economic Knowledge* (Cambridge; New York: Cambridge University Press, 1991).

60 Paul A. Samuelson, *Foundations of Economic Analysis* (Cambridge, MA: Harvard University Press, 1947).

61 See Backhouse, *Becoming Samuelson*, part III.

62 Robert Solow to Paul Samuelson, December 20, 1946, Samuelson papers, box 70, folder Solow. Solow seems to have encountered Samuelson's approach to economics very early, as Debreu recalled: "I suppose I became aware of Samuelson in Salzburg in the summer of 1948 … where Leontief and Bob Solow came over; Solow was a little young but was very aware of the work of Samuelson," interview with Debreu in Weintraub, *Stabilizing Dynamics*, 140.

63 See Ingrao and Israel, *Invisible Hand*, 262; Roger E. Backhouse, "Revisiting Samuelson's *Foundations of Economic Analysis*," *Journal of Economic Literature* 53, no. 2 (2015): 326–50, 340.

64 An essential foundation for chemistry, the principle applied thermodynamics to the study of chemical reactions, which Antoine Laurent de Lavoisier had described in terms of a balance sheet method listing inputs and outputs. The algebraic expression allowed for simple formulations mediating between various spheres of nature as well as various aspects of Enlightenment culture through a universal method. Le Chatelier in turn was himself a government adviser and occupied with the organization of scientific research under the conditions of Taylorism using the principle. At Harvard, the Pareto group around Lawrence J. Henderson, biochemist and sociologist, linked the notion of economic equilibrium in Pareto's sociology with the Le Chatelier principle as well as with Cannon's concept of homeostasis to analyze social phenomena in terms of thermodynamical and physiological systems. See Bernadette Bensaude-Vincent and Valeria Mosini, "Between Economics and Chemistry: Lavoisier's and Le Chatelier's Notions of Equilibrium," in *Equilibrium in Economics: Scope and Limits*, edited by Valeria Mosini (New York: Routledge, 2007), 45–59.

65 Samuelson's use of mathematics was essentially shaped by Wilson, professor of Vital Statistics, part-time member of the economics department, and himself a student of Josiah W. Gibbs, the major reference for thermodynamic reasoning in the 1930s. See Juan Carvajalino, "Samuelson's Operationally Meaningful Theorems: Reflections of E. B. Wilson's Methodological Attitude," *Journal of Economic Methodology* 25, no. 2 (2018): 143–59; Backhouse, *Becoming Samuelson*, part II; Weintraub, *Stabilizing Dynamics*, chapter 3.

66 See Jean-Pierre Dupuy, *On the Origins of Cognitive Science: The Mechanization of the Mind* (Cambridge, MA: MIT Press, 2009), 189, n. 28.

67 Mary S. Morgan, *The World in the Model: How Economists Work and Think* (Cambridge: Cambridge University Press, 2012), 20.

68 Robert M. Solow, "On the Structure of Linear Models," *Econometrica* 20 no. 1 (1952): 29–46.

69 See Marcel Boumans, "Dynamizing Stability," in *Robert Solow and the Development of Growth Economics* (supplement to *History of Political Economy* 41), edited by Mauro Boianovsky and Kevin D. Hoover (Durham, NC: Duke University Press, 2009), 127–46.

70 Robert Solow to Harold Kuhn, June 27, 1955, Solow papers, box 57, file K: 1 of 4. Solow spoke about the concepts of decomposability and reducibility. What is today known as the Perron–Frobenius theorem involved the concept of decomposable systems, which allowed the application of the theory of Markov chains to properties of nonnegative matrices. The theory of positive or nonnegative matrices was essential in linear economics as the inputs in processes of production needed to be either positive or zero.

71 As Marcel Boumans delineates, the innovative aspect of Solow's paper was that it applied the mathematics of eigenvalues and eigenvectors instead of the more laborious application of principal minors, which were used in the relevant studies by Lloyd Metzler and David Hawkins, and Herbert A. Simon. See Boumans, "Dynamizing Stability," 127–46.

72 He recommended the application of a theorem by German mathematician Helmut Wielandt, who had demonstrated some results of the work of Frobenius "in a simpler, more elegant style." Israel Herstein to Robert Solow, February 5, 1952, Solow papers, box 55, file H: 2 of 3. In the following months, Herstein published his comments in *Econometrica*. Together with Debreu he then translated Wielandt's article and circulated it as a Cowles Commission Discussion Paper, which was eventually published in 1953.

73 Robert Solow to Israel Herstein, February 15, 1952, Solow papers, box 54, file H: 2 of 3. On economic theory itself following "a principle of economy," which is essential to the integrity of the "liberal oikodicy," see Joseph Vogl, *The Specter of Capital* (Stanford, CA: Stanford University Press, 2015), 35.

74 See Philip Mirowski, *Machine Dreams: How Economics Became a Cyborg Science* (Cambridge: Cambridge University Press, 2002), 409. Solow and Debreu had met at the 1948 summer school in Salzburg, Austria, mentioned in note 63, which was co-organized by Leontief (List titled "Economic students," Leontief papers, HUG 4517.30, box 8, folder Salzburg Seminar, Courtesy of the Harvard University Archives).

75 Robert Solow to Gerard Debreu and Israel Herstein, February 5, 1952, Solow papers, box 54, file D: 3 of 4.

76 Solow, "Note on Dynamic Multipliers," 307, n. 4.

77 Solow, "Note on the Price Level," 79; Robert M. Solow, "Growth Theory and After," *American Economic Review* 78, no. 3 (1988): 307–17, 309.

78 See Backhouse, "Revisiting Samuelson's *Foundations of Economic Analysis*," 347. On Samuelson's combination of mathematics and economic meaning, see Carvajalino, "Samuelson's Operationally Meaningful Theorems," 154.

79 Cf. Bensaude-Vincent and Mosini, "Between Economics and Chemistry," 56.

80 Samuelson himself had a lifelong interest in thermodynamics, which did not translate into publications such as *Foundations*.

81 Solow, "How Did Economics Get That Way," 98–99.

82 Council of Economic Advisers, "Economic Report of the President Transmitted to the Congress, January 6, 1950" (Washington, DC: Government Printing Office, 1950), 80.

83 On these two mutually exclusive ideas of development, see Michele Alacevich, "Early Development Economics Debates Revisited," *Journal of the History of Economic Thought* 33, no. 2 (2011): 145–71.

84 Albert O. Hirschman, *The Strategy of Economic Development* (New Haven, CT: Yale University Press, 1963 [1958]), 52, cited in Michele Alacevich, *The Political Economy of the World Bank: The Early Years* (Stanford, CA: Stanford University Press, 2007), 71.

85 John von Neumann, "A Model of General Economic Equilibrium," *Review of Economic Studies* 13, no. 1 (1945): 1–9, 1–2. The paragraph is based on joint work with Roger E. Backhouse, "Mathematics and the Language of Economics" (paper presented at the Workshop "Language(s) and Language Practices in Business and the Economy," Vienna University of Economics and Business, October 23–25, 2014). On the 1937 model and how Neumann came to frame an economic as a mathematical problem, to which he had already found a solution, see Juan Carvajalino, "Unlocking the Mystery of the Origins of John von Neumann's Growth Model," *History of Political Economy* 53, no. 4 (2021): 595–631.

86 David G. Champernowne, "A Note on J. v. Neumann's Article on 'A Model of Economic Equilibrium," *Review of Economic Studies* 13, no. 1 (1945): 10–18, 10.

87 Champernowne, "A Note," 12. The commentary did not criticize the (at the time straightforward) assumption that any natural factors of production (land, air, water, raw materials) were available in unlimited quantities.

88 While his model was widely received among mathematical economists, Neumann himself never wrote anything else on competitive economic analysis. In fact, his and Morgenstern's *Theory of Games and Economic Behavior* opposed competitive and strategic behavior even though their theorems could be reduced to one another mathematically. See Düppe and Weintraub, "Siting the New Economic Science," 474.

89 Robert M. Solow and Paul A. Samuelson, "Balanced Growth under Constant Returns to Scale," *Econometrica* 21, no. 3 (1953): 412–24, 417. A formal difference was that, in place of Neumann's multiple processes with fixed coefficients, Solow and Samuelson assumed a continuous, monotonic production function with constant returns to scale. As Samuelson acknowledged in a letter to James Tobin, the bulk of the paper was contributed by Solow (Paul Samuelson to James Tobin, no date, Solow papers, box 61 file T: 2 of 2).

90 Solow and Samuelson, "Balanced Growth," 412.

91 Tjalling Koopmans to Robert Solow and Paul Samuelson, September 22, 1954, Solow papers, box 57 file K: 1 of 4.

92 Undated manuscript, Solow papers, box 57 file K: 1 of 4.

93 See, for instance, Theodore E. Harris, R-381-PR, "The Theory of Branching Processes," A Report prepared for United States Air Force Project RAND (Santa Monica, CA: The RAND Corporation, May 1964), v.

94 Akin to the nineteenth-century system builders on whom he drew, Lotka aimed to construct a holistic theory by setting up analogies between epidemiology, demography, physical biology, chemical processes, biological, social, and economic interactions. For Lotka as a link between late nineteenth- and early twentieth-century thinkers and late twentieth-century systems ecology, see Ariane Tanner, *Die Mathematisierung des Lebens. Alfred James Lotka und der energetische Holismus im 20. Jahrhundert* (Tübingen: Mohr Siebeck, 2017).

95 See Backhouse, *Becoming Samuelson*, 219–22. In contrast to E. O. Wilson, who later presented ant colonies as "factories" for the production of queens, here no terminology from other fields was used. On Wilson's linear programming model, see Paul Erickson, "Theorizing Application," in *Becoming Applied: The Transformation of Economics after 1970* (supplement to *History of Political Economy* 49, edited by Roger E. Backhouse and Béatrice Cherrier (Durham, NC: Duke University Press, 2017), 58–77, 70.

96 Lotka himself did not link his version of the Lotka–Volterra model to energetics. As philosophers of science Tarja Knuuttila and Andrea Loettgers have pointed out, he also thought of it as freed from disciplinary and theoretical specificities and applicable to a whole range of cases. See Tarja Knuuttila and Andrea Loettgers, "Modelling as Indirect Representation? The Lotka–Volterra Model Revisited," *British Journal for the Philosophy of Science* 68 (2017): 1007–36, 1026. Neither Lotka nor Vito Volterra, however, spoke of a "model" or described their work in terms of "modeling."

97 Judy L. Klein, *Statistical Visions in Time: A History of Time Series Analysis, 1662–1938* (Cambridge: Cambridge University Press, 1997), 220.

98 On Georgescu-Roegen's work and the differences to neoclassical modeling, see François Allisson and Antoine Missemer, "Some Historiographical Tools for the Study of Intellectual Legacies," *Studies in History and Philosophy of Science Part A* 84 (2020): 132–41, 135–6; Quentin Couix, "Natural Resources in the Theory of Production: The Georgescu-Roegen/Daly versus Solow/Stiglitz Controversy," *The European Journal of the History of Economic Thought* 26, no. 6 (2019): 1341–78. On Georgescu-Roegen's reproach that neoclassical modeling amounted to nothing more than "paper-and-pencil exercises," a term that Solow and modelers of his ilk used in the affirmative (Chapter 5), see Alberto Fragio, *Historical Epistemology of Ecological Economics: Essays on the Styles of Economic Reasoning* (Cham: Springer, 2022), 86.

99 On the notion of "limited physics transfer," see Marcel Boumans, "Paul Ehrenfest and Jan Tinbergen: A Case of Limited Physics Transfer," in *Non-Natural Social Science* (supplement to *History of Political Economy* 25), edited by Neil de Marchi (Durham, NC: Duke University Press, 1993): 131–56. The argument for similarities in mathematical structure does not say more about specific modeling

strategies and interpretations that made a mathematical form useful for a particular modeling endeavor. There are many ways in which mathematical forms can be adapted in specific model construction practices. On the Lotka–Volterra equations as an exemplar for the concrete situatedness of economists' use of "templates" from biology, see Knuuttila and Loettgers, "Modeling as Indirect Representation?"; Hsiang-Ke Chao, "Three Kinds of the Lotka–Volterra Model Transfer from Biology to Economics," *Synthese* 202, no. 4 (2023): 124.

100 P. H. Leslie, "On the Use of Matrices in Certain Population Mathematics," *Biometrika* 33, no. 3 (1945): 183–212. As did linear programmers, Leslie emphasized the "great economy in the use of symbols" of expressing fertility and mortality rates in the form of a matrix (and the age distribution as a vector) rather than in the ordinary form of a continuous system expressed in differential and integral calculus (202).

101 Solow, "Note on the Price Level," 75.

102 In correspondence, Solow already spoke of "a neo-classical model" (Robert Solow to Wassily Leontief, November 12, 1952, Solow papers, box 57, file L: 2 of 2).

103 Combining the disciplines of economics, sociology, and psychology, the department was a "catch-all department," as Solow retroactively described it, "like a category marked 'other' in an engineering school." Robert Solow, in an interview with Philippe Fontaine (September 2009), cited in Roger E. Backhouse and Philippe Fontaine, "Conclusions: The Identity of Economics – Image and Reality," in *The Unsocial Social Science? Economics and Neighboring Disciplines since 1945* (supplement to *History of Political Economy* 42), edited by Roger E. Backhouse and Philippe Fontaine (Durham, NC: Duke University Press, 2010), 343–51, 347. For the institutional history of the department see Cherrier, "History of Economics at MIT."

104 The Committee on Educational Survey, "Report to the Faculty of the Massachusetts Institute of Technology" (Cambridge: The Technology Press, 1949), 36, available at https://facultygovernance.mit.edu/sites/default/files/reports/1949-12_Report_of_the_Committee_on_Educational_Survey.pdf, last accessed April 19, 2024. On the longer history of engineers' self-promotion as presenting exceptional mental discipline, which qualified them for shaping public policies, see Amy Sue Bix, "The Wider Context of Samuelson's MIT Textbook: Depression-Era Discussions about the Value of Economics Education for American Engineers," in *Economics and Engineering: Institutions, Practices, and Cultures* (supplement to *History of Political Economy* 52), edited by Pedro Garcia Duarte and Yann Giraud (Durham: Duke University Press, 2020), 31–58, 55.

105 See Béatrice Cherrier, "The Rise of Economics as Engineering II: The Case of MIT," *Institute for New Economic Thinking*, April 24, 2013, available at www.ineteconomics.org/perspectives/blog/the-rise-of-economics-as-engineering-ii-the-case-of-mit, last accessed July 27, 2023. "A program in Economics here involves something over half the course time devoted to physics, mathematics, and engineering," Solow wrote on behalf of one of his students, who was excellent in "the Social Science subjects" of mathematical statistics and accounting but failed the engineering classes (Robert Solow to Dorothy Sutherland, July 2, 1952, Solow papers, box 53, file B: 6 of 7).

106 Solow, "Note on the Price Level," 75.

107 Solow, "Note on the Price Level," 75.

108 Solow, "Note on the Price Level," 76.

109 Solow, "Note on the Price Level," 75. In a letter to Debreu and Herstein, he described his general research interests as dynamic input–output systems "of Leontief–Georgescu–Roegen type" and "particularly the price and interest theories to be associated with this" (Robert Solow to Gerard Debreu and Israel Herstein, February 5, 1952, Solow Papers, box 54, file D: 3 of 4).

110 Solow, "Note on the Price Level," 79 and 77.

111 All: Solow, "Note on the Price Level," 77. On the physical–marginalist notion of capital and its others, see Jonathan Levy, "Capital as Process and the History of Capitalism," *Business History Review* 91, no. 3 (2017): 483–510, 492.

112 Solow, "Note on the Price Level," 79.

113 Both: Solow, "Note on the Price Level," 75.

114 Solow, "Note on the Price Level," 74.

115 On the concept of affordance, see James J. Gibson, *The Ecological Approach to Visual Perception* (New York: Taylor & Francis, 1986), chapter 2.

116 Robert M. Solow, *Growth Theory: An Exposition* (New York: Oxford University Press, 1970), 1.

117 On typical model narratives, see Bernhard Kleeberg, "Factual Narrative in Economics," in *Narrative Factuality: A Handbook*, edited by Monika Fludernik and Marie-Laure Ryan (Berlin: De Gruyter, 2019), 379–90, 381.

118 Solow, *Growth Theory*, 2.

119 Geoffrey C. Harcourt, "Some Cambridge Controversies in the Theory of Capital," *Journal of Economic Literature* 7, no. 2 (1969): 369–405, 387.

120 Solow, "On the Structure of Linear Models," 32, 29.

121 Solow, "Note on the Price Level," 77.

122 Dorfman et al., *Linear Programming and Economic Analysis*, 350–1.

123 Thinking about the *Anschaulichkeit* of material models, Thomas Brandstetter has suggested that "illusory aesthetic effects" precede and enable the view of a model as a symbolic representation. From such a perspective, the sensual experience in the interaction with the artifact precedes the more narrowly defined epistemic notions of intelligibility or similarity. Thomas Brandstetter, "Täuschend ähnlich: Bemerkungen zur Geschichte des Modellexperiments," *Berichte zur Wissenschaftsgeschichte* 34, no. 3 (2011): 207–23, 220.

124 Marx W. Wartofsky, "The Model Muddle. Proposals for an Immodest Realism (1966)," in *Models: Representation and the Scientific Understanding*, edited by Marx W. Wartofsky (Dordrecht: D. Reidel Publishing Company, 1979), 1–11, 1.

5

Model Talk

A model, the previous chapters have suggested, is a quite tricky object, not only in the sense that it is hard to fix its meaning but also in that its specific character depends on the interactions it is involved in. The multivalent nature of models provoked many different attempts at understanding on behalf of modelers. They developed a range of conceptions of what models were and did, what modeling involved as a practice, and what a modeling science should deliver. Views on modeling were as diverse as the practices of modeling and thus formed a rather variable hodgepodge of attitudes, beliefs, and arguments. At the outset of this book, the philosopher and historian of science Marx Wartofsky was intrigued by "the proliferation of strange and unrelated entities which come to be called models" in the arts and the sciences in the 1960s.[1] In the perspective of scientist practitioners the situation was more problematic – to such an extent that by the end of the decade a mathematician could lament in *Science* magazine that "the term *model* is used (and misused) in many ways."[2] In economics as well a variety of model conceptions were on the table "What is a model? It is not a word with a very precise meaning," the linear programmer and economic modeler Richard Goodwin noted in the early 1950s.[3] He picked up on economists' adoption of the language and practice of modeling in the immediate postwar era that came hand in hand with a concern for the foundations and quality of the knowledge gained by the new "tools and techniques."[4] What a model signified depended not only on the particularities of the relevant research but also on the specific ways this research was embedded in a variety of political uses, social meanings, and cultural associations.

This chapter investigates how Solow and his colleagues tried to make sense of their modeling work between the mid-1950s and early 1970s, often in reaction to fundamental critique. In regard to experiments with material models, the historian of science Thomas Brandstetter has framed modelers' reflections on the relation between their artifacts and whatever they were supposed to represent as "metatheories." These metatheories resulted from modelers' need to explain themselves, to clarify the epistemic prerequisites of modeling.[5] In such "model-talk," as Wartofsky called it, "models inhabit a limbo between worlds." They are assigned neither to the "blood-and-guts world of real objects and processes" nor to "the cognitive world of purported truths."[6] Similarly, economic modelers positioned their artifacts somewhere in between. In the preceding chapters I have situated Solow's model on different trajectories that spotlighted how the model was treated as a concrete artifact and, often enough, supplemented with economists' distancing gestures: We are analyzing the model, not the world. At the same time, they assigned their models the status of tools, useful for all kinds of action. This chapter tunes in to economists' model talk. Trying to make sense of what they were doing, they portrayed modeling as a practice – as an acquired craft that combined particular skills with a way of thinking that could not be readily formalized. In particular when directed at outside critics, model talk entangled epistemic with cultural, political, and social aspects. For this reason, I will delineate how the multifaceted character and interpretative openness of models made economists use a whole range of narratives and cultural symbolism in a mission to clarify and control model conceptions.

The model talk that follows did not amount to a formal set of methodological reflections. In addition to economists' view of their activities involved in modeling, it spoke to themes in the philosophy of science, picked up on epistemological vocabulary, and strained to link political-economic divides with methodological standpoints. Keen on convincing critics who did not understand or approve of the new formalism, mathematical modelers sometimes alluded to seemingly logical-positivist or Popperian frameworks through the use of terms such as "hypotheses testing" or "falsification."[7] The utterings that interest me most, however, are more strongly related to their research work. They were made in various contexts (lectures, debates, correspondence), sometimes spontaneously, always bound to the specific situation in which they were made and the dynamics of the larger exchange in which they were embedded. In any case, they did not grow from a modeler's attempt to offer a formalized epistemology of modeling. Emphasizing the casual appearance of such framings, I see them as an essential part of the practice of modeling. This does not mean that historical actors were more truthful on these occasions than in their published work. But neither was their model talk simply meaningless spiel.

Not least, model talk spoke to a frustration of critics and proponents of the new economics alike. Legitimizing technicality contributed to both methodological self-reflection and struggles for expert authority. Economists both explicitly and implicitly communicated a strong sense of what it meant to be a modeler and which epistemic ideals this involved. In this sense, model talk also alluded to "the right stuff" that made a good modeler.[8] Apart from gendered associations that accompanied debates about mathematics in economics from the start, the right stuff also involved cultural stereotypes. An example is the English economist J. R. (Dick) Sargent's presentation "Are American Economists better?" In 1960, at a dinner talk at the Political Economy Club at Nuffield College, he presented a dazzling view of neoclassical modeling as a practice: "No American economist ever thinks; he uses his analytical tools to arrive at meaningful theorems."[9] Using Solow's "Contribution to the Theory of Economic Growth" as an exemplar to dismiss an "English economics" represented by Joan Robinson's work, Sargent celebrated American economics as the more scientific, experimental, and professional way. Infused with the (folklore American) "spirit of innovation and exploration," Solow would distinguish himself not by following a strict set of mathematical rules but by "being careless," by departing "from the standards of rigour."[10] Whereas the modeler, indeed in a truly virile manner, gave "ideas a run," Robinson, "like a wise nurse, wags her head and warns. A steady hand is all very well, so long as its grip is not around one's throat."[11] Prejudicial exaggerations and discriminatory framings like this all-too-common dismissal of Robinson accompanied model talk when it sought to differentiate mathematical modeling from other styles of reasoning that raised questions modelers deemed irrelevant or not manageable in the realm of "science."[12]

Sargent's example illustrates how model talk tapped into different registers that are commonly neglected by methodological discussion but still equipped the practice of mathematical modeling with a cultural repertoire that accompanied its rise in the 1960s. In the following sections I focus on three themes that come up in model talk surrounding Solow's model: (1) The notion of modeling as a trial-and-error exploratory practice, which came with perceiving mathematical models as prototypes, that is, assigning them preliminary status; (2) the essential orientation of the modeling endeavor to be useful for policy-making, which equipped the model with the suggestive power of visualizing a world that could be established; and (3) the performance of the *scientific persona* of the modeler-economist as a technical worker and modest "little thinker" who worked for the social good. These three themes reflect some of the issues that were at stake when modelers grappled with the complexity of their small-scale, so-called simple theoretical models.

PRELIMINARY MODELING

Mathematical modeling has been contested as a suitable practice of fabricating economic knowledge since the beginning. In the 1950s and 1960s, mathematical economists mainly encountered critique from two (sometimes opposing) sides: For trying to become a proper science at all and for not trying hard enough. Peter Drucker, a professor of management at New York University, who frequently called for the end of the so-called Keynesian revolution, gnawed at the "sterility" of economic theory: "One look at the *American Economic Review*, the house organ of the profession in this country, will show that while a great many good people ... are hard at work, they are mostly producing minor refinements in tools of doubtful application." In 1957, the same year Solow published his technique for measuring "technical change" (Chapter 2), Drucker's criticism built on a growing literature that scathed mathematical economics for its scientistic pretense.[13] With a nod to the similar critiques by Austrian economists Friedrich Hayek and Robert Nef, he denied economics as a whole any scientific status. Others thought that it was just neoclassical modelers in particular who were on the wrong path. One of the new critical books in that vein was *The Failures of Economics* (1955) by the economist Sidney Schoeffler, which had generated some uproar in the discipline. In a logical-positivist vein, Schoeffler claimed that economics failed as a modern science for its inability to state immutable laws and to predict economic events. Compared to the natural sciences, it only provided a "messy" type of knowledge, which amounted to nothing more than "makeshifts and expedients."[14]

From early on in his career, Solow engaged with critical commentaries when it came to the limited epistemological capacities of mathematical economics. He usually argued from the point of view of a practitioner, molding his experience in tinkering with mathematical models into arguments against a methodological critique that, to him, was just too abstract. In a review of Schoeffler's "thoughtful and provocative" book, he delivered one of his first responses to the critics. Though many of Schoeffler's points hit right home, Solow argued, his problem was "an excessively literal view of scientific method."[15] In a breezy manner that would become typical of his interventions, Solow did make a case for the technicality of economic argument. But, in doing so, he argued against "the received view":

Economics should neither emulate the physical sciences, nor should it aim to arrive at "true" knowledge, exact predictions, or precise probability statements. Instead, it was about "indirect reasoning," about guesswork and hunches: "Perhaps one can hope for occasional flashes of insight that ... enable us to say something useful about the gross consequences of, say, particular tax laws."[16] Solow directed attention to the practice of modeling and took issue with the strict separation between science and art. To Schoeffler, there was no science of economics but, on the one hand, a science of decision-making, which was a field of logic, and, on the other, a practical art of economic policy-making, comparable to medicine. Solow, in contrast, echoed the preamble to his 1956 paper and maintained that "at a certain level all science is art."[17] His way of approaching the model muddle was to stay as close as possible to the intricacies of the activity of modeling. Instead of delving into the underdetermined meaning of models as ready-made products, he emphasized their role in economists' research practices. Linking a model's capacities with the modeler's dexterity and creativity, Solow highlighted the importance of conceiving of mathematical modeling as a craft.

Speaking about modeling as a practical activity in the 1950s was not specific to Solow but pervaded the model-based literature on growth and business cycles. Evsey Domar, for instance, one of the claimed constructors of the Harrod–Domar model, described model construction as "a very subtle art."[18] The term hinted at certain skills the practitioner needed to build a good model. "The most important part of the economist's art," wrote James S. Duesenberry in his work on business cycles and growth, was "knowing how to simplify one's description of reality without neglecting anything essential."[19] Once the model was completed, the analyst could engage in a trial-and-error process of toying or tinkering. "I like playing with models," Goodwin noted in the abovementioned manuscript.[20] His account illustrates how modeling economists highlighted the playful character of their work. Having been denied tenure at Harvard (where he had also taught Solow, Chapter 4), Goodwin had just moved to England and escaped possible McCarthyite harassment.[21] At his new post, he defended his way of theorizing against "some embattled member of the Older School of Economists." Dramatically titled "The Confessions of an Unrepentant Model Builder," the manuscript emphasized the practical virtues of building "one's own model and then work[ing] it."[22] Against the "strong empiricist and positivist tradition," Goodwin argued that a model "never tells us anything about the 'real' world."[23] The point of modeling was precisely that the modeler could freely design a new world and then investigate it without being all too burdened by its relation to reality.

Small-scale models such as Solow's had a specific role to play. Chapter 4 showed how the model developed as a miniature of dynamic linear models. Economists' model talk frequently related a small artifact back to bigger ones: Working with them was widely seen as a substitute for manipulating larger or more complex models. Experimenting with input–output models or the new large-scale macroeconometric models required an extensive research infrastructure, large amounts of data, the requisite computing capacities, personnel, and the relevant coordination activities. In contrast, constructing and manipulating a small-scale model was a rather inexpensive way of doing economics. These superior economies of what Solow later called "small-scale handicraft operations" did not only extend to the financial and organizational efforts.[24] They were also more efficient on an epistemic level: With their small scale, these models could open up a space to ask questions that could not otherwise be raised. Dealing with larger systems of equations was computationally too laborious, in particular in the early 1950s when computing capacities were low. Larger-scale econometric models, which combined Keynesian modeling and data such as those constructed by Solow's MIT colleague Lawrence Klein, "hamper[ed] the needed experimentation."[25] In a similar vein, Leontief, director of the Harvard Economic Research Program, maintained that the purpose of dynamic input–output models, which were only of little use to empirical analysis, planning, or prediction, was that they enabled theoretical "small-scale experiments."[26]

The conception of small-scale modeling as an exploratory practice hinged on the view of mathematical models as concrete artifacts. In the mid-1950s, several economists took up the vocabulary of control engineering and drew analogies between servomechanisms and macroeconomic concepts, which mimicked reasoning in terms of physical analogs.[27] When Oskar Morgenstern explicated how models were used to investigate "the general properties of a system by its manipulation on the basis of a theory of the system," he compared them with models in aeronautics.[28] Instead of computing the breaking point or determining it with a real airplane, a model was "put into a wind-tunnel and is exposed to stresses until it breaks."[29] Such experiments could be conducted numerous times with various alterations of the model. Similarly, Richard Stone argued almost a decade later that "the only practical course is to build a prototype and then improve on it in the light of experience and needs."[30] The essential characteristic of the model prototype was its tentativeness. "One has to start somewhere. One knows perfectly well that one's prototype model will not be a very perfect tool, but the really important thing is that one should set it up, see how the parts of the system interact, and check how the relationships of the model work out in practice."[31] The comparison of mathematical models to the objects of aeronautic laboratories, which were crucial for the conquest of both air and space, was by no means restricted to economics. Claude Lévi-Strauss argued that the human sciences should make use of "reduced models," just like those "which aerodynamic analysis tests in its wind channels."[32] Similar to mathematical economics, here, the research object of ethnological study was a system of relations, the "social structure." This structure was given by the constructed model, which, in turn, was understood as a concrete object. Symptomatic of the multiplicity of model conceptions, Lévi-Strauss used a variety of cursory references and associations. He mentioned Neumann and Morgenstern's *Theory of Games and Economic Behavior* and compared the mechanical models of anthropology (which, as a field, dealt with observations that were not amenable to statistical and probabilistic analysis) with the small-scale models of an apprentice to qualify as a master artisan.[33]

The conception of modeling as experimenting with a prototype hinted at the preliminary character of small-scale models. They did not directly provide detailed analysis or numerical knowledge for the questions of theory or policy-making but were one component of a larger endeavor. Solow embedded the growth model in an epistemology that related to the tentativeness of small-scale, "qualitative" knowledge.[34] "I am trying to express an attitude towards the building of very simple models," he stated in a paragraph of concluding thoughts to his book *Growth Theory: An Exposition* (1970).[35] On its hundred pages, Solow laid out growth theory as he had been teaching it to successive classes of graduate students at MIT. Very simple models provided undiscovered worlds, exploratory sites for the modeler. "If you want to know what it's like out there, it's all right to send two or three fellows in sneakers to find out the lay of the land and whether it will support human life." Solow recognized that the knowledge ("whatever analytical insights") gained through investigating a small-scale model world did not "lead directly to prescription for policy or even to detailed diagnosis." Neither, he wrote in response to a frequent criticism by the late 1960s, were they merely "a game": They would prove useful for further modeling endeavors, namely the construction of "larger-scale econometric models" – an "altogether bigger operation" that was not as "glamorous."[36]

What Solow termed a "reconnaissance exercise" went beyond the sense of priority in a chronology of events. For one, it related to the forward-moving, imaginary character of modeling. As I have argued throughout the previous chapters, it was, in the first place, about creating an artificial world. This world was based on existing knowledge, which was not deemed sufficiently workable. Due to its new form, the small-scale model could be explored. At least from hindsight, the framing in terms of reconnaissance alluded to expansionist and extractivist settings, from military connotations to the idea of outer space as the final frontier, to the American Frontier with its imagined empty space. In a different way from Solow, the macroeconometric modeler Arthur S. Goldberger directly referred to the Frontier when honoring earlier contributions: "Students of the American West will recall that before the pioneers arrived, explorers had already charted the territory. Then, while one group of pioneers was pitching its tents, forging tools, sowing seeds, and building model cabins, a second wagon train had followed a different trail and found its promised land."[37] Here, the pioneers were small-scale modelers. Taking Solow's metaphor further, it was small-scale modelers whose job was precisely to exclude all kinds of factors from their models, to ignore most of what was around, and to focus in the first place on the new construction.

Second, reconnaissance modeling was about testing something out, a rather simple and low-cost action, which, in case it was successful, provided the ground for a more expensive and expansive project. Domar argued in that vein against the critique that economic models were an "oversimplification": "It is easy enough to add a few more variables," at least as long the result was still manageable.[38] In this sense, the small-scale model was part of what Tjalling Koopmans, director of the Cowles Commission and frequent correspondent of Solow, called a "sequence of models." In his often-cited treatise on model methodology, he argued that small-scale models were protected from the "reproach of unreality."[39] They simply provided a first prearrangement for something that was yet to come. In the realm of theory, a simple model was, ideally, to be extended and complicated. In empirical estimation, economists described the relationship between theoretical construction and empirical measurement as an iterative process. The initial formulation of a model was such that it could be implemented with existing data. Once more empirical material was available, the model could be adapted, for instance, extended by adding new variables. Solow's notion of "reconnaissance exercise" related in particular to macroeconometric models as they were constructed from the mid-1950s onward. For their larger-scale econometric estimation, the initial, small-scale model served as a prototype, which could be adapted and extended in order to provide numbers on the behavior of output, employment, the wage rate, price level, interest rate, and other variables.

During the 1960s, with the rising availability of electronic computers, these models became bigger in that the variables were broken down into more detail – a development sketched in the Epilogue. From this perspective, modeling was an open-ended process, and models were always preliminary.[40]

Frequently, economists portrayed the tentativeness of small-scale models as a didactic device, which provided yet another argument for the preliminary value of small-scale models. Morgenstern, very critical of his fellow economists' way of dealing with empirics, ascribed analogue models "superior pedagogic value."[41] More on the affirmative side when it came to econometric estimation, Solow's MIT colleague Klein presented the Keynesian model of income determination as a "pedagogical model" that had "teaching attributes." In the second edition of *The Keynesian Revolution* (making a case for socialist planning against Keynes, the "glorifier of bourgeois life") he argued that the simple model provided "a crude framework for thinking and illustrating main ideas."[42] The philosopher and historian of science Marcel Boumans has argued in his account of economists' modeling strategies that small-scale models "provide[d] a kind of understanding one at least could communicate to students or colleagues."[43] Such a view brought together modelers with otherwise different epistemic stances such as Herbert Simon and Robert Lucas.

The preliminary status that economists attributed to small-scale models meant that they provided a first step in a specific direction and acted as a guide for successive projects. They came with restrictions as to which ways they could be extended and what kinds of factors could be added. The great danger of this kind of modeling, as proponents of other modeling styles maintained, was that it curtailed analysis from the start. Echoing broader debates at the time, the urban economist Harry W. Richardson, for instance, took issue with small-scale models that "illustrious economists," one of them being Solow, had built for this field of so-called applied economics.[44] The policy problem in question was the "allocation" of metropolitan space to housing and traffic. Solow's model relied on what he called "a series of drastic simplifying assumptions" in order "to work out a fairly general (though abstract) theory," which boiled down to "the analysis of a single austere example."[45] In Richardson's view, the model contributed nothing of value. The differential equation techniques required the exclusion of all kinds of factors that were so important to the field of urban economics, worst of all by reducing space and neglecting nonlinearities. As a consequence, the model simply replicated established results and encouraged the "revival of dead issues" that had been tackled by urban economists decades before.[46] The great danger of modeling in the style of "MIT economics," Richardson highlighted, was that its specific mathematics only allowed it to deal with the simplest cases, thus becoming incapable of providing knowledge useful for policy-making. Referring to Jay Forrester's work (also at MIT), whose system dynamics models were foundational for the Club of Rome's *Limits to Growth*, published two years prior, Richardson made a case for nonlinearity, system simulation, and models that had no analytical solutions. "It would be a disaster if a policy-oriented field such as urban economics went the way of growth theory."[47]

In a seemingly annoyed reply, Solow went back to his idea of simple models as reconnaissance exercises and highlighted their use for policy-purposes. As a matter of course, he yawned, his model was not of direct use for policy-making. While he agreed with items on Richardson's "list of desiderata," he thought it absurd to try to include all these factors at once. In fact, "serious research" was all about focusing on a few factors. A "pencil-and-paper model" provided a first step for more extensive modeling – in the form of a whole collection of several easily manageable models and in the form of a large-scale simulation model. While the former case risked ignoring important interactions, the extension in the latter came "at the cost that no one can fully understand what is happening in the bowels of the machine."[48] Solow's point was that these different modeling strategies were complementary. Richardson shuddered to think that urban economics could turn into growth theory, where a whole cohort of professors and students created a vast variety of neoclassical growth models, adding ever more factors to a transparent and manageable pencil-and-paper-form.[49] In contrast, Solow emphasized that small-scale mathematical models could equally provide building blocks for constructing more complex, empirical models, which in turn provided concrete, numerical knowledge for policy-making. The dynamic between small and large forms made him double down on the mediated importance of pencil-and-paper models for public policy – a further layer of model talk that provided the neoclassical growth model with specific meaning.[50]

MODELS AS POLICY VISIONS

The model talk of MIT's economists in the 1950s and 1960s situated theoretical small-scale models in the larger project of providing technical knowledge for economic governance. Much later, in conversation, Solow spoke of his modeling practice as "engineering in the design sense," which he linked to his working home at MIT. "I lived my whole professional life in an engineering school," Solow explained, "and so the notion that one of the functions of a professor of engineering is not necessarily to build a bridge but to design a bridge ... came perfectly naturally to us at MIT."[51] This quote brings together the idea of a mathematical model as concrete artifact and its tentativeness as a design for building something in the world. Other modelers used the language of design more systematically, though equally as a way to align modeling with "the professions" rather than the sciences. Most prominently, Herbert Simon, who grappled with the various design functions of models and later titled his memoirs *Models of My Life*, noted that it was not only engineers who designed: "Everyone designs who devises courses of action aimed at changing existing situations into preferred ones."[52] Devising company plans, the work of a physician, and the design for a social welfare policy were thus similar kinds of action. In fact, Solow's model fed into the architecture of model infrastructures of policy-making. In this setting, it contributed to calculating a balanced growth path in the remote future and the factors that could contribute to increasing that growth – as illustrated in the Epilogue. For now, I will focus on the role of the neoclassical growth model in the new economics of the early 1960s. In the model talk of economists at the Council of Economic Advisers (CEA), this theoretical model became an important part of a governmental endeavor, if only in a quite elusive sense. It provided the vision of an ideal world that could be established through the right, expert-led policies.

Situated at MIT, Solow linked his theoretical work more strongly to policy questions than did other mathematical economists at the time. So much so that Simon, being asked to recommend Solow as a member of the President's Science Advisory Committee (PSAC) at the California Institute of Technology, only ranked him third after Kenneth Arrow (and sociologist James Coleman): "Robert Solow (44), MIT, is a mathematical economist, in the same class as Arrow, but he has perhaps been more concerned with national economic policy, hence is perhaps slightly less appropriate than Arrow for PSAC purposes."[53] This was in 1968. At the beginning of the decade, the political influence of macroeconomists reached new heights during the Kennedy administration.[54] Solow joined Kennedy's CEA under Walter Heller, whose new economics was *TIME* front-cover material and launched a veritable hype around "Kennedy's economic planners."[55] Historians have painted the Council as a key means of economists' influence in this period, especially under the Democratic presidencies of Truman, Kennedy, and Johnson.[56] While there are reasons to doubt the CEA's potency, economists certainly took it seriously as a channel for influencing both executive and legislative action and, in some cases, public opinion.[57] After a drought in presence due to a less active policy stance during the Eisenhower administration, with the coming of the Kennedy administration, economists thought that they had revived their "influence at the top," as Solow celebrated in 1961 in a letter to a colleague:

Things are different now. Just count. Paul Samuelson and Dick Musgrave and countless others have been advising Kennedy since summer. Paul was offered the chairmanship of the Council of Economic Advisers and turned it down. It went instead to Walter Heller … Jim Tobin will be a member of the Council of Economic Advisers and he is as good an economist as we have. Bob Roosa is undersecretary of the Treasury. Speaking of RAND, Charlie Hitch … has just been appointed Assistant Secretary of Defense. Even more important, [this] will make the technical jobs in Washington attractive and professional economists will be influencing policy from its start.[58]

Distributed across the executive branch, macroeconomic experts did not necessarily agree on which economic issues government should focus on. Growth, however, remained a major goal and vehicle of government policies and, with the Cold War growing tenser, became an ever more pressing issue. After the recession of 1958 and the launch of Sputnik I in 1957, Evsey Domar, who frequently turned up in the previous pages as a growth economist but who was also an expert on the Soviet Union, testified in a hearing before the Joint Economic Committee Congress in 1959 that Soviet growth was "so far above our own" that it should in fact "worry us."[59] Despite an abundance of growth studies, the federal government had, in his eyes, not done "anything really important" to seriously push growth rates.[60] In the same vein, economist Edward Denison used Cold War imperatives to assert the need for a more aggressive politics of growth in his prominent 1962 book *The Sources of Economic Growth in the United States*. Based on investigations into the causes for productivity increases along the lines discussed in Chapter 2, Denison argued that it was the job of "economic science … to offer a 'menu' of possible ways to affect the rate of growth."[61] In his 1960 presidential campaign, Kennedy promised 5 percent annual growth and his economic advisers agreed that the US economy had to grow faster than in previous years, both in order to achieve domestic goals and to succeed in economic competition with the USSR.

In the wartime project of actively furthering growth, the technical expertise of economists that built on mathematical and statistical methods earned its own label: "growthmanship." First used in a derogatory way by Richard Nixon in the Presidential election, insinuating that growth was the single political goal of his opponent Kennedy's "great ends" campaign, the term was eventually adopted by the latter's economists such as Solow.[62] Within Heller's CEA, he was charged with drafting the policy repertoire for an extended politics of growth. The first pages of the 1962 "Economic Report of the President" reinforced the power of "well-timed support" of policies to stabilize and foster the national economy.[63] As in earlier reports, the Council urged cooperation with labor and management as well as the adoption of specific macroeconomic policies to achieve, among other objectives, "our goal of economic growth."[64] In contrast to the reports of 1949 and 1950 (Chapter 2), the 1962 recommendations made ample use of concepts from macroeconomic theory. After all, the new economics of Heller and his successors was a "political economy" with the purpose of "weaving modern economic theory into the fabric of national thinking and policy."[65] The report's reliance on technical knowledge derived from models was most apparent in the chapter devoted to economic growth – planned and coordinated by Solow.[66]

Revisiting the economic record, the report's chapter spoke of growth rates that had been realized and of higher growth rates that would have been possible to realize if stronger stimulating policies had been in place. Such "potential growth" was the growth rate at which the economy fully employed all capital and labor capacities. Such technical concepts conveniently helped to put policy options in a nutshell. Accordingly, the main preoccupation of the Council was "narrowing" the gap between actual and potential growth.[67] The purpose of macroeconomic policies was concurrently defined as keeping the national economy on that potential growth path – alternately termed "the path of steady high employment," "the path of potential GNP," or "the path of full employment growth" or at least keeping deviations from that path as small as possible. Figure 5.1 shows one of the charts that visualized the gap. Potential growth was given by a straight increasing line; the curve that intersected it provided measured GNP values in 1961 prices; and the dashed curves projected three possible trajectories for future GNP numbers.

The potential growth rate related to the concept of potential output, which calculated the maximum achievable production capacity of the economy as a whole. The measure was established in the late 1940s in the administrative realm of national income accounting.[68] In economic theory, the idea that a trustworthy government could realize a full employment equilibrium through encouraging a specific amount of investment had equally been around for some time.[69] Concurrently to Heller's gap-

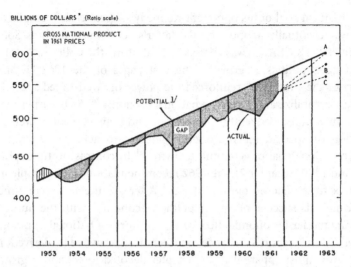

Figure 5.1 The gap to be narrowed: The gap of actual and potential output, "Gross national product, actual and potential, and unemployment rate" (Council of Economic Advisers, "Economic Report 1962," 52)

closing project, the emerging field of development economics calculated the "saving ratio" that was needed to achieve a certain desired growth rate – with the help of the Harrod–Domar model.[70] In all of these projects, the technical language of actual and potential output framed the divergence between them as something possible to be eliminated. Kennedy's CEA Council calculated the possible gains within specific target areas of macroeconomic policies and how they were "allocated" as to reduce the 40 billion dollar gap between actual and potential GNP. The 1962 report suggested that government delivered jobs, research, training, and capital investment in such a way that national production kept pace with rising employment numbers. The characteristics and designs of the short-run policy instruments were detailed in separate chapters. These built on economists' research on possible factors that might close the gap. In a well-received academic paper, Council member Arthur Okun measured the relationship between GNP growth and employment rates to estimate the optimal rate of unemployment. His results then went into figures like Figure 5.1 as an essential assumption for projections.[71] Ultimately, the report argued that if the relevant short-run policies were successful, then lower unemployment would reduce the gap by 15 billion, a larger labor force (through greater demand) would contribute 4 billion, longer hours of work 5 billion, and greater productivity per man-hour (through higher utilization) 16 billion dollars.[72]

Whether the CEA's reports or Heller's more informal memos to Kennedy (as analyzed by the historian of economics Béatrice Cherrier), concrete recommendations were not only framed by empirical estimation and the "what-happens-if"-formats of economic models. They also decisively depended on policy preferences, beliefs, norms, values, and subjective judgment, all of which belonged to the "skills" of the growthmen.[73] An instance is Tobin's note to Samuelson urging him to shape Democratic policies:

> I was a little disappointed with Kennedy's economics in the great debate. I recognize that he's got to talk nonsense about agriculture, as does Nixon. But I was sorry that he [Kennedy] shied off from the idea of a budget surplus, and that he didn't have the guts to say that a tax increase might be necessary to achieve his program . . . I don't like this line that faster growth will automatically bring the tax revenues we need to do the job. How do we get the faster growth? And don't we need more resources to government than automatic growth of taxes will allocate? I believe that in one of your early memos to Kennedy this year, you pointed out that the British people didn't buy this line from the Labor Party. And a great deal of popular comment on the debate the other night suggests that Nixon scored a point on the "how do you pay for it all?" exchange. Do something. Say it isn't so.[74]

Tobin wanted Samuelson (and probably Solow) to advocate for the implementation of tax increases. He was convinced that his colleagues actually had the power to influence policy decisions. Eventually, Solow instead supported a massive tax reduction. First discussed in 1962 and introduced in February 1964, the infamous Kennedy–Johnson tax cut was one of the measures to stimulate economic growth by seeking to spur business investment.[75] Critiques abounded that macroeconomists with their focus on the aggregate ignored distributional effects and that their design favored the richest. Among others, critics were other liberal economists like Keyserling, who had been chair of Truman's CEA (Chapter 2), and John Kenneth Galbraith, who took issue with the new economics on several levels, as the next section will show.[76] In retrospect, historian Eli Cook has interpreted the Democrats' bill as a "sign of things to come."[77] Solow himself explained his support through recourse to the possibilities of practical politics, demonstrating the advisers' willingness to balance political strategy and economics. In conversation, he agreed that there was a greater need for larger federal spending and that the tax reduction would make it harder to achieve that goal. But "it was plain to us that an increase in federal expenditure was politically impossible; the practical choice for expansionary fiscal policy was either tax reduction or nothing."[78] More generally, Edwards and Drane, two economists working on productivity increases of the Australian economy, highlighted that assessing the gap between actual and full-potential growth relied "in part on one's growth-manship and politics, as well as one's analysis."[79] In this marbled realm of economic expertise, the neoclassical growth model merged epistemic vision and the possibilities of administrative–political action.

The CEA's expertise relied on a collection of heterogenous models and calculation techniques rather than one unified overarching framework. This applied to MIT economists' research more generally and set them apart from later developments in the discipline. Solow repeatedly stressed that his research was not invested in a particular model. Even if there was a theoretical opportunity to create an overarching mathematical general framework, the complexities of the economic world (with its uncertainty, limited information, and imperfect competition) demanded a variety of heterogeneous models adjusted to the problem in hand. In the CEA's portrayal of the economy and its future capabilities, the potential growth rate did not coincide with the long-run equilibrium growth path of Solow's model. In fact, it did not even address the long-run, and it was not built on neoclassical assumptions. The impact of the model was less tangible. In combination with other techniques that detailed the effects of short-run policies and investigated disaggregate data, it depicted a possible state that could be implemented through short-run policies. The CEA argued not only for being able to achieve a balance between consumers and business (and banking) but also for a balance between current and future consumption.[80] In a manner not so different from Solow's model, capital accumulation was to keep pace with the growth of the labor force through manipulation of the interest rate. This kind of narrative linkage brought together the long-run of the neoclassical model with short-run, "Keynesian" policies of demand management. According to Solow's own recollections, the 1962 report of Kennedy Council's work relied on an "implicit model of the long run"; both he himself and Tobin kept working on their growth models, "the tools we had in mind when we thought about the macroeconomics of the long run."[81] Increasing potential output, the goal of growth policies was not equivalent to increasing the model's long-term growth rate. However, in the minds of growthmen, these policies still opened the possibility of achieving such a long-term rate, in Solow's words, "if we knew how to achieve it."[82]

The model talk of CEA experts visualized an ideal world of balanced growth which could be reached if the right steps were taken. In this sense, the neoclassical growth model embodied the pragmatic imagination of a possible future world that could be realized through appropriate macro-economic management of the mixed economy. Its neat cosmos exhibited a visionary quality: In the long run, there was another, a better world that was possible to reach if the government took the proper actions in the short run.[83] From this perspective, the model called for the realization of full potential growth and the establishment of perfectly allocating markets. While it did not involve any guidance on which policies would lead to its equilibrium vision, it still entertained the possibility of realizing it. Or, as Solow put it in a heated exchange with Galbraith: "Any economic system can be made to work, if you go at it cleverly."[84]

The prospective realism of a small-scale model drew heavily on the idea that precisely formulated mechanisms were an indispensable means for policy-making.[85] Even economists who worked in contrasting ways appreciated the importance of the kind of coherence and rigor that mathematical models provided. "The desire for determinacy is not merely a product of the professional style," the British economist and Solow's friend Robin Marris wrote in relation to contemporary macroeconomic management. The Fabian, who followed American social criticism and was associated with Keynesian–Marxist approaches, argued that determinate models were "particularly needed by those who wish to evaluate and prescribe" in the form of concrete policy recipes.[86] For Solow, more specifically, they were part of a toolkit that enabled policy to use the market for social ends through taxation and incentives:

I do believe that market forces operate over a large part of the modern economy, sometimes loosely, sometimes tightly. That does not mean that whatever the market turns up is good, or immune from tinkering on the part of the political authority. It does suggest that it will often be efficient to accomplish the social good by *using* the market.[87]

The neoclassical growth model provided a fiction that could be implemented through the governmental use of market forces. As it dispensed with all kinds of complications, it did so efficiently. At the same time, it opened up an indeterminate, muddled space. Beyond the confines of the model, these complications reappeared and gave rise to more model talk, which now sought to bring together epistemological reflections and the political meaning of models.

THE ECONOMIST AS A LITTLE-THINKER

By the end of the 1960s, the economics profession had risen to new heights. Economics was widely accepted as a science; the Swedish national bank established the "Nobel Memorial Prize for Economic Sciences in the memory of Alfred Nobel." At the same time, critiques of neoclassical modeling and its abstractions gained currency across political camps. Whether well-known critical economists such as Robert Heilbroner, representatives of the various rising strands of radical economics, or economic institutions such as the Committee for Economic Development: The focus on macroeconomic management based on the model imagery of a smoothly-working market seemed too far off from contemporary political, social, and economic problems.[88] By their very design, models excluded so many factors from economic reasoning such that economists seemed unable, not interested, or simply unwilling to talk about, for instance, the heavy reliance of Kennedy's growthism on military spending, not to mention their inability to say anything about war, poverty, racial discrimination, or the power of large corporations – a whole "roster of ignored subjects," as Heilbroner put it.[89] The critique not only related to concrete policy measures and larger political agendas. It contested the very foundation of economists' knowledge, its methodological, conceptional, and institutional frameworks.

When it came to American Keynesianism, one of the core reproaches was that its models simply provided market ideology in mathematical disguise. The model imagery, so the critique went, showed profit-maximizing firms and sovereign consumers brought together by a smoothly-working market, which provided them with all information. Joan Robinson's related criticism accompanied Solow's work from his beginnings as an academic economist (Chapter 1). To her, profits, like all other kinds of economic phenomena, were a matter of power and politics, which also framed the division of incomes. In neoclassical models like Solow's, the income distribution appeared to be independent of institutions, social relations, and history. Assuming that profit was related to the productivity of capital, these models justified capitalist profits as rightfully earned.[90] The critique, widely shared among institutionalist, historical, Keynesian, and Marxist camps, gained new steam with the rise of the New Left. Neoclassical models stood for a politics of simple remedies through deficit spending based on the view that government, in the words of Robinson, "can only ask for what business chooses to give" and that only "what's profitable is right."[91]

More than once Solow defended the profession against allegations that economists promoted the omnipotence of the market and actually believed in the realism of their models. Convinced that the state had a considerable role to play, he had particular reason to engage with the reproach that neoclassical modeling was merely laissez-faire ideology in a new guise. Diametrically opposed, Solow made the case that, as scientific tools for economic governance, models based on neoclassical assumptions were in fact essential for progressive politics. Probably referring to an exchange with Robinson, he noted: "One of Cambridge's most distinguished economists, with whom I had been carrying on a rather abstract controversy, once said to me at a party: 'You're not a reactionary; so why don't you agree with me?' I thought it was a good question."[92] Replying to Heilbroner's discussion of values and ideology of the neoclassical mainstream, Solow even emphasized the "radical potential," of economics, "especially along equalitarian lines."[93]

Given the manifold understandings of models' capacities, the practitioners' focus on their tentativeness, and the practical necessity of translating model knowledge into something useful for policy-making, it was not easy to establish clear-cut relationships between economic research, interventionist expertise, and political ideals. A case in point is a polemical exchange between Galbraith, Solow, and Marris in *The Public Interest*. The magazine was founded in 1965 to debate the new social sciences, especially the use of their knowledge for the rational management of a growing welfare state.[94] Before the editors, Daniel Bell and Irving Kristol, became poster boys for neoconservatism at the beginning of the 1970s, most of the magazine's contributors were social scientists who tended to be moderately liberal Democrats. Some of them, including Solow, had highly technical qualifications but belonged to the subset of professors able and willing to write for a nonspecialist audience. The editors saw the style of economics practiced at MIT as especially promising for "nonideological" interventionist social science.[95] In a paper coauthored with the historian of social science Eric Hounshell, we analyze the specific dynamics of the debate to demonstrate how difficult it was for the actors to come to an agreement about the scientific and political character of models.[96] In the following pages, I focus on one dimension of the debate, which provides an example for yet another mode of model talk, its language, and style.

In 1967, the *Public Interest* published Solow's review of Galbraith's new best seller *The New Industrial State* (1967). Carrying forward an argument expounded in *The Affluent Society* (1958), Galbraith combined an analysis of mid-century capitalist society with a scathing portrayal of economists' epistemic failures: Since the large corporation had essentially transformed the reality of American economy, society, and state, economists' conventional efficient-market assumptions of sovereign, rational consumers, and profit-maximizing firms went radically awry. To Galbraith, who offered a very different kind of economic knowledge, modeler-economists either (at best) drastically misunderstood or (at worst) deliberately concealed the destructive drive for growth in contemporary capitalism. The verdict of Solow's review: It was "a book for the dinner table not for the desk."[97] While Galbraith warned his readers that mathematical models were simply proof for "muddled and incomplete thought," Solow presented mathematical modeling as the only proper way to generate reliable knowledge for economic management. "Counting noses or assets and recounting anecdotes are not to the point. What is to the point is a 'model' – a simplified description – of that economy that will yield valid predictions about behavior."[98]

Both the epistemic and political meanings of economic modeling were muddled to such an extent that the adversaries mobilized varied figures and virtues associated with the practice. The construction of *scientific personae* allowed Galbraith and Solow to portray clear gaps between their political positions – much larger gaps than was possible in their discussion of modeling and interventionist knowledge.[99] In contrast to Galbraith, who cast himself as a well-heeled cosmopolitan scholar with astute judgment of social reality, Solow identified with a highly professionalized, seemingly inward-looking community. Paul Samuelson (who, ironically, had wide public recognition as one of Kennedy's main economic advisers and became prominent as a regular columnist for *Newsweek* five years later) captured this in his 1961 AEA presidential address: "Not for us the limelight and the applause . . . in the long run, the economic scholar works for the only coin worth having – our own applause."[100] In a similar manner, Solow's self-fashioning as a technical economist worked decidedly through distancing gestures. He opened his review with a mocking portrait:

> Galbraith is, after all, something special. His books are not only widely read, but actually enjoyed. He is a public figure with some significance; he [has] the power to shake stock prices by simply uttering nonsense. He is known and attended to all over the world. He mingles with the Beautiful People . . . It is no wonder that the pedestrian economist feels for him an uneasy mixture of envy and disdain.[101]

While Galbraith portrayed economists as willing propagandists or unconscious stooges of large corporations and enemies of the common good, Solow depicted his opponent as a superficial, self-satisfied, elitist intellectual whose renown had nothing to do with genuine qualifications and expertise but only his jet-set sheen. A year before the debate, Galbraith counted among the A-list intellectuals invited to Truman Capote's legendary party of the "Establishment" elite.[102] Staging himself as the technical economist, Solow used Galbraith's high-society mingling to deny his opponent any professional and moral credibility. Quoting from *The New*

Industrial State, Solow lampooned the author's elitist posture: "'What is called a high standard of living consists, in considerable measure, in arrangements for avoiding muscular energy, increasing sensual pleasure and for enhancing caloric intake above any conceivable nutritional requirement . . .' One wonders," Solow jabbed, "if that paragraph were written in Gstaad where, we are told, Professor Galbraith occasionally entertains his muse."[103] Unable to recognize social reality (underlined by Solow with a list of poverty statistics) from his alpine retreat, Galbraith imposed his taste on the philistine masses: "It is a very fine line between analytical statements about the creation of wants by advertising and elaborate indications that one believes one's own tastes to be superior to those of the middle classes."[104] In contrast, Solow presented himself as a simple technical worker inveighing against upper-class elitism. Against the backdrop of a smoldering "mass culture debate," Solow not only countered critique of the assumption of the sovereign consumer but also hit hard against what he sketched as intellectualism. In his later reply to Heilbroner, he objected to the concept of false consciousness: "The attack on consumer sovereignty performs the same function as the doctrine of 'repressive tolerance'," he wrote in (taunting) reference to Herbert Marcuse. "If people do not want what I see so clearly they should want, it can only be that they don't know what they really want."[105]

The role of modeling for self-stylization as a simple technical worker, the near identification of the modeler with his little artifacts, became most obvious when Solow differentiated between "big-thinkers" and "little-thinkers."

The world can be divided into big-thinkers and little-thinkers. The difference is illustrated by the old story of the couple who had achieved an agreeable division of labor. She made the unimportant decisions: what job he should take, where they should live, and how to bring up the children. He made the important decisions: what to do about Jerusalem, whether China should be admitted to the United Nations, how to deal with crime in the streets. Economists are determined little-thinkers. They want to know what will happen to the production of houses and automobiles in 1968 if Congress votes a 10 percent surcharge on personal and corporate tax bills, and what will happen if Congress does not.[106]

Skillfully using a gendered language of power, Solow assigned economists the female role in the household, taking care of the daily business of life. The big-thinker, associated with the male role in (outside) the household, in contrast, dealt with the grand political questions of the public sphere. In that setting, it was through painstaking, sober technical work with large numbers that Solow's little-thinker toiled for the social good. But her role was not simply reduced to technical issues; after all, she did make decisions. Both in the practice of modeling and in the realm of expertise, economists certainly needed their subjective judgment, proper statement of their values, and a set of skills. Solow and Galbraith performed different styles of turning economic knowledge into practical politics. Managing the economy required the ability to "navigate the political field," as sociologist Stephanie Mudge has framed it. In her account, the macroeconomist of the 1960s "was part technical engineer, part pragmatic political strategist."[107] While Solow was a member of Kennedy's CEA designing the abovementioned tax cut, Galbraith flatly opposed the CEA's proposition. He "deliberately missed" official meetings and, as his friend and personal adviser, whispered in Kennedy's ear: "I saw the President beforehand and weighed in heavily against the action," Galbraith remembered proudly, "stress[ing] ... that in economics, the majority is always wrong. The tax cut was postponed until next year."[108] Exchanges like the one in the *Public Interest* were essential in performing economists' technical knowledge as workable inputs for politics.

In hindsight, the tools of economic theory ultimately did not deliver on the promise that increased growth and productivity would "lift all boats."[109] From Solow's perspective, however, they did have equalitarian consequences in the field of economics itself, namely as a practice that disciplined reasoning. He was convinced that, independently of the contents of economic analysis, people across political camps would benefit from modeling. "Cold analysis" would eradicate ideological preconceptions of both the students from the New Left as well as conservatives who held on to their "hard-hearted shibboleths ... such as that the free market always leads to better results than would come from intervention, or that public enterprise is inherently wasteful, or that steeply progressive taxation is unjust and inefficient, or that the AFL-CIO runs the country."[110] One possible example for the clarifying work of mathematical models was Tobin's paper on "Money and Income." During the 1950s and 1960s, confrontations between what has been framed as two blocks circled around the relation between changes in money supply and changes in income. Friedman, "a bloody nuisance," as Samuelson would have it, argued that changes in money supply caused changes in nominal income and inflation.[111] In his paper, Tobin presented two models, a "Friedmanian" and an "ultra-Keynesian." The latter generated the same sequence found in Friedman's studies, which Tobin used as a demonstration that Friedman's temporal order could also have been brought about by a different mechanism, in which money had no causality.[112] This was probably what Solow had in mind when he suggested that models improved economists' intellectual capacities in uncovering some shades of ideological prejudice and bias. In helping to expose unclear thought, to compare and fairly judge economic analyses, and in being a learnable craft, modeling also seemed to be able to push equality within the discipline of economics. In retrospect, Solow noted that it was the shift toward modeling that stopped economics from being a "fit conversation piece for ladies and gentlemen."[113] Instead, it had turned into a "self-consciously technical subject, no longer a fit occupation for the gentleman-scholar."[114]

A SMALL BAND OF TECHNICAL INITIATES

By 1970, the construction and application of mathematical models had become the dominant practice, effectively the "proper" way of doing economics. Small-scale models such as the neoclassical growth model had turned into an epistemic norm. MIT's economics department, where Solow spent his whole professional life, had become the epitome of an economics devoted to "precise" reasoning and "technical" knowledge. The connection between small-scale modeling and didactic purposes ran through the previous chapters: from the initial construction of Solow's model as a by-product of other modeling work and pedagogy to modelers' associations that small-scale models were a way of communicating their theories in an intelligible manner. Not least, the Solow model became a common device for familiarizing economics students with modeling as a craft. Even today, economists' model talk links the specific way of modeling with the institution of MIT. Elite economists like Paul Krugman speak of their "MIT style" of doing economics or even the "Bob Solow view of the way to work."[115]

As one of the managers and prominent teachers of the economics department, Solow was a key figure in the transformation of MIT into the center of American economics and is commonly referred to as one of the main architects in building the new economics, in particular in his role as a teacher. "We view ourselves as net exporters of finished economists," Solow noted in correspondence as early as 1956.[116] MIT's students – whether aiming to become modeler-economists themselves, experts in government, or informed businesspersons – trained by working out how to use the tools of economic theory. As the literature on paper tools has noted, this kind of reasoning was not so much about asking whether these tools were right but more about developing "a cache of experience closer in kind to craft skill or artisanal knowledge than to explicit textual information."[117] At MIT, the tooled understanding of economics came along with a collaborative atmosphere and a certain workshop character, expressed, for instance, in the open-door-policy at the department.[118] Solow supervised many more PhD dissertations than his colleagues did; he wrote a great many letters of recommendation for his students to help place them in academe, government, and business; many of them became highly influential economists. In his 1970 book on growth theory, Solow thanked the "generations of students," who did "the hard work of pushing forward the theory of economic growth."[119] MIT's graduates spread a way of thinking, "the technique," as Solow mentioned in conversation, combined with the "model building philosophy" centered on constructing "small, understandable, relatively transparent models."[120] Krugman, one of his students, attributed to Solow the style of applying "small models . . . to real problems, blending real-world observation and a little mathematics to cut through to the core of an issue."[121] And the first person who George Akerlof, yet another Nobelist who had studied at MIT, thanked in his *An Economic Theorist's Book of Tales* was Solow: "Each of the models in this volume is a short statement that focuses on a problem. This method of economic theory was taught by Solow to a generation of graduate students at MIT via the medium of growth models."[122]

The label of an MIT style refers to a specific combination of epistemic and political values, *scientific personae*, and a practice of making and marketing economic knowledge – a compound made up from, among others, the modes of model talk laid out in this chapter. Taking seriously modeling as a practice that encompasses both the work and the performance of economics, the model talk exhibited in these pages presented mathematical models – whether intentionally or not – as much more than analytical tools. Instead of clarifying the model muddle, I set out to highlight its richness. The three themes discussed here related, for one, to the concrete artifactual character that modelers accorded to their models in treating them as prototypes or designs for further projects. The model talk in this chapter also involved the visionary character of Solow's model in the context of macroeconomic management. It also included the various political and power-coded associations that pervaded talk about "the technique." I have emphasized the not-yet-disciplined character of model talk in situations in which economists struggled with both the epistemological and political status of their artifacts. When modeling stabilized as economists' prime mode of reasoning, some of that model talk congealed into what Krugman and others referred to as a "style" and turned into disciplinary language and formalized methodological stances from the 1960s on.[123] That stabilization entailed a variety of social effects.

Historical and sociological studies of science have emphasized that it is the circulation of objects that co-creates collectives in the first place and holds them together. Solow's model was one of the essential didactic devices that provided a clearly delimited world to explore and to play with. In this way, these models unfolded their socially cohesive power – as testified by Krugman. They bound together a thought collective via shared reasoning practices as well as through the personal traits, work attitudes, and wider meanings that were associated with them. Such inclusionary effects of modeling as a research practice had equally exclusionary features, as was even witnessed by contemporary insiders. In the mid-1950s, for instance, David Novick, head of RAND's Cost Analysis Department and hence no stranger to mathematical argument himself, complemented his epistemological critique of mathematical modeling by expounding the social dynamics that came with it: "the present trend to mathematics as a language has cut off a large part of the fraternity from an ability either to read or understand much of the new thinking."[124] The vehemence of economic modelers' snarky replies to what they called a "blast against mathematical economics" was symptomatic of the urgent, somewhat desperate affirmation of the scientific character of the new economics in the 1950s. In a similar vein to Novick, Galbraith, in the debate in the *Public Interest*, countered Solow's attacks by situating his opponent as part of a "small band of technical initiates . . . somewhat like . . . a fraternity, a lodge, or a chess club."[125] Such mocking comments aside, the ideals that organized tightly knit communities around the formulation of precise and clear-cut models also seem to have clashed with the apparent commitment of MIT's modelers to boost the numbers of female and Black American graduate students.[126] In which ways the gendered rhetoric of economics as a science that pervaded the model talk in this chapter fit together with the exclusionary cultures of engineering schools, elite institutions, and the discipline itself – and how all of this contributed to economics lagging behind other academic fields in changing its demographic makeup – are concerns within the profession up until today.[127] And so we add to the list of absences that haunted mathematical models in their epistemic work the lists of exclusions that accompanied the work of models as a social adhesive.

Notes

1 Marx W. Wartofsky, "The Model Muddle. Proposals for an Immodest Realism (1966)," in *Models: Representation and the Scientific Understanding*, edited by. Marx W. Wartofsky (Dordrecht: D. Reidel, 1979), 1.

2 Marc Kac, "Some Mathematical Models in Science," *Science* 166, no. 3906 (1969): 695–9, 695.

3 Massimo Di Matteo, Francesco Filippi, and Serena Sordi, "'The Confessions of an Unrepentant Model Builder': Rummaging in Goodwin's Archive," *Structural Change and Economic Dynamics* 17, no. 4 (2006): 400–14, 408. This paper provides the transcript of Goodwin's handwritten manuscript (on pages 407–11) supposedly prepared as an address to be given to undergraduate students at the University of Cambridge. Goodwin's work played a role in Chapter 4, when Solow took up his research on the "matrix multiplier," one of the earliest uses of the Perron-Frobenius theorem in economics.

4 See Joel Isaac, "Tool Shock: Technique and Epistemology in the Postwar Social Sciences," in *The Unsocial Social Science? Economics and Neighboring Disciplines since 1945* (supplement to *History of Political Economy* 42), edited by Roger E. Backhouse and Philippe Fontaine (Durham, NC: Duke University Press, 2010), 133–64.

5 Thomas Brandstetter, "Täuschend Ähnlich – Bemerkungen Zur Geschichte Des Modellexperiments," *Berichte zur Wissenschaftsgeschichte* 34, no. 3 (2011): 207–23.

6 Wartofsky, "Model Muddle," 3. On this in-between status of models in economic methodology, see Marcel Boumans, "Models in Economics," in *The Elgar Companion to Economics and Philosophy*, edited by John Bryan Davis, Alain Marciano, and Jochen Runde (Cheltenham, UK: Edward Elgar, 2004), 260–82.

7 For an account of Popperian critiques of economics, see D. Wade Hands, *Reflection without Rules: Economic Methodology and Contemporary Science Theory* (Cambridge: Cambridge University Press, 2001), section 7.1.1.

8 Philosopher Isabelle Stengers described the "right stuff" that made a good scientist as "having faith that what a scientific question doesn't make count, doesn't count; a faith that defines itself against doubt." For her, the project of modern science is "well and truly virile in the sense that it is part of masculine heroism to make an abstraction of one's own interests, of one's prejudices, and to resist the temptations and seductions of questions that would lead one astray." I would extend her view to include the doubts and hesitations in model talk, which I see as a corollary of the making of a clean and closed world. Isabelle Stengers, *Another Science Is Possible: A Manifesto for Slow Science*, translated by Stephen Muecke (Cambridge, MA: Polity, 2018), 36 and 34.

9 J. R. Sargent, "Are American Economists Better?" *Oxford Economic Papers* 15, no. 1 (1963): 1–7, 2.

10 Sargent, "Are American Economists Better?" 3–4.

11 Sargent, "Are American Economists Better?" 3.

12 By the time Sargent gave his talk, "English" economics had already experienced several developments in mathematical economics and econometrics and was not the somewhat exegetic theoretical endeavor that Sargent portrayed. See Roger E. Backhouse, "The Changing Character of British Economics," in *The Post-1945*

Internationalization of Economics (supplement to *History of Political Economy* 28), edited by A. W. Coats (Durham, NC: Duke University Press, 1996), 33–60. Only a year later, Sargent founded the Department of Economics at the University of Warwick, modeled after the kind of "American economics" he had identified in his talk. It was also Sargent who invited Solow to give the Radcliffe Lectures that resulted in *Growth Theory*.

13 Peter F. Drucker, "Review of New Thinking in Economic Theory, by Sidney Schoeffler and Neil W. Chamberlain," *Review of Politics* 18, no. 3 (1956): 359–62, 359. For an intellectual biography and the political philosophy of Drucker as a thinker of what he himself denoted "knowledge work," see Nils Gilman, "The Prophet of Post-Fordism: Peter Drucker and the Legitimation of the Corporation," in *American Capitalism: Social Thought and Political Economy in the Twentieth Century*, edited by Nelson Lichtenstein (Philadelphia: University of Pennsylvania Press, 2006), 109–32.

14 Sidney Schoeffler, *The Failures of Economics: A Diagnostic Study* (Cambridge, MA: Harvard University Press, 1955), 153.

15 Robert M. Solow, "Review of The Failures of Economics: A Diagnostic Study by Sidney Schoeffler," *Review of Economics and Statistics* 39, no. 1 (1957), 96–98, 97.

16 Solow, "Review of The Failures of Economics," 98. Through a variety of comparisons (quality control for electronic computers, entomology, and molecular biology) and references (the mathematician George Polya's *Plausible Inference* and philosopher of science Stephen Toulmin's comparison of models with maps), Solow argued that it was not about asking whether an economic law was true but whether it held in any particular situation.

17 Solow, "Review of The Failures of Economics," 98. The preamble of his "Contribution to the Theory of Economic Growth" spoke about the "art of theorizing," see Chapter 1. Much later, Solow put it in the following way: "What model building probably isn't, is a science, in the sense that I doubt that you can reduce model building to a model of model building," interview with Verena Halsmayer, May 3, 2011.

18 Evsey D. Domar, "Economic Growth: An Econometric Approach," *American Economic Review* 42, no. 2 (1952): 479–95, 484.

19 James S. Duesenberry, *Business Cycles and Economic Growth* (New York: McGraw-Hill, 1958), 14–15. In the book, Duesenberry argued against the view that depressions could be portrayed as a repetitive cyclical mechanism. He was later involved in the construction of the Brookings model, one of the best-known large-scale econometric models.

20 Richard Goodwin, "The Confessions of an Unrepentant Model Builder" (transcript), in Di Matteo et al. "'The Confessions of an Unrepentant Model Builder': Rummaging in Goodwin's Archive," *Structural Change and Economic Dynamics* 17, no. 4, 2006: 407–11, 408.

21 See Frederic Lee, *A History of Heterodox Economics: Challenging the Mainstream in the Twentieth Century* (New York: Routledge, 2009), 239, n41. At Cambridge, Goodwin continued his work in linear programming and on the interaction between long-run growth and business cycles.

22 Goodwin, "Confessions of an Unrepentant Model Builder," 408. His account of modeling emerged from early debates on growth and cycles in England, which

revolved around Hicks's 1950 book on the trade cycle and Robinson's work on accumulation. See Di Matteo et al., "Confessions of an Unrepentant Model Builder."

23 Goodwin, "Confessions of an Unrepentant Model Builder," 408.

24 Robert M. Solow, "Cowles and the Tradition of Macroeconomics" (presentation at The Cowles Fiftieth Anniversary Celebration, June 3, 1983), 16, available at https:// cowles.yale.edu/sites/default/files/2022-12/50th-solow.pdf, last accessed April 20, 2024.

25 Robert M. Solow, "Economic Model-Building. Review of Klein, L. R. (1950) *Economic Fluctuations in the United States, 1921–1941*, New York: John Wiley," *Mechanical Engineering*, 72, no. 12 (1950): 990–1, 991.

26 Wassily Leontief et al., eds., *Studies in the Structure of the American Economy: Theoretical and Empirical Explorations in Input–Output Analysis* (New York: Oxford University Press, 1953), 62. On the HERP and Leontief's work, see Chapter 3.

27 Around that time, the MIT political scientist and cybernetician Karl Deutsch, who collaborated with Solow, criticized the social sciences for endorsing mechanistic and organismic models rather than information-feedback systems. See Ronald Kline, "How Disunity Matters to the History of Cybernetics in the Human Sciences in the United States, 1940–80," *History of the Human Sciences* 33, no. 1 (2020): 12–35, 19. I discussed the view of small-scale models as prototypes in Verena Halsmayer, "From Exploratory Modeling to Technical Expertise: Solow's Growth Model as a Multi-Purpose Design," in *MIT and the Transformation of American Economics* (supplement to *History of Political Economy* 46), edited by E. Roy Weintraub (Durham, NC: Duke University Press, 2014), 229–51, 241–3.

28 Oskar Morgenstern, "Experiment and Large Scale Computation in Economics," in *Economic Activity Analysis*, edited by Oskar Morgenstern (New York: Wiley, 1954), 484–549, 499.

29 Morgenstern, "Experiment and Large Scale Computation," 501.

30 Richard Stone, "The Analysis of Economic Systems," in *Semaine d'Etude Sur Le Role de l'Analyse Econometrique Dans La Formulation de Plans de Developpement*, Pontificiae Academiae Scientiarum Scripta Varia 28 (Vatican City: Pontificiae Academiae Scientiarum, 1965), 3–88, 84.

31 Stone, "Analysis of Economic Systems," 112.

32 My translation of "reduzierte Modelle zu Hilfe zu nehmen (so jene, welche die Aerodynamik in ihren Windkanälen erprobt)," Claude Lévi-Strauss, "Wissenschaftliche Kriterien in den Sozial- und Humanwissenschaften," in *Strukturale Anthropologie*, edited by Claude Lévi-Strauss, translated by Eva Moldenhauer, Hans Henning Richter, and Traugott König, vol. II (Frankfurt: Suhrkamp, 1992), 325–50, 338, cited in Michael Bies, "Das Modell als Vermittler von Struktur und Ereignis. Mechanische, statistische und verkleinerte Modelle bei Claude Lévi-Strauss," *Forum Interdisziplinäre Begriffsgeschichte* 5, no. 2 (2016): 43–54, 52.

33 On Lévi-Strauss's modeling philosophies, see Bies, "Das Modell als Vermittler von Struktur und Ereignis," and Bernard Dionysius Geoghegan, *Code: From Information Theory to French Theory* (Durham: Duke University Press, 2023), chapter 4.

34 Proponents of the first epistemology were, for instance, Milton Friedman and Robert Lucas. See Marcel Boumans, *How Economists Model the World into Numbers* (New York: Routledge, 2005), 179.

35 The book, printed in 1970 by Oxford University Press, was based on six Radcliffe Lectures delivered at the University of Warwick in December 1968 and January 1969.

36 All: Solow, *Growth Theory*, unnumbered page after 104. In his usual nonchalant manner, he proceeds: "But it may be what God made graduate students for. Presumably he had something in mind."

37 Arthur S. Goldberger, "Structural Equation Methods in the Social Sciences," *Econometrica* 40, no. 6 (1972): 979–1001, 979. I am grateful to Eric Hounshell for pointing me to this paper.

38 Domar, "Economic Growth," 484.

39 Tjalling C. Koopmans, *Three Essays on the State of Economic Science* (New York: McGraw-Hill Book Company, 1957), "The Construction of Economic Knowledge," 127–66, 142.

40 For a taxonomy of exploratory functions of scientific models, see Axel Gelfert, *How to Do Science with Models: A Philosophical Primer* (Cham: Springer, 2016), chapter 3.

41 Morgenstern, "Experiment and Large Scale Computation," 504.

42 Lawrence R. Klein, *The Keynesian Revolution*, 2nd ed. (London: Macmillan, 1968), 78, 193. On Klein's stances on Keynes/ianism, see Erich Pinzón-Fuchs, "Lawrence R. Klein and the Making of Large-Scale Macroeconometric Modeling, 1938–55," in *The History of Macroeconometric Modeling* (supplement of *History of Political Economy* 51, no.3), edited by Kevin D. Hoover, Marcel Boumans, and Pedro Garcia Duarte (Durham, NC: Duke University Press, 2019), 401–23, 408–10; Timothy Shenk, "Taking Off the Neoliberal Lens: The Politics of the Economy, the MIT School of Economics, and the Strange Career of Lawrence Klein," *Modern Intellectual History* 20, no. 4 (2023): 1194–218, 1208–16.

43 Boumans, *How Economists Model the World into Numbers*, 180.

44 Harry W. Richardson, "A Comment on Some Uses of Mathematical Models in Urban Economics," *Urban Studies* 10, no. 2 (1973): 259–66, 259. The other model Richardson chided was constructed by James Mirrlees. I am grateful to Béatrice Cherrier for making me aware of the exchange. See Béatrice Cherrier, "Mathiness in Context: Richardson, Solow and Mirrlees Debate the Uses of Math in Urban Economics in the 1970s," *The Undercover Historian: Beatrice Cherrier's Blog*, October 21, 2015, available at https://beatricecherrier.wordpress.com/2015/10/21/mathiness-in-context-richardson-solow-and-mirrlees-debate-the-uses-of-maths-in-urban-economics-1973, last accessed April 20, 2024.

45 Robert M. Solow, "Congestion, Density and the Use of Land in Transportation" *Swedish Journal of Economics* 74, no. 1 (1972): 161–73, 161.

46 Richardson, "Comment on Some Uses of Mathematical Models," 259.

47 Richardson, "Comment on Some Uses of Mathematical Models," 260.

48 All: Robert Solow, "Rejoinder to Richardson: I," *Urban Studies* 10, no. 2 (1973): 267. Solow had used the language of "pencil and paper models" before, see Robert M. Solow, *Capital Theory and the Rate of Return* (Amsterdam: North-Holland, 1963), 56–7; Robert Solow to Howard Nicholson, November 13, 1969, Solow

papers, box 58, file N: 2 of 2. The notion appeared in late-nineteenth-century mathematical biology and highlighted modelers' conception of mathematical models as concrete objects. See Michael Friedman and Karin Krauthausen, "How to Grasp an Abstraction: Mathematical Models and Their Vicissitudes between 1850 and 1950. Introduction," in *Model and Mathematics: From the 19th to the 21st Century*, edited by Michael Friedman and Karin Krauthausen (Cham: Springer International Publishing, 2022), 1–49, 36.

49 A survey article in growth theory had already noted in 1964 that, while it had certainly provided problems with "intellectual fascination," modeling exercises with neoclassical growth models were starting to become "frivolous." See F. H. Hahn and R. C. O. Matthews, "The Theory of Economic Growth: A Survey," *Economic Journal* 74, no. 296 (1964): 779–902, 890. On the shriveling of growth theory between 1970 and the mid-1980s, see Snowdon and Vane, *Conversations with Leading Economists*, 586.

50 Solow, "Rejoinder to Richardson," 267.

51 Robert Solow, interview with Verena Halsmayer, May 3, 2011. See also Halsmayer, "From Exploratory Modeling to Technical Expertise"; Verena Halsmayer, "Der Ökonom als 'Engineer in the Design Sense' – Modellierungspraxis und professionelles Selbstverständnis in Robert Solows 'Contribution to the Theory of Economic Growth,'" *Berichte zur Wissenschaftsgeschichte* 36, no. 3 (2013): 245–59.

52 Herbert A. Simon, *The Sciences of the Artificial* (Cambridge, MA: MIT Press, 1969), 111.

53 Herbert Simon to Lee DuBridge, December 19, 1968, Carnegie Mellon University Archives, Digital Collections, Herbert Simon, Series: Consulting, Folder Box: 51, Folder Number 3832, Folder Title: President's Science Advisory Committee: Correspondence, Doc Number: 63, available at http://doi.library.cmu.edu/10.1184/pmc/simon/box00051/fld03832/bdl0008/doc0002, last accessed April 20, 2024. I am grateful to Eric Hounshell for sharing this material.

54 Elizabeth Popp Berman, *Thinking like an Economist: How Efficiency Replaced Equality in U.S. Public Policy* (Princeton: Princeton University Press, 2022), 25.

55 *TIME Magazine*, March 3, 1961. Heller's CEA involved, among others, James Tobin, Kermit Gordon, Gardner Ackley, and Arthur Okun. Solow was appointed senior economist from February 1961 to February 1962 and remained a consultant for Heller for some time. See Application for a NSF senior postdoctoral fellowship October 10, 1962, Solow papers, box 58, file N: 1 of 2.

56 See Robert M. Collins, *More: The Politics of Economic Growth in Postwar America* (Oxford: Oxford University Press, 2000), 52–63; Michael A. Bernstein, *A Perilous Progress: Economists and Public Purpose in Twentieth-Century America* (Princeton: Princeton University Press, 2011).

57 Timothy Mitchell has argued that the establishment of the CEA may have been a "pyrrhic victory." At the same time as it institutionalized their advice, the CEA also cordoned off and thereby contained the power of professional economists. In contrast with economists in upper-level bureaucratic positions, CEA members had no decision-making powers: Their advice and forecasts could be easily disregarded. See Timothy Mitchell, "Economentality: How the Future Entered Government," *Critical Inquiry*, no. 40 (2014): 479–507, 490–1. Cf. Craufurd D. Goodwin, "The Patrons of Economics in a Time of Transformation," in *From*

Interwar Pluralism to Postwar Neoclassicism (supplement to *History of Political Economy* 30), edited by Mary S. Morgan and Malcolm Rutherford (Durham, NC: Duke University Press, 1998): 53–81, 79.

58 Robert Solow to Dick Sargent, January 5, 1961, Solow papers, box 60, file S: 1 of 7.

59 Evsey D. Domar, "Statement," in *Comparisons of the United States and Soviet Economies. Hearings before the Joint Economic Committee Congress of the United States. First Session* (Washington: United States Government Printing Office, 1960), 245–48, 247.

60 Domar, "Statement," 247. Apart from fully utilizing productive capacities, Domar suggested focusing on education, science, and technology.

61 Both: Edward F. Denison, *The Sources of Economic Growth in the United States* (New York: Committee for Economic Development, 1962), 1–2. Denison was part of the group that developed the first national income and product statistics in the 1940s and was heavily involved with Kuznets's projects, see Chapter 2.

62 See Mauro Boianovsky and Kevin D. Hoover, "In the Kingdom of Solovia: The Rise of Growth Economics at MIT, 1956–1970," in *MIT and the Transformation of American Economics* (supplement to *History of Political Economy* 46), edited by E. Roy Weintraub (Durham, NC: Duke University Press, 2014), 198–228, 199.

63 Council of Economic Advisers, "Economic Report of the President (January 1962)," (Washington: Government Printing Office, 1962), 7.

64 Both: Council of Economic Advisers, "Economic Report 1962," 9.

65 Walter W. Heller, *New Dimensions of Political Economy: The Godkin Lectures at Harvard University* (Cambridge, MA: Harvard University Press, 1966), vii. The notion of "new economics" already described statistical and mathematical methods in the 1940s but was popularized by Heller to market his approach to economic management. On the 1949 and 1950 reports and the politics of growth, see Chapter 2.

66 On writing the chapter, see Robert M. Solow, "Growth Theory and After," *American Economic Review* 78, no. 3 (1988): 307–17, 310; Robert M. Solow, "The Kennedy Council and the Long Run," in *Economic Events, Ideas and Policies: The 1960s and After*, edited by G. L. Perry and James Tobin (Washington, DC: Brookings Institution, 2000), 111–35, 112. From a senior professional staff of nineteen economists and statisticians, Solow was assisted by Dick Attiyeh, Sidney Winter, and Roy Wehrle (Council of Economic Advisers, "Economic Report 1962," 196).

67 See Heller's summary of the CEA's policies, Heller, *New Dimensions of Political Economy*, chapter 2. On Heller's memos and his excessive use of "the gap," see Béatrice Cherrier, "How to Write a Memo to Convince a President: Walter Heller, Policy-Advising, and the Kennedy Tax Cut," *Œconomia* 9, no.2 (2019): 315–35.

68 While growth research hitherto had focused on depicting past production, it was Kuznets who computed an ideal capacity both for the present and the future. See Onur Özgöde, "Institutionalism in Action: Balancing the Substantive Imbalances of 'the Economy' through the Veil of Money," *History of Political Economy* 52, no. 2 (2020): 307–39, 330–1.

69 On the basis of the accelerator, Domar, for instance, had raised the question, "if income was guaranteed to grow at the equilibrium rate – would that call forth sufficient investment to generate the needed income?" Evsey D. Domar, "Capital

Expansion, Rate of Growth, and Employment," *Econometrica* 14, no. 2 (1946): 137–47, 145.

70 See Mauro Boianovsky, "Beyond Capital Fundamentalism: Harrod, Domar and the History of Development Economics," *Cambridge Journal of Economics* 42, no. 2 (2018): 477–504, 486. Until today, policy models of financial institutions like the World Bank relate to Harrod–Domar models and are used to calculate a "financing gap," how much funds and aid a specific country needed, though it was obvious that GDP numbers did not react in the way that these models presumed. Examples from Guyana in the 1980s to Lithuania in the 1990s abound. See William Easterly, *The Elusive Quest for Growth: Economists' Adventures and Misadventures in the Tropics* (Cambridge, MA: MIT Press, 2002), 35–7.

71 See Cherrier, "How to Write a Memo to Convince a President," section 1.

72 Council of Economic Advisers, "Economic Report 1962," 108.

73 Béatrice Cherrier has studied how Heller communicated the CEA's expertise to policy-makers. She emphasizes that experts themselves explicitly recognized that setting target levels for policy objectives was obviously a normative task, "How to Write a Memo to Convince a President," section 3.

74 James Tobin to Paul Samuelson, September 29, 1960, Solow papers, box 61, file T: 2 of 2.

75 See Berman, *Thinking like an Economist*, 34; Collins, *More*, 53.

76 Aurélien Goutsmedt, "How the Phillips Curve Shaped Full Employment Policy in the 1970s: The Debates on the Humphrey–Hawkins Act," *History of Political Economy* 54, no. 4 (2022): 619–53, 624–5.

77 Eli Cook, *The Pricing of Progress: Economic Indicators and the Capitalization of American Life* (Cambridge, MA: Harvard University Press, 2017), 263.

78 Private correspondence with Verena Halsmayer, September 17, 2014.

79 H. R. Edwards and N. T. Drane, "The Australian Economy," *Economic Record* 39, no. 87 (1963): 259–81, 259.

80 This illustrates Timothy Mitchell's argument about how such a mode of government (balancing opposite interests through utilizing a calculated economic future) was an effect of "the economy." See Mitchell, "Economentality," 492.

81 Robert M. Solow, "The Kennedy Council and the Long Run," in *Economic Events, Ideas and Policies: The 1960s and After*, edited by G. L. Perry and James Tobin (Washington, DC: Brookings Institution, 2000), 111–35, 112.

82 Solow, "Kennedy Council and the Long Run," 113. He proceeded: "We (or I, anyway) thought of growth theory as being the macroeconomics of a national economy that always – by hook or by crook – manages to keep its actual aggregate output very close to its potential output." Thinking of the long-run growth rate itself as a malleable object was only a later development in the so-called endogenous growth theory from the mid-1980s onward.

83 Cf. John Toye, "Solow in the Tropics," in *Robert Solow and the Development of Growth Economics* (supplement to *History of Political Economy* 41) edited by Mauro Boianovsky and Kevin D. Hoover (Durham, NC: Duke University Press, 2009), 221–40, 222.

84 Robert M. Solow, "The Truth Further Refined: A Comment on Marris," *The Public Interest*, no. 11 (1968): 47–52, 52.

85 Literary scholar Joseph Vogl has noted that economists' "realism is prospective; it is always anticipating a virtual reality which it projects into objects and relations," Joseph Vogl, *The Specter of Capital* (Stanford, CA: Stanford University Press, 2015), 36.

86 Robin Marris, "Preface for Social Scientists," in *The Corporate Economy: Growth, Competition, and Innovative Potential*, edited by Robin Marris and Adrian Wood (Cambridge, MA: Harvard University Press, 1971), xv–xxvi, xx. On Marris, see Adrian Wood, "Robin Marris (1924–2012)," in *The Palgrave Companion to Cambridge Economics*, edited by R. A. Cord (London: Palgrave Macmillan UK, 2017), 893–914.

87 Robert M. Solow, "A Rejoinder," *The Public Interest*, no. 9 (1967): 118–9, 119.

88 On the New Left critique of economics, see Tiago Mata, *Radical Expectations: How the New Left Changed Economics* (Cambridge: Cambridge University Press, forthcoming); on the Committee for Economic Development and its critique of neo-classical economics, see Amy C. Offner, *Sorting out the Mixed Economy: The Rise and Fall of Welfare and Developmental States in the Americas* (Princeton: Princeton University Press, 2019), chapter 6, in particular p. 204.

89 Robert L. Heilbroner, "On the Limited 'Relevance' of Economics," *The Public Interest* 21 (1970): 80–93, 83. When Solow joined the CEA, Robert McNamara's Department of Defense absorbed 10 percent of national income, one-half of every tax dollar. See the documentary *The Fog of War: Eleven Lessons from the Life of Robert S. McNamara* (directed by Errol Morris), min. 5:00. Kennedy had in fact built up the most powerful military force in history, see Collins, *More*, 56–7.

90 Cf. Maurice Dobb, *Theories of Value and Distribution since Adam Smith: Ideology and Economic Theory* (London: Cambridge University Press, 1973), 35.

91 See Soma Golden, "Economist Joan Robinson, 72, Is Full of Fight," *New York Times*, March 23, 1976, available at www.nytimes.com/1976/03/23/archives/econo mist-joan-robinson-72-is-full-of-fight-economist-joan-robinson.html, last accessed May 7, 2024.

92 Solow, "Truth Further Refined," 52.

93 Robert M. Solow, "Science and Ideology in Economics," *The Public Interest* 21 (1970): 94–107, 98.

94 In its 1965 inaugural issue, editors Bell and Kristol announced their commitment to nonideological inquiry (neither "liberal, conservative, or radical"), complementing the anti-utopianism of Bell's *The End of Ideology: On the Exhaustion of Political Ideas in the Fifties* (1960). See Daniel Bell and Irving Kristol, "What Is the Public Interest?," *The Public Interest* 1 (1965): 3–5, 4.

95 Already in 1966, Bell tried to commission Solow to write an article about whether the new economics could already manage the economy effectively: "Even more broadly, would you assume that all this, socialist as well as capitalist economics can come within neo-classical models?," Daniel Bell to Robert Solow, June 7, 1966, Solow papers, box 52, file B: 4 of 7. Solow never wrote the requested article, but the themes were at the center of his other contributions to the *Public Interest*.

96 Eric Hounshell and Verena Halsmayer, "How Does Economic Knowledge Have a Politics? On the Frustrated Attempts of John K. Galbraith and Robert M. Solow to Fix the Political Meaning of Economic Models in The Public Interest," *KNOW*:

A Journal on the Formation of Knowledge 4, no. 2 (2020): 263–93. The following paragraphs are adapted from the paper.

97 Robert M. Solow, "The New Industrial State, or, Son of Affluence," *The Public Interest*, no. 9 (1967): 100–108, 101.

98 Solow, "New Industrial State," 103.

99 In the history of science, *scientific personae* bring together ways of life and forms of knowledge. They are cultural figures formed through habits, mental conditions, and material techniques within specific historical contexts. See Lorraine Daston and H. Otto Sibum, "Introduction: Scientific Personae and Their Histories," *Science in Context* 16, no. 1–2 (2003): 1–8.

100 Paul Samuelson, "Economists and the History of Ideas," *American Economic Review* 52, no. 1 (1962): 1–18, at 18. Cited in Marion Fourcade, *Economists and Societies: Discipline and Profession in the United States, Britain, and France, 1890s to 1990s* (Princeton: Princeton University Press, 2009), 110. Indeed, Solow had public appearances in, among others, *The New Republic*, *The New York Times Book Review*, and *The Public Interest*. On economists in the public sphere, see Tiago Mata and Steven G. Medema, "Cultures of Expertise and the Public Interventions of Economists," in *The Economist as Public Intellectual* (supplement to *History of Political Economy* 45), edited by Tiago Mata and Steven G. Medema (Durham, NC: Duke University Press, 2013), 1–19.

101 Solow, "New Industrial State," 100. According to Solow, Galbraith shared that power with Fed chairman William McChesnay, who did not take Galbraith's political positions but was an opponent of Heller in the struggle for political influence – as a noneconomist.

102 On Galbraith and his insider/outsider role, see David Halberstam, "The Importance of Being Galbraith," *Harper's Magazine*, November 1 (1967): 47–54.

103 Solow, "New Industrial State," 104.

104 Solow, "Rejoinder," 119.

105 "It is said that ordinary people cannot be entrusted with the judgment of their own welfare, not even with the choice of the things they buy." Solow, "Science and Ideology," 105.

106 Solow, "New Industrial State," 100–1.

107 Stephanie L. Mudge, *Leftism Reinvented: Western Parties from Socialism to Neoliberalism* (Cambridge, MA: Harvard University Press, 2018), 374. Many thanks to Eric Hounshell for pointing me to this part.

108 John Kenneth Galbraith, *Ambassador's Journal: A Personal Account of the Kennedy Years* (Boston: Houghton Mifflin, 1969), 338. Solow recounted another such occasion to a colleague: Swedish economists "had just won a long, hard battle" over interest rates at their central bank. "Then Ken breezed into Stockholm on his way from somewhere, had dinner with the big shots, casually told them [to change their policy] . . . Then he breezed out again, having undone years of careful education . . . Who wouldn't grind his teeth?" Robert Solow to Richard "Dick" Sargent, January 5, 1961, Solow papers, box 60, file S: 1 of 7.

109 Solow himself claimed that inequality was one of the fields where his reasoning changed significantly. During his time at the CEA, the top 1 percent earned a 12.6 percent of GDP; the bottom 50 percent earned 19.5 percent; today these percentages have reversed. See Peter Dizikes, "The Productive Career of Robert Solow,"

December 27, 2019, available at www.technologyreview.com/2019/12/27/131259/ the-productive-career-of-robert-solow, last accessed May 7, 2024.

110 Both Solow, "Science and Ideology," 98.

111 Paul Samuelson to Alvin Hansen, January 18, 1966, Solow papers, box 60, file S, 6 of 7.

112 James Tobin, "Money and Income: Post Hoc Ergo Propter Hoc?" *Quarterly Journal of Economics* 84, no. 2 (1970): 301–17. See Tarja Knuuttila, "Epistemic Artifacts and the Modal Dimension of Modeling," *European Journal for Philosophy of Science* 11, no. 3 (2021), section 4.

113 Robert M. Solow, "The Wide, Wide World of Wealth," *New York Times Sunday Book Review*, March 20, 1988, available at www.nytimes.com/1988/03/20/books/ the-wide-wide-world-of-wealth.html, last accessed April 20, 2024.

114 Robert M. Solow, "How Did Economics Get That Way and What Way Did It Get," *Daedalus* 126 (2005): 87–100, 89.

115 Paul Krugman, "Incidents from My Career," 1995, available at www.princeton .edu/~pkrugman/incidents.html, last accessed April 20, 2024. On Solow's model as a teaching device, see also Halsmayer, "From Exploratory Modeling to Technical Expertise," 243–5.

116 Solow, in a letter to Domar, cited in Béatrice Cherrier, "Toward a History of Economics at MIT, 1940–72," in *MIT and the Transformation of American Economics* (supplement to *History of Political Economy* 46), edited by E. Roy Weintraub (Durham, NC: Duke University Press, 2014), 15–44, 25. For a quantitative study of the spread of MIT's students, Andrej Svorenčík, "MIT's Rise to Prominence: Outline of a Collective Biography," in *MIT and the Transformation of American Economics* (supplement to *History of Political Economy* 46), edited by E. Roy Weintraub (Durham, NC: Duke University Press, 2014), 109–33.

117 David Kaiser, *Drawing Theories Apart: The Dispersion of Feynman Diagrams in Postwar Physics* (Chicago: University of Chicago Press, 2005), 356. See also Ursula Klein, "Paper Tools in Experimental Cultures," *Studies in History and Philosophy of Science Part A* 32, no. 2 (2001): 265–302.

118 See the many celebratory remarks on Solow's legacy as a teacher in Dizikes, "Productive Career of Robert Solow."

119 Solow, *Growth Theory*, vi.

120 Both: Robert Solow, interview with Verena Halsmayer, May 3, 2011.

121 Krugman, "Incidents from My Career."

122 George A. Akerlof, *An Economic Theorist's Book of Tales* (Cambridge: Cambridge University Press, 2009), vii. Among MIT's alumni who received the Nobel Memorial Prize of the Swedish national bank are Joseph Stiglitz, Lawrence Klein, and Robert Mundell.

123 I owe the expression of "disciplinary language" to an exchange with Marcel Boumans.

124 David Novick, "Mathematics: Logic, Quantity, and Method," *The Review of Economics and Statistics* 36, no. 4 (1954): 357–8, 358. Novick's main argument was that logical consistency alone neither implied relevance nor relation "to the facts of the real world" (357). Paul A. Samuelson, "Introduction: Mathematics in Economics – No, No or Yes, Yes, Yes?" *The Review of Economics and Statistics* 36, no. 4 (1954): 359. On the symposium, see Philip Mirowski, *Machine Dreams: How*

Economics Became a Cyborg Science (Cambridge: Cambridge University Press, 2002), 396–406, emphasizing two different approaches for developing a mathematical social science at RAND; Camila Orozco Espinel, "How Mathematical Economics Became (Simply) Economics: The Mathematical Training of Economists during the 1940s, 1950s and 1960s in the United States" (Center for the History of Political Economy at Duke University Working Paper Series, No. 2020-11, November 16, 2020), 7–12, available at https://ssrn.com/abstract= 3731733, last accessed May 7, 2024, focusing on the economists' case for mathematical training.

125 John Kenneth Galbraith, "A Review of a Review," *The Public Interest* no. 9 (1967): 109–18, 118.

126 In contrast to Harvard, Yale, Penn, and Columbia, MIT had not produced a Black American PhD in economics by the beginning of the 1970s. Apparently, the faculty started a "unique and extraordinary" affirmative action effort (predominantly Richard Eckaus, Samuelson, Solow, and Peter Temin), which was stopped after a few years. See William Darity and Arden Kreeger, "The Desegregation of an Elite Economics Department's PhD Program: Black Americans at MIT," in *MIT and the Transformation of American Economics* (supplement to *History of Political Economy* 46), edited by E. Roy Weintraub (Durham, NC: Duke University Press, 2014): 317–36, 326.

127 For recent perspectives from within the US discipline, see, for instance, the discussions at the panel session *How Can Economics Solve Its Gender Problem?* at the 2019 annual meeting of the American Economic Association in Atlanta, available at www.aeaweb.org/webcasts/2019/how-can-economics-solve-gender-problem, last accessed April 20, 2024; and Committee on Equity, Diversity and Professional Conduct, "AEA Professional Climate Survey: Final Report," September 15, 2019, available at www.aeaweb.org/resources/member-docs/final-climate-survey-results-sept-2019, last accessed April 20, 2024.

Epilogue

"Once we attend to the miniature world, the outside world stops and is lost to us," Susan Stewart notes in her account of miniatures in the arts and literature. Using the example of a toy, she describes miniatures as worlds of "arrested life."[1] One way of looking at models is to understand them as manifestations of a desire for control or reflections of human anxiety compensating for a chaotic world. Solow's model presented an orderly world on an equilibrium growth path. Everything beyond that world – from natural resources to distribution to power – was relegated to the realm of the unknown, at least for the time being. In this sense, the model offered a retreat; it was a small-scale space protected from contamination by an outside world that could not be scaled down. Critics of mathematical economics have frequently written about its fictional abstractions in these terms. One such critic, Sidney Schoeffler, whom we encountered in Chapter 5, wondered whether the reason that economists stuck with models that were, to him, so obviously inadequate from a scientific and logical point of view was that they satisfied specific psychological needs. "Unbearable facts are eliminated and desires are satisfied by imagery so that man can live in harmony with himself and with his environment," he quoted from the psychology literature.[2] Like Stewart's miniatures, mathematical models might compensate for the order and calm that a real world lacks. Historians of economics have inquired into how general equilibrium analysis fulfilled a need for protection for the mathematical economist Gerard Debreu, a retreat from the complications and frictions of his lived experience.[3] "Finding equilibrium," in Till Düppe's and E. Roy Weintraub's account, was not simply a matter of devising the most depersonalized and aloof axiomatic system. It was also an expression of the lives of their protagonists.[4]

In contrast to general equilibrium theorists, the modelers in this book were not in the first place concerned with the formulation of abstract axiomatic worlds. Their epistemic values were different. They focused on "practicability," on a model being "useful" and "realistic enough." Still, concepts of economic equilibrium, the harmony of interests, and perfect rationality also informed their reasoning. Solow's model was indeed a prime visualization of such a well-running world, as Schoeffler would have it, a "wish-fulfilling intellectual imagery."[5] The model supported the belief that capitalism was not a series of erratic and arbitrary fluctuations and crises. Yet the protagonists of this book did not suppose an automatic harmony of market mechanisms. Rather than a flight from the world, they thought that their models provided them with an opportunity to, as a maker of different kinds of miniatures has put it, "confront, question, critique, or consider it."[6] Their epistemic virtues, I have argued, were tightly interlinked with their stance toward economic management. These modelers not only believed in the manageability of the economy, but they actually wanted to help manage it themselves. It is in this way that models prompted economists to emphasize the irregular, nonsystematic element of economic phenomena, the "cacophony of the marketplace," as Solow once put it.[7] Such an epistemological stance came along with several tensions linked to the ambiguity and openness of their models rather than the closure they provided.

My approach in this book was to take seriously the many ways in which economists treated models as artifacts. In the context of specific practices, models were not fixed, closed-off realities. They were made, used, adapted, and repurposed; they prompted questions, raised problems, and motivated action; they excluded issues, made some things invisible, and drew their "builders" and "users," as the historical actors put it, into their highly specific worlds. At the same time, they were not as clean-cut as one would want to believe; they allowed for different and sometimes contradictory interpretations. Their ultimate indeterminacy raised a variety of model talk concerning both their economic contents and their meanings in research and policy-making (Chapter 5). The past chapters led through different encounters with Solow's model. My central question was what this "simple" model was and did (Chapter 1). Due to its small scale and particular form, the model was able to interact with various other forms of economic knowledge and take on several roles. When Solow aimed to create a simple model for his students, the by-product of his more complex modeling work turned out to be a contribution to growth theory (Chapter 4). In effect, it introduced a specific way of theorizing and, in the eyes and hands of growth modelers, came to provide a more general case that confined other approaches to special cases. It also equipped economists with what they appreciated as an easy-to-use and more efficient technique of measuring growth and its factors than existing gauges (Chapter 2). And it figured as a simpler version of more complex, quantitative models, interpreted as providing "qualitative" knowledge (Chapter 3). Modelers compared the work it did with literary miniatures such as "parables" or "fables," for it enabled them to tell clean-cut stories about how modern growth worked. In this way, the different trajectories in this book showed how the model shifted gears, changed purposes, appearances, and meanings depending on its specific engagements.

Theoretical model, instrument of measurement, a means of storytelling, a didactic device – all this happened at and around Solow's desk. From there, and simultaneously from the desks where other versions of the neoclassical growth model were constructed, it circulated widely. It was adapted, extended, and applied in a variety of projects, in different fields over many decades. In the realm of economic theory, "the Solow model" became one of the dominant workhorse models that defined what was accepted as economic knowledge. Economists replaced parameters and equations with different formulations, clarified the model's interrelationships, searched for more solid foundations for its results, and generalized its outcomes. Such work could, for instance, use the "elegant" curve of the neoclassical growth model as a graphic device to show that it became "unmanageable" when land was included.[8] In the form of the model, the notion of economic growth made its way as a useable concept into other areas of economists' study such as development economics, cycles, and public finance. In 1987, when Solow was awarded the Sveriges Riksbank Prize in Economic Sciences in Memory of Alfred Nobel, the model was said to have sparked "hundreds of theoretical and empirical articles." It had become, as the press release from the Royal Swedish Academy of Sciences announced, a "framework for structuring modern macroeconomic theory."[9] On the occasion of his Nobel lecture, Solow noted in an ironic tone that "'the neoclassical model of economic growth' started a small industry."[10] If we take these utterings at face value, how can we account for the model's tenacity?

Given that I have emphasized the many roles the model played in the 1950s and the 1960s, it probably will not come as a surprise that economists of later decades praised its versatility. It is telling that they compared the Solow model to the Feynman diagrams in theoretical physics, taking "abstract concepts of equilibrium over time" and "shaping them into tools for ordinary economists."[11] Introduced as a bookkeeping device for simplifying calculations in quantum electrodynamics in the late 1940s, the Feynman diagrams were adopted in a variety of fields. The historian David Kaiser has argued that these now routine diagrammatic applications "helped to transform the way physicists saw the world, and their place within it."[12] Similarly, the Solow model – in concert with a whole collection of small- and larger-scale models – acted as an agent of disciplinary change that transformed both economists' reasoning practices as well as the domain of economic expertise. That economists draw the comparison with the Feynman diagrams is telling in yet another way. It supports the argument that economists themselves understood a model as a specific kind of concrete artifact. The economists who adopted and continued work on Solow's model spoke of a "machinery," an "apparatus," a "tool," and an "instrument."[13] They considered it the right tool for a job. In fact, it turned into different tools for many jobs.

Throughout this book I have argued that Solow's model, and the forms of knowledge it built upon, already framed the jobs it was supposed to do and prefigured the very problems it should solve. This was not entirely obscure to practitioners. After all, the model was not appreciated for any specific realism, empirical correctness, or explanatory power. In the first place, this practice of mathematical modeling was not about forging an agreement between theory and a reality but, akin to a technological practice, about fixing together various bits of knowledge, making things work, and thereby creating an artifactual reality in its own right.[14] The Feynman diagrams, as many other examples from the history of science, had been introduced as "convenient ways to talk about the world," but already in the next generation of practitioners they acquired an "added sense of realism."[15] Similarly, as the following two examples will illustrate, the consolidation of Solow's model had implications for "economic growth" as an economist-made technophenomenon.[16] Here, the passing of time is essential. "The Solow model" was implemented in long-lasting constellations used by successive groups of economists who had learned economic modeling as a craft and were trained in treating mathematical models as concrete artifacts. In the following section I will sketch two trajectories that indicate the uses of the model in the 1970s and 1980s, namely in a field of economic measurement called "growth accounting" and in the establishment of epistemic infrastructures for policy-making. These trajectories point at the different chronologies that unfold when focusing on the level of the artifacts and infrastructures of economic knowledge rather than the rise and fall of theoretical and political ideas.

NEOCLASSICAL GROWTH IN ACTION

The perhaps most enduring way in which the neoclassical growth model has left its imprint on economic knowledge is its use as a device for measurement. In Chapter 2, I showed how economists appreciated it as a more efficient procedure for measuring the factors of growth than existing indices. The superior economy of this instrument of measurement, however, came at great costs. For one, it cast the economy as a whole, its growth, and the role of productivity in neoclassical terms. Whatever did not fit into this rendition of the economy – the ever-extendable list of things that were excluded from the model – was neatly tucked away in a "residual." Such a device created a strict boundary between what was known (meaning that it was part of the model), and what was unknown (the "rest"). The first category involved conventional measures of capital and labor. The residual contained not only measurement errors but all kinds of things that played a role in the world of economic practices but were not specifically measured: From inequality to various types of capital to all kinds of cultural, social, and temporal factors that affected measures of GNP. In this sense, the numbers that the neoclassical model created could just as well be read as measures of the enormous distance between the model and the world it was intended to gauge. But, while others spoke of a "measure of our ignorance," Solow strikingly framed the residual as "technical progress." He was aware of and outspoken about the stakes of his interpretative maneuver. The procedure required, he noted with a seeming shrug of the shoulders, more than a deliberate suspension of disbelief.[17] Once others applied the model as a measuring device, such qualifications were easily waived.

Soon, the model came to set the terms of debate over "technical change." It was employed to measure growth and productivity of national economies, industries, and individual firms. While Solow had qualified his use of "technical change" as "a shorthand expression for *any kind of shift* in the production function," for the most part the literature using the model simply carried on with the label.[18] A 1963 study of growth and productivity of the Australian economy, for example, employed "the method ... developed by R. M. Solow."[19] The lower table in Figure E.1 shows the relevant development of the index of "technical progress," here still put in quotes. Similarly, a paper measuring the rate of technical change in the Indian Tata Iron and Steel Company (TISCO) noted that "the method of estimation chosen is that of Professor Solow."[20] Another example was a paper on "technological change" in US agriculture, which featured a table visualizing the application of "the Solow model" (Figure E.2).[21]

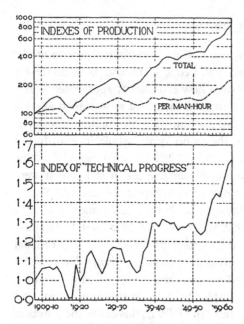

Figure E.1 The "index of 'technical proress'"
(Edwards and Drane, "Australian Economy," 268)

TABLE 2. APPLICATION OF THE SOLOW MODEL TO AGRICULTURE

Year	Employment in Agriculture (thousands)[1]	Capital in Agriculture in 1910–14 dollars (millions)[2]	Agricultural Gross Product 1910–14 dollars (millions)[3]	Share of Capital in Output[4]	ΔA/A from Formula 2[5]	% of Tech. Change Previous Decade	Tech. Change Function A(t)[6]
	(1)	(2)	(3)	(4)	(5)	(6)	(7)
	Assuming All Labor at Market Wage						
1850	4,902	13,650	1,628	.000			1.00000
1860	6,208	18,743	2,317	.000	.1237	1 1/8	1.12375
1870	6,850	19,758	2,713	.298	.0566	1/2	1.18732
1880	8,585	27,819	4,028	.303	.1476	3/8	1.36252
1890	9,938	33,707	4,992	.224	.0584	1/2	1.44213
1900	10,912	40,307	6,187	.271	.1065	1	1.59488
1910	11,592	45,367	6,708	.395	.0013	1/8	1.59700
1920	11,449	49,842	7,471	.436	.0809	3/4	1.72620
1930	10,472	49,160	8,660	.567	.2280	2 1/8	2.11970
1940	9,163	48,472	9,632	.516	.2010	1 7/8	2.54580
1950	6,906	53,693	11,778	.504	.3846	3 1/8	3.50482
1958				.226	.4204	4 1/2	5.03177

Figure E.2 The "Application of the Solow model to agriculture"
(Lave, "Empirical Estimates of Technological Change," 944)

In these early instances, the model was applied as it was, leaving its form intact and keeping Solow's label for the rest. It was used as a simple tool to measure productivity in datasets that, with a couple of reformulations, fit its format. Critics maintained that the residual captured all kinds of things and was not actually to be taken as "technical change." Even Solow himself asked economists not to equate technical change in common speech ("inventions. . . like the electric light or the automobile or the electronic computer") with the statistical constructs of econometric research. "Economists, who give the impression of having invented the idea of technological progress in the past 6 or 7 years," he mused, "have something much more pedestrian in mind." Rather than talking about technological progress, they should use "the pedestrian label of 'increase in output per unit of input'. It is a statistical artifact."[22] This came at a point in Solow's career when he started to more frequently urge his colleagues not to mistake the categories of econometric analysis for real-world entities. Irrespective of the intentions of its constructor, the model gained a life of its own as an easy-to-use measuring device.

The history of science has emphasized that the circulation of knowledge consists of practices of transformation, adaptation, and reinterpretation. The central point is that these processes are productive and not merely applications by passive recipients. This is also true for an area of research between economics and economic history called "growth accounting," for which Solow's model is said to have "laid the foundation."[23] The field, picking up pace in the 1960s and active until the present day, built on both aggregate production functions and index number constructions as its major instruments. What came to be called the "Solow residual" had a major role to play, not only as a common tool but also as a frequent contrasting foil for approaches that did not use a neoclassical production function.[24] The overarching aim of growth accounting was to include ever more additional factors of production. This was an attempt to curtail the list of absences that came with the model. But, in order to make the model measure more things, these had first to be brought into a form that fit the model-guided measurement procedure. In the decades to come, intangible factors of production such as "knowledge" or "education," for instance, were recast as quantitative entities so that they could enter the growth accounting framework. Approaches that used the neoclassical growth model as a measuring device added ever more items as parameters in the production function: Organizational characteristics, human capital in the forms of education and health, population changes, or government policies. Once researchers committed to using that tool, they had to turn the things they wanted to know into inputs that fit the model. This is not only about the affordances and the limitations that come with an instrument's use. As the model framed ways of thinking, seeing, and acting, it guided perception. Once it became the standard of the field, it essentially prefigured the object it was supposed to measure.

As an instrument of measurement, the Solow model's rendition of the economy not only affected economists' ideas and theories. The quantitative kind of knowledge it provided was explicitly thought to be useful in economic expertise and policy-making. In this way, its restrictive imaginary power extended directly to economic governance, where the Solow residual was widely treated as a straightforward yardstick to allocate resources "in the interests of economic growth."[25] Chapter 2 showed how national accounts captured the economic benefits of public expenditure, thus providing quantitative arguments for state investments. At the same time, this meant subjecting policy to an economic evaluation. The neoclassical growth model took part in this broader trend as it became one crucial instrument to measure how all kinds of factors contributed to the increase of national income and thus, so the argument commonly went, to progress. Of the various factors for cutting down the Solow residual, it was especially aggregate statistics of "research and development" that policy-makers picked as a parameter to fine-tune the growth of the national economy.[26] Policies directed at growth and focusing on the economic value of scientific knowledge were simpler to advance than policies that aimed at other results (such as, for instance, pushing for more effective pharmaceuticals). The promotion of policies for stimulating technological innovation relied to a great extent on aggregate time series production function regressions. Here, Solow's model presented processes of knowledge-making in the form of a production function, measured in terms of inputs and outputs. It thus contributed to a development that reduced the realm of the economic to efficiency calculations and subordinated public policies to that realm.[27]

With the "Solow Residual," the model had a scintillating career in the world of economic expertise. Yet there was another, less visible way in which it contributed so-called technical knowledge for economic governance. From the 1960s onward, when economic planning rose to new prominence, Solow's model was integrated in the epistemic infrastructure of policy-making. Large-scale macroeconometric forecasting and planning models figured as decision support systems in a variety of institutions from planning offices and institutions in public administration to central banks and businesses.[28] Economists argued that these models provided a more systematic character to the knowledge used in governance as it was able to lay out the assumed consequences of various possible policies and added a long-term purview. Providing such an overhead perspective, models were intended to enable planners to figure out ways to better order the whole. Most planning and forecasting models worked as evaluation tools measuring potential effects of policies on national economic growth. Examples stretch from the Federal Republic of Germany (putting the macroeconomic goals of growth and stability into its constitution in 1967), to Colombia's *Plan Decenal* (which was essential for the collaboration between the National Front, the US, and international lenders), to Belgium's planning model MARIBEL (which was only introduced in 1970 to promote "democratic" decision-making).[29] While the concrete purposes, the institutional embedding of planning, and its effects on policy-making differed widely, macroeconometric models commonly included projections of the long-run and established specific growth targets. Here, the neoclassical growth model had a special role to play.

When it came to integrating growth, most macroeconometric models included a neoclassical framework. In the short-run, they afforded an analysis of policy effects, in which the role of demand was crucial. In their portrayal of the long-run, however, demand had no role to play. In these long-run scenarios, markets were assumed to work smoothly. This was the "land of the margin" that Solow had invoked in his 1956 paper, the cosmos of the neoclassical growth model (Chapter 1). This is not to say that it was precisely Solow's model that circulated. As I have mentioned several times, Solow's was not the only formulation of a neoclassical growth model. In particular, when it came to policy modeling, Tinbergen's version was probably closer to the minds of planners. One example for the employment of the small-scale model, however, is a project that directly linked to Solow's paper – the Norwegian planning model. Illustrating the porousness of the boundaries between governmental expertise and academic work, Norwegian planner Leif Johansen both extended the neoclassical growth model as a contribution to economic theory and made Solow's model an essential part of the architecture of a quantitative multi-sector growth model for planning purposes.[30] This model, in turn, was implemented as part of a computerized infrastructure for administrative decision-making in the Norwegian ministry of finance in the late 1960s.[31]

In the Norwegian planning system, the neoclassical growth model contributed to calculating both a balanced growth path in the remote future and the factors that would increase that growth. Johansen's

"Multi-Sectoral Study of Economic Growth" (1960) presented a model economy that consisted of several sectors and was supposed to show the effects of changes (for example, technological progress) on various sectors of the economy and their relationship to one another (such as the redistribution of labor and capital between the sectors). Using data from Norwegian national accounts, the model was implemented numerically to provide a guide to macroeconomic planning. In all of this, the (adapted) neoclassical growth model served as a kind of design for establishing and checking the behavior of the larger-scale model. Since Johansen thought it would be difficult "to see the macroeconomic implications of a multi-sector model," he used the small-scale model as a benchmark for judging the larger model's behavior. Only if it corresponded to the behavior of the smaller one was it to be considered reasonable.[32] Like many others who used and extended Solow's model, Johansen stressed its operational practicability and functional simplicity. Here, the model became part of a larger-scale construction that carried most of its phenomenotechnical characteristics: The economy created was a system of efficient production, which, in the neoclassical long-run, grew without frictions on a balanced growth path. Based on the assumptions of the efficient utilization of resources and consumer sovereignty, questions of distribution or any other kind of concerns that went beyond efficiency were excluded from the start.

As a part of planning models, Solow's model fit perfectly in the environments of interventionism and the mixed economy from where it came. Similar to the way Solow made sense of his modeling practice, Johansen emphasized that equilibrium was not achieved automatically by the forces of the market: It had to be maintained by active policy. His model provided "a background and a framework for the continuous flow of decisions" within the realm of policy-making.[33] In the technical framework of 1960s macroeconomic planning, a variety of political strategies were viable. In each case, however, the major point of reference was growth. In that vein, Johansen stressed the possibility of creating the appropriate institutions for implementing "a continuous and balanced growth process with full employment of both labor and capital equipment."[34] Being a life-long card-carrying member of the Norwegian Communist Party, he himself did so with an eye on Soviet planning.

The concrete architectures of macroeconomic planning models differed, and their institutional embedding framed the way in which the knowledge they provided wielded influence on policy-making. At their core, however, all these modeling projects adhered to a similar epistemology and ontology: It was not about an "as if," a hypothetical on whose ground government should act. Recall the often-cited methodological stance associated with Milton Friedman that one should proceed working with a model *as if* its assumptions were true – as long as its predictions were accurate. In Chapter 1 I have compared that perspective with Solow's 1956 preamble that the crucial assumptions needed to be "realistic enough." As vague as that formulation might be, it put a prime on the concrete modeling situation, the problem at hand, and the role of the modeler's skills in judging the adequacy of an assumption. Similarly, in the eyes of their constructors, large-scale planning models did not provide a glance into the future "as if" their assumptions were true. The projects discussed in these pages were embedded in a discourse that was all about "what happens if." Planners designed a menu of possible actions that in turn generated a set of different outcomes. Here, economic expertise was neither predictive nor probabilistic. Instead, planning models were tools for imagining possible future worlds that might very well be realized.[35]

As a design for econometric planning, the Solow model contributed to the quantitative generation of possible future worlds that could be achieved through macroeconomic management. The rationale was the following: Since prices and wages did not adjust quickly enough to bring markets into equilibrium in the short-run, the main task of economic expertise was to manage aggregate demand. Once a certain rate of employment was reached, market competition would establish an efficient allocation of resources. Whatever issues specific markets might exhibit, economic expertise was able to provide appropriate knowledge for intervening to foster competitive markets.[36] In this sense, planning models were part of a program that they themselves shaped. It was about making the economy that they depicted resemble the model ever more closely, making it akin to a determinate and predictable system.

I have argued that the ambiguity of mathematical models was conducive to their application to policy design. Several political programs could be supported by the same models, but on the flipside a model came with a variety of closures, which tended to become invisible when models turned into standards. Over and over, modelers in the previous chapters spoke of their models as tools but did not, contrary to what we might expect, argue for their neutrality. For the philosopher Alain Badiou, probably taking a swipe at contemporary French planning at the end of the 1960s, these models figured as a "technical image of the interests of the bourgeois class," readily "objectify[ing] class objectives."[37] Johansen, in contrast, stressed a certain ideological flexibility of models: Planning techniques could be used to achieve the "goals of a central power complex," and be employed "in the interest of one particular class."[38] This, however, did not mean that he thought of models as neutral. Clearly, they promoted a kind of policy-making that gave priority to "total efficiency and the development of consumption."[39] Once the model system for macroeconomic planning was established, implicit assumptions were consolidated, and the values and goals embodied by the model were not questioned further.

The model infrastructure of policy-making that evolved from the interventionism of the 1950s and 1960s remained rather stable. Despite the collapse of the Bretton–Woods system and debt crises, the vision of a future world of perfect efficiency and balanced growth seems to have translated well into the 1970s and beyond, as did the role of growth as the benchmark par excellence. The Norwegian system of planning models is indeed active until the present day, for forecasting as well as in the design of policy programs.[40] This is similar in the US, at least according to Gregory Mankiw, who in the 2000s bemoaned that the infrastructure of policy-making relied on the same old models. To him, developments in macroeconomic theory since the 1970s "had only minor impact on the practical analysis of monetary or fiscal policy."[41] A glance at the scarce literature on the practices of providing economic knowledge for governance suggests that, alongside the establishment of DSGE (dynamic stochastic general equilibrium) models in the early 2000s, existing models were adapted and became more detailed with new, more fine-grained variables. The very foundational architecture of these models, in particular a specific kind of "Keynesian" structural equation model, remained relatively stable, both in Treasury Departments and at the FED, for instance.[42]

The examples of growth accounting and planning models illustrate how a small-scale model, a clean zone of domesticated experience, could take on a life independently of the model constructors and have effects in policy-making – not simply through its aesthetic appeal but, more concretely, as a suitable component for the epistemic infrastructures of economic expertise. That it fit existing governmental technologies (national income accounts, productivity measurements, input–output models) was no accident but built in. It neatly blended in and provided an efficient mechanism that calculated the effects of various factors on "long-term growth," which was not only limitless through the power of technological progress but also worked entirely without paying attention to the distribution of income. The two examples I provided highlighted the ability of the model to be extended, put together with other models, and adapted to new data sets and new computing capacities. The work of modeling is rarely finished:

Both the work on and of the model go on. In a way, the neoclassical growth model became a representation of the preferred form of accepted economic analysis and of what economists considered worth investigating. It was not only about the acceptance of a specific technique but the hegemony of a specific kind of problematization. Due to its inherent ambiguity and suggestive power, however, its consolidation came with ironic twists – which brings us back to where this book started.

AFTERLIFE

The Introduction opened with Amartya Sen's 1970 letter to Solow pointing to a certain ambiguity of the model's status as a "model." Was it a mimetic portrayal of the world or was it a fictional world that could be established? In the chapters of this book, I traced some of the model's trajectories as an artifact with its various transformations and interpretations as a "model." The previous section already indicated that such an approach blurs the idea of contained schools or paradigms. This is the case even if we stick with the realm of economic theory. The exchange between Sen and Solow took place at a time when growth theory was the epitome of the field of economics, not least through MIT's modelers who were on the top of the profession. Together with their students, they worked extensively on the neoclassical growth model, including, for instance, multiple sectors and the depreciation on capital. In 1964, Samuelson's *Economics*, the dominant textbook then in its sixth edition, received a chapter on growth – not merely in the sense of rising GDP or measurements of growth and productivity but in the model-sense of an equilibrium growth path. By the end of the decade, the first anthologies collecting the essential contribution to the field came out, among them Sen's, and the first textbook on growth theory offered a consolidated introduction for graduate students in 1970.[43] Already in the course of the 1970s neoclassical growth theory and its specific style of modeling stopped being the exemplar of what was considered high theory. And yet, this was not the end of Solow's model.

In 1974, Evsey Domar bemoaned that "simple models [were] not popular anymore."[44] The ebbing of growth theory as a field resulted, in part, from the dissolution of the bipartisan consensus on New Deal liberalism, which was linked with the stagflation crisis and the rising cultural critique of growth, abundance, and consumerism. At the same time, growth modeling stopped being a separate field and became part of general economics. This was related to a new vogue in economic theory, new classical macroeconomics, which pushed the concepts of "microfoundations" and "rational expectations," challenging "Keynesian" economics. The crux of what has come down as "the Lucas critique" was that Keynesian models did not account for agents' expectations and behavior in reaction to policy changes such as a tax increase.[45] The new classicals' idea was to bring together microeconomics (as the study of utility-maximizing rational actors) with the macroeconomic realm of growth, inflation, and unemployment. In the previous chapters we encountered several attempts to relate the whole with the parts, depictions of the macroeconomy with portrayals of firms, sectors, or industries. By the beginning of the 1970s, new classicals did so by modeling "representative agents" (one "representative" profit-maximizing firm and one "representative" utility-maximizing household). In a way, the new classical critique proceeded with the familiar argument that proper scientific economics had to be rigorous. But how different was this desire for an overarching mathematical framework from the approach followed by the modelers discussed in this book. Though Solow's model was also based on the assumption of perfect competition, it had not provided an explicit formulation. Again, it was this openness that made it adaptable to the new fashion in economic theory. At the same time, engaged in different modeling practices, it changed its very status as a model.[46]

When, from the late 1970s onward, modeling practices in economic theory diversified and a whole variety of models emerged and spread, Solow's was readily integrated. Focusing on its persistence highlights the model's ability to transgress the boundaries of different theoretical "schools." This holds in particular when it comes to the theoretical debates around a new major research object, the so-called real business cycle. The basic idea was to merge long-run growth with short-run business cycles in an overarching mathematical framework. The relevant models adopted, as historians of economics Tiago Mata and Francisco Louçã have demonstrated, a neoclassical production function. The question of how to do so sparked controversy between two schools, "New Classical" and "New Keynesian" macroeconomics. In particular, "the interpretation of the Solow residual became a crucial item of that debate."[47] While theoretical outlooks and disciplinary as well as political alignments differed, all the involved parties relied on the residual, "weaponizing" it for their diverging purposes.[48] Another example for the model changing its status is the revival of neoclassical growth theory from the mid-1980s onward under the label of "endogenous growth theory." The new models built on the concepts of market clearing and perfect foresight just as before, but they endogenized the previously exogenous factor "technical progress," which meant it became a part of the model. Technical progress was now treated as just another good produced and purchased on markets. Named "human capital devoted to research" or "stock of knowledge," a new variable entered the growth model, leaving its basic architecture intact.[49] In a process of consolidation, Solow's model, created at a specific time and place and with a specific purpose, had turned into an essentially unchallenged routine. In this sense, the model has had a buoyant, very successful career. Its epistemological and ontological framings, however, were diverse, which makes it in fact worrisome to speak of the same model.

Following a particular scholarship on modeling, I have maintained throughout this book that a model is embedded in different engagements that decisively frame its character. In the mid-1950s, Solow's model had been part of an endeavor that celebrated the opportunity to experience the workings of a mathematical world, to test ideas, and to extend the dimensions of economic imagination without having to pay too much attention to empirical reality. Solow and economists of his ilk appreciated a model's playful character, its exploratory and, above all, its preliminary form. They pleaded for multi-purpose toolboxes to deal flexibly with specific problems at hand. They highlighted the artificiality of their closed worlds and factored in the role of their skills, judgment, and values. And yet, when these economists' toolboxes stabilized, their models gained a much more steadfast character than their initial framing as exploratory worlds actually allowed for. Between the 1960s and 1980s, mathematical forms and the epistemic norms that accompanied them became increasingly autonomous from their artificers and their specific sites. It is here that the power of models became even more manifest, the power to draw users into their worlds of domesticated experience. By the end of the 1980s, a survey of economic graduate students at elite universities captured a profession that had more appreciation for mathematical technicalities than for dealing with economic problems of whatever they saw as the real world.[50] Also the essential framing of Solow's model (and hereby of "growth") in economic theory changed: In the new endogenous growth theory, the long-term growth rate itself seemed to be malleable. While before, long-term growth was taken as an imaginary trend that could in principle be implemented, it was now something existing in the world.[51] Similarly, in real business cycle theory, "what-if" had turned into "as-if." Solow himself was highly critical, as real business cycle theory took, he argued, "the construction . . . as a model of the actual capitalist world."[52]

The frustration of the historical actors speaks to the openness of models. In Solow's own account, there appears to be a break: While he and his colleagues framed growth and technology as state-driven, these were now to be brought about by the workings of the markets. The growthism of the 1980s argued for an automatic trickling-down and thus used growth to legitimize cuts of social measures, decreasing wage rates, and declining employment numbers.[53] In contrast to Solow's view, from the perspective I have taken in this book, however, there was a curious continuity. Thinking back to the early 1950s, the small-scale model came with cautious "qualifications" that highlighted some of its absences and warned the reader of taking it too literally. Such caveats replaced an earlier way of presenting mathematical economic knowledge. In his account of dynamic instability, Harrod, for instance, had emphasized the lack of certainty in an essayistic treatment circling around a mathematical framework (Chapter 1). Solow's work separated the mathematics and the verbal treatment. Now the model constituted the very object of analysis; it provided secure knowledge. Uncertainty was relegated to the qualifications, a verbal account of how the model was not straightforwardly related to anything beyond its boundaries. It was strikingly easy for subsequent modelers to dispense with such contained paragraphs of doubt. By constructing mathematical models and treating them as some kind of material objects, the economists in this book had created artifactual realities, which developed a life of their own. The list of absences, which had an eerie presence in their writings, vanished when models became increasingly autonomous. Once integrated into different kinds of practice, Solow's model was not only interpreted differently but – given it consisted of the combination of algebraic equations, diagrammatic visualization, and verbal accounts – indeed became a different "model." Regardless of initial intentions and of the modeler's protest, it turned, in some quarters, into a carrier of a market fundamentalist world view and an exemplar for the belief in the omnipotence of markets.

Notes

1   Susan Stewart, *On Longing: Narratives of the Miniature, the Gigantic, the Souvenir, the Collection* (Durham: Duke University Press, 1993), 67, 57.

2   Walter A. Weisskopf, "Psychological Aspects of Economic Thought," *Journal of Political Economy* 57, no. 4 (1949): 304–14, 305, cited in Sidney Schoeffler, *The Failures of Economics: A Diagnostic Study* (Cambridge, MA: Harvard University Press, 1955), 166.

3   Till Düppe, "Gerard Debreu's Secrecy: His Life in Order and Silence," *History of Political Economy* 44, no. 3 (2012): 413–49.

4   Till Düppe and E. Roy Weintraub, *Finding Equilibrium: Arrow, Debreu, McKenzie and the Problem of Scientific Credit* (Princeton: Princeton University Press, 2014), xxi.

5 Weisskopf, "Psychological Aspects of Economic Thought," 309, cited in Schoeffler, *Failures of Economics*, 167.

6 Dr. K, "Miniature Manifesto Part 2: Stop Quoting Susan Stewart," *The Wonder of Miniature Worlds*, June 1, 2015, available at https://thewonderofminiatures.home.blog/2015/06/01/miniature-manifesto-part-2-stop-quoting-susan-stewart, last accessed April 21, 2024.

7 Robert M. Solow, "Review of The Failures of Economics: A Diagnostic Study by Sidney Schoeffler," *Review of Economics and Statistics* 39, no. 1 (1957): 96–8, 96. In the decades to come, Solow also worked with models that were not (always) self-correcting. Having lost his name to the growth model, however, these were far less received. See Robert M. Solow and Joseph E. Stiglitz, "Output, Employment, and Wages in the Short Run," *Quarterly Journal of Economics* 82, no. 4 (1968): 537–60; Frank Hahn and Robert Solow, *A Critical Essay on Modern Macroeconomic Theory* (Cambridge, MA: MIT Press, 1998).

8 Everett E. Hagen, "Population and Economic Growth." *American Economic Review* 49, no. 3 (1959), 310–27, 316. On the stabilization of growth theory, see Mauro Boianovsky and Kevin D. Hoover, "In the Kingdom of Solovia: The Rise of Growth Economics at MIT, 1956–1970," in *MIT and the Transformation of American Economics* (supplement to *History of Political Economy* 46), edited by E. Roy Weintraub (Durham, NC: Duke University Press, 2014), 198–228; Philip Mirowski, *Science-Mart: Privatizing American Science* (Cambridge, MA: Harvard University Press, 2011), 71–2.

9 Press Release for the Royal Swedish Academy of Sciences, "The Nobel Memorial Prize in Economics 1987," *Scandinavian Journal of Economics* 90, no. 1 (1988): 1–5, 3.

10 Both: Robert M. Solow, "Growth Theory and After," *American Economic Review* 78, no. 3 (1988): 307–17, 308.

11 Avinash Dixit, "Growth Theory after Thirty Years," in *Growth/Productivity/Unemployment: Essays to Celebrate Bob Solow's Birthday*, edited by Peter Diamond (Cambridge, MA: MIT Press, 1990), 3–22, 3.

12 David Kaiser, *Drawing Theories Apart: The Dispersion of Feynman Diagrams in Postwar Physics* (Chicago: University of Chicago Press, 2005), 4.

13 See, for instance, Francis M. Bator, "On Capital Productivity, Input Allocation and Growth," *Quarterly Journal of Economics* 71, no. 1 (1957): 86–106, 95, n5; Dixit, "Growth Theory after Thirty Years," 3.

14 On the related distinction between science and technoscience on the level of research objects, see Bernadette Bensaude-Vincent, Sacha Loeve, Alfred Nordmann, and Astrid Schwarz, "Matters of Interest: The Objects of Research in Science and Technoscience," *Journal for General Philosophy of Science* 42, no. 2 (2011): 365–83.

15 Kaiser, *Drawing Theories Apart*, 368–9.

16 On my use of Bachelard's phenomenotechnique, see the Introduction.

17 Robert M. Solow, "Technical Change and the Aggregate Production Function," *Review of Economics and Statistics* 39, no. 3 (1957): 312–20, 312. See also the final section of Chapter 2.

18 Solow, "Technical Change and the Aggregate Production Function," 312.

19 H. R. Edwards and N. T. Drane, "The Australian Economy," *The Economic Record* 39, no. 87 (1963): 259–81, 266.

20 P. N. Dhar and Om Kar Seth, "The Rate of Technical Progress in the Tata Iron and Steel Company in 1913–56," *Indian Economic Review* 6, no. 1 (1963): 1–19, 2.

21 Lester B. Lave, "Empirical Estimates of Technological Change in United States Agriculture, 1850–1958," *Journal of Farm Economics* 44, no. 4 (1962): 941–52, 944.

22 Robert M. Solow, *Capital Theory and the Rate of Return* (Amsterdam: North-Holland, 1963), 37, cited in Tiago Mata and Francisco Louçã, "The Solow Residual as a Black Box: Attempts at Integrating Business Cycle and Growth Theories," in *Robert Solow and the Development of Growth Economics* (supplement to *History of Political Economy* 41), edited by Mauro Boianovsky and Kevin D. Hoover (Durham, NC: Duke University Press, 2009), 334–55, 335.

23 Press Release from the Royal Swedish Academy of Sciences, "The Nobel Memorial Prize in Economics 1987," *Scandinavian Journal of Economics* 90, no. 1 (1988): 1–5, 3.

24 See Zvi Griliches, "The Sources of Measured Productivity Growth: United States Agriculture, 1940–60," *Journal of Political Economy* 71, no. 4 (1963): 331–46, 331. For a detailed portrayal of the epistemic dynamics in the field of growth accounting, see Jeff Biddle, *Progress Through Regression: The Life Story of Empirical Cobb-Douglas Production Function* (Cambridge: Cambridge University Press, 2021), 257–95. For practitioners' surveys, see Dale W. Jorgenson, "Productivity and Economic Growth," in *Fifty Years of Economic Measurement: The Jubilee of the Conference on Research in Income and Wealth*, edited by Ernst R. Berndt and Jack E. Triplett (Chicago: University of Chicago Press, 1991), 19–118; Zvi Griliches, "The Discovery of the Residual: An Historical Note" (NBER Research Working Paper 5348, New York, 1995), available at www.nber.org/papers/w5348, last accessed April 21, 2024. For a discussion of different measurement procedures for economic growth in economics and economic history, see Nicholas Crafts, "Solow and Growth Accounting: A Perspective from Quantitative Economic History," in *Robert Solow and the Development of Growth Economics* (supplement to *History of Political Economy* 41), edited by Mauro Boianovsky and Kevin D. Hoover (Durham, NC: Duke University Press, 2009): 200–20.

25 Robert M. Solow, "Technical Progress, Capital Formation and Economic Growth," *American Economic Review* 52, no. 2 (1962): 76–86, 86.

26 On the American development of the object of R&D, see Sarvnaz Lotfi, "Capitalizing the 'Measure of Our Ignorance': A Pragmatist Genealogy of R&D" (Dissertation, Virginia Polytechnic Institute and State University, 2020).

27 See Daniel Hirschman and Elizabeth Popp Berman, "Do Economists Make Policies? On the Political Effects of Economics," *Socio-Economic Review* 12, no. 4 (2014): 779–811, 796; Mirowski, *Science-Mart*, 73. Again, Solow himself criticized the approach: "There is an internal logic – or sometimes non-logic . . . the 'production' of new technology may not be a simple matter of inputs and outputs," Robert M. Solow, "Perspectives on Growth Theory," *Journal of Economic Perspectives* 8 (1994): 45–54, 52, cited in Mirowski, *Science-Mart*, 73.

28 See the contributions to Marcel Boumans and Pedro Garcia Duarte, eds., *The History of Macroeconometric Modeling* (special issue of *History of Political Economy* 51, no 3) (Durham, NC: Duke University Press, 2019). More specifically on the use of macroeconometric models in central banks, see Juan Acosta and Béatrice Cherrier, "The Transformation of Economic Analysis at the Board of

Governors of the Federal Reserve System during the 1960s," *Journal of the History of Economic Thought* 43, no. 3 (2021): 323–49.

29 Alexander Nützenadel, *Stunde der Ökonomen: Wissenschaft, Politik und Expertenkultur in der Bundesrepublik 1949–1974* (Göttingen: Vandenhoeck & Ruprecht, 2005), 308–16; Andrés M. Guiot-Isaac, "Persuasion and Trust: The Practical Functions of Time-Fixed Development Plans, Colombia 1958–1970" (manuscript, October 2023, under review with *Science in Context*); Zoé Evrard, "The Belgian 'Impossible Scenario' of 1980: Reinventing Planning in Times of 'Crisis'" (manuscript, January 2023, under review with *Science in Context*).

30 Leif Johansen, "Substitution versus Fixed Production Coefficients in the Theory of Economic Growth: A Synthesis," *Econometrica* 27, no. 2 (1959): 157–76; Leif Johansen, *A Multi-Sectoral Study of Economic Growth* (Amsterdam: North-Holland, 1960).

31 The following paragraphs build on Verena Halsmayer, "A Model to 'Make Decisions and Take Actions: Leif Johansen's Multisector Growth Model, Computerized Macroeconomic Planning, and Resilient Infrastructures for Policymaking," in *Becoming Applied: The Transformation of Economics after 1970* (supplement to *History of Political Economy* 49), edited by Roger E. Backhouse and Béatrice Cherrier (Durham, NC: Duke University Press, 2017), 158–86. On the construction of the multisector growth model and the role of Solow's model, see also Olav Bjerkholt, "The Making of the Leif Johansen Multi-Sectoral Model," *History of Economic Ideas* 17, no. 3 (2009): 103–26.

32 Johansen, *Multi-Sectoral Study of Economic Growth*, 24.

33 Johansen, *Multi-Sectoral Study of Economic Growth*, 45.

34 Johansen, *Multi-Sectoral Study of Economic Growth*, 45.

35 On the epistemologies of econometric planning, see Verena Halsmayer, "Ökonometrisches Planen," in *Enzyklopädie der Genauigkeit*, edited by Markus Krajewski, Antonia von Schöning, and Mario Wimmer (Konstanz: Konstanz University Press, 2021), 304–14. On the opposition of "as if" and "what if" in different calculational techniques, see William Deringer's contribution to a review symposium on Jens Beckert's *Imagined Futures*, William Deringer, "Just Props?: Calculation and the Capitalist Imagination," *Socio-Economic Review* 15, no. 1 (2017): 244–9.

36 Cf. Roger E. Backhouse, "Economics," in *The History of the Social Sciences Since 1945*, edited by Roger E. Backhouse and Philippe Fontaine (Cambridge: Cambridge University Press, 2010), 38–70, 55.

37 Alain Badiou, *The Concept of Model: A Introduction to the Materialist Epistemology of Mathematics*, edited and translated by Zachary Luke Fraser and Tzuchien Tho (Melbourne: re.press, 2007 [1970]), 12.

38 Leif Johansen, *Lectures on Macroeconomic Planning*, Vol. 1, General Aspects (Amsterdam: North-Holland, 1977), 50.

39 Johansen, *Lectures on Macroeconomic Planning*, 51.

40 See Halsmayer, "Model to 'Make Decisions and Take Actions'," 178–81.

41 N. Gregory Mankiw, "The Macroeconomist as Scientist and Engineer," *The Journal of Economic Perspectives* 20, no. 4 (2006): 29–46, 42, cited in Timothy Shenk, "Taking Off the Neoliberal Lens: The Politics of the Economy, the MIT School of Economics, and the Strange Career of Lawrence Klein," *Modern Intellectual History*, 20, no. 4 (2023): 1994–218, 1209.

42 See Aurélien Goutsmedt, "Macroeconomics at the Crossroads: Stagflation and the Struggle between 'Keynesian' and New Classical Macroeconometric Programs" (working paper, 2019), available at https://aurelien-goutsmedt.com/publication/ stagflation-crossroad, last accessed April 22, 2024. On the curious persistence of macroeconometric models, see Aurélien Goutsmedt, Francesco Sergi, Béatrice Cherrier, Juan Acosta, François Claveau, and Clément Fontan, "To Change or Not to Change: The Evolution of Forecasting Models at the Bank of England" (working paper, October 23, 2021), available at https://aurelien-goutsmedt.com/ publication/model-boe, last accessed April 22, 2024. Pedro Garcia Duarte and Francesco Sergi, "Computer Operators and Software Engineers at Data Resources Inc.: An Oral History (1969–1983)," working paper, 2022, available at www.anpec .org.br/encontro/2022/submissao/files_I/i1-28da31598a4ffae2309bf75d1399ac6d .pdf, last accessed April 22, 2024.

43 Joseph E. Stiglitz and Hirofumi Uzawa, eds., *Readings in the Modern Theory of Economic Growth* (Cambridge, MA: MIT Press, 1969); Edwin Burmeister and Rodney Dobell, *Mathematical Theories of Economic Growth* (New York: Macmillan, 1970). An earlier, widely-read survey article was F. H. Hahn and R. C. O. Matthews, "The Theory of Economic Growth: A Survey," *The Economic Journal* 74, no. 296 (1964): 779–902. See Boianovsky and Hoover, "In the Kingdom of Solovia," 219–20.

44 Evsey D. Domar, "Lessons from Growth Models," Lecture delivered at the University of the Philippines, Domar Papers, box 9, David M. Rubenstein Rare Book and Manuscript Library, Duke University, cited in Boianovsky, "Modeling Economic Growth," 430.

45 On Lucas's critique and reactions to it, see Michel de Vroey, *A History of Macroeconomics from Keynes to Lucas and Beyond* (New York: Cambridge University Press, 2016), chapter 9; Aurélien Goutsmedt, Erich Pinzón-Fuchs, Matthieu Renault, and Francesco Sergi, "Reacting to the Lucas Critique," *History of Political Economy* 51, no. 3 (2019): 535–56. On the new classical macroeconomics, the rational expectations movement, and microfoundations, see Pedro Garcia Duarte and Tadeu Lima, "Introduction: Privileging Micro over Macro? A History of Conflicting Positions," in *Microfoundations Reconsidered: The Relationship of Micro and Macroeconomics in Historical Perspective*, edited by Pedro Garcia Duarte and Tadeu Lima (Cheltenham, UK: Edward Elgar, 2013), 1–8.

46 Marcel Boumans has framed the changes in the 1980s in terms of "a shift from a control engineering approach to an information engineering methodology." His stance links to this book in that the change from what has been called "Keynesian economics" and "new classical economics" was not a simple intellectual matter, neither in terms of ideas nor in terms of methods. Rather, it was about "drastic changes to the mathematical toolbox, concepts, and research strategies since the 1980s," which had not only methodological but also ontological implications. See Marcel Boumans, "The Engineering Tools That Shaped the Rational Expectations Revolution," in *Economics and Engineering: Institutions, Practices, and Cultures* (supplement to *History of Political Economy* 52), edited by Pedro Garcia Duarte and Yann Giraud (Durham, NC: Duke University Press, 2020): 143–67.

47 Tiago Mata and Francisco Louçã, "The Solow Residual as a Black Box: Attempts at Integrating Business Cycle and Growth Theories," in *Robert Solow and the*

Development of Growth Economics (supplement to *History of Political Economy* 41), edited by Mauro Boianovsky and Kevin D. Hoover (Durham, NC: Duke University Press, 2009), 334–55, 341.

48 Aurélien Saïdi, "How Saline Is the Solow Residual? Debating Real Business Cycles in the 1980s and 1990s," *History of Political Economy* 51, no. 3 (2019): 579–99.

49 On the revival of neoclassical growth in the form of endogenous growth theory, see David Warsh, *Knowledge and the Wealth of Nations: A Story of Economic Discovery* (New York: Norton, 2007).

50 David Colander and Arjo Klamer, "The Making of an Economist," *The Journal of Economic Perspectives* 1, no. 2 (1987): 95–111.

51 Robert M. Solow, "The Kennedy Council and the Long Run," in *Economic Events, Ideas and Policies: The 1960s and After*, edited by G. L. Perry and James Tobin (Washington, DC: Brookings Institution, 2000), 111–35, 112–13.

52 He proceeded: "What we used to call business cycles – or at least booms and recessions – are now to be interpreted as optimal blips in optimal paths in response to random fluctuations in productivity and the desire for leisure." Solow, "Growth Theory and After," 310.

53 Robert M. Collins, *More: The Politics of Economic Growth in Postwar America* (Oxford: Oxford University Press, 2000), chapter 6; Matthias Schmelzer, *The Hegemony of Growth: The OECD and the Making of the Economics Growth Paradigm* (Cambridge: Cambridge University Press, 2016), 267.

Acknowledgments

Reading the final version of the manuscript that will be published in about a year, I am all the more aware of how much it took to bring this project to an end. It is the result of a process of growing apart from and at the same time deepening my understanding of economic reasoning – a process that started when I was writing my master's thesis in economics and continued to study history. Both fascinated and alienated by small-scale mathematical models, I searched for ways to study that kind of reasoning and its many politics from an epistemological and historiographical distance. Having moved between different fields of scholarship, I want to thank the many people who contributed to this book at different stages by creating spaces to speak freely and giving some sense of belonging.

There are not enough words to thank Eric Hounshell for his intellectual companionship and the many ways our collaboration made academic work deeply rewarding. Without his sometimes astounding interest in debating the intricacies of economic knowledge, his unwavering support in difficult times, and his careful editing of the manuscript, this book would look very different. Monika Wulz has not only been a friend but also a most serious and inspiring interlocutor, in particular when it came to the challenges of writing in between fields and of dealing with the politics of academic life. The collective support, focused discussion, and shared insights into the vagaries of research in the history of economics of Cléo Chassonnery-Zaïgouche, Roni Hirsch, and Maria Bach has meant a lot, especially in times when writing felt debilitating.

At Cambridge University Press, I would like to thank Harro Maas for his trust in commissioning the manuscript in the first place. The expert editorial support of Philip Good, Sable Gravesandy, Laura Blake, and their team helped me turn the manuscript into a book.

This publication would not have been possible without the continuous and profound conversations at the Chair of Science Studies at the University of Lucerne. This was the place that allowed me to deepen my understanding of research as a material as well as historical practice. Several chapters were first discussed in our colloquium and benefited greatly from the participants' close critical engagement. I am grateful to Christoph Hoffmann for providing this space, the time, and his appreciation of the understated. Kris Decker unfailingly asked the most disarming questions.

While growing ever more into the history of science, I appreciated the lasting ties to historians and philosophers of economics, who have supported this project ever since its beginnings as my doctoral dissertation. I am grateful to Roger Backhouse for his willingness to share ideas and material, his helpful feedback at various stages, and his thoughtful reading of the entire manuscript. I am indebted to the enthusiasm of Marcel Boumans, from whom my initial understanding of modeling as a research practice has benefitted profoundly and who has discussed several of the chapters. I would like to thank Mary Morgan for her precise commentary and constructive criticism, from which I was lucky to benefit during my stay at the London School of Economics and in the discussions of a reading group on models as cultural artifacts. A research stay at the Center for the History of Political Economy at Duke University enabled me to do the core archival research. I am grateful to the faculty and fellows, in particular to Kevin Hoover and Roy Weintraub, whose interest in the larger project on which this book is based was crucial not only for the first decisive steps of my thesis but also for my decision to keep working on it.

In addition to those already mentioned, many colleagues and friends read draft chapters and provided feedback along the way. I am immensely thankful for their time and generosity in sharing their expertise: Amanar Akhabbar, Jérôme Baudry, Jeff Biddle, Jarosław Boruszewski, Vincent Carret, Natalia Carrillo-Escalera, Nat Dyer, Max Ehrenfreund, Aurélien Goutsmedt, Sandra Gratwohl, Florian Huber, Hyo Yoon Kang, Tarja Knuuttila, Sarvnaz Lotfi, Sergio F. Martínez Muñoz, Richard Nelson, Krzysztof Nowak-Posadzy, David Phillipy, Flurin Rageth, Mario Schulze, Mischa Suter, Sarine Waltenspül, and Anne-Marie Weist.

I have presented parts of this book to several audiences over the past years. The conversations helped me shape my arguments and better understand their location and bearing. In particular, I am indebted to the participants of the Séminaire romand d'histoire des sciences et des techniques at the University of Lausanne and of the seminar "Numbers &

Measurement" of the SPHERE laboratory at the Université Paris Cité. Their feedback provided the impetus for the last phase of revisions and led, I believe, to a much stronger manuscript.

Thoroughly taken apart, rewritten, and extended in terms of both the historical material and the analytical perspective taken, this book is based on my dissertation. Béatrice Cherrier, Pedro Garcia Duarte, Till Düppe, Pirmin Fessler, Yann Giraud, Jérémy Grosman, Catherine Herfeld, Max Kasy, Peter Lindner, Tiago Mata, Ina Matt, Birgit Nemec, Alyssa Schneebaum, Andrej Svorenčík, Manuel Wäckerle, and Christina Wessely have all inspired and backed my project in one way or another. Thank you.

In times of academic precarity I was privileged to have four years of financial and intellectual support through the PhD program "The Sciences in Historical, Philosophical, and Cultural Contexts" at the University of Vienna. I am grateful to the faculty and fellows. Mitchell Ash agreed to advise my dissertation after he had, years earlier, supported the idea of looking at the history of economics as part of the history of science. I first encountered the history and philosophy of economics in Karl Milford's PPE course at the University of Vienna. I am most grateful for his never-ending interest in (controversial) discussion. Way back, a reading group on historiography, organized by Rosa Costa and Stefan Probst, was pivotal in opening up the worlds of historical epistemology to me.

Finally, I would like to express my gratitude to the late Robert Solow for taking the time for two interviews and sharing his thoughts on my work. Even though not much of the interviews found its way into these pages, our conversations helped me to look at modeling as something done by people at specific times and places. Looking back, they might also have prompted me to clearly differentiate between model and modeler, and to pay attention to the various ways in which Solow's model has turned into my, the historian's, artifact.

For helping me during my archival research I am thankful to the staff of the Rubinstein Rare Book and Manuscript Library (Economists Papers Project, Duke University), in particular Kate Collins, the Collections of the Harvard University Archives, and the King's College Archive Centre (University of Cambridge). Günther Müller of the Vienna University library kindly made sure that I had all the literature I needed for writing my dissertation; Matthew Panhans helped me with archival research at Duke; Selina Buser provided editing assistance when finishing up the manuscript at the University of Lucerne; the detailed index was made by Simon Reading; and Meike Lauggas helped me to better understand academic demands and rites.

This project has received funding from the Chair of Science Studies at the University of Lucerne, the Faculty of Humanities and Social Sciences at the University of Lucerne, the Center for the History of Political Economy at Duke University, the KLI Institute (Klosterneuburg), and the Austrian Science Fund (FWF, W1228-G18). I am grateful to Andy Solow and his siblings for permission to quote from Solow's papers; Robert C. Merton for permission to quote from Samuelson's papers; Harvard University for permission to quote from material held in the Harvard University Archives; and the Carnegie Mellon University Archives for permission to quote from materials they hold. Some portions of this book rely on materials and analysis that I have previously published. The first four sections of Chapter 3 extend an analysis published on pages 162–7 of Verena Halsmayer, "Artifacts in the Contemporary of Economics," in *A Contemporary Historiography of Economics*, ed. Till Düppe and E. Roy Weintraub (London: Routledge, 2018), 157–76, reproduced by permission of Taylor and Francis Group, LLC, a division of Informa plc. The fourth section of Chapter 1 is based on Verena Halsmayer and Kevin D. Hoover, "Solow's Harrod: Transforming Macroeconomics Dynamics into a Model of Long-Run Growth," *European Journal for the History of Economic Theory* 23 (2016): 71–97, reprinted by permission of Taylor & Francis Ltd, http://www.tandfonline.com; the third section of Chapter 5 draws on Eric Hounshell and Verena Halsmayer, "How Does Economic Knowledge Have a Politics? On the Frustrated Attempts of John K. Galbraith and Robert M. Solow to Fix the Political Meaning of Economic Models in The Public Interest," *KNOW* 4, no. 2 (2020): 263–93, reproduced by courtesy of the University of Chicago.

References

Abramovitz, Moses. "Economics of Growth." In *Survey of Contemporary Economics*, edited by Bernard F. Haley, 132–78. Homewood, IL: Richard D. Irwin, Inc., 1952.

"Resource and Output Trends in the United States Since 1870." *American Economic Review* 46, no. 2 (1956): 5–23.

Thinking about Growth and Other Essays on Economic Growth and Welfare. Cambridge: Cambridge University Press, 1989.

Acosta, Juan, and Béatrice Cherrier. "The Transformation of Economic Analysis at the Board of Governors of the Federal Reserve System during the 1960s." *Journal of the History of Economic Thought* 43, no. 3 (2021): 323–49.

Akerlof, George A. *An Economic Theorist's Book of Tales.* Cambridge: Cambridge University Press, 2009.

Akhabbar, Amanar. "The Case against 'Indirect' Statistical Inference: Wassily Leontief's 'Direct Induction' and the Structure of American Economy, 1919–29." In *Exploring the History of Statistical Inference in Economics*, edited by Jeff Biddle and Marcel Boumans, 259–92. Supplement to *History of Political Economy* 53. Durham, NC: Duke University Press, 2021.

"Wassily Leontief as an Econometrician, and the Expansion of the Field of Direct Observation." Working paper, August 2022.

Akhabbar, Amanar, Gabrielle Antille, Emilio Fontela, and Antonio Pulido. "Input–Output in Europe: Trends in Research and Applications." *OEconomia* 1, no. 1 (2011): 73–98.

Alacevich, Michele. "Early Development Economics Debates Revisited." *Journal of the History of Economic Thought* 33, no. 2 (2011): 145–71.

The Political Economy of the World Bank: The Early Years. Stanford, CA: Stanford University Press, 2007.

Alhadeff, Charlotte P., and David A. Alhadeff. "Recent Bank Mergers." *Quarterly Journal of Economics* 69, no. 4 (1955): 503–32.

Allisson, François, and Antoine Missemer. "Some Historiographical Tools for the Study of Intellectual Legacies." *Studies in History and Philosophy of Science Part A* 84 (2020): 132–41.

Amadae, Sonja M. *Rationalizing Capitalist Democracy: The Cold War Origins of Rational Choice Liberalism.* Chicago: University of Chicago Press, 2003.

Anand, Ibanca. "Resisting Narrative Closure: The Comparative and Historical Imagination of Evsey Domar." In *Narrative in Economics: A New Turn on the Past*, edited by Mary S. Morgan and Thomas S. Stapleford, 497–521. Supplement to *History of Political Economy* 55. Durham, NC: Duke University Press, 2023.

Asimakopulos, Athanasios. "Harrod on Harrod: The Evolution of a Line of Steady Growth." *History of Political Economy* 17, no. 4 (1985): 619–35.

Aslanbeigui, Nahid, and Guy Oakes. *The Provocative Joan Robinson: The Making of a Cambridge Economist*. Durham, NC: Duke University Press, 2009.

Aspromourgos, Tony. "On the Origins of the Term 'Neoclassical'." *Cambridge Journal of Economics* 10, no. 3 (1986): 265–70.

Assous, Michaël. "Solow's Struggle with Medium-Run Macroeconomics, 1956–95." *History of Political Economy* 47, no. 3 (2015): 395–417.

Assous, Michaël, and Vincent Carret. *Modeling Economic Instability: A History of Early Macroeconomics*. Cham: Springer, 2022.

Aujac, Henri. "Leontief's Input–Output Table and the French Development Plan." In *Wassily Leontief and Input–Output Economics*, edited by Michael L. Lahr and Erik Dietzenbacher, 65–89. Cambridge: Cambridge University Press, 2004.

Bachelard, Gaston. *The New Scientific Spirit*, translated by Arthur Goldhammer. Boston, MA: Beacon Press, 1984 [1934].

Backhouse, Roger. "The Changing Character of British Economics." In *The Post-1945 Internationalization of Economics*, edited by A. W. Coats, 33–60. Supplement to *History of Political Economy* 28. Durham, NC: Duke University Press, 1996.

"Economics." In *The History of the Social Sciences since 1945*, edited by Roger E. Backhouse and Philippe Fontaine, 38–70. Cambridge: Cambridge University Press, 2010.

Founder of Modern Economics: Paul A. Samuelson. Vol. 1: Becoming Samuelson. New York: Oxford University Press, 2017.

"Linear Programming and Economic Analysis: The Collaboration between Samuelson, Dorfman and Solow, 1949–1958," Working paper, version 1, September 2012.

"MIT and the Other Cambridge." In *MIT and the Transformation of American Economics*, edited by E. Roy Weintraub, 252–71. Supplement to *History of Political Economy* 46. Durham, NC: Duke University Press, 2014.

The Ordinary Business of Life: A History of Economics from the Ancient World to the Twenty-First Century. Princeton: Princeton University Press, 2004.

"Paul Samuelson, RAND and the Cowles Commission Activity Analysis Conference, 1947–1949." Working paper, version 2, October 2012.

"Revisiting Samuelson's Foundations of Economic Analysis." *Journal of Economic Literature* 53, no. 2 (2015): 326–50.

Backhouse, Roger E., and Béatrice Cherrier. "'It's Computers, Stupid!' The Spread of Computers and the Changing Roles of Theoretical and Applied Economics." In *The Age of the Applied Economist: The Transformation of Economics Since the 1970s*, edited by Roger E. Backhouse and Béatrice Cherrier, 103–26. Supplement to *History of Political Economy* 49. Durham, NC: Duke University Press, 2017.

Backhouse, Roger E., and Harro Maas. "Marginalizing Maclaurin: The Attempt to Develop an Economics of Technological Progress at MIT, 1940–50." *History of Political Economy* 48, no. 3 (2016): 423–47.

Backhouse, Roger E., and Philippe Fontaine. "Conclusions: The Identity of Economics: Image and Reality." In *The Unsocial Social Science? Economics and Neighboring Disciplines since 1945*, edited by Roger E. Backhouse and Philippe Fontaine, 343–51. Supplement to *History of Political Economy* 42. Durham, NC: Duke University Press, 2010.

Backhouse, Roger E., and Verena Halsmayer. "Mathematics and the Language of Economics." Paper presented at the Workshop "Language(s) and Language Practices in Business and the Economy." Vienna University of Economics and Business, October 23–25, 2014.

Badiou, Alain. *The Concept of Model: An Introduction to the Materialist Epistemology of Mathematics*, edited and translated by Zachary Luke Fraser and Tzuchien Tho. Transmission. Melbourne: re.press, 2007 [1970].

Balisciano, Márcia L. "Hope for America: American Notions of Economic Planning between Pluralism and Neoclassicism, 1930–1950." In *From Interwar Pluralism to Postwar Neoclassicism*, edited by Mary S. Morgan and Malcolm Rutherford, 153–78. Supplement to *History of Political Economy* 30. Durham, NC: Duke University Press, 1998.

Ballandonne, Matthieu, and Goulven Rubin. "Robert Solow's Non-Walrasian Conception of Economics." *History of Political Economy* 52, no. 5 (2020): 827–61.

Ballard, Charles L., and Marianne Johnson. "Applied General Equilibrium Analysis." In *Becoming Applied: The Transformation of Economics after 1970*, edited by Roger E. Backhouse and Béatrice Cherrier, 78–102. Supplement to *History of Political Economy* 49. Durham, NC: Duke University Press, 2017.

Bänziger, Peter-Paul, Marcel Streng, and Mischa Suter. "Histories of Productivity: An Introduction." In *Histories of Productivity: Genealogical Perspectives on the Body and Modern Economy*, edited by Peter-Paul Bänziger and Mischa Suter, 5–10. London: Routledge, 2018.

Barro, Robert J., and Xavier Sala-i-Martín. *Economic Growth*. Cambridge, MA: MIT Press, 2003.

Bateman, Bradley W. "Clearing the Ground: The Demise of the Social Gospel Movement and the Rise of Neoclassicism in American Economics." In *From Interwar Pluralism to Postwar Neoclassicism*, edited by Mary S. Morgan and Malcolm Rutherford, 29–52. Supplement to *History of Political Economy* 30. Durham, NC: Duke University Press, 1998.

Bator, Francis M. "On Capital Productivity, Input Allocation and Growth." *Quarterly Journal of Economics* 71, no. 1 (1957): 86–106.

Baumol, William J. "Formalisation of Mr. Harrod's Model." *Economic Journal* 59, no. 236 (1949): 625–9.

Bell, Daniel. *The End of Ideology: On the Exhaustion of Political Ideas in the Fifties*. Glencoe, IL: Free Press, 1960.

Bell, Daniel, and Irving Kristol. "What Is the Public Interest?" *The Public Interest* 1 (1965): 3–5.

Benanav, Aaron. "How to Make a Pencil." *Logic*, December 20, 2020. Available at https://logicmag.io/commons/how-to-make-a-pencil, last accessed April 18, 2024.

Bensaude-Vincent, Bernadette, Sacha Loeve, Alfred Nordmann, and Astrid Schwarz. "Matters of Interest: The Objects of Research in Science and Technoscience." *Journal for General Philosophy of Science* 42, no. 2 (2011): 365–83.

Bensaude-Vincent, Bernadette, and Valeria Mosini. "Between Economics and Chemistry: Lavoisier's and Le Chatelier's Notions of Equilibrium." In *Equilibrium in Economics: Scope and Limits*, edited by Valeria Mosini, 45–59. New York: Routledge, 2007.

Berman, Elizabeth Popp. *Thinking like an Economist: How Efficiency Replaced Equality in U.S. Public Policy*. Princeton: Princeton University Press, 2022.

Bernstein, Michael A. *A Perilous Progress: Economists and Public Purpose in Twentieth-Century America*. Princeton: Princeton University Press, 2001.

Besomi, Daniele. "Harrod's Dynamics and the Theory of Growth: The Story of a Mistaken Attribution." *Cambridge Journal of Economics* 25 (2001): 79–96.

The Making of Harrod's Dynamics. London: Macmillan, 1999.

Bessner, Daniel. *Democracy in Exile: Hans Speier and the Rise of the Defense Intellectual*. Ithaca: Cornell University Press, 2018.

Biddle, Jeff. *Progress through Regression: The Life Story of Empirical Cobb–Douglas Production Function*. Cambridge: Cambridge University Press, 2021.

Biddle, Jeff, and Marcel Boumans. "Exploring the History of Statistical Inference in Economics: Introduction." In *Exploring the History of Statistical Inference in Economics*, edited by Jeff Biddle and Marcel Boumans, 1–24. Supplement to *History of Political Economy* 53. Durham, NC: Duke University Press, 2021.

Bies, Michael. "Das Modell als Vermittler von Struktur und Ereignis. Mechanische, statistische und verkleinerte Modelle bei Claude Lévi-Strauss." *Forum Interdisziplinäre Begriffsgeschichte* 5, no. 2 (2016): 43–54.

Bivar, Venus. "Historicizing Economic Growth: An Overview of Recent Works." *The Historical Journal* 65, no. 5 (2022): 1470–89.

Bix, Amy Sue. "The Wider Context of Samuelson's MIT Textbook: Depression-Era Discussions about the Value of Economics Education for American Engineers." In *Economics and Engineering: Institutions, Practices, and Cultures*, edited by Pedro Garcia Duarte and Yann Giraud, 31–58. Supplement to *History of Political Economy* 52. Durham, NC: Duke University Press, 2020.

Bjerkholt, Olav. "The Making of the Leif Johansen Multi-Sectoral Model." *History of Economic Ideas* 17, no. 3 (2009): 103–26.

"Wassily Leontief and the Discovery of the Input–Output Approach." Memorandum, No. 18. Oslo University, Department of Economics, 2016. Available at https://EconPapers.repec.org/RePEc:hhs:osloec:2016_018, last accessed April 18, 2024.

"When Input–Output Analysis Came to Norway." *Structural Change and Economic Dynamics* 6 (1995): 319–30.

Bjerkholt, Olav, and Heinz D. Kurz, eds. "The History of Input–Output Analysis, Leontief's Path and Alternative Tracks." Special issue, *Economic Systems Research* 18, no. 4 (2006): 331–426.

Blaug, Mark, and Peter Lloyd, eds. *Famous Figures and Diagrams in Economics*. Cheltenham, UK: Edward Elgar, 2010.

Bockman, Johanna. *Markets in the Name of Socialism. The Left-Wing Origins of Neoliberalism*. Stanford, CA: Stanford University Press, 2011.

Boianovsky, Mauro. "Beyond Capital Fundamentalism: Harrod, Domar and the History of Development Economics." *Cambridge Journal of Economics* 42, no. 2 (2018): 477–504.

"Modeling Economic Growth: Domar on Moving Equilibrium." *History of Political Economy* 49, no. 3 (2017): 405–36.

Boianovsky, Mauro, and Kevin D. Hoover. "In the Kingdom of Solovia: The Rise of Growth Economics at MIT, 1956–1970." In *MIT and the Transformation of American Economics*, edited by E. Roy Weintraub, 198–228. Supplement to *History of Political Economy* 46. Durham, NC: Duke University Press, 2014.

eds. *Robert Solow and the Development of Growth Economics*. Supplement to *History of Political Economy* 41. Durham, NC: Duke University Press, 2009.

Boruszewski, Jarosław, and Krzysztof Nowak-Posadzy, "Economic Models as Cultural Artifacts: A Philosophical Primer." *Filozofia Nauki (The Philosophy of Science)* 29, no. 3 (2021): 63–87.

Boulding, Kenneth. "In Defense of Statics." *Quarterly Journal of Economics* 69, no. 4 (1955): 185–502.

Boumans, Marcel. "Dynamizing Stability." In *Robert Solow and the Development of Growth Economics*, edited by Mauro Boianovsky and Kevin D. Hoover, 127–46. Supplement to *History of Political Economy* 41. Durham, NC: Duke University Press, 2009.

"The Engineering Tools That Shaped the Rational Expectations Revolution." In *Economics and Engineering: Institutions, Practices, and Cultures*, edited by Pedro Garcia Duarte and Yann Giraud, 143–67. Supplement to *History of Political Economy* 52, Durham: Duke University Press, 2020.

"The History of Mathematisation in Economics." Manuscript submitted to the elements series in the history of economics, Cambridge University Press, October 2023.

How Economists Model the World into Numbers. New York: Routledge, 2005.

"Logical Positivism and Leontief." Working paper, University of Amsterdam, 2012.

"Materials Selection in Economic Modeling." *Synthese* 201, no. 4 (2023): 125.

"Models in Economics." In *The Elgar Companion to Economics and Philosophy*, edited by John Bryan Davis, Alain Marciano, and Jochen Runde, 260–82. Cheltenham, UK: Edward Elgar, 2004.

"Observations in a Hostile Environment: Morgenstern on the Accuracy of Economic Observations." In *Observing the Economy: Historical Perspectives*, edited by Harro Maas and Mary S. Morgan, 114–36. Supplement to *History of Political Economy* 44. Durham, NC: Duke University Press, 2012.

"Paul Ehrenfest and Jan Tinbergen: A Case of Limited Physics Transfer." In *Non-Natural Social Science*, edited by Neil de Marchi, 131–56. Supplement to *History of Political Economy* 25. Durham, NC: Duke University Press, 1993.

Boumans, Marcel, and Pedro Garcia Duarte, eds. *The History of Macroeconometric Modeling*. Special Issue of *History of Political Economy* 51, no. 3. Durham, NC: Duke University Press, 2019.

Boumans, Marcel, and Ariane Dupont-Kieffer, eds. *Histories of Econometrics*. Supplement to *History of Political Economy* 43. Durham, NC: Duke University Press, 2011.

Brand, Stewart. *II Cybernetic Frontiers*. New York: Random House, 1974.

Brandstetter, Thomas. "Täuschend ähnlich – Bemerkungen zur Geschichte des Modellexperiments." *Berichte zur Wissenschaftsgeschichte* 34, no. 3 (2011): 207–23.

Breslau, Daniel. "Economics Invents the Economy: Mathematics, Statistics, and Models in the Work of Irving Fisher and Wesley Mitchell." *Theory and Society* 32, no. 3 (2003): 379–411.

Breslau, Daniel, and Yuval Yonay. "Beyond Metaphor: Mathematical Models in Economics as Empirical Research." *Science in Context* 12 (1999): 317–32.

Brinkley, Alan. "The National Resources Planning Board and the Reconstruction of Planning." In *The American Planning Tradition: Culture and Policy*, edited by Robert Fishman, 173–91. Baltimore: Johns Hopkins University Press, 2000.

Buck-Morss, Susan. "Envisioning Capital. Political Economy on Display." *Critical Inquiry* 21, no. 2 (1995): 434–67.

Burmeister, Edwin, and Rodney Dobell. *Mathematical Theories of Economic Growth.* New York: Macmillan, 1970.

Burns, Arthur F., and Wesley C. Mitchell. *Measuring Business Cycles.* New York: NBER, 1946.

Buttrick, John. "A Note on Professor Solow's Growth Model." *Quarterly Journal of Economics* 72, no. 4 (1958): 633–6.

Camic, Charles. "On Edge: Sociology during the Great Depression and the New Deal." In *Sociology in America: A History*, edited by Craig Calhoun, 225–80. Chicago: University of Chicago Press, 2007.

 Veblen: The Making of an Economist Who Unmade Economics. Cambridge, MA: Harvard University Press, 2020.

Canaday, Margot. "Building a Straight State: Sexuality and Social Citizenship under the 1944 G.I. Bill." *Journal of American History* 90, no. 3 (2003): 935–57.

Canguilhem, Georges. *Études d'Histoire et de Philosophie des Sciences*, 3rd ed. Paris: Vrin, 1975.

Carret, Vincent. "Wassily Leontief's Research Program: Science, Beliefs, Institutions." *History of Political Economy* 56, no. 4 (2024): 653–84.

Carson, Carol. "The History of the United States National Income and Product Accounts: The Development of an Analytical Tool." *Review of Income & Wealth* 21 (1975): 153–81.

Carter, Anne P. "Leontief's 'Stuff': An Archeology of Input–Output Material." *OEconomia* 1, no. 1 (2012): 51–9.

Carvajalino, Juan. "Samuelson's Operationally Meaningful Theorems: Reflections of E. B. Wilson's Methodological Attitude." *Journal of Economic Methodology* 25, no. 2 (2018): 143–59.

 "Unlocking the Mystery of the Origins of John von Neumann's Growth Model." *History of Political Economy* 53, no. 4 (2021): 595–631.

Champernowne, David G. "A Note on J. v. Neumann's Article on 'A Model of Economic Equilibrium'." *Review of Economic Studies* 13, no. 1 (1945): 10–18.

Chao, Hsiang-Ke. "Three Kinds of the Lotka–Volterra Model Transfer from Biology to Economics." *Synthese* 202, no. 4 (2023): 124.

Chao, Hsiang-Ke, and Harro Maas, eds. "Special Issue: Thinking and Acting with Diagrams." *East Asian Science, Technology and Society: An International Journal* 14, no. 2 (2020).

Cheng, Chung-Tang. "Guy H. Orcutt's Engineering Microsimulation to Reengineer Society." In *Economics and Engineering: Institutions, Practices, and Cultures*, edited by Yann Giraud and Pedro Garcia Duarte, 191–217. Supplement to *History of Political Economy* 52. Durham, NC: Duke University Press, 2020.

Cherrier, Béatrice. "A History of Economics at MIT." In *MIT and the Transformation of American Economics*, edited by E. Roy Weintraub, 15–44. Supplement to *History of Political Economy* 46. Durham, NC: Duke University Press, 2014.

"How to Write a Memo to Convince a President: Walter Heller, Policy-Advising, and the Kennedy Tax Cut." *Œconomia* 9, no. 2 (2019): 315–35.

"Mathiness in Context: Richardson, Solow and Mirrlees Debate the Uses of Math in Urban Economics in the 1970s." *The Undercover Historian: Beatrice Cherrier's Blog* (blog), October 21, 2015. Available at https://beatricecherrier.wordpress.com/2015/10/21/mathiness-in-context-richardson-solow-and-mirrlees-debate-the-uses-of-maths-in-urban-economics-1973, last accessed April 20, 2024.

"The Price of Virtue: Some Hypotheses on How Tractability Has Shaped Economic Models." *Œconomia* 13, no. 1 (2023): 23–48.

"The Rise of Economics as Engineering II: The Case of MIT." *Institute for New Economic Thinking* (blog), April 24, 2013. Available at www.ineteconomics.org/perspectives/blog/the-rise-of-economics-as-engineering-ii-the-case-of-mit, last accessed July 27, 2023.

"Toward a History of Economics at MIT, 1940–72." In *MIT and the Transformation of American Economics*, edited by E. Roy Weintraub, 15–44. Supplement to *History of Political Economy* 46. Durham, NC: Duke University Press, 2014.

Chimisso, Cristina. "Narrative and Epistemology: Georges Canguilhem's Concept of Scientific Ideology." *Studies in History and Philosophy of Science Part A* 54 (2015): 64–73.

Chimisso, Cristina and Nicholas Jardine. "Hélène Metzger on Precursors: A Historian and Philosopher of Science Confronts Her Evil Demon." *HOPOS: The Journal of the International Society for the History of Philosophy of Science* 11, no. 2 (2021): 331–53.

Clement, Douglas. "Interview with Robert Solow." *The Region. Banking and Policy Issues Magazine*, September 1, 2002. Available at www.minneapolisfed.org/publications_papers/pub_display.cfm?id=3399, last accessed April 22, 2024.

Cohen, Avi J., and Geoffrey C. Harcourt. "Whatever Happened to the Cambridge Capital Theory Controversies?" *Journal of Economic Perspectives* 17, no. 1 (2003): 199–214.

Cohen, Lizabeth. *A Consumers' Republic: The Politics of Mass Consumption in Postwar America*. New York: Vintage Books, 2004.

Cohen-Cole, Jamie. *The Open Mind: Cold War Politics and the Sciences of Human Nature*. Chicago: Chicago University Press, 2014.

Colander, David, and Arjo Klamer. "The Making of an Economist." *The Journal of Economic Perspectives* 1, no. 2 (1987): 95–111.

Collins, Robert M. *More: The Politics of Economic Growth in Postwar America*. Oxford: Oxford University Press, 2000.

The Committee on Educational Survey. "Report to the Faculty of the Massachusetts Institute of Technology." Cambridge: The Technology Press, 1949. Available at https://facultygovernance.mit.edu/sites/default/files/reports/1949-12_Report_of_the_Committee_on_Educational_Survey.pdf, last accessed April 19, 2024.

Committee on Equity, Diversity and Professional Conduct. "AEA Professional Climate Survey: Final Report," September 15, 2019. Available at www.aeaweb.org/resources/member-docs/final-climate-survey-results-sept-2019, last accessed April 20, 2024.

Cook, Eli. *The Pricing of Progress: Economic Indicators and the Capitalization of American Life*. Cambridge, Mass.: Harvard University Press, 2017.

Copeland, Morris A., and E. M. Martin. "The Correction of Wealth and Income Estimates for Price Changes." In *Studies in Income and Wealth*, edited by Conference on Research in National Income and Wealth, vol. 2, 85–135. New York: NBER, 1938.

Couix, Quentin. "Natural Resources in the Theory of Production: The Georgescu-Roegen/Daly versus Solow/Stiglitz Controversy." *The European Journal of the History of Economic Thought* 26, no. 6 (2019): 1341–78.

Council of Economic Advisers. "Business and Government: Fourth Annual Report to the President." Washington, DC: Government Printing Office, 1949.

"Economic Report of the President: Transmitted to the Congress, January 28, 1954." Washington, DC: Government Printing Office, 1954.

"Economic Report of the President (January 1962)." Washington, DC: Government Printing Office, 1962.

"Economic Report of the President: Transmitted to the Congress, January 7." Washington, DC: Government Printing Office, 1949.

"Economic Report of the President Transmitted to the Congress, January 6, 1950." Washington, DC: Government Printing Office, 1950.

Crafts, Nicholas. "Solow and Growth Accounting: A Perspective from Quantitative Economic History." In *Robert Solow and the Development of Growth Economics*, edited by Mauro Boianovsky and Kevin D. Hoover, 200–20. Supplement to *History of Political Economy* 41. Durham, NC: Duke University Press, 2009.

Crowther-Heyck, Hunter. "Patrons of the Revolution: Ideals and Institutions in Post-War Behavioral Science." *Isis* 97, no. 3 (2006): 420–46.

Dale, Edwin L., Jr. "Electronic Calculator Delivered to Bureau of Census: Science and Industry are Aided by New Electronic Calculators." *New York Herald Tribune*, 5 August 1951, Grace Murray Hopper Collection, Press Clippings, box 5, folder 24 (https://sova.si.edu/details/NMAH.AC.0324?s=0&n=10&t=C&q=&i=0#ref400).

Darity, William, and Arden Kreeger. "The Desegregation of an Elite Economics Department's PhD Program: Black Americans at MIT." In *MIT and the Transformation of American Economics*, edited by E. Roy Weintraub, 317–36. Supplement to *History of Political Economy* 46. Durham, NC: Duke University Press, 2014.

Daston, Lorraine. "The Coming into Being of Scientific Objects." In *Biographies of Scientific Objects*, edited by Lorraine Daston, 1–14. Chicago: University of Chicago Press, 2000.

Daston, Lorraine, and H. Otto Sibum. "Introduction: Scientific Personae and Their Histories." *Science in Context* 16, no. 1–2 (2003): 1–8.

Davis, Hiram S. *Productivity Accounting*. Philadelphia: University of Pennsylvania Press, 1955.

De Vroey, Michel. *A History of Macroeconomics from Keynes to Lucas and Beyond*. New York: Cambridge University Press, 2016.

De Vroey, Michel, and Kevin D. Hoover, eds. *The IS-LM Model: Its Rise, Fall, and Strange Persistence*. Supplement to *History of Political Economy* 36. Durham, NC: Duke University Press, 2004.

De Vroey, Michel, and Pedro Garcia Duarte. "In Search of Lost Time: The Neoclassical Synthesis." *The B.E. Journal of Macroeconomics* 13, no. 1 (2013): 1–31.

Dekker, Erwin. *Jan Tinbergen (1903–1994) and the Rise of Economic Expertise.* Cambridge: Cambridge University Press, 2021.

Denison, Edward F. *The Sources of Economic Growth in the United States.* New York: Committee for Economic Development, 1962.

Deringer, William. *Calculated Values: Finance, Politics, and the Quantitative Age.* Cambridge, MA: Harvard University Press, 2018.

"Just Props?: Calculation and the Capitalist Imagination." *Socio-Economic Review* 15, no. 1 (2017): 244–9.

Desrosières, Alain. "Managing the Economy." In *The Cambridge History of Science, VII: The Modern Social Sciences,* edited by Theodore M. Porter and Dorothy Ross, 553–64. Cambridge: Cambridge University Press, 2003.

The Politics of Large Numbers: A History of Statistical Reasoning. Cambridge, MA: Harvard University Press, 1998.

Dhar, P. N., and Om Kar Seth. "The Rate of Technical Progress in the Tata Iron and Steel Company in 1913–56." *Indian Economic Review* 6, no. 1 (1963): 1–19.

Di Matteo, Massimo, Francesco Filippi, and Serena Sordi. "'The Confessions of an Unrepentant Model Builder': Rummaging in Goodwin's Archive." *Structural Change and Economic Dynamics* 17, no. 4 (2006): 400–14.

Didier, Emmanuel. *America by the Numbers: Quantification, Democracy, and the Birth of National Statistics,* translated by Priya Vari Sen. Cambridge, MA: MIT Press, 2020.

Dixit, Avinash. "Growth Theory after Thirty Years." In *Growth/Productivity/Unemployment: Essays to Celebrate Bob Solow's Birthday,* edited by Peter Diamond, 3–22. Cambridge, MA: MIT Press, 1990.

Dizikes, Peter. "The Productive Career of Robert Solow," December 27, 2019. Available at www.technologyreview.com/2019/12/27/131259/the-productive-career-of-robert-solow/, last accessed April 15, 2024.

Dobb, Maurice. *Theories of Value and Distribution since Adam Smith: Ideology and Economic Theory.* Cambridge: Cambridge University Press, 1973.

Domar, Evsey D. "Capital Expansion, Rate of Growth, and Employment." *Econometrica* 14, no. 2 (1946): 137–47.

"Comment," in *Capital Formation and Economic Growth,* edited by Moses Abramovitz, 107–11. Princeton: Princeton University Press, 1955.

"Economic Growth: An Econometric Approach." *American Economic Review* 42, no. 2 (1952): 479–95.

"On Total Productivity and All That." *Journal of Political Economy* 70, no. 6 (1962): 597–608.

"Statement." In *Comparisons of the United States and Soviet Economies. Hearings before the Joint Economic Committee Congress of the United States. First Session,* 245–8. Washington: United States Government Printing Office, 1960.

Dorfman, Robert. "In Appreciation of Wassily Leontief." *Structural Change and Economic Dynamics* 6 (1995): 305–8.

Dorfman, Robert, Paul Samuelson, and Robert M. Solow. *Linear Programming and Economic Analysis.* New York: McGraw-Hill, 1958.

Dostaler, Gilles. *Keynes and His Battles.* Cheltenham, UK: Edward Elgar, 2007.

Douglas, Paul H. *The Theory of Wages.* New York: MacMillan, 1934.

Dr. K. "Miniature Manifesto Part 2: Stop Quoting Susan Stewart." *The Wonder of Miniature Worlds* (blog), June 1, 2015. Available at https://thewonderofminiatures .home.blog/2015/06/01/miniature-manifesto-part-2-stop-quoting-susan-stewart, last accessed April 21, 2024.

Drucker, Peter F. "Review of New Thinking in Economic Theory, by Sidney Schoeffler and Neil W. Chamberlain." *Review of Politics* 18, no. 3 (1956): 359–62.

Duarte, Pedro Garcia, and Tadeu Lima. "Introduction: Privileging Micro over Macro? A History of Conflicting Positions." In *Microfoundations Reconsidered: The Relationship of Micro and Macroeconomics in Historical Perspective*, edited by Pedro Garcia Duarte and Tadeu Lima, 1–8. Cheltenham, UK: Edward Elgar, 2013.

Duarte, Pedro Garcia, and Francesco Sergi. "Computer Operators and Software Engineers at Data Resources Inc.: An Oral History (1969–1983)." Working paper, 2022. Available at www.anpec.org.br/encontro/2022/submissao/files_I/i1-28da31598a4ffae2309bf75d1399ac6d.pdf, last accessed April 22, 2024.

Duesenberry, James S. *Business Cycles and Economic Growth*. New York: McGraw-Hill, 1958.

Duncan, Joseph W., and William C. Shelton. *Revolution in United States Government Statistics, 1926–1976*. Washington, DC: US Department of Commerce, Office of Federal Statistical Policy and Standards, 1978.

Düppe, Till. "Gerard Debreu's Secrecy: His Life in Order and Silence." *History of Political Economy* 44, no. 3 (2012): 413–49.

Düppe, Till, and E. Roy Weintraub, *Finding Equilibrium: Arrow, Debreu, McKenzie and the Problem of Scientific Credit*. Princeton: Princeton University Press, 2014.

"Siting the New Economic Science: The Cowles Commission's Activity Analysis Conference of June 1949." *Science in Context* 27, no. 3 (2014): 453–83.

Dupuy, Jean-Pierre. *On the Origins of Cognitive Science: The Mechanization of the Mind*. Cambridge, MA: MIT Press, 2009.

Easterly, William. *The Elusive Quest for Growth: Economists' Adventures and Misadventures in the Tropics*. Cambridge, MA: MIT Press, 2002.

Edwards, H. R., and N. T. Drane. "The Australian Economy." *Economic Record* 39, no. 87 (1963): 259–81.

Edwards, Paul N., Lisa Gitelman, Gabrielle Hecht, Adrian Johns, Brian Larkin, and Neil Safier. "AHR Conversation: Historical Perspectives on the Circulation of Information." *The American Historical Review* 116, no. 5 (2011): 1392–435.

Eisner, Robert. "On Growth Models and the Neo-Classical Resurgence." *The Economic Journal* 68, no. 272 (1958): 707–21.

Epple, Moritz. "'Analogien', 'Interpretationen', 'Bilder', 'Systeme' und 'Modelle': Bemerkungen zur Geschichte abstrakter Repräsentationen in den Naturwissenschaften seit dem 19. Jahrhundert." Edited by Eva Axer, Eva Geulen, and Alexandra Heimes. *Forum Interdisziplinäre Begriffsgeschichte* 5, no. 1 (2016): 11–30.

"Between Timelessness and Historiality: On the Dynamics of the Epistemic Objects of Mathematics." *Isis* 102, no. 3 (2011): 481–93.

Erickson, Paul. "Theorizing Application." In *Becoming Applied: The Transformation of Economics after 1970*, edited by Roger E. Backhouse and Béatrice Cherrier, 58–77. Supplement to *History of Political Economy* 49. Durham, NC: Duke University Press, 2017.

The World the Game Theorists Made. Chicago: The University of Chicago Press, 2015.

Erickson, Paul, Judy L. Klein, Lorraine Daston, Rebecca Lemov, Thomas Sturm, and Michael D. Gordin. *How Reason Almost Lost Its Mind: The Strange Career of Cold War Rationality*. Chicago: The University of Chicago Press, 2013.

Espahangizi, Kijan, and Monika Wulz. "The Political and the Epistemic in the Twentieth Century: Historical Perspectives." *KNOW: A Journal for the Formation of Knowledge* 4, no. 2 (2020): 161–74.

Evans, W. Duane, and Marvin Hoffenberg. "The Interindustry Relations Study for 1947." *The Review of Economics and Statistics* 34, no. 2 (1952): 97–142.

Evrard, Zoé. "The Belgian 'Impossible Scenario' of 1980: Reinventing Planning in Times of 'Crisis'." April 2024, under review with *Science in Context*.

Fabricant, Solomon. "Economic Progress and Economic Change: Thirty-Fourth Annual Report." New York: NBER, 1954, available at www.nber.org/books/ annu54-1, last accessed April 15, 2024.

The Output of Manufacturing Industries, 1899–1937. New York: NBER, 1940.

Feder, Barnaby J. "Man in the News: Robert Merton Solow; Tackling Everyday Economic Problems." *The New York Times*, October 22, 1987, available at www .nytimes.com/1987/10/22/business/man-in-the-news-robert-merton-solow-tack ling-everyday-economic-problems.html, last accessed April 19, 2024.

Federici, Silvia. "The Restructuring of Housework and Reproduction in the United States in the 1970s (1980)." In *Revolution at Point Zero: Housework, Reproduction, and Feminist Struggle*, edited by Silvia Federici, 41–53. Oakland, CA: PM Press, 2012.

Findlay, Ronald. "Economic Growth and the Distributive Shares." *The Review of Economic Studies* 27, no. 3 (1960): 167–78.

Fioramonti, Lorenzo. *Gross Domestic Problem: The Politics behind the World's Most Powerful Number*. London: Zed Books, 2013.

Fleck, Ludwik. *Genesis and Development of a Scientific Fact*. Chicago: University of Chicago Press, 1979.

Fogel, Robert W., Enid M. Fogel, Mark Guglielmo, and Nathaniel Grotte. *Political Arithmetic: Simon Kuznets and the Empirical Tradition in Economics*. Chicago: University of Chicago Press, 2013.

Foley, Duncan K. "An Interview with Wassily Leontief." *Macroeconomic Dynamics* 2, no. 1 (1998): 116–40.

Foucault, Michael. *Fearless Speech*. Edited by Joseph Pearson. Los Angeles: Semiotext (e), 2001.

Fourcade, Marion. *Economists and Societies: Discipline and Profession in the United States, Britain, and France, 1890s to 1990s*. Princeton: Princeton University Press, 2009.

Fragio, Alberto. *Historical Epistemology of Ecological Economics: Essays on the Styles of Economic Reasoning*. Cham: Springer, 2022.

Friedman, Michael, and Karin Krauthausen. "How to Grasp an Abstraction: Mathematical Models and Their Vicissitudes Between 1850 and 1950. Introduction." In *Model and Mathematics: From the 19th to the 21st Century*, edited by Michael Friedman and Karin Krauthausen, 1–49. Cham: Springer International Publishing, 2022.

Friedman, Milton. *Essays in Positive Economics*. Chicago: University of Chicago Press, 1953.

Frydl, Kathleen J. *The GI Bill*. New York: Cambridge University Press, 2009.

Galbraith, John Kenneth. *Ambassador's Journal: A Personal Account of the Kennedy Years*. Boston: Houghton Mifflin, 1969.

"A Review of a Review." *The Public Interest* no. 9 (1967): 109–18.

Gass, Saul I. "Model World: A Model Is a Model Is a Model Is a Model." *Interfaces* 19, no. 3 (1989): 58–60.

Gelfert, Axel. *How to Do Science with Models: A Philosophical Primer*. Cham: Springer, 2016.

Geoghegan, Bernard Dionysius. *Code: From Information Theory to French Theory*. Durham, NC: Duke University Press, 2023.

"From Information Theory to French Theory: Jakobson, Lévi-Strauss, and the Cybernetic Apparatus." *Critical Inquiry* 38 (2011): 96–126.

Georgescu-Roegen, Nicholas. "The Aggregate Linear Production Function and Its Applications to von Neumann's Economic Model." In *Activity Analysis of Production and Allocation: Proceedings of a Conference*, edited by Tjalling C. Koopmans, 98–116. New York: John Wiley & Sons, 1951.

Gerovitch, Slava. "Roman Jakobson und die Kybernetisierung der Linguistik in der Sowjetunion." In *Die Transformation des Humanen: Beiträge Zur Kulturgeschichte der Kybernetik*, edited by Michael Hagner and Erich Hörl, 229–74. Frankfurt: Suhrkamp, 2008.

Gerstle, Gary. *American Crucible: Race and Nation in the Twentieth Century*. Princeton: Princeton University Press, 2016.

Giacovelli, Sebastian and Andreas Langenohl. "Temporalitäten in der wirtschaftswissenschaftlichen Modellbildung: Die Multiplikation von Zeitlichkeit in der Neoklassik." In *Die Innenwelt der Ökonomie: Wissen, Macht und Performativität in der Wirtschaftswissenschaft*, edited by Jens Maeße, Hanno Pahl, and Jan Sparsam, 33–53. Wiesbaden: Springer VS, 2017.

Gibson, James J. *The Ecological Approach to Visual Perception*. New York: Taylor& Francis, 1986.

Gilbert, Milton, Georg Jaszi, Charles F. Schwartz, and Edward F. Denison. "National Income and Product Statistics of the United States, 1929–1946." *Survey of Current Business* 27 (1947): 1–54.

Gilman, Nils. "The Prophet of Post-Fordism: Peter Drucker and the Legitimation of the Corporation." In *American Capitalism: Social Thought and Political Economy in the Twentieth Century*, edited by Nelson Lichtenstein, 109–32. Philadelphia: University of Pennsylvania Press, 2006.

Giraud, Yann. "Legitimizing Napkin Drawing: The Curious Dispersion of Laffer Curves, 1978–2008." In *Representation in Scientific Practice Revisited*, edited by Catelijne Coopmans, Janet Vertesi, Michael E. Lynch, and Steve Woolgar, 269–90. Cambridge, MA: MIT Press, 2014.

"Negotiating the 'Middle-of-the-Road' Position: Paul Samuelson, MIT, and the Politics of Textbook Writing, 1945–55." In *MIT and the Transformation of American Economics*, edited by E. Roy Weintraub, 134–52. Supplement to *History of Political Economy* 46. Durham, NC: Duke University Press, 2014.

Goldberger, Arthur S. "Structural Equation Methods in the Social Sciences." *Econometrica* 40, no. 6 (1972): 979–1001.

Golden, Soma. "Economist Joan Robinson, 72, Is Full of Fight." *New York Times*, March 23, 1976. Available at www.nytimes.com/1976/03/23/archives/economist-joan-robinson-72-is-full-of-fight-economist-joan-robinson.html, last accessed April 11, 2024.

"Leontief Relates Economic Theory to Fact. Professor's Research Project Perfects Input–Output Analysis." *The Harvard Crimson*, December 17, 1959. Available at www.thecrimson.com/article/1959/12/17/loentief-relates-economic-theory-to-fact, last accessed April 18, 2024.

Goodwin, Craufurd D. "The Patrons of Economics in a Time of Transformation." In *From Interwar Pluralism to Postwar Neoclassicism*, edited by Mary S. Morgan and Malcolm Rutherford, 53–81. Supplement to *History of Political Economy* 30. Durham, NC: Duke University Press, 1998.

Goodwin, Richard. "The Confessions of an Unrepentant Model Builder." Transcript, in Di Matteo et al. 'The Confessions of an Unrepentant Model Builder': Rummaging in Goodwin's Archive." *Structural Change and Economic Dynamics* 17, no. 4 (2006): 407–11.

Goutsmedt, Aurélien. "How the Phillips Curve Shaped Full Employment Policy in the 1970s: The Debates on the Humphrey–Hawkins Act." *History of Political Economy* 54, no. 4 (2022): 619–53.

"Macroeconomics at the Crossroads: Stagflation and the Struggle between 'Keynesian' and New Classical Macroeconometrics Programs." Working paper, 2019. Available at https://aurelien-goutsmedt.com/publication/stagflation-crossroad, last accessed April 22, 2024.

Goutsmedt, Aurélien, Erich Pinzón-Fuchs, Matthieu Renault, and Francesco Sergi. "Reacting to the Lucas Critique." *History of Political Economy* 51, no. 3 (2019): 535–56.

Goutsmedt, Aurélien, Francesco Sergi, Béatrice Cherrier, Juan Acosta, François Claveau, and Clément Fontan. "To Change or Not to Change: The Evolution of Forecasting Models at the Bank of England." Working paper, October 23, 2021. Available at https://aurelien-goutsmedt.com/publication/model-boe, last accessed April 22, 2024.

Gram, Harvey, and G. C. Harcourt. "Joan Robinson and MIT." *History of Political Economy* 49, no. 3 (2017): 437–50.

Green, H. A. John. "Growth Models, Capital and Stability." *The Economic Journal* 70, no. 277 (1960): 57–73.

Griliches, Zvi. "The Discovery of the Residual: An Historical Note." NBER Research Working Paper 5348. New York, 1995. Available at www.nber.org/papers/w5348, last accessed April 21, 2024.

"The Sources of Measured Productivity Growth: United States Agriculture, 1940–60." *Journal of Political Economy* 71, no. 4 (1963): 331–46.

Guiot-Isaac, Andrés M. "Persuasion and Trust: The Practical Functions of Time-Fixed Development Plans, Colombia 1958-1970." Manuscript, October 2023, under review with *Science in Context*.

Hagemann, Harald. "Leontief and His German Period." *Russian Journal of Economics* 7 (2021): 67–90.

Hagen, Everett E. "Population and Economic Growth." *American Economic Review* 49, no. 3 (1959): 310–27.

Hahn, F. H. "The Stability of Growth Equilibrium." *Quarterly Journal of Economics* 74, no. 2 (1960): 206–26.

Hahn, F. H., and R. C. O. Matthews. "The Theory of Economic Growth: A Survey." *Economic Journal* 74, no. 296 (1964): 779–902.

Hahn, Frank, and Robert Solow. *A Critical Essay on Modern Macroeconomic Theory.* Cambridge, MA: MIT Press, 1998.

Halberstam, David. "The Importance of Being Galbraith." *Harper's Magazine*, November 1, 1967, 47–54.

Haley, Bernard F. *A Survey of Contemporary Economics.* Homewood, IL: Richard D. Irwin, Inc., 1952.

Hall, Robert L., and Charles J. Hitch. "Price Theory and Business Behaviour." *Oxford Economic Papers* 2, no. 1 (1939): 12–45.

Halsmayer, Verena. "Der Ökonom als 'Engineer in the Design Sense' – Modellierungspraxis und professionelles Selbstverständnis in Robert Solows 'Contribution to the Theory of Economic Growth'." *Berichte zur Wissenschaftsgeschichte* 36, no. 3 (2013): 245–59.

"Following Artifacts." *History of Political Economy* 50, no. 3 (2018): 629–34.

"From Exploratory Modeling to Technical Expertise: Solow's Growth Model as a Multi-Purpose Design." In *MIT and the Transformation of American Economics*, edited by E. Roy Weintraub, 229–51. Supplement to *History of Political Economy* 46. Durham, NC: Duke University Press, 2014.

"A Model to 'Make Decisions and Take Actions': Leif Johansen's Multisector Growth Model, Computerized Macroeconomic Planning, and Resilient Infrastructures for Policymaking." In *Becoming Applied: The Transformation of Economics after 1970*, edited by Roger E. Backhouse and Béatrice Cherrier, 158–86. Supplement to *History of Political Economy* 49. Durham, NC: Duke University Press, 2017.

"Ökonometrisches Planen." In *Enzyklopädie der Genauigkeit*, edited by Markus Krajewski, Antonia von Schöning, and Mario Wimmer, 304–14. Konstanz: Konstanz University Press, 2021.

Halsmayer, Verena, and Kevin D. Hoover. "Solow's Harrod: Transforming Macroeconomics Dynamics into a Model of Long-Run Growth." *European Journal for the History of Economic Theory* 23 (2016): 71–97.

Hands, D. Wade. *Reflection without Rules: Economic Methodology and Contemporary Science Theory.* Cambridge: Cambridge University Press, 2001.

Harcourt, Geoffrey C. "Some Cambridge Controversies in the Theory of Capital." *Journal of Economic Literature* 7, no. 2 (1969): 369–405.

Some Cambridge Controversies in the Theory of Capital. Cambridge: Cambridge University Press, 1972.

Harcourt, Geoffrey C., and Prue Kerr. *Joan Robinson.* Basingstoke: Palgrave Macmillan, 2009.

Harris, Seymor. "A Postscript of the Editor." *The Review of Economics and Statistics* 36, no. 4 (1954): 382–6.

Harris, Theodore E. "The Theory of Branching Processes." R-381-PR, A Report prepared for United States Air Force Project RAND. Santa Monica, CA: The RAND Corporation, May 1964.

Harrod, R. F. "An Essay in Dynamic Theory." *The Economic Journal* 49, no. 193 (1939): 14–33.

"What Is a Model?" In *Value, Capital and Growth. Papers in Honour of Sir John Hicks*, edited by J. N. Wolfe, 173–92. Edinburgh: Edinburgh University Press, 1968.

Hayek, Friedrich. "The Use of Knowledge in Society." *American Economic Review* 35, no. 4 (1945): 519–30.

Heilbroner, Robert L. "On the Limited 'Relevance' of Economics." *The Public Interest* 21 (Fall 1970): 80–93.

Heller, Walter W. *New Dimensions of Political Economy: The Godkin Lectures at Harvard University*. Cambridge, MA: Harvard University Press, 1966.

Henderson, James M. and Richard E. Quandt. "Walras, Leontief, and the Interdependence of Economic Activities: Comment." *Quarterly Journal of Economics* 69, no. 4 (1955): 626–31.

Heyck, Hunter. *Age of System: Understanding the Development of Modern Social Science*. Baltimore: Johns Hopkins University Press, 2015.

Hilgers, Philipp von. "Zur Einleitung: Eine Epoche der Markovketten." In *Andrej A. Markov: Berechenbare Künste*, edited by Philipp von Hilgers and Wladimir Velminski, 9–27. Zürich: diaphanes, 2007.

Hirsch, Eric. *Acts of Growth: Development and the Politics of Abundance in Peru*. Stanford, CA: Stanford University Press, 2022.

Hirschman, Albert O. *The Strategy of Economic Development*, 52. New Haven, CT: Yale University Press, 1963 [1958].

Hirschman, Daniel. "Rediscovering the 1%: Knowledge Infrastructures and the Stylized Facts of Inequality." *American Journal of Sociology* 127, no. 3 (2021): 739–86.

Hirschman, Daniel, and Elizabeth Popp Berman. "Do Economists Make Policies? On the Political Effects of Economics." *Socio-Economic Review* 12, no. 4 (2014): 779–811.

Hitchcock, Frank L. "The Distribution of a Product from Several Sources to Numerous Localities." *Journal of Mathematics and Physics* 20 (1941): 224–30.

Hoffman, Allison. "Economist Paul Samuelson Dead at 94: Smart, Jewish Keynesian Somehow Succeeded." *Tablet*, December 14, 2009. Available at https://tabletmag .com/scroll/22290/economist-paul-samuelson-dead-at-94, last accessed April 19, 2024.

Hoffmann, Christoph. *Die Arbeit der Wissenschaften*. Zürich: diaphanes, 2013.

Hogan, Warren P. "Technical Progress and Production Functions." *Review of Economics and Statistics* 40 (1958): 407–11.

Hoover, Kevin D. "Microfoundational Programs." In *Microfoundations Reconsidered: The Relationship of Micro and Macroeoconomics in Historical Perspective*, edited by Pedro Garcia Duarte and Gilberto Tadeu Lima, 19–61. Cheltenham, UK: Elgar, 2012.

Hounshell, Eric, and Verena Halsmayer. "How Does Economic Knowledge Have a Politics? On the Frustrated Attempts of John K. Galbraith and Robert M. Solow to Fix the Political Meaning of Economic Models in *The Public Interest*." *KNOW: A Journal on the Formation of Knowledge* 4, no. 2 (2020): 263–93.

Hounshell, Eric T. "A Feel for the Data: Paul F. Lazarsfeld and the Columbia University Bureau of Applied Social Research." Dissertation, UCLA Los Angeles, 2017.

How Can Economics Solve Its Gender Problem? Panel at the 2019 annual meeting of the American Economic Association. Atlanta, 2019. Available at www.aeaweb.org/

webcasts/2019/how-can-economics-solve-gender-problem, last accessed April 20, 2024.

Ingrao, Bruna, and Giorgio Israel. *The Invisible Hand: Economic Equilibrium in the History of Science*. Cambridge, MA: MIT Press, 1990.

Isaac, Joel. "Tool Shock: Technique and Epistemology in the Postwar Social Sciences." In *The Unsocial Social Science? Economics and Neighboring Disciplines since 1945*, edited by Roger E. Backhouse and Philippe Fontaine, 133–64. Supplement to *History of Political Economy* 42. Durham, NC: Duke University Press, 2010.

Iverson, Kenneth E. "Machine Solutions of Linear Differential Equations Applications to a Dynamic Economic Model." Doctoral Thesis, Harvard University, 1954.

Jacoby, Russell. *The Last Intellectuals: American Culture in the Age of Academe*. New York: Basic Books, 1987.

Johansen, Leif. *Lectures on Macroeconomic Planning, Vol. 1, General Aspects*. Amsterdam: North-Holland, 1977.

A Multi-Sectoral Study of Economic Growth. Amsterdam: North-Holland, 1960.

"Substitution versus Fixed Production Coefficients in the Theory of Economic Growth: A Synthesis." *Econometrica* 27, no. 2 (1959): 157–76.

Johnson, Edgar A. J. "The Encyclopedia of the Social Sciences." *Quarterly Journal of Economics* 50, no. 2 (1936): 355–66.

Jorgenson, Dale W. "Productivity and Economic Growth." In *Fifty Years of Economic Measurement: The Jubilee of the Conference on Research in Income and Wealth*, edited by Ernst R. Berndt and Jack E. Triplett, 19–118. Chicago: University of Chicago Press, 1991.

Kac, Marc. "Some Mathematical Models in Science." *Science* 166, no. 3906 (1969): 695–9.

Kaiser, David. *Drawing Theories Apart: The Dispersion of Feynman Diagrams in Postwar Physics*. Chicago: University of Chicago Press, 2005.

Katznelson, Ira. *Fear Itself: The New Deal and the Origins of Our Times*. New York: Liveright, 2013.

Kendrick, John W. "Productivity Trends: Capital and Labor: NBER Interim Report 1956." New York: NBER, 1956. Available at www.nber.org/chapters/c5596, last accessed April 15, 2024.

King, Willford I. *The Wealth and Income of the People of the United States*. New York: MacMillan, 1915.

Klaassen, L. H., L. M. Koyck, and H. J. Witteveen, eds. *Jan Tinbergen: Selected Papers*. Amsterdam: North-Holland, 1959.

Kleeberg, Bernhard. "Factual Narrative in Economics." In *Narrative Factuality: A Handbook*, edited by Monika Fludernik and Marie-Laure Ryan, 379–90. Berlin: De Gruyter, 2019.

Klein, Judy L. "Shotgun Weddings in Control Engineering and Postwar Economics, 1940–72." In *Economics and Engineering: Institutions, Practices, and Cultures*, edited by Pedro Garcia Duarte and Yann Giraud, 115–42. Supplement to *History of Political Economy* 52. Durham, NC: Duke University Press, 2020.

Statistical Visions in Time: A History of Time Series Analysis, 1662–1938. Cambridge: Cambridge University Press, 1997.

Klein, Lawrence R. *The Keynesian Revolution*, 2nd ed. London: Macmillan, 1968.

Klein, Ursula. "Paper Tools in Experimental Cultures." *Studies in History and Philosophy of Science Part A* 32, no. 2 (2001): 265–302.

Kline, Ronald. *The Cybernetics Moment, or, Why We Call Our Age the Information Age.* Baltimore: Johns Hopkins University Press, 2015.

"How Disunity Matters to the History of Cybernetics in the Human Sciences in the United States, 1940–80." *History of the Human Sciences* 33, no. 1 (2020): 12–35.

Knuuttila, Tarja. "Epistemic Artifacts and the Modal Dimension of Modeling." *European Journal for Philosophy of Science* 11, no. 3 (2021): 65.

"Imagination Extended and Embedded: Artifactual versus Fictional Accounts of Models." *Synthese* 198, no. S21 (2021): 5077–97.

Models as Epistemic Artefacts: Toward a Non-Representationalist Account of Scientific Representation. Philosophical Studies from the University of Helsinki 8. Helsinki: Department of Philosophy, 2005.

Knuuttila, Tarja, and Andrea Loettgers. "Modelling as Indirect Representation? The Lotka–Volterra Model Revisited." *British Journal for the Philosophy of Science* 68 (2017): 1007–36.

Knuuttila, Tarja T., and Mary S. Morgan. "Models and Modelling in Economics." In *Philosophy of Economics*, edited by Uskali Mäki, vol. 13, 49–87. Handbook of the Philosophy of Science. Amsterdam: Elsevier Scientific, 2012.

Kohli, Martin C. "Leontief and the U.S. Bureau of Labor Statistics, 1941–1954: Developing a Framework for Measurement." In *The Age of Economic Measurement*, edited by Judy L. Klein and Mary S. Morgan, 190–212. Supplement to *History of Political Economy* 30. Durham, NC: Duke University Press, 2001.

Koopmans, Tjalling C., ed. *Activity Analysis of Production and Allocation.* Cowles Commission Monograph 3. New York: John Wiley and Sons, 1951.

"Analysis of Production as an Efficient Combination of Activities." In *Activity Analysis of Production and Allocation*, edited by Tjalling C. Koopmans, 33–97. Cowles Commission Monograph 3. New York: John Wiley and Sons, 1951.

Three Essays on the State of Economic Science. New York: McGraw-Hill Book Company, 1957.

Krämer, Sybille. "Mathematizing Power, Formalization, and the Diagrammatical Mind or: What Does 'Computation' Mean?" *Philosophy & Technology* 27, no. 3 (2014): 345–57.

Kregel, Jan A. "Economic Dynamics and the Theory of Steady Growth: An Historical Essay on Harrod's 'Knife Edge'." *History of Political Economy* 12, no. 1 (1980): 97–123.

Krislov, Joseph. "The Extent and Trends of Raiding among American Unions." *Quarterly Journal of Economics* 69, no. 1 (1955): 145–52.

Krugman, Paul. "Incidents from My Career," 1995. Available at www.princeton.edu/~pkrugman/incidents.html, last accessed April 20, 2024.

Kurz, Heinz D., and Neri Salvadori. *Theory of Production: A Long-Period Analysis.* Cambridge: Cambridge University Press, 1995.

Kuznets, Simon. "Comment." In *A Survey of Contemporary Economics*, edited by Bernard F. Haley, 178–81. Homewood, IL: Richard D. Irwin, Inc., 1952.

"Measurement: Measurement of Economic Growth." *The Journal of Economic History* 7 (1947): 10–34.

"National Income." In *Encyclopedia of the Social Sciences*, edited by Edwin R. A. Seligman, vol. 11, 205–44. New York: MacMillan, 1933.

National Income: A Summary of Findings. New York: NBER, 1946.

National Income and Its Composition, 1919–1939, vol. 1. New York: NBER, 1941.

La Grandville, Olivier. "The 1956 Contribution to Economic Growth Theory by Robert Solow: A Major Landmark and Some of Its Undiscovered Riches." *Oxford Review of Economic Policy* 23, no. 1 (2007): 15–24.

Lange, Oskar. *Introduction to Economic Cybernetics.* Oxford: Pergamon Press, 1970.

Langenohl, Andreas. "Neoklassische Polychronie. Die Temporalitäten Algebraischer Modelle bei Alfred Marshall," edited by Eva Axer, Eva Geulen, and Alexandra Heimes. *Forum Interdisziplinäre Begriffsgeschichte* 5, no. 1 (2016): 102–14.

Lave, Lester B. "Empirical Estimates of Technological Change in United States Agriculture, 1850–1958." *Journal of Farm Economics* 44, no. 4 (1962): 941–52.

Lee, Frederic. *A History of Heterodox Economics: Challenging the Mainstream in the Twentieth Century.* New York: Routledge, 2009.

Leonard, Robert. *Von Neumann, Morgenstern, and the Creation of Game Theory. From Chess to Social Science, 1900–1960.* Cambridge: Cambridge University Press, 2010.

Leontief, Wassily. "Academic Economics." *Science* 217 (1982): 104–5.

"The Balance of the Economy of the USSR." In *Foundations of Soviet Strategy for Economic Growth, Selected Short Soviet Essays 1924–1930,* edited by Nicolas Spulber, 88–94. Bloomington, IN: Indiana University Press, 1964.

"Comment on Chipman, in *The Technology Factor in International Trade,* edited by Raymond Vernon, 132–7. New York: Columbia University Press, 1970.

"Die Bilanz der Russischen Volkswirtschaft. Eine Methodologische Untersuchung." *Weltwirtschaftliches Archiv* 22, no. 2 (1925): 338–44.

Essays in Economics. New York: Routledge, 1966.

"Interrelation of Prices, Output, Savings, and Investment." *Review of Economics and Statistics* 19, no. 3 (1937): 109–32.

"Output, Employment, Consumption and Investment." *Quarterly Journal of Economics* 58, no. 2 (1944): 290–313.

"The Problems of Quality and Quantity in Economics." *Daedalus* 88, no. 4 (1959): 622–32.

"Recent Developments in the Study of Interindustrial Relationships." *American Economic Review* 39, no. 3 (1949): 211–25.

"Theoretical Assumptions and Non-Observed Facts." *American Economic Review* 61 (1971): 1–7.

"What an Economic Planning Board Should Do." *Challenge* 17, no. 3 (1974): 35–40.

Leontief, Wassily, Hollis B. Chenery, Paul G. Clark, James S. Duesenberry, Allen R. Ferguson, Anne P. Grosse, Robert N. Grosse, Mathilda Holzman, Walter Isard, and Helen Kistin. *Studies in the Structure of the American Economy: Theoretical and Empirical Explorations in Input–Output Analysis.* New York: Oxford University Press, 1953.

Lepenies, Philipp. *The Power of a Single Number: A Political History of GDP.* New York: Columbia University Press, 2016.

Leslie, P. H. "On the Use of Matrices in Certain Population Mathematics." *Biometrika* 33, no. 3 (1945): 183–212.

Lévi-Strauss, Claude. "Wissenschaftliche Kriterien in den Sozial- und Humanwissenschaften." In *Strukturale Anthropologie,* edited by Claude Lévi-

Strauss, translated by Eva Moldenhauer, Hans Henning Richter, and Traugott König, vol. II, 325–50. Frankfurt a.M.: Suhrkamp, 1992.

Levitt, Theodore. "The Lonely Crowd and the Economic Man." *Quarterly Journal of Economics* 70, no. 1 (1956): 95–116.

Levy, Jonathan. "Capital as Process and the History of Capitalism." *Business History Review* 91, no. 3 (2017): 483–510.

Little, I. M. D. "Classical Growth." *Oxford Economic Papers* 9, no. 2 (1957): 152–77.

Lotfi, Sarvnaz. "Capitalizing the 'Measure of Our Ignorance': A Pragmatist Genealogy of R&D." Dissertation, Virginia Polytechnic Institute and State University, 2020.

Louçã, Francisco. *The Years of High Econometrics. A Short Story of the Generation That Reinvented Economics.* London: Routledge, 2007.

Maas, Harro. "Making Things Technical: Samuelson at MIT." In *MIT and the Transformation of American Economics*, edited by E. Roy Weintraub, 272–94. Supplement to *History of Political Economy* 46. Durham, NC: Duke University Press, 2014.

Maas, Harro, and Mary S. Morgan. "Observation and Observing in Economics." In *Observing the Economy*, edited by Harro Maas and Mary S. Morgan, 1–24. Supplement to *History of Political Economy* 44. Durham, NC: Duke University Press, 2012.

Macekura, Stephen. "Development and Economic Growth: An Intellectual History." In *History of the Future of Economic Growth: Historical Roots of Current Debates on Sustainable Degrowth*, edited by Iris Borowy and Matthias Schmelzer, 120–8. New York: Routledge, 2017.

The Mismeasure of Progress: Economic Growth and Its Critics. Chicago: University of Chicago Press, 2020.

Mahalanobis, Prasanta C. "Some Observations on the Process of Growth of National Income," *Sankhyā: The Indian Journal of Statistics* 12, no. 4 (1953): 307–12.

Maier, Charles S. "The Politics of Productivity: Foundations of American International Economic Policy after World War II." *International Organization* 31, no. 4 (1977): 607–33.

Mäki, Uskali. *The Methodology of Positive Economics: Reflections on the Milton Friedman Legacy.* Cambridge: Cambridge University Press, 2009.

Maniglier, Patrice. "What Is a Problematic?" *Radical Philosophy* 173 (2012): 21–3.

Mankiw, N. Gregory. "The Macroeconomist as Scientist and Engineer." *The Journal of Economic Perspectives* 20, no. 4 (2006): 29–46.

Marglin, Stephen A. *Raising Keynes: A Twenty-First-Century General Theory.* Cambridge, MA: Harvard University Press, 2021.

Marris, Robin. "Preface for Social Scientists." In *The Corporate Economy: Growth, Competition, and Innovative Potential*, edited by Robin Marris and Adrian Wood, xv–xxvi. Cambridge, MA: Harvard University Press, 1971.

Mata, Tiago. "Constructing Identity: The Post Keynesians and the Capital Controversies." *Journal of the History of Economic Thought* 26, no. 2 (2004): 241–59.

Mata, Tiago, and Francisco Louçã. "The Solow Residual as a Black Box: Attempts at Integrating Business Cycle and Growth Theories." In *Robert Solow and the Development of Growth Economics*, edited by Mauro Boianovsky and Kevin D. Hoover, 334–55. Supplement to *History of Political Economy* 41. Durham, NC: Duke University Press, 2009.

Mata, Tiago, and Steven G. Medema. "Cultures of Expertise and the Public Interventions of Economists." In *The Economist as Public Intellectual*, edited by Tiago Mata and Steven G. Medema, 1–19. Supplement to *History of Political Economy* 45, Durham, NC: Duke University Press, 2013.

Matthews, R. C. O. "The Work of Robert M. Solow." *Scandinavian Journal of Economics* 90, no. 1 (1988): 13–16.

McCloskey, Deirdre. "History, Differential Equations, and the Problem of Narration." *History and Theory* 30 (1991): 21–36.

M'charek, Amade. "Race, Time and Folded Objects: The HeLa Error." *Theory, Culture & Society* 31, no. 6 (2014): 29–56.

McKinley, Erskine. "The Problem of 'Underdevelopment' in the English Classical School." *Quarterly Journal of Economics* 69, no. 2 (1955): 235–52.

Medina, Eden. *Cybernetic Revolutionaries: Technology and Politics in Allende's Chile.* Cambridge, MA: MIT Press, 2011.

Metzger, Hélène. *Newton, Stahl, Boerhaave et la doctrine chimique.* Paris: Blanchard, 1974 (1930).

Miller, Peter, and Nikolas Rose. "Governing Economic Life." *Economy and Society* 19, no. 1 (1990): 1–31.

Mills, Frederick C. *Productivity and Economic Progress.* NBER Occasional Paper 38. New York: NBER, 1952.

Mirowski, Philip. *Machine Dreams: How Economics Became a Cyborg Science.* Cambridge: Cambridge University Press, 2002.

Science-Mart: Privatizing American Science. Cambridge, MA: Harvard University Press, 2011.

"Twelve Theses Concerning the History of Postwar Neoclassical Price Theory." In *Agreement on Demand: Consumer Theory in the Twentieth Century*, edited by Philip Mirowski and Wade D. Hands, 343–79. Supplement to *History of Political Economy* 38. Durham, NC: Duke University Press, 2006.

Mirowski, Philip, and Edward M. Nik-Khah. *The Knowledge We Have Lost in Information: The History of Information in Modern Economics.* Oxford: Oxford University Press, 2017.

Mitchell, Herb F. "The Machine Solution of Simultaneous Linear Systems." Doctoral Thesis, Harvard University, 1948.

Mitchell, Timothy. "Economentality: How the Future Entered Government." *Critical Inquiry* 40, no. 4 (2014): 479–507.

"Fixing the Economy." *Cultural Studies* 12, no. 1 (1998): 82–101.

Morgan, Mary S. *The History of Econometric Ideas.* Historical Perspectives on Modern Economics. Cambridge: Cambridge University Press, 1990.

"Making Measuring Instruments." In *The Age of Economic Measurement*, edited by Judy L. Klein and Mary S. Morgan, 235–51. Supplement to *History of Political Economy* 33. Durham, NC: Duke University Press, 2001.

"Seeking Parts, Looking for Wholes." In *Histories of Scientific Observation*, edited by Lorraine Daston and Elizabeth Lunbeck, 303–25. Chicago: University of Chicago Press, 2011.

"Technocratic Economics: An Afterword." In *Economics and Engineering: Institutions, Practices, and Cultures*, edited by Yann Giraud and Pedro Garcia

Duarte, 294–304. Supplement to *History of Political Economy* 52. Durham, NC: Duke University Press, 2020.

The World in the Model: How Economists Work and Think. Cambridge: Cambridge University Press, 2012.

Morgan, Mary S., and Malcolm Rutherford. "American Economics: The Character of the Transformation." In *From Interwar Pluralism to Postwar Neoclassicism*, edited by Mary S. Morgan and Malcolm Rutherford, 1–26. Supplement to *History of Political Economy* 30. Durham, NC: Duke University Press, 1998.

Morgenstern, Oskar. "Experiment and Large Scale Computation in Economics." In *Economic Activity Analysis*, edited by Oskar Morgenstern, 484–549. New York: John Wiley & Sons, 1954.

Mudge, Stephanie L. *Leftism Reinvented: Western Parties from Socialism to Neoliberalism.* Cambridge, MA: Harvard University Press, 2018.

Murphy, Frederic H., and Venkat Panchanadam. "Understanding Linear Programming Modeling through an Examination of the Early Papers on Model Formulation." *Operations Research* 45, no. 3 (1997): 341–56.

National Bureau of Economic Research. *Income in the United States: Its Amount and Distribution, 1909-1919, Vols. 1 and 2.* New York: NBER, 1921/1922.

National Planning Association. *National Budgets for Full Employment.* Washington, DC: National Planning Association, 1945.

Nelson, Richard R. "Numbers and Math Are Nice, But . . ." *Biological Theory* 10, no. 3 (2015): 246–52.

von Neumann, John. "A Model of General Economic Equilibrium." *Review of Economic Studies* 13, no. 1 (1945): 1–9.

von Neumann, John, and Oskar Morgenstern. *Theory of Games and Economic Behavior.* Princeton: Princeton University Press, 1944.

Nevin, Edward. "Professor Hansen and Keynesian Interest Theory." *Quarterly Journal of Economics* 69, no. 4 (1955): 637–41.

Nik-Khah, Edward. "George Stigler, the Graduate School of Business, and the Pillars of the Chicago School." In *Building Chicago Economics*, edited by Robert Van Horn, Philip Mirowski, and Thomas A. Stapleford, 116–48. Cambridge: Cambridge University Press, 2011.

Novick, David. "Mathematics: Logic, Quantity, and Method." *The Review of Economics and Statistics* 36, no. 4 (1954): 357–58.

Nützenadel, Alexander. *Stunde der Ökonomen: Wissenschaft, Politik und Expertenkultur in der Bundesrepublik 1949-1974.* Kritische Studien zur Geschichtswissenschaft, Bd. 166. Göttingen: Vandenhoeck & Ruprecht, 2005.

Nye, David E. *Consuming Power: A Social History of American Energies.* 3. print. Cambridge, MA: MIT Press, 2001.

O'Bryan, Scott. *The Growth Idea: Purpose and Prosperity in Postwar Japan.* Honolulu: University of Hawaii Press, 2009.

Offner, Amy C. *Sorting out the Mixed Economy: The Rise and Fall of Welfare and Developmental States in the Americas.* Princeton: Princeton University Press, 2019.

Orozco Espinel, Camila. "How Mathematical Economics Became (Simply) Economics: The Mathematical Training of Economists during the 1940s, 1950s and 1960s in the United States." Center for the History of Political Economy at Duke University

Working Paper Series, No. 2020-11, November 16, 2020. Available at https://ssrn
.com/abstract=3731733, last accessed April 22. 2024.

O'Sullivan, Mary A. "A Confusion of Capital in the United States." In *The Contradictions of Capital in the Twenty-First Century: The Piketty Opportunity*, edited by Pat Hudson and Keith Tribe, 131–66. Newcastle: Agenda Publishing, 2016.

Özgöde, Onur. "Institutionalism in Action: Balancing the Substantive Imbalances of 'the Economy' through the Veil of Money." *History of Political Economy* 52, no. 2 (2020): 307–39.

Perlman, Mark, and Morgan Marietta. "The Politics of Social Accounting: Public Goals and the Evolution of the National Accounts in Germany, the United Kingdom and the United States." *Review of Political Economy* 17, no. 2 (2005): 211–30.

Pilvin, Harold. "Full Capacity vs. Full Employment Growth." *Quarterly Journal of Economics* 67, no. 4 (1953): 545–52.

Pinzón-Fuchs, Erich. "Lawrence R. Klein and the Making of Large-Scale Macroeconometric Modeling, 1938–55," in *The History of Macroeconometric Modeling*, edited by Kevin D. Hoover, Marcel Boumans, and Pedro Garcia Duarte, 401–23. Supplement of *History of Political Economy* 51, no. 3. Durham, NC: Duke University Press, 2019.

Polenske, Karen R. "Leontief's 'Magnificent Machine' and Other Contributions to Applied Economics." In *Wassily Leontief and Input–Output Economics*, edited by Michael L. Lahr and Erik Dietzenbacher, 9–29. Cambridge: Cambridge University Press, 2004.

Porter, Theodore M. "Locating the Domain of Calculation." *Journal of Cultural Economy* 1, no. 1 (2008): 39–50.

"Speaking Precision to Power: The Modern Political Role of Social Science." *Social Research* 73, no. 4 (2006): 1273–94.

Trust in Numbers: The Pursuit of Objectivity in Science and Public Life. Princeton, NJ: Princeton University Press, 1996.

Prescott, Edward C. "Robert M. Solow's Neoclassical Growth Model: An Influential Contribution to Economics." *The Scandinavian Journal of Economics* 90, no. 1 (1988): 7–12.

Press Release from the Royal Swedish Academy of Sciences. "The Nobel Memorial Prize in Economics 1987." *The Scandinavian Journal of Economics* 90, no. 1 (1988): 1–5.

Productivity Measurement Advisory Service of the European Productivity Agency. "In This Number." *Productivity Measurement Review* 16 (1959): 3–4.

"Program of the Sixty-Fourth Annual Meeting of the American Economic Association." *American Economic Review* 42, no. 2 (1952): viii–xi.

Rheinberger, Hans-Jörg. "Gaston Bachelard and the Notion of 'Phenomenotechnique'." *Perspectives on Science* 13, no. 3 (2005): 313–28.

"Reassessing the Historical Epistemology of Georges Canguilhem." In *Continental Philosophy of Science*, edited by Gary Gutting, 187–97. Malden, MA: Blackwell Publishing Ltd, 2005.

Richardson, Harry W. "A Comment on Some Uses of Mathematical Models in Urban Economics." *Urban Studies* 10, no. 2 (1973): 259–66.

Robinson, Joan. "History versus Equilibrium." *Indian Economic Journal* 21, no. 3 (1974): 202–13.

"The Production Function and the Theory of Capital." *Review of Economic Studies* 21, no. 2 (1953–54): 81–106.

Rothschild, Emma. "Where Is Capital?" *Capitalism: A Journal of History and Economics* 2, no. 2 (2021): 291–371.

de Rouvray, Cristel Anne. "Economists Writing History: American and French Experience in the Mid 20th Century." PhD dissertation, London School of Economics and Political Science, 2005.

Rutherford, Mark. *The Institutionalist Movement in American Economics, 1918–1947: Science and Social Control.* Cambridge: Cambridge University Press, 2011.

Saïdi, Aurélien. "How Saline Is the Solow Residual? Debating Real Business Cycles in the 1980s and 1990s." *History of Political Economy* 51, no. 3 (2019): 579–99.

Samuelson, Paul. "Abstract of a Theorem Concerning Substitutability in Open Leontief Models." In *Activity Analysis of Production and Allocation*, edited by Tjalling C. Koopmans, 142–46. Cowles Commission Monograph 3. New York: John Wiley and Sons, 1951.

Economics: An Introductory Analysis. New York: McGraw-Hill Book Company, Inc., 1948.

"Economists and the History of Ideas." *American Economic Review* 52, no. 1 (1962): 1–18.

Foundations of Economic Analysis. Cambridge, MA: Harvard University Press, 1947.

"Introduction: Mathematics in Economics: No, No or Yes, Yes, Yes?" *The Review of Economics and Statistics* 36, no. 4 (1954): 359.

"Robert Solow: An Affectionate Portrait." *The Journal of Economic Perspectives* 3, no. 3 (1989): 91–7.

"Unemployment Ahead." *The New Republic*, September 11, 1944.

Samuelson, Paul A., and Robert M. Solow. "A Complete Capital Model Involving Heterogeneous Capital Goods." *Quarterly Journal of Economics* 70, no. 4 (1956): 537–62.

Sargent, J. R. "Are American Economists Better?" *Oxford Economic Papers* 15, no. 1 (1963): 1–7.

Schabas, Margaret. *The Natural Origins of Economics.* Chicago: University of Chicago Press, 2006.

Schelling, Thomas C. "Capital Growth and Equilibrium." *American Economic Review* 37, no. 5 (1947): 864–76.

Schlombs, Corinna. *Productivity Machines: German Appropriations of American Technology from Mass Production to Computer Automation.* Cambridge, MA: MIT Press, 2019.

Schmelzer, Matthias. *The Hegemony of Growth: The OECD and the Making of the Economics Growth Paradigm.* Cambridge: Cambridge University Press, 2016.

Schmelzer, Matthias, Andrea Vetter, and Aaron Vansintjan. *The Future Is Degrowth: A Guide to a World beyond Capitalism.* New York: Verso, 2022.

Schmidgen, Henning. "Figuren des Zerebralen in der Psychologie von Gilles Deleuze." In *Ecce Cortex: Zur Geschichte des Modernen Gehirns*, edited by Michael Hagner, 317–49. Göttingen: Wallstein, 1999.

Schmookler, Jacob. "The Changing Efficiency of the American Economy, 1869–1938." *Review of Economics and Statistics* 34, no. 3 (1952): 214–31.

Schoeffler, Sidney. *The Failures of Economics: A Diagnostic Study.* Cambridge, MA: Harvard University Press, 1955.

Sedgewick, Augustine. "Against Flows." *History of the Present: A Journal of Critical History* 4, no. 2 (2014): 143–70.

Sen, Amartya. *Growth Economics: Selected Readings*. Harmondsworth, Middlesex: Penguin Books, 1970.

Sent, Esther-Mirjam. "Engineering Dynamic Economics." In *New Economics and Its History*, edited by John B. Davis, 41–62. Supplement to *History of Political Economy* 29. Durham, NC: Duke University Press, 1998.

Shenk, Timothy. "Taking Off the Neoliberal Lens: The Politics of the Economy, the MIT School of Economics, and the Strange Career of Lawrence Klein." *Modern Intellectual History* 20, no. 4 (2023): 1194–218.

Shishido, Shuntaro. "Japan's Economic Growth and Policy-Making in the Context of Input–Output Models." In *Wassily Leontief and Input–Output Economics*, edited by Michael L. Lahr and Erik Dietzenbacher, 294–310. Cambridge: Cambridge University Press, 2004.

Simon, Herbert A. "A Behavioral Model of Rational Choice." *Quarterly Journal of Economics* 69, no. 1 (1955): 99–118.

The Sciences of the Artificial. Cambridge, MA: MIT Press, 1969.

Skocpol, Theda. *Social Policy in the United States: Future Possibilities in Historical Perspective*. Princeton NJ: Princeton University Press, 1995.

Smith, Vernon L. "The Theory of Capital." *American Economic Review* 52, no. 3 (1962): 481–91.

Snowdon, Brian, and Howard R. Vane. *Conversations with Leading Economists: Interpreting Modern Macroeconomics*. Cheltenham: Elgar, 1999.

Solow, Robert M. "A Rejoinder." *The Public Interest* no. 9 (1967): 118–9.

Capital Theory and the Rate of Return. Amsterdam: North-Holland, 1963.

"Congestion, Density and the Use of Land in Transportation." *Swedish Journal of Economics* 74, no. 1 (1972): 161–73.

"A Contribution to the Theory of Economic Growth." *Quarterly Journal of Economics* 70, no. 1 (1956): 65–94.

"Cowles and the Tradition of Macroeconomics." presentation at The Cowles Fiftieth Anniversary Celebration, June 3, 1983. Available at https://cowles.yale.edu/sites/default/files/2022-12/50th-solow.pdf, last accessed April 20, 2024.

"On the Dynamics of the Income Distribution." A Thesis Presented in Partial Fulfillment of the Requirements for the Degree of Doctor of Philosophy in the Department of Economics, Harvard University, 1951. microfilm Duke University.

"Economic Model-Building. Review of Klein, L. R. (1950) Economic Fluctuations in the United States, 1921–1941, New York: John Wiley." *Mechanical Engineering* 72, no. 12 (1950): 990–1.

Growth Theory: An Exposition. New York: Oxford University Press, 1970.

"Growth Theory and After." *American Economic Review* 78, no. 3 (1988): 307–17.

"Heavy Thinker. Review of Prophet of Innovation: Joseph Schumpeter and Creative Destruction by Thomas K. McCraw." *New Republic*, May 21, 2007. Available at www.newrepublic.com/article/heavy-thinker, last accessed April 22, 2024.

"How Did Economics Get That Way and What Way Did It Get." *Daedalus* 126 (2005): 87–100.

"The Kennedy Council and the Long Run." In *Economic Events, Ideas and Policies: The 1960s and After*, edited by G. L. Perry and James Tobin, 111–35. Washington, DC: Brookings Institution, 2000.

"The New Industrial State, or, Son of Affluence." *The Public Interest* 9 (1967): 100–8.

"A Note on Dynamic Multipliers." *Econometrica* 19, no. 3 (1951): 306–16.

"A Note on the Price Level and Interest Rate in a Growth Model." *Review of Economic Studies* 21, no. 1 (1953–54): 74–9.

"Perspectives on Growth Theory." *Journal of Economic Perspectives* 8 (1994): 45–54.

"The Production Function and the Theory of Capital." *Review of Economic Studies* 23, no. 2 (1955–56): 101–8.

"Rejoinder to Richardson: I." *Urban Studies* 10, no. 2 (1973): 267.

"Review Koopmans Activity Analysis of Production and Allocation." *American Economic Review* 42, no. 3 (1952): 424–9.

"Review of The Failures of Economics: A Diagnostic Study by Sidney Schoeffler." *Review of Economics and Statistics* 39, no. 1 (1957): 96–8.

"Robert M. Solow: Biographical." NobelPrize.org. Nobel Prize Outreach AB 2023, November 28, 2023. Available at www.nobelprize.org/prizes/economic-sciences/1987/solow/biographical, last accessed April 19, 2024.

"Science and Ideology in Economics." *The Public Interest* 21 (1970): 94–107.

"The State of Macroeconomics." *Journal of Economic Perspectives* 22, no. 1 (2008): 243–46.

"On the Structure of Linear Models." *Econometrica* 20, no. 1 (1952): 29–46.

"Swan, Trevor W." In *An Encyclopedia of Keynesian Economics*, edited by Thomas Cate, 594–7. Northampton, MA: Edward Elgar, 2013.

"Technical Change and the Aggregate Production Function." *Review of Economics and Statistics* 39, no. 3 (1957): 312–20.

"Technical Progress, Capital Formation and Economic Growth." *American Economic Review* 52, no. 2 (1962): 76–86.

"The Truth Further Refined: A Comment on Marris." *The Public Interest* 11 (1968): 47–52.

"Unemployment as a Social Problem." In *Choice, Welfare, and Development. A Festschrift in Honour of Amartya K. Sen*, edited by K. P. Pattanaik Basu and K. Suzumura, 313–22. Oxford: Clarendon Press, 1995.

"The Wide, Wide World of Wealth." *New York Times Sunday Book Review*, March 20, 1988. Available at www.nytimes.com/1988/03/20/books/the-wide-wide-world-of-wealth.html, last accessed April 20, 2024.

Solow, Robert M., and Paul A. Samuelson. "Balanced Growth under Constant Returns to Scale." *Econometrica* 21, no. 3 (1953): 412–24.

Solow, Robert M., and Joseph E. Stiglitz. "Output, Employment, and Wages in the Short Run." *Quarterly Journal of Economics* 82, no. 4 (1968): 537–60.

Speich Chassé, Daniel. *Die Erfindung des Bruttosozialprodukts: Globale Ungleichheit in der Wissensgeschichte der Ökonomie*. Kritische Studien zur Geschichtswissenschaft, Bd. 212. Göttingen: Vandenhock & Ruprecht, 2013.

"When Economics Went Overseas: Epistemic Problems in the Macroeconomic Analysis of Late Colonial Africa." In *Science, Africa and Europe: Processing Information and Creating Knowledge*, edited by Martin Lengwiler, Nigel Penn, and Patrick Harries, 237–55. London: Routledge, 2019.

Spulber, Nicolas, ed. *Foundations of Soviet Strategy for Economic Growth, Selected Short Soviet Essays 1924–1930*. Bloomington: Indiana University Press, 1964.

Stapleford, Thomas. *The Cost of Living in America: A Political History of Economic Statistics*. Cambridge: Cambridge University Press, 2009.

"Defining a 'Living Wage' in America: Transformations in Union Wage Theories, 1870–1930." *Labor History* 49, no. 1 (2018): 1–22.

"Historical Epistemology and the History of Economics: Views through the Lens of Practice." *Research in the History of Economic Thought and Methodology* 35A (2017): 113–45.

"Shaping Knowledge about American Labor: External Advising at the U.S. Bureau of Labor Statistics in the Twentieth Century." *Science in Context* 23, no. 2 (2010): 187–220.

Steedman, Ian, ed. *Socialism & Marginalism in Economics 1870–1930*. London: Routledge, 1995.

Stengers, Isabelle. *Another Science Is Possible: A Manifesto for Slow Science*, translated by Stephen Muecke. Cambridge, MA: Polity, 2018.

Stewart, Susan. *On Longing: Narratives of the Miniature, the Gigantic, the Souvenir, the Collection*. Durham, NC: Duke University Press, 1993.

Stigler, George J. "The Cost of Subsistence." *Journal of Farm Economics* 27, no. 2 (1949): 303–14.

"The Division of Labor Is Limited by the Extent of the Market." *Journal of Political Economy* 59, no. 3 (1951): 185–93.

Trends in Output and Employment. New York: NBER, 1947.

Stiglitz, Joseph E., and Hirofumi Uzawa, eds. *Readings in the Modern Theory of Economic Growth*. Cambridge, MA: MIT Press, 1969.

Stone, Richard. "The Analysis of Economic Systems." In *Semaine d'Etude Sur Le Role de l'Analyse Econometrique Dans La Formulation de Plans de Developpement*, edited by Pontificia Academia Scientiarum, 3–88. Pontificiae Academiae Scientiarum Scripta Varia 28. Vatican City: Pontificiae Academiae Scientiarum, 1965.

"Review of Commodity Flow and Capital Formation by S. Kuznets." *The Economic Journal* 49, no. 194 (1939): 308–9.

"The Use and Development of National Income and Expenditure Estimates." In *Lessons of the British War Economy*, edited by Daniel N. Chester, 83–101. Cambridge: Cambridge University Press, 1951.

Studenski, Paul. *The Income of Nations: Theory, Measurement, and Analysis*. New York: New York University Press, 1958.

Suter, Mischa. *Geld an der Grenze: Souveränität und Wertmaßstäbe im Zeitalter des Imperialismus 1871–1923*. Berlin: Matthes & Seitz, 2024.

Suzuki, Tomo. "The Epistemology of Macroeconomic Reality: The Keynesian Revolution from an Accounting Point of View." *Accounting, Organizations and Society* 28, no. 5 (2003): 471–517.

Svorenčík, Andrej. "MIT's Rise to Prominence: Outline of a Collective Biography." In *MIT and the Transformation of American Economics*, edited by E. Roy Weintraub, 109–33. Supplement to *History of Political Economy* 46. Durham, NC: Duke University Press, 2014.

Swan, Trevor W. "Economic Growth and Capital Accumulation." *Economic Record* 32, no. 2 (1956): 334–61.

"Growth Models: Of Golden Ages and Production Functions." In *Economic Development with Special Reference to East Asia*, edited by Kenneth Berrill, 3–18. London: Palgrave Macmillan UK, 1964.

Swedberg, Richard. *Economics and Sociology: Redefining Their Boundaries: Conversations with Economists and Sociologists*. New Jersey: Princeton University Press, 1990.

Tanner, Ariane. *Die Mathematisierung des Lebens. Alfred James Lotka und der energetische Holismus im 20. Jahrhundert.* Tübigen: Mohr Siebeck, 2017.

Tellmann, Ute. *Life & Money: The Genealogy of the Liberal Economy and the Displacement of Politics.* New York: Columbia University Press, 2018.

Thomas, William. *Rational Action: The Sciences of Policy in Britain and America, 1940–1960.* Cambridge, MA: MIT Press, 2015.

Tinn, Honghong. "Modeling Computers and Computer Models: Manufacturing Economic-Planning Projects in Cold War Taiwan, 1959–1968." *Technology and Culture* 59, no. 4 (2018): 66–99.

Tobin, James. "A Dynamic Aggregative Model." *Journal of Political Economy* 62, no. 2 (1955): 103–15.

"Money and Income: Post Hoc Ergo Propter Hoc?" *Quarterly Journal of Economics* 84, no. 2 (1970): 301–17.

Tomlinson, Jim. "The Politics of Economic Measurement: The Rise of the 'Productivity Problem' in the 1940s." In *Accounting as Social and Institutional Practice*, edited by Anthony G. Hopwood and Peter Miller, 168–89. Cambridge: Cambridge University Press, 1999.

Tooze, Adam. "Die Vermessung der Welt. Ansätze zu einer Kulturgeschichte der Wirtschaftsstatistik." In *Wirtschaftsgeschichte als Kulturgeschichte. Dimensionen eines Perspektivenwechsels*, edited by Hartmut Berghoff and Jakob Vogel, 325–51. Frankfurt am Main: Campus Verlag, 2004.

"The Gatekeeper." *London Review of Books*, April 22, 2021. Available at www.lrb.co .uk/the-paper/v43/n08/adam-tooze/the-gatekeeper, last accessed April 11, 2024.

"Imagining National Economies: National and International Economic Statistics, 1900–1950." In *Imagining Nations*, edited by Geoffrey Cubitt, 212–84. Manchester: Manchester University Press, 1998.

Statistics and the German State, 1900–1945: The Making of Modern Economic Knowledge. Cambridge: Cambridge University Press, 2001.

Toye, John. "Solow in the Tropics." In *Robert Solow and the Development of Growth Economics*, edited by Mauro Boianovsky and Kevin D. Hoover, 221–40. Supplement to *History of Political Economy* 41. Durham, NC: Duke University Press, 2009.

Universities – National Bureau Committee on Economic Research. "Problems in the Study of Economic Growth." New York: NBER, 1949.

U.S. National Resources Planning Board. "National Resources Development: Report for 1943. Part I. Post-War Plan and Program." Washington, DC, 1943.

Uzawa, Hirofumi. "On a Two-Sector Model of Economic Growth." *The Review of Economic Studies* 29, no. 1 (1961): 40–7.

Vanoli, André. *A History of National Accounting.* Amsterdam: IOS Press, 2005.

Vogl, Joseph. *The Specter of Capital.* Stanford, CA: Stanford University Press, 2015.

Warsh, David. *Knowledge and the Wealth of Nations: A Story of Economic Discovery.* New York: Norton, 2007.

Wartofsky, Marx W. "Introduction." in *Models: Representation and the Scientific Understanding*, edited by Marx W. Wartofsky, xiii–xxvi. Dordrecht: D. Reidel Publishing Company, 1979.

"The Model Muddle: Proposals for an Immodest Realism (1966)." In *Models: Representation and the Scientific Understanding*, edited by Marx W. Wartofsky, 1–11. Dordrecht: D. Reidel Publishing Company, 1979.

"Telos and Technique: Models as Modes of Action (1968)." In *Models: Representation and the Scientific Understanding*, edited by Marx W. Wartofsky, 140–53. Dordrecht: D. Reidel Publishing Company, 1979.

Weintraub, E. Roy. "Autobiographical Memory and the Historiography of Economics." In *A Contemporary Historiography of Economics*, edited by Till Düppe and E. Roy Weintraub, 9–21. London: Routledge, 2018.

"Commentary on Learning Economic Method from the Invention of Vintage Models by Bert Hamminga." In *Post-Popperian Methodology of Economics: Recovering Practice*, edited by Neil De Marchi, 355–73. Boston: Kluwer Academic Publishers, 1988.

How Economics Became a Mathematical Science. Durham, NC: Duke University Press, 2002.

"MIT's Openness to Jewish Economists." In *MIT and the Transformation of American Economics*, edited by E. Roy Weintraub, 45–59. Supplement to *History of Political Economy* 46. Durham, NC: Duke University Press, 2014.

Stabilizing Dynamics: Constructing Economic Knowledge. Cambridge: Cambridge University Press, 1991.

Weisskopf, Walter A. "Psychological Aspects of Economic Thought." *Journal of Political Economy* 57, no. 4 (1949): 304–14.

Wendler, Reinhard. *Das Modell zwischen Kunst und Wissenschaft*. Munich: Wilhelm Fink Verlag, 2013.

Wood, Adrian. "Robin Marris (1924–2012)." In *The Palgrave Companion to Cambridge Economics*, edited by R. A. Cord, 893–914. London: Palgrave Macmillan UK, 2017.

Wright, David. "Mr. Harrod and Growth Economics." *Review of Economics and Statistics* 31, no. 4 (1949): 322–8.

Wulwick, Nancy. "The Mathematics of Economic Growth." Working Paper No. 38. Jerome Levy Institute, 1990.

Wulz, Monika. *Erkenntnisagenten: Gaston Bachelard und die Reorganisation des Wissens*. Kaleidogramme 61. Berlin: Kulturverl. Kadmos, 2010.

Yarrow, Andrew L. *Measuring America: How Economic Growth Came to Define American Greatness in the Late Twentieth Century*. Amherst: University of Massachusetts Press, 2010.

Young, Warren. *Harrod and His Trade Cycle Group. The Origins and Development of the Growth Research Programme*. London: MacMillan, 1998.

Zauberman, Alfred. "A Note on Soviet Capital Controversy." *Quarterly Journal of Economics* 69, no. 3 (1955): 445–51.

Zenawi, Meles. "States and Markets: Neoliberal Limitations and the Case for a Developmental State." In *Good Growth and Governance in Africa: Rethinking Development Strategies*, edited by Akbar Noman, Kwesi Botchwey, Howard Stein, and Joseph E. Stiglitz, 140–74. Oxford: Oxford University Press, 2012.

Archive Material

Edwin B. Wilson Papers. Harvard University Archives, Harvard University.

Grace Murray Hopper Collection. Archives Center, National Museum of American History.

Herbert A. Simon Papers. Carnegie Mellon University Archives, Carnegie Mellon University.

Joan V. Robinson Papers. King's College Archive Centre, Cambridge University.

Joseph Alois Schumpeter papers. Harvard University Archives, Harvard University.

Paul A. Samuelson Papers. Economists' Papers Archive, David M. Rubenstein Rare Book & Manuscript Library, Duke University.

Robert M. Solow Papers. Economists' Papers Archive, David M. Rubenstein Rare Book & Manuscript Library, Duke University.

Wassily Leontief Personal Archive. Harvard University Archives, Harvard University.

Further Material

Robert M. Solow, interview with Verena Halsmayer, May 3, 2011.

private correspondence with Verena Halsmayer, September 17, 2014.

Index

References to figures are in *italics*

Other Books in the Series (*continued from page ii*)

Printed in the United States
by Baker & Taylor Publisher Services